CONTENTS

EDITORS' PREFACE

Longman A level Study Guides, written by experienced examiners and teachers, aim to give you the best possible foundation for success in your course. Each book in the series encourages thorough study and a full understanding of the concepts involved, and is designed as a subject companion and study aid to be used throughout the course.

Many candidates at A-level fail to achieve the grades which their ability deserves, owing to such problems as the lack of a structured revision strategy, or unsound examination technique. This series aims to remedy such deficiencies, by encouraging a realistic and disciplined approach in preparing for and taking exams.

The largely self-contained nature of the chapters gives the book a flexibility which you can use to your advantage. After starting with the background to the A-, AS-level and Scottish Higher courses and with details of the syllabus coverage, you can read all other chapters selectively, in any order appropriate to the stage you have reached in your course.

Geoff Black and Stuart Wall

A-LEVEL
AND AS-LEVEL

ECONOMICS

Barry Harrison

LONGMAN

LONGMAN A AND AS - LEVEL REVISE GUIDES

Series editors
Geoff Black and Stuart Wall

Titles available:
Accounting
Art and Design
Biology
Business Studies
Chemistry
Computer Science
Economics
English
French
Geography
German
Government and Politics
Law
Mathematics
Modern History
Physics
Psychology
Sociology

Addison Wesley Longman Limited
Edinburgh Gate, Harlow,
Essex CM20 2JE, England
and Associated Companies throughout the world.

First published 1990
Second edition 1995 ISBN 0 582 27688 8
Third impression 1998

British Library Cataloguing in Publication Data
A catalogue record for this book is available from the British Library

Set in 10/12pt Century Old Style

Produced by Addison Wesley Longman Singapore Pte Ltd
Printed in Singapore

ACKNOWLEDGEMENTS

The author is grateful to the following examination boards for permission to reproduce their questions.

   Associated Examining Board (AEB)
   Northern Ireland Council for Curriculum Examinations and Assessment (NICCEA)
   Scottish Examination Board (SEB)
   University of Cambridge Local Examinations Syndicate (UCLES)
   Edexcel Foundation (London) (ULEAC)
   University of Oxford Delegacy of Local Examinations (ODLE)
   Welsh Joint Education Committee (WJEC)

These Boards accept no responsibility for the accuracy of the answers provided. They are the responsibility of the author alone.

   I am also grateful to the Controller of Her Majesty's Stationery Office, and to Lloyds Bank PLC for permission to reproduce material from their *Economic Bulletin*.

AUTHOR'S NOTE

This book aims to promote thorough understanding of those topics most frequently examined at Advanced Level. To achieve this, careful attention is given to explaining points of detail so that a clear understanding of each topic is encouraged. All teachers know that a topic which is understood is easily remembered!

In a subject such as Economics where change is frequent, it is important to be up-to-date if success in the examination is to be achieved. Recent editions of conventional textbooks are very useful here, but they rarely give guidance on how material can be arranged to answer examination questions. Nor do they show how recent examination questions reflect the changing emphasis placed on the different aspects of each topic. This book includes Tutor's Answers, Student's Answers and Outline Answers to recent examination questions. There are also Review Sheets at the end of each chapter to help you check your understanding of what you have read. In all cases the aim is to show how familiar principles can be used to answer different questions and to provide a guide to the standard required for success.

I am pleased to acknowledge the helpful advice and encouragement provided by George Stanlake throughout the writing of this book. His comments led to many improvements in the clarity of the text. I am also grateful to my wife Lea who typed most of the book and who, along with my children Paul, Matthew and Simon, provided much encouragement. The editors of the series also provided encouragement and I am grateful for this. Finally I would like to take this opportunity of thanking my former teachers for all the help they have given in the past.

NAMES AND ADDRESSES OF THE EXAM BOARDS

Associated Examining Board (AEB)
Stag Hill House
Guildford
Surrey GU2 5XJ

University of Cambridge Local Examinations Syndicate (UCLES)
Syndicate Buildings
1 Hills Road
Cambridge CB1 1YB

Northern Examinations and Assessment Board (NEAB)
Devas Street
Manchester M15 6EX

Edexcel Foundation (London) (ULEAC)
Stewart House
32 Russell Square
London WC1B 5DN

Northern Ireland Council for Curriculum, Examinations and Assessment (NICCEA)
29 Clarendon Road
Belfast BT1 3BG

Oxford and Cambridge Schools Examination Board (OCSEB)
Purbeck House
Purbeck Road
Cambridge CB2 2PU

The Oxford Delegacy is also administered
from this address.

Scottish Examination Board (SEB)
Ironmills Road
Dalkeith
Midlothian EH22 1LE

Welsh Joint Education Committee (WJEC)
245 Western Avenue
Cardiff CF5 2YX

EXAMINATION TECHNIQUES

GETTING STARTED

All of the examinations covered by this book include an essay or free response paper. Many include a multiple-choice paper and a stimulus or data response paper. The aim of this chapter is to provide guidance on how to prepare for your own examination and how to approach different types of examination question.

All candidates are assessed on their performance in the examination room for what is a relatively short period of time. However, this does not mean that there is a short cut to success. Success will only come as the result of consistent effort, thorough preparation and careful revision. A surprising number of students pay only lip service to this simple statement of fact, but experienced teachers will know that preparation for the final examination cannot be left until the last few weeks before the examination. Instead, throughout your course, you should regularly check your understanding of the basic concepts that have been covered. As part of this process of regular revision you should set down *outline* answers to past examination questions. Chapters 2–17 of this book contain recent examination questions set by the various examining boards and outline answers to these questions are also included. You should attempt all the questions set on the topics relevant to your own course. Even though some of the questions will not have appeared in the particular examination for which you are entered, preparing an outline answer to all the questions will develop your understanding of each topic.

Having completed an answer, or the outline of an answer, check your own approach against that given in the text. The answers given in the text are not to be considered as definitive; indeed, in some cases, it is possible to approach questions in a fundamentally different way. Nevertheless, by comparing your own answer with the one given in the text, it will usually be possible to assess whether your own approach is along the right lines as well as identify any mistakes you may have made. This is extremely important, since it is essential to learn from your mistakes if you are to improve your understanding of the subject. If, after comparing your answer with the one suggested in the text, you are unsure about the validity of your approach, check with your course tutor.

You will also find an **actual student answer** to a past question in each chapter. Look at the **examiner comments** on the strengths and weaknesses of that answer. This will give you a good idea of what the examiner is looking for in an answer. The **tutor's answer** included in each chapter should also give you guidance on what the examiner is looking for. Finally you can try the questions in the **Review Sheets** at the end of each chapter. These will help you to check your understanding of what you have read in that chapter.

ESSENTIAL PRINCIPLES

ESSAY WRITING TECHNIQUES

During your course you will probably be required to produce essays for marking by the course tutor. Sometimes the marks obtained will count towards the final grade awarded on completion of the course, but more often essays (and other assignments) are simply set as an aid to understanding and learning. In either case you should ensure that each essay is written to the highest standard you are capable of achieving at that time.

Remember that writing essays sometimes involves drawing on knowledge from several parts of the course. The only way to be sure that you are answering a question fully is to understand all the topics that have been covered. To do this you must regularly revise the topics covered in class; a good rule of thumb is to spend about half an hour each week revising and testing your understanding of topics already covered.

❝ *Regular revision is the key* ❞

Writing essays which are consistently of a high standard involves taking pride in your work as well as paying careful attention to many other points. These will be the subject of the remainder of this section.

PREPARING YOUR ESSAY

Obtain the essay title as early as possible and consider it carefully. Think what it means and what it is asking you to do. If you are unsure, a useful tip is to try to write in your own words on a sheet of rough paper what you think the essay title means. For example, if the essay title is: 'What are the reasons for government intervention in a market economy?' it is asking you 'Why do governments interfere with a market economy?' and to answer this you must state and explain these reasons.

PLANNING YOUR ESSAY

Once you have decided what the title means, you can plan what to put in your answer. Make a list of the following things:

What to put in your introduction
In general, this should be very brief and to the point. It is best to include a **definition** of the central topic of your essay where this is appropriate. For example, if an essay title asks you to 'Explain, what is meant by ...' or 'Define ...' then it is best to start with a definition. Therefore, in answer to the question 'Explain, with the use of relevant examples, what is meant by the term opportunity cost', you might begin by writing: '*Opportunity cost* is usually defined as ...'. Even where you are not specifically asked to define or describe something, it is good sense to do so; look out for this. For example, the title 'Economic goods are scarce goods – explain the meaning of this statement', doesn't actually ask you to define 'economic goods' but you must do so if you are to explain the meaning of the statement. As well as a definition, it is usually helpful to outline, in the introduction, the stages that will appear in your argument.

❝ *Definitions are important* ❞

What to put in the body of your essay
Note down the major items you will be dealing with. Consider how to divide these up into separate paragraphs. Remember that each separate item should be dealt with in a separate paragraph. At this stage you should note down examples or facts that you intend to use, diagrams that you will draw, and additional definitions that you will state.

Whether to write a separate conclusion or not
In general, put one in. It will in any case serve as a useful summary of what you have said in your answer. For example, if you are asked 'Give the reasons for government intervention in a market economy', in your final paragraph you could write: 'We have outlined five reasons for government intervention in a market economy. These are; the instability that might arise in a market economy; the possibility of exploitation by monopolies; the extent to which inequalities occur; the hardship caused by economic change and the desire to alter the use of resources when social and private values are different.' Sometimes the essay title itself will be a question, so that in your conclusion you must actually state what your answer has been.

❝ *Review your findings* ❞

WRITING YOUR ESSAY

Write neatly and legibly. Follow your plan. Take care to express your ideas correctly and in a way that is intelligible to others. Remember that all the sentences in one paragraph should be concerned with the same point and should follow logically from each other when you are outlining the argument. In general, do not use abbreviations. Do, however, make sure that you phrase things in a way that is appropriate to the title, so that it is clear that you are answering the question. Avoid making a numbered list of items; each point must be described in a complete sentence. For example, where you are describing the measures used in regional policy, one sentence could begin: 'One measure used in regional policy is ...'. The second measure might be described in a sentence that starts: 'Another measure used is ...' and so on.

Always try to write an essay to the best of your ability. If you do this, your essay technique will gradually improve. This is very important because if you do not learn to write clear, logical and well-reasoned essays in class or at home, success will be more difficult to achieve in the examination itself.

CHECKING YOUR ESSAY

Answer the question set

Once you have finished writing, do not think the essay is ready to be handed in; first it must be checked by you. Look at your plan and check that you have included in your essay everything you intended to. It is amazing how easy it is to overlook something when you are busy writing. Check that you have really written a full and complete answer to the question. Have you dealt with all the parts to the question? Have you explained and described everything as fully as you could? It is a good idea to do this check some time *after* you have written the essay. Coming to it afresh will allow you to consider it more carefully.

LEARNING FROM YOUR MISTAKES

Learn from your mistakes

When the marked essay is returned to you, don't file it away and forget about it. You will find it difficult to improve your techniques unless you learn from your mistakes. This means reading over your essay after it has been marked, taking note of the comments that have been added and thinking about how it could be improved. This will dramatically reduce the likelihood of your making the same mistake twice and, coupled with regular revision, will markedly increase your chances of success in the examination.

DATA RESPONSE TECHNIQUES

Many of the major examining boards now include **data response** (i.e. stimulus-based) questions on their Economics papers. Some boards set a compulsory data response paper, as in the GCE A-level papers set by the University of London Examinations and Assessment Council and the Associated Examining Board. However, others, such as the Oxford Delegacy of Local Examinations offer candidates the option of answering data response questions. Broadly there are three types of data response question:

- those based on hypothetical data;
- those based on factual data;
- those based on newspaper articles, or on extracts from official reports, etc.

Much of what has been written above about essays is still important, but because of the nature of data response questions it is impossible to give specific guidance on how to construct an answer. For example, in some cases it might be appropriate to include an introduction, but in others, where the question is highly structured and consists of several different parts, this might not be necessary.

What can be said is that, in all types of data response question, the purpose of giving data is to enable you to demonstrate an understanding of the principles contained in the data. In order to demonstrate understanding you must consider both the assumptions implicit in the data and the implications of any trends shown in the data.

❝ Remember to use the data given ❞

This is very important because it enables examiners to distinguish between candidates who understand economic principles and can apply them, and candidates who have simply memorised them. When answering data response questions, examples should be taken from the data in order to illustrate your answer. This can sometimes be done by extracting the appropriate figures from the material given. At other times, it is necessary to manipulate figures to obtain examples or to highlight trends in the data.

One point you should remember is that data response questions which involve arithmetic calculations are often easier than they at first appear. The best way to approach these is to use the information you are given to obtain, by calculation, as much additional information as will be helpful to you in tackling the question. Once you have obtained this it is often very easy to see the answer to particular parts of the question. However, do not neglect to mention the economic principles on which your answer is based. It is not your arithmetic ability which is being tested, but your ability to understand and apply economic principles.

MULTIPLE-CHOICE TECHNIQUES

Like data response questions, multiple-choice questions (sometimes called items) are becoming an increasingly common feature of examinations in Economics. The most widely used type of multiple-choice question is the simple completion question. This consists of an opening statement (referred to as the **stem**) followed by a series of responses. Only one response (the **key**) correctly completes the statement in the stem, or answers the question it poses. The remaining responses are simply **distractors**. On the face of it, they appear as though they could be correct, but they are not. They are there simply to attract the unwary or the ill-prepared.

In the examination, the multiple-choice paper will consist of a relatively large number of questions (usually 30 or 50) to be answered in a relatively short period of time. This is the major advantage, as an examination method, of multiple-choice questions; they make it possible to test, in an examination, a wide range of subject knowledge and understanding. Such breadth of coverage is impossible to achieve by any other means under examination conditions.

Because multiple-choice questions can test both descriptive knowledge and analytical ability, they are not only a useful method of examining, but also an invaluable aid to learning. During your course you will find it very useful to assess your progress by using multiple-choice questions, whether you take a multiple-choice paper in the examination or not. Remember that each question has only one key, so a good check of your understanding would be your awareness of not only why the key is correct, but also why the other responses are incorrect.

REVISION

There are no hard and fast rules about when to begin final revision for the examination. This depends on the individual, the type of examination, the time available, and so on. All that can be said is that if you are to give yourself the maximum chance of success, thorough revision of all the syllabus is required. Nothing can be left out, otherwise you might find that there are compulsory questions you cannot answer, and that your choice of essay or data response questions is restricted. You should therefore begin revision at a fairly early stage and indeed final revision should simply build on an already solid foundation established by regular revision during your course.

❝ A revision plan can help ❞

It is probably best to begin revision by making a detailed **plan** of when each topic is to be covered. You should make every effort to stick to this plan. However, do remember that you are likely to find revision relatively easy at the start, but more difficult towards the end. Your plan should allow for this, and also for the fact that the more difficult topics will take longer to revise than others. You should take great care, therefore, to ensure that your plan sets realistic targets. Sticking to the plan will lead to growing confidence as you progress from one topic to the next and as your understanding of the subject as a whole grows.

How to revise is very much a personal matter, but you might find the following practical hints useful.

1 Rewrite your course notes on any topic in shortened form, using headings and making lists of points.
2 Learn these lists; it is useful to remember how many points there are in each list, e.g. learn that there are three types of injection into the circular flow of income.
3 Make a separate list of clear and concise definitions.

Some revision hints

4 Draw the main diagrams or charts used in any topic.
5 Write down some key facts and figures that you might learn.
6 Write down any examples or cases that illustrate important principles.
7 Learn these definitions, diagrams, facts and examples by rewriting them from memory and checking them against your notes.
8 Practise past examination questions and especially multiple-choice items and data response questions. For essays, remember there are two things to practise:

- planning your answer;

- writing it in the time allowed.

IN THE EXAMINATION

Follow the instructions

Before attempting any examination paper you must carefully read the instructions on the front of the examination paper. You must follow these instructions to the letter, noting in particular the total number of questions which must be attempted, and the number that should be attempted from each section. You should also note the total time allowed for completing the paper and bear this in mind when allocating time between questions. The remainder of this section provides guidance on how to approach the different types of examination question in the exam room.

ESSAYS

Choosing questions
Choose essay questions very carefully: read through all the questions, marking those that you think you might be able to answer. For these questions consider whether you can actually answer all the parts, as there is usually little point in attempting a question if you cannot answer all of it. Then choose the appropriate number of questions out of those that you can answer, selecting those that you feel you can answer best. Remember that your aim is to show the examiner that you know and understand Economics; don't think that you can give a good answer to a question just because it is easy to answer without using Economics.

Answer plan
Plan what to put in your answer; write this down so that you can follow your plan. Think very carefully about actually answering the question. Note how many marks are allocated to each part of the answer. This is a guide as to how important each part is, so it also tells you how long to spend on each part.

Answer carefully
Write your answer carefully, expressing ideas precisely, using supporting evidence whenever available. Don't be vague and do give examples. Follow the rubric, i.e. set out your answer in the same way that the question has been set out; if the question is divided into two parts, (a) and (b), so your answer must be similarly divided. Make a note of the time you begin each question and spend only the appropriate amount of time on it. This is important because if you are to succeed to the best of your ability you must complete the paper.

Referring back
Keep referring back to the question and to your plan. It is easy, under examination conditions, to wander off the point and to include irrelevant material. Marks are not usually deducted for this, but economists know that the opportunity cost is very high. Time spent discussing irrelevant material is no longer available to discuss relevant material! The penalty for this kind of error might therefore be very serious. It only takes a short while to check that you are following your plan and that what you have written is relevant to the question that has been set.

Keep the question in mind

Answer check
If you have any time left after completing your answers, check your work for errors and omissions. These can easily creep in under examination conditions.

DATA RESPONSE

Again, much of the suggested approach to the essay paper is still relevant here. However, in addition to thinking about the questions, it is necessary to consider how, in each case, the data can be *used* to answer the question. This almost certainly means recognising the economic principles illustrated by, or contained within, the data. On a first reading, this is not an easy task and you should not abandon the idea of attempting a question merely because it is not immediately apparent how to answer it. A second or third reading will often provide you with insights that a first reading does not.

MULTIPLE-CHOICE

All questions on the multiple-choice paper are compulsory, and you will have to work fairly rapidly through them to complete this paper. Despite this, don't try to do too much in your head. If you do, you are likely to become confused or to overlook some important point. Instead, draw diagrams, write down formulae to help you, and work fully through any calculations.

Because you must work quickly through this paper, it is particularly important to read each stem carefully. Under examination pressure it is easy to overlook a vital word. This is especially true where questions begin with a negative stem such as 'Which one of the following is not an invisible export?' Before putting down your answer on the examination paper, therefore, you should quickly glance at the stem to ensure that you have not made an obvious error in your choice of response.

On this type of paper, there will inevitably be some questions which are easier than others. Because of this you should not spend too much time on one question. If you are struggling with a particular question, it is best to miss it out and to go on to the next one. Remember to mark the question you have missed out, and be careful not to put the answer to succeeding questions in the wrong place. This is very easily done when you are using a computer marked card to record your answers. The only certain way to avoid doing this is to check the question number and answer number before recording your response. Do not forget to go back and answer any questions you have missed out. If you are still unable to answer them, eliminate any responses you know to be incorrect and make a guess from the remainder. You have at least a 20 per cent chance of being right where the question has five responses, and at least a 25 per cent chance where it has four! Eliminating incorrect responses increases the chance of being right still further.

> ❝ **You can eliminate incorrect responses** ❞

TOPICS AND COURSES

Table 1.1 gives a broad indication of the topics and courses for which this book will be useful. Check your own syllabus.

As we note below, the A-Level and AS-Level Economics syllabuses were revised in 1995 to bring them into line with the National Curriculum. Along with other A-Level subject syllabuses, a *subject core* was identified for Economics consisting of a body of knowledge, understanding and skills considered essential to advanced level study. All the revised syllabuses now incorporate that core, and indeed go beyond it to specify what subject matter they will assess you on. In fact very little has been taken out of the new A-Level syllabuses, though there has been some change of emphasis, such as more attention to the causes and consequences of market failure, to the use of aggregrate demand/aggregate supply analysis in macroeconomics, to regulation/deregulation issues, etc. The questions set on these syllabuses will also pay rather more attention to skills involving application and data handling. Again, check your own examination board syllabus for more detailed information on topics and assessment arrangements.

MODULAR COURSES

In Economics, as in other subjects, there has been considerable interest in the possible provision of courses which are assessed in discrete units or 'modules' throughout the course. Nuffield Economics has provided this type of course for some time, and Cambridge (UCLES) now offers modular A-level and AS-level Economics courses as alternatives to its standard (linear) courses which are still on offer.

CHAPTER AND TOPIC	A-LEVEL								SCOTTISH HIGHER
	AEB	UCLES*	NEAB	ULEAC	NICCEA	ODLE	O&C	WJEC	SEB
2 The economic problem	✓	✓	✓	✓	✓	✓	✓	✓	✓
3 Production, costs and returns	✓	✓	✓	✓	✓	✓	✓	✓	✓
4 Demand, supply and price	✓	✓	✓	✓	✓	✓	✓	✓	✓
5 Perfect competition and monopoly	✓	✓	✓	✓	✓	✓	✓	✓	✓
6 Imperfect competition	✓	✓	✓	✓	✓	✓	✓	✓	✓
7 The structure of industry	✓	✓	✓	✓	✓	✓	✓	✓	✓
8 National income accounting	✓	✓	✓	✓	✓	✓	✓	✓	✓
9 National income determination	✓	✓	✓	✓	✓	✓	✓	✓	✓
10 Wages and trade unions	✓	✓	✓	✓	✓	✓	✓	✓	✓
11 Interest, rent and profit	✓	✓	✓	✓	✓	✓	✓	✓	✓
12 Money and banking	✓	✓	✓	✓	✓	✓	✓	✓	✓
13 The value of money	✓	✓	✓	✓	✓	✓	✓	✓	✓
14 International trade and protection	✓	✓	✓	✓	✓	✓	✓	✓	✓
15 The balance of payments and exchange rates	✓	✓	✓	✓	✓	✓	✓	✓	✓
16 Public finance	✓	✓	✓	✓	✓	✓	✓	✓	✓
17 Management of the economy	✓	✓	✓	✓	✓	✓	✓	✓	✓

* Linear and modular courses available

Table 1.1 Topics and courses

THE 'CORE' AT A-LEVEL

The *core* at A- (and AS-) level has been identified as:

■ The market mechanism.

■ Causes of, and responses to, market failure.

■ The national economy (including the structure and essential determinants of international trade).

You will find the topic areas covered in the seventeen chapters of this book cover these essential microeconomic and macroeconomic features within the core. They will also cover the majority of additional and optional materials required by your own particular examination board for purposes of assessment. If you are in any doubt as to your own syllabus, or the methods of assessment you will face, you should contact your own examination board.

For Economics, the core will normally be around 50 per cent of all you will learn at A-level. It will, however, usually be 100 per cent of all you will learn at AS-level.

A FINAL WORD

When you first start your course, set your sights on obtaining the highest grade. Stick to your aim throughout the course and gear the level of your effort accordingly. Pay particular attention to those topics which you do not fully understand and never assume that an individual topic is unimportant. In a subject like Economics, topics often interrelate and a full understanding of one topic is impossible without a full understanding of others. Remember that if you do find a topic difficult, other students will also find it difficult. This is why it is important to persevere. Not everyone succeeds in the examination, but those who persevere in seeking to overcome their problems have a clear advantage. At the end of the day, the highest grade is particularly important because few people achieve it. This book cannot guarantee success, but if used correctly, it should prove to be a valuable aid.

Further reading
Harrison, *Studying Economics at A Level*, Longman 1989.
Stanlake and Harrison, *A Macroeconomics Workbook*, Longman 1984.

THE ECONOMIC PROBLEM: RESOURCE ALLOCATION

ECONOMIC TERMINOLOGY

SCARCITY AND CHOICE

OPPORTUNITY COST

THE MARKET ECONOMY

THE CENTRALLY PLANNED ECONOMY

THE MIXED ECONOMY

GETTING STARTED

Economics is the study of how society makes choices about *what* output is to be produced, *how* this output is to be produced and *for whom* it is to be produced. In other words, it is the study of how society allocates its scarce resources among competing alternatives. The economic resources referred to in this definition are usually classified as: land, labour, capital and enterprise. This subject is covered extensively in Chapter 3 but the point to note here is that all societies must decide how to allocate their limited resources to given ends. The study of Economics is largely concerned with this problem, and how society deals with it.

As well as being aware of the subject content, it is also important to be aware of the *methodology* used in the study of Economics. In fact, Economics is often termed a 'social science': 'science', because the approach used has much in common with that of the natural scientist, studying Chemistry or Physics for example; 'social', because the subject matter is the human being.

The basic approach is referred to as *scientific method*, but because we are concerned with analysing the behaviour of human beings, the controlled experiments of the 'natural sciences' (in which a single factor affecting the result can be excluded) are impossible in the study of Economics. This makes it more difficult for economists to link cause and effect. Another problem for economists is that *individual* human beings react differently to external events, making predictions more difficult. Fortunately, it is often easier to predict the reaction of *groups* of individuals to events because extreme reactions tend to cancel each other out.

As with any science, the main aim of Economics is to develop theories (or hypotheses) which can help to explain the events we observe. There are two main ways of developing such theories. One is the *deductive* approach; here a theory is proposed, logical deduction is then applied to develop predictions, and a test is made of these predictions against the facts. For instance, one theory is that the amount of a commodity consumers wish to purchase will usually vary with its price. This prediction can then be tested against how consumers actually behave. If the facts do not support the theory it must be rejected in favour of other theories which better explain actual observations. An alternative way of developing a theory is to use the *inductive* approach. The facts themselves are the starting point for this approach, with any observed pattern or regularity in the facts giving the economist some guidance. He or she must then work backwards to induce a theory which, by logical deduction, actually predicts the pattern of facts observed. For example, we might observe that unemployment tends to rise in the winter and fall in the summer. Having observed this regular pattern, we might produce a theory to explain it which could then be tested against the facts in the normal way.

ESSENTIAL PRINCIPLES

ECONOMIC TERMINOLOGY

Normative and positive statements

One very important point arising out of the application of scientific method to Economics is that care must be taken to avoid **normative statements**. These are matters of opinion which cannot be proved or disproved by reference to the facts, since they are based on *value judgements*. Normative statements can easily be recognised because they often contain verbs such as 'should' or 'ought'. For instance, to say that, 'The government's main aim should be the control of inflation', is a normative statement, since its validity cannot be checked against any facts. It is a statement with which we may either agree or disagree, but there is no way of proving that it is correct or incorrect. It is a matter of *opinion* rather than a matter of fact.

66 Distinguish normative from positive 99

This contrasts markedly with **positive statements**. The accuracy of positive statements can be checked against the facts and they can be *proved* correct or incorrect. Therefore, to say that, 'The rate of inflation in the UK over the last twelve months has been 6 per cent', is a positive statement. By reference to the facts, it can be proved to be correct or incorrect. Any statement which can be checked against the facts is a positive statement.

The distinction between positive and normative statements is particularly important in a subject like Economics which embraces many controversial topic areas, since there is often a great temptation to express personal opinions which have little to do with any facts. It is irrelevant whether you personally approve or disapprove of trade unions, centrally planned economies, membership of the EU or government policy in general. These are political matters and opinions can be expressed through the ballot box. As economists, it is much more important to explain how institutions operate, the effect of their operation on the allocation of resources, the way in which they are likely to change in the future, and so on.

Micro and macro

Another very important distinction to be aware of is that between micro and macro economics. These terms come from the Greek words for 'small' and 'large'. **Microeconomics** is therefore concerned with the behaviour of small parts of the economy, such as an individual or a firm. It focuses on such topics as the wage rate in a particular occupation or the price of a particular product. **Macroeconomics** on the other hand deals with the economy as a whole and is concerned with such aggregates as unemployment, the rate of interest or the levels of exports and imports. The reason for the distinction is that small changes, such as a change in the price of a box of matches, have no effect on the economy as a whole. However, the distinction is not always as clear as this. A change in the price of oil might well have microeconomic and macroeconomic implications.

Note: Some of the topics covered in this chapter can be illustrated using supply and demand diagrams. A full explanation of these is not given until Chapter 4, so they are therefore omitted from this chapter. However, when you have read Chapter 4, refer back to this chapter and use supply and demand diagrams to explain how the price mechanism operates.

SCARCITY AND CHOICE

THE ECONOMIC PROBLEM

The economic problem is summed up in two key words, **scarcity** and **choice**. To the economist, scarcity has a very specific meaning and does not simply mean rare as many people often assume. To the economist, something is scarce if society desires more of it than is currently available. By this definition most goods and services are scarce. After all, we can all think of things we desire which we do not currently possess: more records, more clothes, more cars and so on.

ECONOMIC CHOICES

66 Resource allocation is the basic problem 99

The basic economic problem confronting all societies is how to allocate scarce resources between alternative uses. Resources are scarce because the collective desires of society for consumption at any moment in time exceed the ability to satisfy those desires. Because there are insufficient resources to produce all that is desired, society is forced to make choices. These choices are:

- **What** output will be produced? It is obvious that if society cannot produce all it desires, it must choose which goods and services to produce from the available resources. Any decision about what items to produce also implies a decision about how much of these items to produce. However, because resources are scarce, more of one thing implies less of something else.

⁶⁶ What, how and for whom? 99

- **How** shall the output be produced? Society must decide not only what output is to be produced, but also how the output is to be produced. There are various ways of producing any given output. In many of the world's poorer countries production is often *labour-intensive* (i.e. uses large amounts of labour relative to other factors of production) while production of the same goods in the richer countries is often *capital-intensive* (i.e. uses large amounts of capital relative to other factors of production). For example, this is true of most agricultural production.

- **For whom** shall the output be produced? Clearly if an output is produced there must be some means of allocating it to consumers and of deciding who receives what. In other words, society must decide how its output is to be distributed.

The way in which society makes these choices gives rise to different economic systems and these are considered later in this chapter.

OPPORTUNITY COST

Because all output is created from scarce resources, it follows that these resources have alternative uses. How many uses can you think of, for timber or labour, for example? However, once resources have been used to produce a particular type of output they are no longer available to produce a different type of output. In choosing which goods and services will be produced from scarce resources, society also chooses which goods and services it will do without. If resources are used to produce one thing, society is forced to do without those other things that might have been produced from the same resources. This is very important to the economist and in choosing what to produce (or consume), the next most desired alternative sacrificed is referred to as the **opportunity cost** (or real cost) of what is produced (or consumed).

⁶⁶ Be familiar with opportunity cost 99

In taking decisions about production and consumption, both policy-makers and private individuals are concerned with the concept of opportunity cost. For example, a local authority might be considering the construction of a new educational college. If land and capital are used to build houses, they cannot also be used to build the college. In this case, we say that the opportunity cost of additional housing is the college which is sacrificed.

ECONOMIC GOODS AND FREE GOODS

It is clear that opportunity cost only arises when production or consumption involves foregoing an alternative. However, consumption of some goods involves no sacrifice and consequently has no opportunity cost. These goods are not created from scarce resources and are available in such abundance relative to the demand for them that it is possible for one person to consume them to complete satiety, i.e. until no more are required, without depriving anyone else of consumption. Such goods are referred to as **free goods**. The most often quoted example of a free good is fresh air, but there are many other examples, such as sand in the desert.

⁶⁶ Economic goods have an opportunity cost 99

Economists distinguish free goods, which do not embody scarce resources, from those goods which do, by referring to the latter as **economic goods**. Because only economic goods have an opportunity cost (since free goods are not created from scarce resources), the three basic choices referred to earlier (What? How? and For whom?) only refer to choices concerning economic goods.

⁶⁶ Free goods have no opportunity cost 99

The term 'free goods' sometimes causes confusion. Not all goods and services for which no charge is made are free goods. Some 'goods', such as state education or 'free' concerts, are made available without direct charge to consumers, but they are still created from scarce resources. Therefore, in providing them, the alternatives that those resources could have produced are foregone so they are economic goods and not free goods. Remember – if there is an opportunity cost, then the goods are not free goods even if no charge is made for them.

PRODUCTION POSSIBILITY CURVES

One way of representing the range of possible choices available to society is in the form of a **production possibility curve**. Such a curve is illustrated in Fig. 2.1 and for simplicity it is assumed that society can only produce two goods, X and Y.

Because society has only a limited amount of resources, there is an upper limit on the amount of output that can be produced at any moment in time. A production possibility curve therefore shows the maximum output that society can produce given its existing resources. In other words, all points *on* the curve represent points at which the economy is operating at full productive capacity, i.e. full employment. Any point *inside* the curve must, therefore, indicate that there are unemployed resources in the economy. Thus, at point R in Fig. 2.1 there are unemployed resources in the economy, whereas at points S and T there is full employment.

A production possibility curve shows what society can produce with *existing* resources at any moment in time. However, over time, society's ability to produce output will increase because of improvements in the productivity of labour, greater technological progress, an increase in the size of the labour force and so on. Whatever the cause, if society's ability to produce output increases, this will be represented by an outward movement of the entire production possibility curve.

It might seem unrealistic to show the production possibilities available to society by considering only two goods. After all, a developed economy such as the UK produces a whole range of different goods and services. However, it is not necessarily unrealistic to concentrate on only two goods, as in Fig. 2.1. For example, good X could be output provided through the *public* sector, i.e. state-provided activities, whereas good Y could represent output provided through the *private* or market sector. Yet again, good X might represent the goods produced for immediate consumption (*consumer goods*) or goods such as machines (*capital goods*) which are used to produce other goods. Even more fundamentally, we could consider the choice as being between *tangible goods* (X) and *services* (Y), and so on.

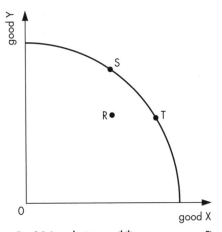

Fig. 2.1 A production possibility curve

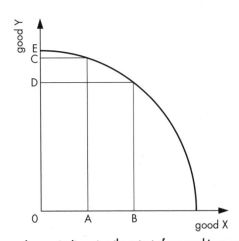

Fig. 2.2 Change in opportunity cost as the output of one good increases

Production possibility curves and opportunity cost

We can illustrate the principle of opportunity cost using a production possibility curve. The curve shows the maximum amount of one good that can be produced, given that a particular quantity of another good is required. For example, in terms of Fig. 2.2, if the economy is currently producing OC of good Y, the *maximum* amount of good X that can be produced is OA. However, if OB of good X is required, the *maximum* amount of good Y that can be produced is OD. In other words, the *opportunity cost* of an additional AB units of good X, is CD units of good Y, because this is the amount of good Y that must be foregone or *sacrificed* in order to have the additional units of good X.

It is also important to note that the shape of the production possibility curve indicates that the opportunity cost of any given increase in the output of one good will change as we move along the production possibility curve. For example, we have already seen that the opportunity cost of increasing the output of good X by AB units when we move from an output of OA of good X to an output of OB of good X, is CD of Y. However, if we increase the output of good X from zero to OA (roughly the same increase in the output of good X as AB) then the opportunity cost is much lower at only EC units of good Y. In other words, the opportunity cost increases as the output of any good increases.

There are several reasons for this, but the most obvious is that not all resources are equally well suited to the production of both goods. Some resources are better suited to the production of goods than others and when resources specialise in producing the goods in which they are most efficient, higher levels of output will be produced. For example, at point E we are using some resources to produce good Y which are not well suited to the production of this good and therefore they are not very productive. Because of this, initially, it is possible to produce good X at a relatively low opportunity cost by diverting those resources away from good Y which are better suited to the production of good X. Note, however, that as the production of good X increases, the opposite occurs, and the opportunity cost of producing extra units of X starts to increase.

EXTERNALITIES, SOCIAL COSTS AND PRIVATE COSTS

66 Be familiar with externalities 99

One important aspect of production and consumption in modern economies is that they frequently give rise to **externalities**. These are the spill-over effects of production and consumption which affect society as a whole rather than just the individual producers or consumers. Externalities might impose costs on society such as air pollution from the operation of motor vehicles or river pollution from the dumping of waste materials. On the other hand, externalities might confer benefits (negative costs) such as the general increase in property values in a particular street that results from individual improvements to property. It is important to note that any costs and benefits resulting from externalities are not solely borne by the individuals or firms responsible for them. Instead they are borne by *all* the individuals or firms affected by them.

66 Private and social costs can differ 99

To derive the full **social costs** of production, we must add the costs (or benefits) of these externalities to the **private costs** of production, such as labour costs, raw material costs, etc. We shall see later that the existence of externalities has an important bearing on the allocation of resources to different uses in the economy.

THE MARKET ECONOMY

While the nature of the choices confronting all societies is the same, they sometimes adopt different methods of dealing with them. One method is to allow choices to be resolved by the free play of *market forces* (supply and demand), and in this case we say that resources are allocated through the *price mechanism*. This simply means that individuals, as consumers, freely choose which goods and services they will purchase, and producers freely decide which goods and services they will provide. Because of this, market economies are often referred to as free enterprise or *laissez faire* (leave well alone) economies.

CHARACTERISTICS OF THE MARKET ECONOMY

Limited role for the state

Market economies are characterised by an almost total lack of government intervention. Indeed, in a strictly free enterprise economy, the only major role performed by the government would be that of creating a framework of rules or laws within which both private individuals and firms could conduct their affairs. Such roles would be necessary since, in their absence, there would be no protection from such activities as the addition of harmful substances to products, the false labelling of contents, fraudulent behaviour and so on.

The right to own and dispose of private property

One of the most important features of this kind of economic system is the right of individuals to own private property, and in particular to own and dispose of land and capital as factors of production. This is extremely important, and means that any individual possessing the necessary factors of production, or resources, is free to undertake production. Indeed, in the absence of government intervention, they are free both to undertake production and to decide what they will produce.

Despite this, the decision to produce is not always undertaken by those individuals who own the necessary factors of production. Sometimes, these are hired out to other individuals. Those individuals who do undertake production are known as **entrepreneurs**. Since the entrepreneur hires the factors of production or uses those currently in his/her ownership, he/she is a *risk-taker*, and since the entrepreneur also decides how resources will be organised and what they will produce, he/she is also a *decision-taker*. The entrepreneurial function is therefore that of risk-taker and decision-taker.

The existence of the profit motive

In making decisions about production, entrepreneurs are guided by the **profit motive**. In other words, the motivating force for the entrepreneur is assumed to be self-interest, with entrepreneurs producing whatever offers them greatest profit. Because of this, price changes provide signals to producers, and because of the effect of price changes on profit, producers react to these signals.

66 Price acts as a signal 99

Reliance on the price mechanism to allocate resources

This is the most fundamental characteristic of market economies. Decisions about consumption are undertaken by millions of different people, each freely expressing their preferences for different goods and services. Decisions about production, on the other hand, are undertaken by tens of thousands of producers who freely decide which goods and services they are going to provide. There is little or no direct communication between each of these groups, and yet any change in the preferences of consumers is accurately and quickly transmitted to producers via its effect on the prices of goods and services which producers provide. These price changes ensure that the decisions of producers and consumers, although taken independently, are usually compatible with one another (see Chapter 4).

66 Prices co-ordinate the decisions of producers and consumers 99

How do price changes achieve this? Consider, as an example, the case of a good which suddenly becomes more popular so that there is a market shortage at the *existing* price. In these circumstances, the price of the good will rise so as to ration the available supply. However, the rise in price will make production of that commodity more profitable. Output will therefore expand as producers are now able to attract resources away from alternative uses by the offer of higher rewards. The process will operate in reverse when a product becomes less popular. It is particularly important to note that, because of their impact on price, changes in consumer demands lead to changes in the allocation of resources. Because of this, the consumer is said to be 'sovereign' in market economies.

ADVANTAGES AND DISADVANTAGES OF MARKET ECONOMIES

Advantages

- **What is produced is dictated by the demands of consumers** One of the main advantages of the market mechanism is that consumers, by their own actions, dictate the pattern of production. Because of this, the consumer is said to be 'sovereign' in market economies. By continuing to consume a commodity they are, in effect, voting for its continued production. By consuming more of a commodity, they are voting more resources into the production of that commodity and, because resources have alternative uses, they are voting fewer resources into the production of other commodities.

- **Producers have an incentive (the profit motive) to respond quickly to changes in consumer demands** However, this simple explanation does not fully convey the significance of the price mechanism's operation. Not only do producers have an incentive to respond to changes in consumer preferences, they also have an incentive to respond quickly and efficiently. Because there is freedom to own and hire the factors of production in free market economies, any producer who does not respond quickly to changes in consumer preferences will soon be driven out of business by those who do respond quickly. In other words, the price mechanism answers both the 'What' and the 'How' questions.

- **Competition encourages firms to use the least-cost method of production** Additionally, it is argued that the freedom to undertake production ensures a high degree of competition in the economy. This is extremely important and competition is the main regulator of economic efficiency in market economies. Any improvement in a firm's efficiency will lower its costs relative to its competitors and hence raise its profits from a given value of sales. It might also enable the more efficient firms to lower their prices relative to other firms, with the aim of attracting more consumers and further increasing profits.

  Thus, the clear implication is that competition benefits the consumer. It encourages efficiency and lower prices, and might also encourage improvements in the nature of the products that firms produce. The incentive for firms to be efficient in market economies is, therefore, a powerful one. The more efficient firms make higher profits, while the least efficient firms are forced out of business because they are unable to compete with the lower prices offered by more efficient firms.

66 **Advantage of market economies** 99

- **Resources are allocated to their 'optimum', or most efficient, use** The price mechanism clearly encourages efficiency in production and distribution, but it is also claimed that its operation leads to an optimum, or ideal, allocation of resources. This is because the price consumers are willing to pay for a commodity represents their valuation of the resources used to produce that commodity. In other words, price is a measure of the value consumers place on a commodity. On the other hand, the cost of producing a commodity is the cost producers pay to attract resources away from other uses. In other words, financial costs of production are a measure of the opportunity cost of production. An optimum allocation of resources exists when the value society places on another unit of the commodity (shown by the price they are willing to pay for it) exactly equals the cost of attracting resources away from alternative uses (i.e. its opportunity cost). This must be so because if alternatives were more highly valued, resources would move into their production because entrepreneurs would offer them higher rewards. This is precisely what happens when demand for a good increases. Its price is bid up and production expands as resources are attracted away from alternatives. When price equals opportunity cost a **Pareto optimum** allocation of resources is said to exist and this simply means that it is no longer possible to make one person better off without simultaneously making someone else worse off.

Disadvantages

- **Prices reflect private costs rather than social costs** It seems, therefore, that the market mechanism operates with great efficiency in the allocation of resources. In practice, however, this is unlikely to be true. One reason for this is that an efficient or optimum allocation of resources can only exist when all prices in the economy fully reflect the *social* costs of production and consumption. However, prices in market economies are based entirely on *private* costs of production. Thus, if a product imposes relatively large social costs on society, then the free operation of the price mechanism will not lead to an optimum allocation of resources. This is simply because the social costs of production will be greater than the private costs, and hence market price will be less than the real (social) opportunity cost of production.

  The fact that price is less than the full (social) costs of production leads to a higher level of consumption, and therefore production, than would happen if costs were based on the full social costs of production. In other words, society would over-produce this commodity, and under-produce others where social costs of production are less than private costs. In this case, it is possible for society as a whole to increase its welfare by a reallocation of resources from those commodities which are over-produced in relation to the optimum level, to those which are under-produced. Thus, where social costs of production exist, the free operation of the price (or market) mechanism will *not* lead to the most efficient allocation of resources.

■ **Public goods and merit goods** The price mechanism might also fail to allocate resources efficiently because it leads to the non-production of pure public goods and the under production of merit goods (see pp. 20–21).

■ **The economy is often unstable** Free market economies are inherently unstable because of the ever-changing pattern of consumer demands. This has serious repercussions. A fall in demand for one industry's product is likely to lead to unemployment in that industry. This might adversely affect whole regions in which an industry is localised. More serious still is the unemployment which results from a general fall in consumer demand. In the absence of government intervention this might be heavy and persistent. Such unemployment represents inefficiency in the market mechanism, because an economy with unemployed resources is working below its productive potential. Hence, the output of goods and services is less than would be achieved if the economy operated at maximum efficiency. This provides justification for government intervention in the economy and the adoption of policies designed to improve the mobility of capital and labour.

❝❝ Disadvantages of market economies ❞❞

■ **There is inequality in the distribution of income and wealth** Free market economies are also criticised because they lead to considerable inequality in the distribution of income and wealth. Those who own land and capital derive incomes from hiring them out, but the vast majority of people have nothing but their labour to sell. In addition, when instability in the economy leads to unemployment, the limited role for the government implies an absence of state aid in the form of income support for example. Similarly those with relatively low incomes or with relatively large families receive no kind of state aid. This degree of inequality is unacceptable to most people.

THE CENTRALLY PLANNED ECONOMY

An alternative method of allocating resources is for the government to issue directives or instructions to firms indicating what they should produce, the quantities that should be produced, and so on. In some cases, this might be accompanied by complete physical rationing among consumers, but it is more usual to allow consumers a large degree of choice over the items they purchase.

The problems of planning

One obvious problem for this kind of system is to ensure that the demands of consumers matches the output of firms. We have seen that the price mechanism performs this function in free enterprise economies, but in centrally planned economies producers will only follow the instructions they are given. In this type of system, the mechanism which 'signals' shortages of some commodities can often be the existence of long queues and empty shelves; while the signal for surpluses of other commodities is often the accumulation of stocks.

❝❝ Planners must consider all the linkages between outputs ❞❞

Another problem faced by the planners is to ensure that the target levels of output assigned to various industries are compatible with each other. For example, in giving the steel industry a target level of output, the planners must take into consideration the target levels of output assigned to other industries which use steel, such as car manufacturing and ship building. Similarly, when assigning a target to the steel industry, the planners must ensure that a sufficient supply of coal is available to the steel industry. Hence the target given to the coal industry must take account of the target given to the steel industry and so on. The particular target levels of output assigned to different industries will reflect the balance struck by the planners between the production of *consumer goods* and the production of *capital goods*. They face a further problem of estimating the *pattern* of consumer demands so that they can decide which consumer goods and services to produce and which capital goods to produce. This is an extremely difficult task since consumer demands are constantly changing and mistakes are costly in terms of wasted resources. For example, if it is decided to increase the production of a particular consumer good in the expectation of rising demand, this will also require the production of additional capital goods which might be specific to the production of that consumer good. If demand for this consumer good actually falls rather than rises, resources will be wasted until the plan can be altered.

It is clear that any attempt to plan the economy is a complex operation and although plans would normally be expected to run for several years, in the former Soviet Union plans were often revised more frequently to take account of changes in consumer demands, technological change, the effects of the weather on agricultural production, and so on. Nevertheless, it is sometimes claimed that centrally planned economies have many advantages over market economies. The most commonly suggested advantages and disadvantages are summarised below.

Advantages of centrally planned economies

- **Production is not undertaken for profit**   It is argued, therefore, that there is greater likelihood of both public goods and merit goods being provided (see pp 20–21); the government simply has to issue a directive to ensure production.

- **Demerit goods can be controlled**   The production and consumption of demerit goods, which impose relatively large social costs on society, can be limited or prevented altogether; this might be done by using taxes (or subsidies) to bring prices more fully into line with social costs, or by direct restrictions on production and consumption.

- **Greater equality is a possibility?**   It is sometimes suggested that there is likely to be greater equality in the distribution of income and wealth in centrally planned economies. This is because the factors of production, with the exception of labour, are owned by the state, so that it is impossible for anyone to derive incomes from hiring out land and capital. Similarly, in a fully centrally planned economy, there are no private entrepreneurs who derive profits from combining the factors of production.

- **Greater stability is possible**   It is claimed that centrally planned economies are likely to be far more stable than market economies. Economic management is entirely in the hands of the government, and consumers have far less power to influence production. Thus, if consumer demand for a particular good falls, it will not necessarily lead to unemployment in the industry. Initially, the planners might maintain production at existing levels and gradually reduce it over time by not replacing workers who leave the industry through retirement, etc. Any surplus output accumulated as a result of this might be sold abroad at reduced prices. It is clear that this could not happen where production is undertaken for profit, since such a policy would undoubtedly reduce the profitability of an industry.

> 66 Central planning does have some advantages, as well as disadvantages 99

Disadvantages of centrally planned economies

- **The loss of consumer sovereignty**   There is general agreement among the critics of this system that an important disadvantage of centrally planned economies is the loss of consumer sovereignty. In other words, the state decides what is to be produced, and consumers have much less influence over production than in market economies. Because of this there are likely to be shortages of certain commodities and surpluses of others, with no automatic mechanism for their removal.

- **The growth of bureaucracy**   There may be a tendency towards larger bureaucratic structures; government planning departments, rather than decentralised markets, govern resource allocation in such economies. The opportunity cost of employing people to gather information, process it and formulate plans, etc., is the alternative output these people could otherwise have produced.

> 66 There may be fewer incentives 99

- **The demotivation factor**   Another important criticism of centrally planned economies is that because the profit motive is absent, there is less incentive to increase efficiency. In market economies, any increase in the efficiency of firms will lower costs of production and increase profits. This provides a powerful incentive to increase efficiency. For instance, it encourages the use of the latest advances in technology in the production process, i.e. **process innovation**, and the quest for new processes and products via research and development expenditure. However, production is not undertaken for profit in centrally planned economies, so there is less incentive to increase efficiency. Indeed, it is sometimes suggested that because any increase in efficiency will lead the planners to raise the target levels of output assigned to an industry, industries in such economies have an incentive *not* to increase efficiency. Whatever the truth of this, there is no doubt that a great deal of industry in the former centrally planned economies was considerably less efficient than industry in the West, where the profit motive guides producers.

■ **The absence of competition** It is also suggested that the absence of competition in centrally planned economies is a disincentive to efficiency. There is less competition among firms in such economies, since each firm simply responds to the instructions it receives from the planners. So long as planners issue instructions for the continued production of any good or service this will be provided, even if firms make a loss (i.e. costs of production exceed sales revenue) in undertaking the production. Any loss that does arise will be underwritten by the state. The absence of competition might therefore discourage moves towards greater efficiency which, in a competitive market economy, would be necessary for the firm to survive. The ultimate sanction against inefficient firms in a market economy is that if they do not earn profits they will eventually be forced into liquidation.

66 **Some problems with central planning** 99

■ **Controlling social costs** Despite the claim that planners *can* take account of the full social costs of production and influence the allocation of resources accordingly, in the former Soviet Union and Eastern bloc countries this was almost certainly *not* done. On the contrary, the environment was treated as a free resource and pollution of the environment was on a scale unimaginable in the West. Untreated waste, often of a toxic nature, was routinely dumped into rivers or on landfill sites. Such landfill sites were frequently close to towns and cities and waste was not always buried. Dense clouds of pollution overhung many towns and cities as factories and chimneys emitted their waste into the environment.

■ **Stability of employment** There is evidence that while high and stable levels of employment existed in certain Eastern bloc countries, this was achieved by overmanning and inefficiency in the allocation of resources. Indeed the problem was made worse because factory managers tended to hoard labour, partly because targets were often raised suddenly and without warning.

■ **Price controls** These were frequently used in centrally planned economies in order to achieve greater equality. However, relatively low prices encourage over-consumption and this has been one of the main reasons for shortages, for example of foodstuffs in many Eastern bloc countries. Here again the result is inefficiency in the allocation of resources.

There is another problem. Shortages create a demand for imports, but allowing the free import of goods and services was often inconsistent with the plan for the economy. Hence, trade had to be restricted in centrally planned economies and, as we shall see in Chapter 14, international trade can have an important effect on the efficiency with which resources are used and therefore on the growth of living standards. By curbing trade, the former Soviet Union and the other planned economies limited their opportunities for faster economic growth.

The collapse of planning

The planned economies of the former USSR collapsed into chaos at the end of the 1980s. However, the newly independent states still faced severe problems. In the former USSR, total output fell by over 20 per cent between 1989 and 1992, while investment in new machinery, plant and equipment fell by around 50 per cent and inflation reached record levels. Indeed inflation in Russia in 1992 was well over 1,000 per cent. For the former centrally planned economies, inflation is a new phenomenon. Under the previous planned system, prices were controlled and any shortages of goods simply led to long queues and empty shelves. As price controls were relaxed, however, prices soared to such an extent that for many people simply feeding themselves became a daily struggle. In more recent years, strict targets have been established for controlling the growth of the money supply and, in consequence, inflation has fallen though it is still at levels unthinkable in the West. (The relationship between changes in money growth and inflation is discussed fully on in Chapter 13.)

One popular myth is that the problems of the former centrally planned economies stem from too rapid a pace of economic reform following the introduction of President Gorbachev's *perestroika* (restructuring) programme. In fact the pace of economic reform had little to do with the collapse of the planned economies; rather it was due to the fact that the planning process simply ceased to function. As the desire for independence of the different republics which made up the former USSR grew, they broke away from the USSR, but often paying too little attention to the integrated system of which they had formed a part. The situation was exacerbated because, under the old planning system, production had been concentrated in specific areas. For example, it has been estimated that three-quarters of the most common 6,000 products had been produced in only *one* establishment per product. As the newly independent states broke away from the former USSR, they ceased to export these products to other parts of the Soviet Union and were often unable to find alternative markets. Further, with no other source of supply available for such products, the planning process collapsed within the territories which remained within the former USSR.

The break up of the Soviet Union caused another problem, particularly for the biggest Republic, Russia. The newly independent states ceased to remit tax revenues to Moscow. Partly as a result of this, and partly as a result of falling oil revenues and falling output generally, the budget deficit (the difference between government expenditure and government revenue) has soared. To finance this gap, the Russian government has simply printed more money, resulting in a rapidly spiralling inflation, which inevitably leads to a misallocation of resources and a disruption of production.

Economic Reform in Eastern Europe

The nature of economic reform in the former USSR differs from country to country, but we can identify some necessary changes if these countries are to move away from planning and towards a market economy.

- **The legality of private ownership of property must be established**
  Without private ownership, the incentive to produce those goods society most desires are produced will be absent, as will the incentive to improve quality, design, delivery and so on.

- **Price stability must be restored** Many of the newly independent states face inflation on a scale unthinkable in Western Europe. When prices rise rapidly, it is difficult for producers to make decisions about what to produce, because they cannot distinguish between a rise in prices for their product due to a change in society's preferences, and a general rise in prices as a result of inflation. However, it is important that price stability is not created merely by *controlling prices*. When prices are controlled, it becomes impossible for the price mechanism to provide appropriate *signals* to producers about changes in the preferences of society for different goods and services.

- **Regulations which prevent competition must be dismantled** It is often argued that competition encourages economic efficiency and that where regulations restrict or stifle competition, resources cannot be allocated efficiently. As well as deregulating some markets, it will be necessary to *create* others. In particular, it will be necessary to create a capital market where the savings of society can be borrowed by entrepreneurs and where individuals and organisations can buy and sell shares in newly privatised companies.

THE MIXED ECONOMY

66 Most economies are mixed 99

We have seen that both free enterprise and centrally planned economies have their respective advantages and disadvantages. For this reason neither is found in its extreme form in the economies of the world. It is often suggested that the economy of Hong Kong comes closest to being a free enterprise economy, but with the collapse of Communism in Eastern Europe there are few examples of planned economies in the world today. In fact all economies are mixed economies and contain features of market economies and features of planned economies. The difference being that in Hong Kong there is less government intervention in the economy and greater reliance on the price mechanism to allocate resources than in some other economies.

Because the role that the government performs in the economy differs between countries, it is difficult to be precise about the exact nature of the mixed economy. Nevertheless, we can identify certain functions performed by the government in most mixed economies, and these are examined below. We should remember, however, that the *extent* of the government's involvement in performing these functions will vary from economy to economy.

THE PROVISION OF PUBLIC GOODS

Characteristics of public goods

66 **Know about public goods** 99

This is a very important role for the government, because certain **public goods** are essential for the operation of developed economies. A public good has a number of characteristics. One is **non-excludability,** which means that they cannot be provided for one citizen without simultaneously becoming available to others. In other words, once a public good is provided, it is often difficult to actually stop a person consuming an extra unit if they wish to do so. This is true in the case of a lighthouse or street lighting, for example. If a lighthouse is constructed, it is impossible to stop shipping in its vicinity from using it. Similarly, if street lighting is provided, it is impossible to prevent any passer-by from taking advantage of it. Charges cannot therefore be levied on public goods because the benefits cannot be denied to those who refuse to pay.

Another characteristic of public goods is **non-exhaustibility** which means that consumption of an extra unit by one person does not diminish the amount available for consumption by others. In other words, once the public good is provided, the additional cost of making it available to an extra consumer is zero. Defence and law and order are often called public goods. An extra person can usually be defended by the armed forces, or be protected by the police and judiciary, at no extra cost! Since the opportunity cost is zero, resources will be allocated more efficiently if no charge is made for public goods.

THE PROVISION OF MERIT GOODS

66 **Merit goods are different** 99

As well as providing public goods, the government also undertakes to provide many other goods and services which add to the quality of life but which are not pure public goods. **Merit goods** do not possess the same characteristics as public goods; for instance people can be excluded from consuming them. They could therefore be provided through the market mechanism. However, many are deliberately provided free of charge through public bodies because their consumption confers relatively large social benefits on society which far outweigh their cost of provision. Examples of merit goods include state education, public health care, municipal housing, and so on.

Arguments for state provision of merit goods

- It encourages a greater consumption of goods which confer benefits on society as a whole. For example, providing education freely to children and health care freely to all, should produce a more skilled and healthier workforce. The absence of these would seriously reduce labour productivity and adversely affect living standards. Similarly, economic efficiency, and hence living standards, would be reduced if the state did not provide an adequate road network, and so on.

- Inequality of income would limit their availability to lower income groups. In this sense, the provision of merit goods redistributes income in favour of the poorer members of society. This is one of the main reasons for the provision of municipal housing.

Arguments against state provision

Despite these arguments it is important to remember that there is also a case against the provision of merit goods (and public goods) by the state.

■ Such goods might be freely available to consumers, but they nevertheless must be paid for by the state. This involves higher levels of taxation or government borrowing than might otherwise be the case. The former might have disincentive effects (see Chapter 16) while the latter might be a cause of inflation (see Chapter 13).

■ To provide merit goods freely to all makes no distinction between those who can afford to pay and those who cannot. It might also encourage over-consumption (in relation to the most efficient use of resources) and consequently divert resources away from other, more productive, activities. After all, if something is provided free of charge there is no opportunity cost to the consumer of additional consumption. Because of this, resources might be diverted into activities which, were the consumers asked to pay the true cost of provision, they might opt not to have, preferring instead some alternative which they feel offers better value for money. In other words, a decision by the state to provide merit goods limits consumer choice since it reduces the resources available to produce other goods and services. Providing merit goods through the state might, therefore, lead to a misallocation of resources away from those uses which confer greater benefit on society. This might reduce the growth of living standards below their potential level.

CONTROL OF THE ECONOMY

One of the most important functions governments now perform is that of economic management. In other words, the government attempts to control the economy in order to achieve certain economic objectives. These may be summarised as a high and stable level of employment, stable prices, economic growth, an acceptable distribution of income and wealth and a sustainable balance of payments position with the rest of the world. Governments use a variety of techniques in their efforts to achieve these objectives, and we shall examine these more fully in Chapter 17. It is only important to note here that governments have made the pursuit of economic objectives one of their functions, and that they intervene in the economy to achieve these objectives.

Redistribution of income

Governments intervene in economies to create greater equality in the distribution of income and wealth than would otherwise exist. The most obvious way in which this is done is through a system of **taxation**, where the higher income earners are taxed more heavily than the lower income earners. Greater equality could also be achieved by the government providing certain goods free of charge or at a subsidised rate. Thus, for example, medical care is provided free of charge in the UK, while drugs issued on prescription are heavily subsidised. Finally, greater equality might be achieved through a **social security system** which provides payments from the state for the sick and aged, as well as to the unemployed and low income earners.

Modifying the system

Governments sometimes place taxes and subsidies on goods and services to influence their prices and hence the volumes produced and consumed. A **tax** on a product usually raises its price and so reduces consumption and therefore production, while a **subsidy** usually lowers price and stimulates consumption and therefore production.

Governments also attempt to modify the operation of the price mechanism by the use of **cost-benefit analysis**. This is a technique which attempts to assess the *net* worth of a particular project, after considering all the private and social costs and benefits arising out of the project. In other words, a money value is assigned to all of the externalities which stem from a project. The net value of externalities is added to the estimated value of private costs and private benefits from a project to give an estimate of its net worth. A positive result indicates that society will be 'better off' if the project goes ahead, whereas a negative result indicates that society will be 'worse off' if the project goes ahead.

❝ Cost-benefit analysis is widely used ❞

Productive efficiency

Governments also intervene in the economy to try and achieve greater efficiency in production. This might mean bringing an entire industry into public ownership, i.e. **nationalisation** or returning a nationalised industry to private hands, i.e. **privatisation**. It might mean removing some of the legal regulations which prevent the emergence of competition in certain industries, i.e. **deregulation**. Greater efficiency in production might require subsidising expenditure on research and development or providing grants to encourage the purchase of new, high technology machinery by firms. It might involve the provision of grants to influence the location of firms, and so on. Of course, any assistance that is given for these purposes is highly selective, and firms do not always qualify for this kind of state aid. Nevertheless, the fact that it is given, implies government involvement in the economy.

GREEN ISSUES

'Green' issues are becoming increasingly important and the *Lloyds Bank Economic Bulletin* of September 1989 (No 129) is entitled *Being Economical with the Environment*. The point is made that most environmental problems arise from externalities. The focus of attention is air pollution and, as with all externalities, those responsible for air pollution often take no account of the effect of their actions on others. For example, one of the main causes of acid rain is the emission of sulphur dioxide into the environment from coal burning power stations. However, if a power station takes no account of this when pricing electricity the entire cost of any externality generated is borne by the community as a whole rather than by consumers of electricity.

Accountability for pollution

Because polluters typically take no (or at least little) account of their action on others, this generally results in the output of polluting industries being greater than is optimal. If polluters were forced to pay for any externalities they impose on society, producers would almost certainly change their techniques of production so as to minimise pollution and consumers would almost certainly choose to consume less of those goods which cause pollution. One solution is therefore to levy a tax on polluters equal to the cost of removing the effect of the externality they generate. This will encourage firms to cut emissions and provides an incentive for them to research ways of permanently reducing pollution. Many economists believe this approach to be preferable to limiting the amount of pollution firms can impose on the environment by regulation. Such an approach provides no incentive to permanently reduce levels of emission.

Political impact

One possible problem with using taxation for this purpose is that to equal the cost of any externality imposed on the community, taxes would need to be set at relatively high levels and this would be politically unpopular. However, it is argued that a relatively small tax, by making consumers more aware of externalities, might bring about a reduction in consumption and therefore encourage producers to reduce pollution emissions. The reduction of taxation on lead free petrol is cited as an example of using taxation policy to bring about environmental benefits.

EXAMINATION QUESTIONS

1 (a) Briefly explain the following terms:
    (i) externalities
    (ii) cost-benefit analysis *(40)*

(b) The government is proposing to build a motorway linking a city with a major port; this motorway would cross an area of outstanding natural beauty. Discuss the problems involved in undertaking a cost-benefit analysis of such a project.

(60)

(ULEAC June 1992)

2 (a) Explain the functions of the price mechanism in a market economy. *(9)*

(b) How might these functions be affected by:

(i) the organisers of the Wimbledon lawn tennis final fixing the price of tickets below the market clearing price? *(8)*

(ii) the government fixing a legal minimum wage above the market clearing wage? *(8)*

(AEB June 1991)

3 Describe the basis of resource allocation in a planned economy and discuss why some planned economies have recently tried to place greater emphasis on market forces.

(UCLES November 1992)

4 Explain how the concept of opportunity cost is relevant in each of the following situations.

(i) A teenager deciding how to spend their weekly pocket money *(4)*

(ii) A student deciding whether to stay at home to revise for an examination or go out to a party *(6)*

(iii) An education board deciding whether to close down a small school in a remote area *(6)*

(iv) A government deciding whether or not to place more emphasis on protecting the environment *(9)*

(NICCEA 1992)

ANSWERS TO EXAMINATION QUESTIONS

TUTOR'S ANSWER TO QUESTION 1

(a) (i) **Externalities** are the spill-over effects of production and consumption that affect society in general rather than simply the individual producer or consumer. For example, when an individual is vaccinated against a particular disease he/she eliminates the possibility of contracting that disease. There is therefore a clear benefit to the *individual*; however, there is also a benefit to *society*. Because those individuals who have been vaccinated do not contract the disease, they cannot pass it on to other members of society who have not been vaccinated. This reduces the possibility of an epidemic. There are also other benefits to society; for example, the smaller the number of people who contract the disease, the fewer the working days lost through illness and the fewer the resources needed for providing health-care for those unfortunate enough to become infected.

An important point about externalities is that they are unpriced by market forces. Because of this, the price mechanism might fail to allocate resources efficiently. Where positive externalities (external benefits) occur there would be under-consumption in relation to the optimum level, and where negative externalities (external costs) occur there would be over-consumption in relation to the optimum level.

(ii) **Cost-benefit analysis** is a technique used to assess the full social costs and benefits of a project; it considers repercussions in the longer term as well as in the short term. The aim is to assign money values to all costs and benefits, including externalities associated with a particular project. External costs, once identified and quantified, are accorded money values along with estimates of raw material costs, labour costs and so on. External benefits of the project must also be identified and quantified along with estimates of any projected revenues, etc.

Having quantified all costs and benefits it would be misleading if all costs were added together and all benefits were added together and then subtracted one from the other. Costs/benefits will be incurred and accrue over a number of years. This is important because a pound received now is worth more than the promise of a pound in the future since it can be invested and earn interest. Similarly costs incurred in the present must be weighted more heavily than costs anticipated in the future. It is therefore necessary to reduce all costs and benefits to their present value by discounting, as explained in part (b) below. Once all costs and benefits have been discounted to present value, if benefits exceed costs then the project will yield a net benefit to society, and vice versa.

(b) There are major problems in carrying out a cost-benefit analysis into the proposed construction of a motorway linking a city with a major port. There would inevitably be problems in estimating input costs such as materials, labour, cost of equipment and so on. Estimates would be particularly difficult to obtain, the longer the project would take to complete. Strictly speaking, it would also be necessary to estimate the maintenance cost over the life of the motorway. If the motorway is to be a toll road then it is also necessary to estimate the anticipated traffic flow and the revenue this will generate over the life of the motorway.

However, the main problems associated with the project are likely to involve the externalities it will generate. We first look at some external costs.

We are told that the proposed motorway would cross an area of outstanding natural beauty. The natural beauty of the area would be lost if the motorway were constructed, but how do we place a value on its loss? Any estimate of the value of lost natural beauty is entirely subjective. After all, beauty is in the eye of the beholder! Nevertheless we clearly have to value the loss of amenity to consumers via damage to the environment.

One technique would be to ask users how much they would require to be compensated for the loss of natural beauty. However, the accuracy of such responses would be highly questionable and in any case if one person claimed it would be impossible to compensate them for the loss of natural beauty, then strictly speaking no cost-benefit analysis could ever show a net benefit to society from constructing the motorway! Analysts must therefore decide for themselves the value of the environment that would be lost. Since such valuations are matters of opinion, their accuracy will remain a matter of doubt and therefore the final result of the cost-benefit analysis, whether it shows an excess of costs over benefits or an excess of benefits over costs, would be questioned by some.

External costs would also be involved in the construction of the motorway. As traffic was diverted to the motorway and additional traffic was generated, pollution in the surrounding area would increase, causing long-term environmental damage. Traffic that was diverted to the motorway would no longer use former routes and if these passed through, or close to, towns and cities, traders might suffer a decline in revenue from passing trade. Again there are problems of how to value these external costs.

Another consideration is how the construction of the motorway is to be financed! If it involves additional taxation, there would be an obvious cost to those who paid the higher taxes. Strictly speaking, the analyst would need to consider the loss to the individual from higher taxation. A millionaire who paid an additional £100 in taxation would experience a smaller loss in terms of satisfaction given up through a lower level of consumption, than the loss of satisfaction experienced by a relatively poor person who paid only an additional £10 in taxation. In practice it would be impossible to value lost satisfaction in this way and this limits the usefulness of cost-benefit analysis. There might also be an additional cost to society. It is alleged that higher taxation has a disincentive effect on those who pay the higher taxes which manifests itself in reduced effort and initiative. To the extent that this is correct, output will be lower than otherwise and this implies that society achieves a lower level of consumption. This will adversely affect the standard of living. Identifying and quantifying the extent of any disincentive effects of higher taxation would cause major problems for the analyst.

The motorway would also confer external benefits on society. One immediate benefit is that constructing a motorway would increase employment. Since the firms which constructed the motorway would produce budgets detailing their anticipated costs, it would be easy to estimate the number of workers who would be employed. Any reduction in unemployment might also save expenditure by the Exchequer on unemployment and social security benefits.

Since the motorway would increase access to a major port, it might have a beneficial effect on international trade. Whether the overall effect on the balance of payments is favourable or not depends on the extent to which exports and imports increase. What is certain is that, if international trade increases, the local economy would benefit and this would be reflected in rising incomes and employment. This is particularly important if the port at the end of the motorway is an area of relatively high unemployment. There would also be benefits to society, not least because rising incomes imply rising tax revenues and this might facilitate a small cut in taxation or increased government expenditure without any need to offset this with higher rates of taxation.

Another possible benefit to society is that by transferring traffic to the motorway there might be a lower level of pollution in towns and cities. It is also possible that there would be less damage to buildings and fewer accidents. Again it would be extremely difficult to quantify these benefits.

Even when values have been assigned to costs and benefits, there is the problem of selecting the appropriate **rate of discount** to reduce future costs and benefits to their present value. The following example is used to explain the importance of selecting an appropriate rate of discount. If a particular project is expected to generate revenues over the next two years of £110m and £121m respectively and the rate of discount is 10 per cent, the *present value* of these expected future revenues is:

$$\frac{£110m}{1.1} + \frac{£121m}{1.1^2} = £200m$$

Now it is clear that, if the rate of discount is greater than 10 per cent, the present value of expected future revenue would be less than £200m. Conversely, if the rate of discount is less than 10 per cent, the present value of expected future revenue will be greater than £200m.

Selecting an appropriate rate of discount is important in the case of a motorway, or any other capital investment with a relatively long expected life, because the bulk of the costs will be incurred during the construction phase, whereas the benefits will accrue over the very long-term. Too high a rate of discount would therefore underestimate benefits relative to costs, and too low a rate of discount would overestimate benefits relative to costs. Selecting an appropriate rate of discount is therefore a major problem facing any cost-benefit analyst. It might seem that the appropriate rate of discount would be the rate used in the private sector. However, public sector investment, such as constructing a motorway has a longer expected life than most private sector investment and, by improving the infrastructure, often confers wider benefits on society.

Clearly a cost-benefit analysis into the proposed motorway would pose many problems and the final result of the analysis would be open to question. On the other hand, by identifying relevant costs and benefits it makes decision taking more rational and thereby aids the decision-making process.

STUDENT'S ANSWER TO QUESTION 2

66 But what *is* the price mechanism? 99

66 A simple demand/supply diagram would help to explain how prices act as signals to producers and consumers 99

66 Good paragraph but you might have gone on to explain why the allocation of resources through the price mechanism is thought to be optimal 99

66 You could present a diagram here showing how setting a maximum price below the equilibrium price leads to excess demand, etc. 99

66 Again, a diagram would help here 99

(a) A market economy exists when there is no government interference to influence the allocation of resources. In market economies, resources are allocated through the price mechanism.

For the price mechanism to allocate resources, it is essential that individuals are free to own the means of production. They will therefore be free to decide which goods and services to produce. They rely on the profit motive to guide them. This simply means they will produce those goods and services which offer them the greatest profit. In a market economy, individuals are also free to choose which goods and services they will consume. Their choice will be influenced by relative prices.

To see how the price mechanism operates let us see what happens when consumers demand more of a particular good. When this happens the price of the good will increase. It will therefore be more profitable than previously and producers will therefore bid resources away from alternative goods and services to take advantage of the higher profits available. This implies that when demand for a particular good increases, output of that good increases. The opposite happens when demand for a particular good falls. It is often said that the consumer is sovereign in market economies because, by changing their demand for different goods and services, they are able to change the range of goods and services produced. The main function of the price mechanism is therefore to allocate resources.

(b) (i) If the price of tickets for the Wimbledon lawn tennis final is fixed below the market clearing price, they will be relatively cheap. In consequence more will be demanded than are available. It will therefore be necessary to ration the available number of tickets. The usual method chosen is 'first come first served'. This simply means that those who are prepared to queue the longest will obtain a ticket. Because of the number of people who want a ticket for the Wimbledon lawn tennis final the time spent queuing might be considerable and the opportunity cost of this will deter many people.

(ii) If a minimum wage is fixed above the market clearing price, this implies that labour will be relatively expensive so the supply of labour will exceed the demand for labour. As a consequence, the minimum wage will cause unemployment. Because the minimum wage will have the force of law, employers will be compelled to pay it. If the price mechanism allocated resources in the labour market unemployment would disappear. The excess supply of labour would lead to a reduction in the wage rate. As the wage rate fell, employers would demand more workers because they are cheaper to employ. On the other hand, the lower wage rate will deter some workers from seeking employment.

66 In both cases you make some interesting points but you do not relate these fully to the operation of the price mechanism. Diagrams, where relevant, can help you to explain the processes involved 99

OUTLINE ANSWERS TO QUESTIONS 3 AND 4

Question 3

In a centrally planned economy, resources are allocated through the decisions of officials rather than by the actions of consumers. To formulate a plan, a great deal of information about the availability of resources must be collected and a great deal of effort expended ensuring that all output decisions are compatible. For example, if planners assign a target to the car industry, they must ensure that sufficient steel is available to meet that target and that sufficient coal is available for the steel industry to meet its target.

There are several problems with this technique of resource allocation which explains why most former centrally planned economies have placed greater emphasis on market forces. You will need to spell out these problems in some detail. These are explained on pp. 16–19.

Question 4

Although you are not specifically asked to do so, it is best to begin your answer to this question by defining opportunity cost. You could then go on to explain its importance in each of the four situations mentioned.

(i) A range of possibilities could be considered here. Pocket money might be spent on a video, a CD, going to a disco and so on. It is important to stress that the opportunity cost, of whatever pocket money is spent on, is the next most desired alternative forgone.

(ii) Here the choices are specified: the student either revises for an examination or goes to a party. Since revision is an important determinant of examination success, the decision involves an assessment of what examination success might lead on to in terms of career prospects. Time is the most valuable resource of all, once it is gone we can never have it back!

(iii) An education board deciding whether to close down a small school in a remote village will need to consider many factors. These might include the financial costs of transporting pupils to an alternative school. Further, if staff are made redundant as a result of the school's closure or are given early retirement, this will involve costs in terms of redundancy payments or increased pensions. There would also be other external costs to consider. How much disruption would be caused to the pupils' education? How would the closure of the school affect the local community and so on?

(iv) The environment is often treated as a free resource by producers who dump waste materials into rivers or pollute the atmosphere with smoke. The opportunity cost of placing more emphasis on protecting the environment depends on several factors, but an important one is the way in which the environment is to be protected. One way to curb pollution is to offer producers a **subsidy** to encourage the use of cleaner technologies. An alternative is to **tax** more heavily those products that pollute the environment. One strategy will place an additional burden on the tax-payer; the other will generate an increase in tax revenue but will involve consumers paying higher prices. In both cases, the opportunity cost will be different.

Further reading

Begg, Dornbusch and Fischer, *Economics* (3rd edn), McGraw-Hill 1991: Ch. 1, Economics and the Economy.
Harrison et al, *Introductory Economics*, Macmillan 1992: Ch. 1, What is Economics?
Samuelson and Nordhaus, *Economics* (14th edn), McGraw-Hill 1992: Ch. 22, The Winds of Change: The Triumph of the Market.
Sloman, *Economics* (2nd edn), Harvester Wheatsheaf 1994: Ch. 1, Introducing Economics.

REVIEW SHEET

1 Define each of the following: then give an example of each type.

Normative statements _____

_____

Example: _____

_____

Positive statements _____

_____

Example: _____

_____

Negative externalities _____

_____

Example: _____

2 Draw a production possibility curve then use your diagram to show what is meant by opportunity cost.

Explanation:

_____

_____

_____

_____

3 List four main advantages of a market economy.

(a) _____

(b) _____

(c) _____

(d) _____

4 List four disadvantages often associated with a market economy.

(a) _____

(b) _____

(c) _____

(d) _____

5 List four advantages often associated with a centrally planned economy.

(a) _____

(b) _____

(c) _____

(d) _____

6 Describe two key characteristics of a public good.

(a) _____

_____

(b) _____

_____

7 What is the difference between a public good and a merit good?

_____

_____

_____

_____

8 Give two reasons for state provision of merit goods.

(a) _____

_____

(b) _____

_____

9 Give two good reasons for the state not providing merit goods.

(a) _____

_____

(b) _____

_____

10 What do you understand by cost-benefit analysis?

_____

_____

_____

_____

11 Describe an example involving the use of cost-benefit analysis in a practical situation.

_____

_____

_____

_____

12 Draw a diagram using a demand and a supply curve to show how equilibrium price is determined in a market.

Now use your diagram to show how price acts as a signal in a market economy to co-ordinate the decisions of consumers and producers.

_____

_____

_____

PRODUCTION, COSTS AND RETURNS

THE FACTORS OF PRODUCTION

DIVISION OF LABOUR

MOBILITY OF THE FACTORS OF PRODUCTION

COMBINING THE FACTORS OF PRODUCTION

THE LAWS OF RETURNS

COSTS OF PRODUCTION

THE FIRM'S REVENUE

APPLIED MATERIALS

GETTING STARTED

Production is defined as any economic activity which satisfies human wants. It therefore refers equally to the creation of goods or to the supply of services. Indeed, to the economist, the chain of production is *only* complete when a good or service is sold to the consumer.

For any community the volume of production depends on many factors, including the quantity and quality of the available resources, the extent to which they are utilised and the efficiency with which they are combined. The volume of production can therefore be increased when more resources or inputs become available, or when existing inputs yield a higher output. The latter is referred to as an increase in **productivity** and is usually measured as average product per worker. Thus productivity rises when average product per worker rises.

When considering the causes of changes in output economists frequently distinguish between the *short* run and the *long* run. These are not fixed time periods, but instead are defined in terms of the time required to bring about changes in the input of various factors of production. Specifically, **the short run** exists when there is at least one fixed factor of production. In other words, the short run refers to a period of time when it is possible to vary the input of some factors of production but impossible to vary the input of at least one other factor. For example, sometimes it is impossible for firms to recruit skilled labour until more workers have been trained, but they usually have little difficulty in recruiting unskilled workers. It is important to note that any factor of production can be fixed in the short run. In contrast, **the long run** is the time period required to bring about a change in the input of *all* the factors of production. In other words, there are no fixed factors of production in the long run.

Marginal product is the *rate* at which total product changes as an additional unit of the variable factor is employed. For instance, the marginal product of labour is usually measured as the change in total output when one more, or one less, worker is employed. The concept of the margin is very important in Economics and you must ensure you are familiar with it and fully understand it. You will see in this chapter that it is also applied to cost. **Marginal cost** is the rate at which total cost changes as output changes. However, at A-level, it is measured as the change in total cost of production when output is increased by one more unit.

Because costs of production vary as output varies, firms must decide what is their most efficient level of output. In fact, there are two kinds of efficiency: *economic* efficiency and *technical* efficiency. Firms are producing at their most economically efficient level when, given their current scale of operations, they are maximising profit, i.e. earning as much profit as possible from the output they currently produce. On the other hand, firms are producing at their most technically efficient level when, given their current scale of production, average cost per unit is minimised. We shall see, in Chapter 5, that only in certain circumstances will these levels of output coincide.

THE FACTORS OF PRODUCTION

ESSENTIAL PRINCIPLES

LAND

Land was defined by early economists to include 'all the free gifts of nature'. It therefore includes the surface area of the planet as well as its mineral and ore deposits. As a factor of production, land has special characteristics. It has no cost of production, is completely fixed in supply, i.e. cannot be reproduced, and cannot be moved from one place to another.

LABOUR

As a factor of production, labour is defined as the physical and mental human effort used to create goods and services. The supply of labour to an economy is therefore very important in determining the level of output an economy is able to produce and depends on such factors as size of the population, length of the working week, number of hours worked per day and so on. However, the quality of labour is also important and this depends on general health and well-being as well as on education and training. More is said about the supply of labour to an economy in Chapter 4.

CAPITAL

Definition
Capital is defined by economists as any man-made asset which is used in the production of further goods and services. In general, it is the use to which a particular asset is put which determines whether it is capital. For example, a motor car used by a salesman would be classed as capital, but a car used for social and domestic purposes would be classed as a consumer good.

Fixed and circulating capital

Fixed vs circulating capital

Economists distinguish between *fixed* capital and *circulating* capital. The former can be used time and again in the production process whereas the latter can only be used once. Fixed capital therefore includes such things as machinery and factory buildings, the road and rail networks, hospitals and educational buildings and so on, whereas circulating capital (also commonly known as working capital) consists of raw materials and work in progress.

Creation of capital
Capital is created from scarce resources and therefore has an opportunity cost. In order to create more capital, it is necessary to consume less so that resources can be released for the production of capital. In other words, to accumulate capital a community must forego current consumption, i.e. the community as a whole must save.

ENTERPRISE

This factor of production is more commonly referred to as **the entrepreneur**. The entrepreneur performs two important roles:

- hiring and combining the other factors of production; and

- risk taking by producing goods and services in anticipation of demand.

DIVISION OF LABOUR

Division of labour refers to the way in which jobs are broken down into their various component parts so that each worker performs only a small part of the entire operation. Because of this, division of labour is often referred to as **specialisation**. In the production of many goods and services, each worker specialises in a single task or small group of related tasks.

ADVANTAGES OF DIVISION OF LABOUR

Increased productivity

Division of labour leads to a far greater average product per worker being achieved than is possible in the absence of specialisation. But why is this increase in productivity possible?

Reasons for specialisation

- Someone who performs the same task every day becomes very skilled at it and is able to work much faster.

- Most of the worker's day is spent on production; no time is wasted moving from work area to work area, or changing one set of tools for another.

- Workers can be trained more quickly since there are fewer skills to learn.

- Breaking production down to a small number of repetitive tasks makes possible the use of specialist machinery which can be kept fully operational throughout the working day; machines are more efficient than humans, so productivity is vastly increased.

- Workers can specialise in performing tasks for which they have a particular aptitude.

Increased standard of living

The greater levels of productivity achieved through division of labour have led to an increase in living standards, since higher productivity leads to lower costs of production and hence to lower prices (see p. 61). The higher level of productivity has also led to a considerable reduction in the length of both the working week and the working year; even so a larger amount of goods and services are produced each year.

Increased range of goods available

The lower cost of production achieved by division of labour, and the consequently lower price of goods and services, has increased the range of goods and services available to most people.

DISADVANTAGES OF DIVISION OF LABOUR

Despite these advantages, division of labour has several disadvantages.

Increased boredom

Greater specialisation results in boredom as workers perform the same tasks throughout the working day. This can lead to low morale, which in turn leads to poor labour relations, higher absenteeism as well as carelessness and an increased number of accidents.

Lack of variety

Problems with specialisation

Output is standardised and large numbers of identical articles are produced. (Remember though, that a greater range of output is still being produced at a lower price; for most people, therefore, a greater variety of output is available.)

Worker interdependence

Specialisation leads to interdependence. Each worker in the production process depends on all other works in the production process. A stoppage by a small group of workers can therefore cause considerable disruption.

SPECIALISATION

Specialisation is now widespread and can be observed in several ways:

- specialisation of *workers* within an industry;

- specialisation of *firms* within an industry, e.g. in the car industry some firms specialise in supplying electrical components or tyres;

- specialisation by *region* – some industries are located in particular parts of the country, e.g. the steel industry in Sheffield; and

- specialisation by *country,* e.g. Brazil which produces coffee or Chile which supplies most of the world's nitrates.

DIVISION OF LABOUR AND THE SIZE OF THE MARKET

Division of labour is only possible if there is a large market. It is useless producing vast quantities of output, even at relatively low prices, if there is only a small market for what is produced. Markets might be limited by several factors:

66 The market can limit specialisation 99

- consumers might demand variety, as with jewellery and *haute couture* clothes;

- some areas are sparsely populated;

- low incomes might restrict 'effective' demand, i.e. demand backed by purchasing power; and

- personal services and repair work are not always easy to split into a number of stages.

MOBILITY OF THE FACTORS OF PRODUCTION

Economists identify two types of mobility: *geographical* mobility and *occupational* mobility. The former refers to a physical movement of a factor of production from one geographical location to another, whereas the latter refers to a factor of production moving from one occupation to another.

IMPORTANCE OF FACTOR MOBILITY

A high degree of factor mobility is considered important to an economy for several reasons.

- The more mobile the factors of production, the easier it is to respond to changes in demand for different goods and services. This makes possible the production of a greater level of output and therefore a higher standard of living. It also reduces unemployment below levels that would otherwise exist.

66 Factor mobility can help 99

- When demand for products increases, prices are pulled upwards and resources are reallocated via the price mechanism. However, when factors of production are mobile, prices are unlikely to rise so quickly, which results in a lower rate of inflation.

- In modern economies, the rate of technological progress is rapid and in order to take full advantage of this, it is necessary to have an adaptable and mobile labour force. Here again the use of new technologies makes possible an improvement in living standards.

- Changes in a country's rate of exchange can lead to sudden changes in the prices of, and demand for, exports and imports (see Chapter 15). Sales and purchases of these are recorded in the balance of payments. If a nation is to have a 'favourable' balance of payments, it will need to take advantage of sudden increases in demand for exports by rapidly producing more output. Extra output may also be needed rapidly to compete with imports. In both cases, mobile factors will help a more rapid output response.

COMBINING THE FACTORS OF PRODUCTION

All production requires the input of resources or factors of production. However, these can often be combined in a variety of ways, sometimes by using more of one factor relative to another, and vice versa. Profit-maximising firms, i.e. firms which aim to make as large a profit as possible, will combine the factors of production so as to minimise the cost of producing any given output.

MEASURING CHANGES IN OUTPUT

Over time, firms vary the level of output they produce within any given period, such as a week or a month. Sometimes they will increase output, sometimes they will reduce it. To do this, they will change the input of factors of production. There are important laws which explain what happens to output as the input of factors of production changes. These are considered below. Here we define some important concepts which are used to explain the laws of returns:

Total product

This is simply the total output a firm produces within a given period of time. For example, the total product of a particular firm might be 1,000 units per week.

Average product

This is usually measured in relation to a particular factor of production, such as labour or capital. Thus the average product of labour is measured as (total product/number of workers). For example, if the total product of the firm is 1,000 units per week and 10 workers are employed, average product per worker is (1,000/10)= 100 units per week. Changes in average product are referred to as changes in **productivity** and we shall see below that changes in productivity have an important impact on the firm's costs of production.

> 66 Know about total, average and marginal product 99

Marginal product

Marginal product is the *rate* at which total product changes as an additional unit of a variable factor is employed. For instance, the marginal product of labour is usually measured as the change in total product when one more worker is employed. If total product when the firm employs 10 workers is 1,000 units per week, and this rises to 1,080 units per week when the firm employs an additional worker, then the marginal product of the last worker is 80 units per week.

THE LAWS OF RETURNS

> 66 These are short run laws 99

Firms can change the level of production by changing the input of the factors of production. Remember though that changes in the input of *all* factors is not possible in the short run as there is at least one fixed factor of production. The **laws of returns** explain the relationship between changes in the input of variable factors and changes in the level of output. The general relationship is summarised in two laws which are sometimes combined into a single law known as **the law of variable proportions**.

The law of increasing returns

This law states that, in the early stages of production, as successive units of a variable factor are combined with a fixed factor, initially, both marginal and average product will rise. In other words, total output will rise more than in proportion to the rise in inputs.

The law of diminishing returns

This law simply states that as successive units of a variable factor are combined with a fixed factor, after a certain point, both marginal product and average product will fall. In other words, total output will rise less than in proportion to the rise in inputs. Eventually total output will even diminish as marginal product becomes negative.

AN ILLUSTRATION OF THE LAWS OF RETURNS

The changing nature of returns to a variable factor can be seen in Table 3.1. We assume that an increasing amount of labour works on a fixed quantity of land, that each worker is homogeneous, i.e. identical to all other workers, and that the techniques of production are unchanged.

It can be seen that up to the employment of the fourth worker, the firm experiences increasing marginal returns because the increase in total product is proportionately greater than the increase in input of the variable factor. This is clearly shown by the rising marginal product of each worker up to the employment of the fourth worker. When marginal product is rising, the rate of increase of total product must also be rising. The main reason why firms experience increasing returns is that there is greater scope for division of labour as the number of workers employed increases.

Diminishing marginal returns set in after the employment of the fifth worker when it is clear that the rate of increase of total product, i.e. marginal product, begins to fall. Diminishing returns set in because the proportions in which the factors of production are employed have become progressively less favourable, reflecting the fact that there are limits to the gains from specialisation. It is useful to note that diminishing marginal returns may occur before diminishing average returns. Even if the marginal product is falling, as long as it is above average product, average product will still rise (see top half of Fig. 3.3 on page 40). Here, diminishing average product only sets in after six workers are employed.

No of workers	Total product	Average product	Marginal product
1	4	4	4
2	10	5	6
3	20	6.7	10
4	35	8.8	15
5	50	10	15
6	60	10	10
7	65	9.3	5
8	65	8.1	0
9	55	6.1	-10

Table 3.1 Changing nature of returns to a variable factor

RETURNS TO SCALE

In the long run, there are no fixed factors and firms can vary the input of all factors of production. When this happens, there has been a change in the scale of production. If a change in the scale of production leads to a more than proportional change in output, firms are subject to increasing returns to scale. For example, if all factor inputs are increased by 10 per cent and output grows by more than this, firms experience increasing returns to scale. These are more generally referred to as **economies of scale**.

It is sometimes suggested that firms might experience constant returns to scale as output grows so that a change in all factor inputs result in an equi-proportional change in output. This is certainly possible but there is no doubt that for the vast majority of firms, as the scale of production increases beyond a certain level, economies of scale quickly give way to **diseconomies of scale** or decreasing returns to scale. Here a change in the input of all factors of production leads to a less than proportional change in output.

Firms are interested in changes in returns because, as we shall see, a change in returns implies a change in a firm's costs. For this reason, economies of scale are sometimes defined as those aspects of increasing size which lead to falling average costs, i.e. cost per unit produced. Diseconomies of scale are those aspects of increasing size which lead to rising average costs.

SOURCES OF ECONOMIES OF SCALE

The source of economies of scale are many and varied, but they are usually grouped into certain categories. More information on economies and diseconomies of scale is given at the end of this chapter in the answers to questions 1 and 2 (pp. 46–50).

Technical economies
These are common in manufacturing, since they relate to the scale of the production unit. There are several reasons why costs might fall as the scale of production increases:

- **Greater scope for division of labour** The larger the size of the production unit, the more men and machines are able to specialise. In the manufacture of motor cars and household durable goods such as televisions and washing machines, the production process can be broken down, in some cases into hundreds of small operations. This facilitates the use of flow line assembly techniques which can have a profound effect on productivity. This gives larger firms a considerable advantage over smaller firms.

■ **Indivisibilities**   Certain items of capital expenditure are relatively expensive and cannot be purchased in smaller or cheaper units, yet they may help raise output substantially. The installation of automatic electronic control systems in industry, although expensive, yields substantial increases in efficiency. The fact that such equipment is indivisible gives larger firms a considerable advantage over smaller firms because the cost of such equipment is relatively high; but the average cost per unit of output falls dramatically as output expands. The use of computers in many large supermarkets to adjust stock levels as goods are sold yields considerable saving in labour time since up–to–the–minute stock checks are now automatically available.

" Reasons for economies of scale "

■ **Economies of linked processes**   Most manufacturing output requires the use of more than one machine. Where machines work at different speeds, large firms are often able to operate more efficiently than small firms. In these circumstances, it will require relatively high levels of output achieved by large firms to enable all the machines to be used to capacity. For instance, suppose two processes, A and B, are needed to produce an item; process A needs a machine which produces 20 units per hour, and process B needs a machine producing 50 units per hour. Only if output is as high as 100 units can both machines be fully used – with five machines in process A and two machines in process B. It is likely that, because of the cost involved, small firms will be unable to purchase machines in sufficient quantities to achieve the full utilisation of machinery. This will give the large firm an advantage over the small firm.

Marketing economies

Marketing embraces many activities, but the main economies of scale in marketing arise from bulk purchasing and/or bulk distribution:

" Non-technical economies of scale are also important "

■ **Economies from bulk purchases**   Large-scale production requires the large-scale input of raw materials. When firms place large orders for raw materials they are able to negotiate bulk discounts which substantially reduce the cost of each unit purchased. In other words, the average cost of materials falls as the quantity purchased increases. The same reasoning explains why large retail chains can sell branded goods more cheaply than small independent retailers.

■ **Economies from bulk distribution**   Where large quantities of output are to be transported, firms can often gain economies. For example, the average cost of transporting a given quantity of oil by sea is much lower when a single super tanker is used than when several smaller tankers are used. Similarly, the increasing use of articulated lorries is evidence that it is cheaper to transport in bulk when using the road network.

Financial economies

Frequently, large firms are able to obtain finance more easily and on more favourable terms than smaller firms. Even a small reduction in the interest rates charged on borrowing, yields substantial savings where relatively large sums are involved.

Risk-bearing economies

A number of advantages can lead to large firms experiencing risk-bearing economies. However, the underlying factor is that large firms frequently engage in a range of diverse activities, so that a fall in the return from any one activity does not threaten the viability of the whole firm.

The law of large numbers involves a different kind of risk-bearing economy. Where demand for a firm's product is uncertain and subject to unpredictable changes, stocks of finished goods will be held to meet any unanticipated increase in demand. Large firms have a considerable advantage over smaller firms here since they are able to hold proportionately lower stocks of finished products, raw materials, spare parts for machinery and so on. For example, firms might well hold the same quantity of spare parts for a particular machine whether they have one machine or four or five, because not all machines will require the same spare part at the same time.

Managerial economies

This source of improved efficiency stems from the fact that large firms are able to offer the rewards necessary to attract the most capable staff whose ability and expertise may well lead to lower average costs.

SOURCES OF DISECONOMIES OF SCALE

While increases in scale frequently confer advantages on firms, in many cases there is a limit to the gains from growth. In other words, there is an optimum level of capacity and increases in scale beyond this level lead to diseconomies of scale which manifest themselves in rising average costs of production. Diseconomies of scale have several sources:

■ **Managerial difficulties**   There is no doubt that the increasing complexity of managing large-scale enterprises is a major source of inefficiency as firms grow beyond a certain size. Managerial expertise of the kind required to run larger and larger firms is relatively fixed in supply even in the long run and as firms grow beyond a certain size it becomes increasingly difficult to control and co-ordinate the various activities of planning, product design, sales promotion, and so on. This is especially true where a diverse range of products is produced and it is an important factor for explaining the emergence of diseconomies of scale.

66 Greater size can bring problems *99*

■ **Low morale**   Organisations which employ large numbers of people sometimes suffer from low morale, perhaps because individuals feel they have little influence on decisions in large firms. Whatever the cause, low morale leads to high rates of absenteeism and a lack of punctuality. It may also lead to a lack of interest in the job which inhibits the growth of productivity and leads to a higher incidence of spoiled work which raises average costs of production and might lead to increased expenditure on quality control.

■ **Higher input prices**   As the scale of production increases, firms require more inputs, and increasing demand for these might bid up factor prices. Additionally, when firms produce on a large scale and rely on full capacity utilisation of capital equipment to gain economies of scale, the power of trade unions is substantially increased. This might enable unions to negotiate wage awards in excess of the growth of productivity, thus increasing average labour costs.

■ **Marketing diseconomies**   There may also be diseconomies associated with the efforts of firms to increase their market share beyond some particular level. It is often the case that firms which already have a significant market share, can only increase that market share by spending proportionately more on certain types of marketing expenditure. For example, if a firm has a market share of 75 per cent, an increase in advertising expenditure of even 100 per cent is unlikely to lead to a market share of 100 per cent. In other words, the advertising expenditure per unit (i.e. one percentage point) of additional market share rises as market share rises. Again, if a manufacturing firm with an 80 per cent market share attempted to supply the remaining retail outlets, including those with a small turnover in out of the way places, it would incur a more than proportionate increase in distribution costs. The point is clear. Beyond a certain market share, firms incur marketing diseconomies of scale and this would pull up long-run marginal and average costs.

COSTS OF PRODUCTION

THE SHORT RUN

In the short run, it is possible to categorise the firm's costs as either *fixed* costs or *variable* costs. Clearly fixed costs are incurred on fixed factors of production and variable costs on variable factors.

Fixed costs

It is impossible to vary the input of fixed factors in the short run, therefore fixed costs do not change as output increases. Additionally, it is important to realise that fixed costs are incurred even when the firm's output is zero. Fixed costs include mortgage or rent on premises, hire purchase repayments, local authority rates, insurance charges, depreciation on assets, and so on. None of these costs is directly related to output and they are all costs which are still incurred in the short run, even if the firm produces no output. They are therefore sometimes referred to as **indirect costs** or **overheads**.

Because total fixed costs are constant with respect to output, *average* fixed costs, i.e. total fixed costs divided by output, decline continuously as output expands (see Table 3.2). Diagrammatically, the behaviour of total fixed costs and average fixed costs as output expands are shown in Fig. 3.1.

Variable costs

66 Variable costs change with output 99

Unlike fixed costs, variable costs are *directly* related to output. When firms produce no output they incur no variable costs, but as output is expanded variable costs are incurred. Because they vary directly with output these costs are sometimes referred to as **direct costs** or supplementary costs. Examples of these costs include costs of raw materials and power to drive machinery, wages of direct labour and so on.

OUTPUT	TOTAL FIXED	TOTAL VARIABLE	TOTAL	MARGINAL	AVERAGE VARIABLE	AVERAGE FIXED	AVERAGE TOTAL
0	100	0	100		0		
				50			
1	100	50	150		50	100	150
				45			
2	100	95	195		47.5	50	97.5
				40			
3	100	135	235		45	33.3	78.3
				30			
4	100	165	265		41.3	25	66.3
				15			
5	100	180	280		36	20	56
				10			
6	100	190	290		31.7	16.7	48.3
				5			
7	100	195	295		27.9	14.3	42.1
				10			
8	100	205	305		25.7	12.5	38.1
				20			
9	100	225	325		25	11.1	36.1
				40			
10	100	265	365		26.5	10	36.5
				60			
11	100	325	425		29.5	9.1	38.6
				85			
12	100	410	510		34.2	8.3	42.5

Table 3.2 Arithmetic example of short run change in costs as output expands

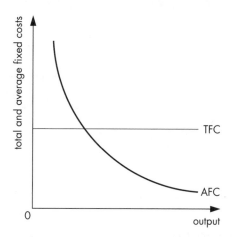

Fig. 3.1 The behaviour of fixed costs as output changes

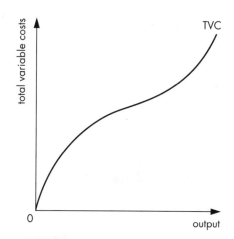

Fig. 3.2 The behaviour of variable costs as output changes

The relationship between marginal costs and variable costs

Marginal cost is the change in total cost when one more unit is produced, and is, therefore, entirely a variable cost. Because, in the short run, only the input of variable factors can be changed, it is clear that the sum of the marginal costs of producing each unit equals the total variable cost of production. Reference to Table 3.2 will confirm this.

Additionally, although variable costs vary directly with output, they are unlikely to vary proportionately because of the effect of increasing and diminishing returns. Figure 3.2 shows the general shape of the total variable cost curve. It is clear that total variable costs at first rise less than proportionately as output expands and the firm experiences increasing returns. Subsequently, as the firm experiences diminishing returns, total variable costs rise more than proportionately as output expands.

The changes in total variable costs brought about by increasing and diminishing returns also imply changes in average variable costs. The relationships between average and marginal product, and average variable and marginal cost are shown in Fig. 3.3. When the firm experiences increasing marginal returns, marginal product rises and marginal cost falls. Conversely, when the firm experiences diminishing marginal returns, marginal product falls and marginal costs rises. However, Fig. 3.3 also shows that when marginal cost is below average variable cost, the latter is falling, and when marginal cost is above average variable cost, the latter is rising. This is because, in the short run, marginal cost is the addition to total variable cost. When the last unit adds less to the total than the current average, then the average must fall. Average variable cost rises, however, when marginal cost lies above it. The implication is that the marginal cost curve cuts the average variable cost curve at its *minimum* point. (Similar reasoning explains why average product rises when marginal product is above it and falls when marginal product is below it, and why the marginal product curve cuts the average product curve at its *maximum* point.)

> 66 Marginal product is related to marginal cost 9 9

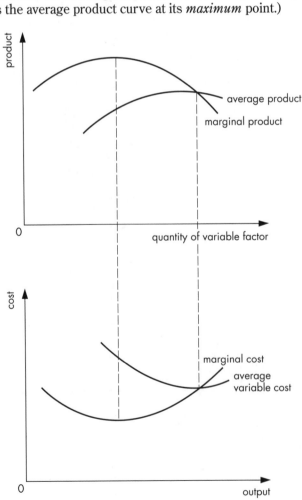

Fig. 3.3 The effect of changes in marginal and average product on marginal and average cost

Average total costs of production

These are more generally referred to simply as average costs, and for any given level of output they are obtained by dividing the total cost of producing that output by the level of the output itself. We know that average fixed costs fall continuously as output expands and that initially, because of increasing average returns, average variable costs fall. It follows that average total costs will fall initially. However, beyond a certain point, average variable costs will begin to rise because of diminishing average returns, and once the rise in average variable costs more than offset the fall in average fixed costs, average total costs will rise. This is clearly shown in Fig. 3.4 which also shows that the marginal cost curve cuts the average total cost curve at the *minimum* point for exactly the same reason that it cuts the average variable cost curve at the minimum point. Table 3.2 (p. 39) provides an arithmetic example of how costs change in the short run, as output expands.

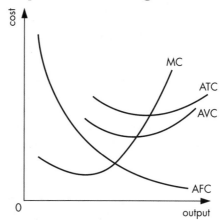

Fig. 3.4 The behaviour of different costs of production

THE LONG RUN

In the short run, the existence of fixed factors means that firms can only increase output by increasing the input of variable factors. In other words, firms have limited capacity. However, in the long run, it is possible for firms to increase capacity. The most obvious reason for doing this is to make possible a greater level of output. However, they might also increase capacity because this will lead to lower average costs of production (economies of scale). Figure 3.5 shows the effect on costs of changes in capacity. Each SAC curve is a short-run average cost curve showing how average cost varies with output with some given level of capacity, i.e. the fixed factor capital.

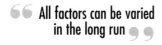 **All factors can be varied in the long run**

If we consider an output OQ, it is clear that the firm can produce this with the level of capacity implied in SAC_1 at an average cost of OC_1 per unit. Alternatively, it could increase capacity to the level implied in SAC_2 giving an average cost of producing OQ units of OC_2. By increasing capacity, the firm lowers its average cost of producing a given output.

More generally, by adjusting capacity in the long run, firms can minimise the cost of producing any given level of output. Indeed, the firm's long-run average cost curve (LAC) shows the minimum average cost of producing any given level of output after adjustments in capacity. It is therefore tangential to all the short-run average cost curves. For this reason, the long-run average cost curve is sometimes referred to as an **envelope curve**, because it supports an infinite number of short-run average cost curves, each reflecting a different level of capacity.

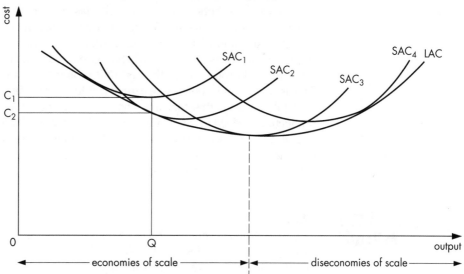

Fig. 3.5 Short-run and long-run costs of production

DECIDING WHETHER TO EXPAND CAPACITY

An important question to consider is whether a firm should increase the input of variable factors to meet an expected increase in sales, or whether it should increase the input of *all* factors by increasing its plant size or building an additional plant. Clearly the fundamental issue here is whether the increase in sales is expected to be permanent or whether it is simply a temporary increase caused by exceptional factors. Only in the former case will the firm have to decide whether to increase capacity by building an additional plant.

66 Factors involved in planning decisions **9 9**

- If the firm's aim is to maximise profit, its decision about whether to expand capacity will depend on the behaviour of costs as output expands. In the short run, the crucial factor is whether it experiences increasing or diminishing returns as output expands. If the firm is experiencing increasing average returns, average cost will be falling, and in these circumstances there might be no cost advantage to the firm in changing the level of capacity. The firm is more likely to seek ways of raising output within the current level of capacity. This might involve using more labour, introducing overtime working, and so on, to raise output.

- If the firm is experiencing diminishing average returns, however, then average cost will be rising. Diminishing returns set in because it is impossible to increase the input of fixed factors in the short run. In the long run, however, it is possible to vary the input of all factors of production and the option of increasing capacity by building an additional plant may well be considered by the firm. It may pursue this option if the increase in capacity leads to lower average costs of production because of economies of scale. In the long run, firms will adjust capacity to produce the required output for economic efficiency (maximum profits) in the most technically efficient (least-cost) way.

THE LEAST-COST COMBINATION

So far, we have implicitly assumed that firms will aim to produce any given level of output in the cheapest possible way. This is a perfectly valid assumption when the ultimate aim of firms is to maximise profit. The combination of factor inputs which minimises the cost of producing any given level of output is referred to as the **least-cost combination**. It is achieved when firms have adjusted their inputs in such a way that for any factor of production, the ratio of its marginal product to price is exactly equal to the ratio of marginal product to price for all other factors of production. In other words, when

66 Least-cost combination of factor inputs **9 9**

$$\frac{\text{marginal product of factor A}}{\text{price of A}} = \frac{\text{marginal product of factor B}}{\text{price of B}}$$

and so on, for all factor inputs.

When this condition is satisfied, the last pound spent on each factor input yields exactly the same return in all cases. It follows that the cost of producing any particular output is at a minimum when this condition is satisfied. It would only be possible to reduce the total cost of producing that output if the last unit of one variable factor added more to total product than the last unit of any other variable factor, per pound spent. This is impossible when the marginal product/price ratios of all factor inputs are equal.

It follows from this that any change in the productivity or the price of a factor of production will lead to factor substitution. For example, if a firm uses two factors, labour and capital, and the price of labour rises while all other things remain equal, firms will cut back on their use of labour and increase their use of capital. This factor substitution will continue until equality between the marginal product/price ratios of both factors is restored.

THE FIRM'S REVENUE

Total revenue

The firm's total revenue (TR) is its total earnings from the sale of its product. Where firms produce a good which is sold to all consumers at the *same* price, total revenue is simply price (P) multiplied by quantity (Q) sold.

$$\text{total revenue} = \text{price} \times \text{quantity}$$
$$\text{TR} = \text{P} \times \text{Q}$$

Average revenue

This is simply total revenue (TR) divided by quantity sold (Q). When firms sell their output to all consumers at the *same* price, it is easy to show that price (P) and average revenue (AR) are identical.

$$\text{average revenue} = \frac{\text{total revenue}}{\text{total output}}$$

$$= \frac{\text{TR}}{\text{Q}}$$

$$= \frac{\text{P} \times \text{Q}}{\text{Q}}$$

$$= \text{P}$$

Marginal revenue

Strictly speaking, this is the *rate* at which total revenue changes as sales change. However, for practical purposes marginal revenue is usually defined as the change in total revenue from the sale of an additional unit.

Deciding whether to produce in the short run and the long run

The distinction between fixed costs and variable costs is important in deciding whether firms should cease production. The firm is obliged to cover its fixed costs whether it undertakes production or not. For example, even when the firm produces no output it still incurs costs such as insurance charges, depreciation on assets, mortgage repayments, rent on premises, and so on. However, variable costs are incurred only when the firm undertakes production. For example, when the firm produces no output it incurs no costs from purchasing raw materials or charges for power to drive the machinery, etc. Once a firm has incurred fixed costs, its decision about whether to continue producing is therefore determined by whether its total revenue (the amount it earns from production) is sufficient to cover its total variable costs. Therefore, we must consider the circumstances in which the firm will be prepared to produce in the short run when fixed costs exist, and the circumstances in which it is prepared to produce in the long run when there are no fixed costs.

Economists treat fixed costs as bygones, i.e. as something which has no influence on decisions taken by the firm in the short run. This is because fixed costs are the same whether or not the firm undertakes production. If total revenue just covers the total variable (running) costs incurred by producing, then the firm is neither better off nor worse off if it continues production. Clearly, if total revenue is greater than total variable costs, then the firm makes at least some contribution towards covering the fixed costs already incurred by continuing in production. To cease production would leave the firm with a loss equal to its fixed costs, whereas if the firm undertakes production it will at least have a surplus over variable costs to set against its fixed costs, therefore incurring a smaller loss.

If the total revenue is less than total variable cost on the other hand, then the firm will be better off by ceasing production altogether. In this situation, the firm's total loss is equal to its fixed cost by not producing, compared with a loss equal to the deficit of variable costs added to the fixed costs if it undertakes production.

If total revenue exactly covers total variable costs this implies that average revenue, that is, price, exactly covers average variable costs.

Firms will therefore undertake production, in the short run, if the price at which their product is sold is at least equal to the average variable cost of production. When average revenue and average variable cost are equal, total revenue is exactly equal to total variable cost. However, unless price at least covers the average total cost, firms experience a loss in the long run, where fixed costs count. By definition, when average revenue exactly equals average total cost, firms break even. While they will be prepared to accept losses in the short run as long as total variable costs are covered,

❝ Short-run conditions ❞

they cannot accept losses in the long run. Therefore, if firms are to continue in production in the long run, the price at which their product is sold must at least equal the average total cost of production.

APPLIED MATERIALS Several studies confirm the existence of falling average costs as output expands up to a certain point. Most studies begin by identifying that level of output where average cost just reaches a minimum, often referred to as the **minimum efficient size** (MES). The effect on cost of a given reduction in output can then be calculated.

GOVERNMENT GREEN PAPER

This approach was adopted by the government in their Green paper entitled *A Review of Monopolies and Mergers Policy* published in 1978. Annexe C of the Green paper summarises the results of various studies into the extent of economies of scale in the UK. Table 3.3 presents a sample from the Review.

PRODUCT	ESTIMATES OF MEPS*	UK-PRODUCED SALES OF PRODUCT	MEPS AS % OF UK PRODUCED SALES
Bread	30 sacks per hour 12–18 sacks per hour	2.2 million tonnes (17.3 million sacks)	about 1% about ½%
Beer	1 million bls p.a. 1–1.5 million bls p.a. 600,000 bls p.a.	35 million bls	about 3% 3–4% about 2%
Cigarettes	36 billion cigarettes p.a.	276 million lb (approx 170 billion cigarettes)	21%
Oil refining	10 million tonnes p.a. 5 million tonnes p.a.	114 million tonnes (crude input)	9% 4%
Detergent powder	70,000 tonnes p.a.	342,000 tonnes	20%
Steel	2–3 million tonnes p.a. 4–9 million tonnes p.a. 4 million tonnes p.a.	about 24 million tonnes (production)	8–12% 17–37% 17%
Electric cookers	300,000 units	1.04 million units	30%
Motor cars	½–1 million units p.a	1.75 million units	29–57%
Commercial vehicles	20,000–30,000 units p.a.	416,000 units	5–7%
Bicycles	160,000 units p.a.	2 million units	8%
Aircraft	'Substantial economies of scale are available'		at least 100%(?)
Synthetic fibres	80,000 tonnes p.a. polymer manufacture	454,000 tonnes (production)	18%
Cotton and synthetic textiles	37.5 million sq. yd (288 Sulzer looms) 1,000 conventional looms	771 million sq. m (production)	6%
Shoes	300,000 pairs p.a. 1 million pairs p.a. 1,200 pairs/day	189 million pairs	0.2% 0.5%
Building bricks	25 million p.a. 50–62.5 million p.a.	7,000 million bricks (5,580 million?)	0.4% 0.7%–0.9%
Cement	200,000 tpa (kiln capacity) 2 million tonnes p.a. 1.2 million tonnes p.a.	17.8 million tonnes	1% 11% 7%
Plasterboard	18–20 million sq. m	104 million sq. m	17–19%
Rubber tyres	5,000 tyres/day	30.3 million tyres (car & van)	about 6%

*For several of the products listed more than one estimate is given.

Table 3.3 Some engineering-type estimates of minimum efficient plant size (MEPS)*

Source: A Review of Monopolies & Merger Policy. A Consultative Document, HMSO 1978.

Despite the date of this publication, it remains the most comprehensive study of this type for the UK. Table 3.4 presents similar but more selective recent data of this type. Note that the third column tells us how much costs increase as a percentage if the plant size is only half that which is technically optimum for the industry.

Industry	MEPS as % of output – EC	MEPS as % of output – UK	% increase in costs for plant at half MEPS
Beer	3	12	5
Bricks	0.2	1	25
Cement	1	10	26
Cigarettes	6	24	2.2
Oil refining	2.6	14	4
Paint	2	7	4.4
Washing machines	10	57	7.5

Table 3.4 Some estimates of scale economies in selected industries

Note: *MEPS = minimum efficient plant size
Source: Based on C.F. Pratten, *Costs of Non-Europe*, Vol. 2, European Commission, 1989.

NEW SHARE ISSUE

Another illustration of how costs and size are related is given in Table 3.5 which shows how the cost of making a new issue of shares (as a percentage of the amount raised) falls as the amount raised increases. We shall see in Chapter 7 that shares are simply a stake in the ownership of a company, but here it is only important to note that the average cost of issuing shares falls as the size of the share issue increases. The data refer to the cost of making a fixed price offer for sale.

AMOUNT RAISED	NO OF FIRMS IN SAMPLE	AVERAGE COST %
Up to £3m	3	17.8
£3–5m	10	11.6
£5–10m	23	8.6
Over £10m	21	4.7

Table 3.5 Costs as a percentage of the amount raised.

Source: Bank of England Quarterly Bulletin, Dec. 1986.

EXAMINATION QUESTIONS

1 (a) Explain the distinction used in cost theory between the 'short run' and the 'long run'. *(5)*
   (b) Explain why a given increase in output for a firm might involve increasing marginal and average costs in the short run, but constant marginal and average costs in the long run. *(15)*
   (c) For what reasons has it been asserted that after some point in the long run average costs of a firm must eventually rise? *(5)*

(WJEC, 1992)

2 (a) What are economies of scale? Illustrate your answer with examples. *(7)*
   (b) Why are such economies only available in the long run? *(8)*
   (c) Since economies of scale exist, why do long-run marginal costs increase ultimately, as output increases? *(10)*

(UCLES November 1988)

3 (a) Explain the distinction between the law of diminishing returns and the concept of returns to scale. *(10)*

(b) Why might these be of use in understanding the output decisions of firms in different industries? *(15)*

(UCLES, June 1993)

4 (a) Describe and explain the behaviour of a firm's average fixed cost and average variable cost as its output increases in the short run. *(15)*

(b) Explain how a firm may use knowledge of

(i) its marginal cost, and *(5)*

(ii) its average variable cost *(5)*

in making decisions about its level of output in the short run.

(Total 25 marks)

(Scottish Higher, 1989)

ANSWERS TO EXAMINATION QUESTIONS

TUTOR'S ANSWER TO QUESTION 1

(a) Economists define the short run as a period of time when the firm operates with at least one fixed factor of production. In other words, the time period under consideration is so short that the input of at least one factor of production cannot be changed. Any factor of production can be fixed and examples might include skilled labour or heavy plant. Because the input of fixed factors cannot be changed, any fixed factor of production will correspond with a fixed cost of production and, by definition, fixed costs of production will not change as output changes.

The long run, on the other hand, is a period of time when there are no fixed factors of production. In other words, all factors of production are variable and therefore the time period under consideration is so long that it is possible to alter the input of all factors of production. Any variable factor of production will correspond with a variable cost of production and as output rises, total variable costs of production will rise.

(b) Marginal cost is the cost of producing an additional unit of output. It therefore consists entirely of the increase in the variable cost of producing an extra unit of output. The firm's average cost of production is its total cost divided by its output. Now the behaviour of marginal cost is determined entirely by the behaviour of marginal product, i.e. the change in output associated with the employment of an additional variable factor of production. The behaviour of average cost, on the other hand, is determined partly by the behaviour of marginal cost and partly by the fact that average fixed cost falls continuously as output expands.

In the short run, as the firm employs more variable factors of production, output will at first rise more than proportionately. Marginal product and average product will tend to rise, primarily because the increased input of variable factors will increase the scope for specialisation. However, there are limits to the gains from specialisation and beyond some point, any further increase in the input of variable factors will result in a less than proportional increase in output. The general relationship between marginal and average product and marginal and average cost is illustrated in Fig. 3.6.

Figure 3.6 shows that, initially, as the input of variable factors increases, marginal product and average product rise and, correspondingly, marginal cost and average cost initially fall. However, as the input of variable factors continues to increase a point is reached after which marginal product and subsequently average product start to fall. Correspondingly, marginal cost, and subsequently average cost, start to rise.

In the long run, there are no fixed factors of production and the behaviour of returns and costs depend entirely on how output changes as all inputs are changed. Now, if a firm experiences economies of scale, output will rise more than

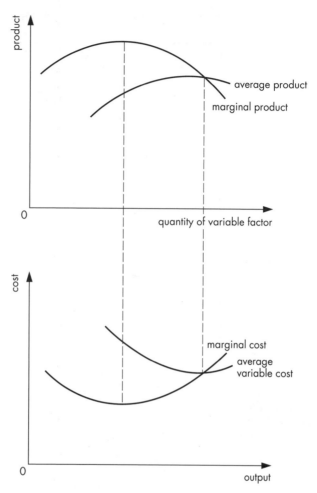

Fig. 3.6

proportionately as the input of variable factors increases. This implies that long-run marginal and average costs will fall. However, if there are no significant economies (or diseconomies) of scale, then as the input of all factors of production increases, output will rise proportionately and this implies that average and marginal cost will both be constant!

(c) It is usually argued that, in the long run, most firms will experience diseconomies of scale as output increases. In these circumstances, the firm increases the input of all factors of production, output rises less than proportionately and therefore long-run marginal and average costs rise as output expands.

There might be several reasons for this. It is often alleged that as firms grow, managerial problems of co-ordination and control increase. This implies that the chain of communication becomes less efficient as the scale of production increases and this inevitably results in cost increases.

Another important source of inefficiency is the effect that increasing size has on morale. It is sometimes alleged that workers feel increasingly isolated as firm size increases and perceive that they have less and less influence on decisions that affect their working lives. Poor morale has an adverse effect on productivity and again would explain why marginal and average costs increase in the long run.

As firms grow they require ever-increasing amounts of inputs and increasing demand for inputs might drive up input prices. If these rise faster than any increase in productivity then here again average and marginal costs will rise in the long run. In addition, firms might experience marketing diseconomies. In order to increase sales, it might become necessary for them to increase disproportionately the amount spent on promoting and advertising their product. In these circumstances, marginal and average costs would again rise in the long run.

STUDENT'S ANSWER TO QUESTION 2

(a) Strictly, firms change the scale of production when there is an equi-proportionate increase in the input of all factors of production. When this leads to a more than proportionate increase in output, firms are said to experience economies of scale. However, it is the effect of this on average cost which is important and, assuming there is no change in the prices of the factors of production, when output rises by proportionately more than inputs, the firm's average costs of production must fall.

> **Good paragraph**

Because of this, economies of scale are more generally defined as those advantages of increasing size which lead to falling average cost.

There are several sources of economies of scale. **Technical economies** are particularly important in manufacturing. For example, the production line in a modern car plant provides the classic example of **division of labour**. In some cases, the production line is almost a mile long and workers along its entire length perform a single or a small number of tasks. The production line also illustrates the **principle of indivisibilities**: it is impossible to have half a production line! Another example of this principle is the employment of specialist staff such as tax accountants in large firms where their specialised abilities can be fully utilised. This is not possible in smaller firms because an individual is not divisible into smaller parts.

> **The main point is that efficient units only come in relatively large sizes**

> **An individual is divisible as a unit of labour. It depends on the number of hours worked**

Firms might also reap substantial **marketing economies**. Particularly important here are the discounts available on bulk purchases. The actual discounts granted to firms is a well-kept secret, but its effect is readily observed in the lower prices charged for many goods by the larger retail outlets. There are also substantial economies available from advertising, especially for firms which produce a variety of products such as manufacturers of household electrical equipment. Here advertising costs per unit are usually lower for larger firms than for smaller firms. But there is another advantage. Advertising one product also advertises the firm's name, which is likely to have a positive effect on the sales of its other products at no extra cost.

> **Why?**

Large firms have an undoubted advantage over smaller firms when raising finance. Quite apart from the fact that they have more assets to pledge as security, they are statistically less likely to default on a loan. Because of this, they are considered to be more credit-worthy borrowers and lower rates of interest are available to them.

> **Another good point**

Risk-bearing economies stem partly from firms diversifying. There are many examples of this. For example, the Imperial Group produces among other things, cigarettes, potato crisps, plasterboard, whisky, and so on. Another kind of risk-bearing economy is the law of large numbers which can be observed in the proportionately smaller number of idle vehicles a bus company maintains to cover unforeseen events such

> **Why?**

as a breakdown, as compared with a smaller bus company.

(b) For purposes of analysis, economists distinguish between the *short* run and the *long* run. This classification takes account of the fact that it is not always easy for firms to change the input of all factors of production and sometimes this can only be achieved after the elapse of a considerable period of time. When firms are unable to change the input of a particular factor of production this factor is described as a *fixed* factor, whereas an input which can readily be increased is described as a *variable* factor. In the long run, all factors of production are variable and therefore the short run exists when the firm has at least one fixed factor of production.

> **Make reference to the time period**

Any factor of production can be fixed. Skilled labour is often difficult to recruit and certain items of capital equipment such as an oil refinery or a dry dock can take a considerable period of time to construct. When firms have a fixed factor of production, any increase in output is only possible by employing additional units of variable factors and working the fixed factor more intensively. However, the existence of the fixed factor indicates that it is impossible for firms to change the scale of production because this requires a change in the input of all factors of production. Since it is impossible for firms to change the scale of production in the short run, economies of scale can only exist in the long run.

> **Only in the short run**

(c) While firms sometimes experience economies of scale as they grow, beyond a certain point they are likely to experience diseconomies of scale. In these circumstances, long-run average costs increase as firms grow. For average costs to be rising long-run marginal costs must be rising and indeed must be above long-run average costs.

> **Good paragraph**

There are many reasons why firms might experience diseconomies of scale. A very important source of such diseconomies is the inability of individuals to manage firms with the same degree of competence as they grow. In large organisations there are several departments; controlling and co-ordinating the activities of these becomes increasingly difficult and is often done less efficiently than in smaller firms. Falling levels of efficiency will put up long-run marginal and average costs of production.

Another important factor is that as profit-seeking organisations grow they will exploit the most profitable opportunities first. However, as they grow they might be forced to accept higher costs. For example, a farmer producing wheat will use the most productive land first but, in order to produce more, might be forced to draw into production land that is less and less productive. Similarly, manufacturing firms might initially locate in the least-cost site but as they grow they might have to be located in higher cost sites. This will clearly raise long-run marginal and average costs of production.

> **Well illustrated**

It is also possible that larger firms will suffer a greater incidence of lost days through strikes and absenteeism. It is sometimes suggested that a possible

```
reason for this is that workers in large firms feel
they have less influence on the activities of the firm
and are less committed to it. If this is true, it would
certainly explain why firms experience higher long-run
average costs beyond a certain size. Indeed, because of
the widespread application of the principle of division
of labour, the absence of a few key workers can cause
severe disruption to production.
     Firms might also experience marketing diseconomies
as they attempt to increase their market share beyond a
certain size. Beyond a certain level each additional
pound spent on marketing activities, such as
advertising, has decreasing impact on sales. As market
share grows, it becomes increasingly difficult to
attract consumers away from alternative brands or to
persuade additional customers to enter the market.
```

❝ This is an excellent answer. Many different examples are used to illustrate points and a very sound understanding is displayed throughout. ❞

OUTLINE ANSWERS TO QUESTIONS 3 AND 4

Question 3

(a) The law of diminishing returns applies in the short run when the firm has at least one fixed factor of production. It would be useful to explain and illustrate this law using a numerical example. Remember to explain that changing returns in the short run are due to specialisation. Initially, as a firm employs more workers, there is greater scope for specialisation. However, beyond some level of output, the existence of a fixed factor imposes a limit on the gains from specialisation.

Returns to scale occur in the long run when all factors of production are variable. A firm experiences economies of scale when a given increase in all inputs leads to a more than proportionate increase in output. It is important to explain the different sources of economies of scale. Beyond some level of output economies of scale give way to diseconomies of scale when a given increase in all inputs leads to a less than proportional change in output. Again it is important to explain why firms might experience diseconomies of scale.

(b) In the short run, diminishing marginal returns imply rising marginal cost and all profit-maximising firms, if they produce at all, will produce along the rising section of the marginal cost curve. Diminishing average returns imply rising average total cost and rising average variable cost. In all profit-maximising industries, it is the intersection of the marginal cost curve with the marginal revenue curve which tells the firm where to produce, but it is the intersection of the average cost curve with the average revenue curve which tells the firm whether to produce at all.

Having explained this, you should then go on to discuss the factors that firms will consider in deciding whether to expand capacity. These are discussed on p. 42.

Question 4

(a) In answering this question, it is necessary to define average fixed costs and average variable costs. Average fixed costs decline continuously in the short run as output expands but, as we have seen, the behaviour of average variable costs is dictated by the laws of returns. In answering this part of the question it is necessary to explain why costs behave as they do and, in particular, to stress the relationship between the behaviour of returns and the behaviour of short-run variable costs.

(b) The importance of marginal costs to firms has been explained earlier. In answering part (ii), it is necessary to explain that if firms are to continue production in the short run, their total revenue must at least cover their total variable costs. This implies that price must exceed the average variable cost. Knowledge of variable costs could therefore influence decisions in the short run.

Further reading

Begg, Dornbusch and Fischer, *Economics* (3rd edn), McGraw-Hill 1991: Ch. 6, Output, supply by firms: revenue and costs, Ch. 8, Developing the theory of supply: costs and production.

Harrison et al, *Introductory Economics*, Macmillan 1992: Ch. 3, The Laws of Returns; Ch. 8, Costs and Revenue.

Lipsey and Harbury, *First Principles of Economics* (2nd edn), Weidenfeld and Nicolson 1992: Ch. 14, Costs of Production.

REVIEW SHEET

1 List five benefits of specialisation (division of labour).

(a) _____

(b) _____

(c) _____

(d) _____

(e) _____

2 List three problems/disadvantages of specialisation.

(a) _____

(b) _____

(c) _____

3 Give four reasons why factor mobility can help an economy.

(a) _____

(b) _____

(c) _____

(d) _____

4 Define each of the following:

Marginal product: _____

_____

Increasing returns: _____

_____

Diminishing retuns: _____

_____

5 Write down a numerical example of your own showing both increasing and diminishing returns.

Number of workers   Total Product Average Product   Marginal Product

6 What do we mean by returns to scale?

_____

_____

_____

_____

7 Identify three sources of *technical* economies of scale. Give examples for each source.

Source 1: _____

Example: _____

Source 2: _____

Example: _____

Source 3: _____

Example: _____

8 Suggest four possible reasons for diseconomies of scale.

(a) _____

(b) _____

(c) _____

(d) _____

9 Draw a diagram showing the relationship between AFC, AVC, ATC and MC.

10 Draw a diagram showing the relationship between short-run average cost and long-run average cost. Explain why you have drawn the diagram in this way.

Explanation: _____

_____

_____

_____

11 Under what circumstances might a firm cease to produce?

In the short run: _____

_____

In the long run: _____

_____

_____

12 What conditions must be satisfied to bring about the least-cost combination of factor inputs? _____

_____

_____

DEMAND, SUPPLY AND PRICE

GETTING STARTED

This chapter looks at the determination of market prices. A market can be defined as any arrangement which brings buyers and sellers of particular products into contact. The collective actions of buyers for a particular product establishes the market demand for that product, and the collective actions of sellers establishes the market supply. The interaction of these forces of demand and supply, i.e. **market forces**, establishes the market price for any given product.

Care must be taken in using the terms demand and supply because they have very precise meanings. Demand does not simply mean the desire to possess. It also means the willingness and ability to purchase articles. Effective demand is therefore the desire to possess something, backed up by the ability to pay for it. However, it is not enough to know the quantity demanded and supplied at particular prices. The time period is also relevant. Producers, for example, are interested in the time period over which demand will materialise. To say that demand is 1,000 units at a price of £2 is an incomplete statement. We need to know whether this quantity will be demanded per day, per week, per month, etc.

At any moment in time, demand and supply are expressed as functions of price. In other words, any other factors which might affect demand or supply are assumed to be constant. The implications of this are discussed later, but because this is a common source of confusion, it is emphasised here.

THE LAW OF DIMINISHING MARGINAL UTILITY

THE DEMAND CURVE

SUPPLY

THE DETERMINATION OF MARKET PRICE

PRICE ELASTICITY OF DEMAND (PED)

PRICE ELASTICITY OF SUPPLY (PES)

THE COBWEB THEOREM

APPLIED MATERIALS

THE LAW OF DIMINISHING MARGINAL UTILITY

66 An important law 99

ESSENTIAL PRINCIPLES

Economists equate the term utility with satisfaction. Utility is important because economists assume that only goods and services which possess it, i.e. which confer satisfaction, will be demanded. Additionally, economists assume that consumers 'act rationally' and this implies that they aim to maximise their total utility, i.e. to gain as much utility as possible, given the limited income they possess and the prices they face. The **law of diminishing marginal utility** simply states that as consumption of a product increases, each successive unit consumed confers less utility than the previous unit. In other words, as consumption increases, marginal utility falls.

CONSUMER EQUILIBRIUM

Equilibrium can be thought of as a state that exists when there is no tendency to change. In the present context, equilibrium will exist when consumers achieve their aim, i.e. maximise satisfaction given their limited income. When this is the case they will have no incentive to change the quantities of the different goods and services they currently purchase, because to do so will result in a reduction in the amount of satisfaction they receive from their purchases. In other words, consumer equilibrium exists when a consumer cannot increase total utility by reallocating expenditure. This occurs when the following condition is satisfied:

66 The condition for maximum utility 99

$$\frac{MU_A}{P_A} = \frac{MU_B}{P_B} = \ldots = \frac{MU_n}{P_n}$$

where
$$\begin{aligned} MU &= \text{marginal utility} \\ P &= \text{price} \\ A, B, \ldots, n &= \text{goods purchased} \end{aligned}$$

This condition simply implies that consumer equilibrium exists when the ratios of marginal utility and price are equal for *all* goods consumed. When this condition is satisfied, it is impossible for the consumer to increase total utility by rearranging purchases because the last pound spent on each good yields the same addition to total utility in all cases. This must maximise total utility because, for example, if the last pound spent on product B yielded more utility than the last pound spent on product A, then the consumer could increase total utility by buying more of B and less of A. This is impossible when the ratios of marginal utility and price are equal, as is illustrated in Table 4.1. It is assumed that only two goods, A which costs £2 per unit and B which costs £4 per unit, are available, and that the consumer has a total budget of £18. Given the consumer's budget, the existing prices, and the levels of utility available from consumption, equilibrium is achieved when 3 units of good A and 3 units of good B are purchased:

i.e. $\dfrac{MU_A}{P_A} = \dfrac{MU_B}{P_B}$ with $\dfrac{10}{2} = \dfrac{20}{4}$

	GOOD A			GOOD B		
QUANTITY CONSUMED	PRICE (£)	TOTAL UTILITY	MARGINAL UTILITY	PRICE (£)	TOTAL UTILITY	MARGINAL UTILITY
1	2	15	15	4	25	25
2	2	27	12	4	48	23
3	2	37	10	4	68	20
4	2	46	9	4	86	18
5	2	53	7	4	102	16
6	2	56	3	4	116	14
7	2	57	1	4	128	12
8	2	55	−2	4	139	11

Table 4.1 Ratios of marginal utility and price

With a budget of £18 it is impossible to achieve a higher level of utility by varying the combination of A and B consumed. For example, if we bought one less B and two more A with the income released, total utility would fall. Not purchasing the third unit of B would lose us 20 units of utility; purchasing the fourth and fifth units of A would only gain us 16 units of utility.

THE DEMAND CURVE

THE INDIVIDUAL'S DEMAND CURVE

Once achieved, equilibrium can only be disturbed if there is a change in some factor that influences the level of consumer satisfaction. This could be the result of a change in the consumer's income, a change in the prices of other goods and services available to consumers, a change in the range or quality of goods and services available, and so on. However, since at any moment in time all factors that affect demand, other than price, are assumed to be constant, it is changes in price which are important to us at present. More specifically, the question we have to answer is this: if all other things remain unchanged, how will a change in the price of one good affect the amount of the good a consumer purchases?

We can answer this question by looking again at Table 4.1. Using the information given here, let us consider what would happen to the amount of good B consumed if there was a reduction in its price from £4 per unit to £2 per unit, and all other things remained unchanged. Because the consumer's aim is to maximise utility, his/her reaction to the price reduction is predictable. He/she will simply rearrange his/her purchases so as to achieve equilibrium following the price reduction. Applying the equilibrium condition:

$$\frac{MU_A}{P_A} = \frac{MU_B}{P_B}$$

> A lower price will mean greater consumption

leads to the conclusion that (with income still £18) the consumer will increase consumption of good B to 7 units, and cut consumption of A to 2 units. When this is done the equilibrium condition is satisfied because:

$$\frac{MU_A}{P_A} = \frac{MU_B}{P_B} \text{ with } \frac{12}{2} = \frac{12}{2}$$

This rearrangement of purchases occurs because as the price of one product falls, the price of obtaining a given level of satisfaction from consuming that product also falls. The price per unit of satisfaction (i.e. utility) obtained from a product therefore becomes cheaper after a price reduction, and a consumer will react by increasing consumption of the product whose price has fallen. The implication is that for the individual consumer, price and quantity demanded vary inversely. This general relationship is illustrated in Fig. 4.1.

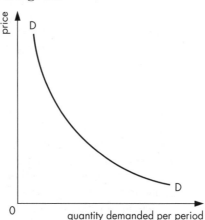

Fig. 4.1 A typical demand curve

So widely applicable is the inverse relationship between price and quantity demand that we refer to Fig. 4.1 as a **normal demand curve**. Any other demand curve is referred to as exceptional, since it is an exception to the general rule that price and quantity demanded vary inversely. Exceptional demand curves are considered later in this chapter.

MARKET DEMAND CURVES

The total market demand for a commodity at any given price is simply the total amount demanded by each consumer at that price. Market demand curves are therefore simply the horizontal summation of each individual's demand curve. Since, for each individual, quantity demanded varies inversely with price, this general relationship will be embodied in the market demand curve. A typical, or normal, market demand curve therefore has the same general shape as the individual's demand curve, illustrated in Fig. 4.1.

A CHANGE IN QUANTITY DEMANDED AND A CHANGE IN DEMAND

Great care must be taken in the use of these terms because, although they appear similar, they imply entirely different things.

A change in quantity demanded

For any product, a change in quantity demanded is always caused by a change in its price. A change in quantity demanded therefore refers to a movement along an existing demand curve. Figure 4.2 is used as a basis for illustration.

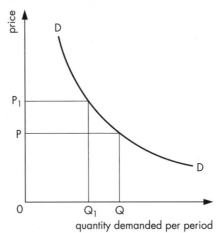

Fig. 4.2 A rise in price leads to a contraction of demand and a fall of price leads to an expansion or extension of demand

💬 Moving along a given demand curve 💬

If price rises from OP to OP_1 then quantity demanded falls from OQ to OQ_1. This is referred to as a reduction in quantity demanded or a **contraction of demand**, i.e. demand contracts from OQ to OQ_1. No other term can be used to describe this. Conversely, if price falls from OP_1 to OP, then quantity demanded rises from OQ_1 to OQ. This rise in quantity demanded can also be referred to as an extension or **expansion of demand**, since demand extends (expands) from OQ_1 to OQ. Again, either of these terms is acceptable, but no other term can be used in this context.

A change in demand

💬 Shifts in the entire demand curve 💬

A change in demand, on the other hand, is caused by a change in some factor other than price. So far we have assumed that at any moment in time price is the only factor that affects demand, all other factors remaining constant. These factors which are assumed to be constant are referred to as the **conditions of demand**, or the parameters of demand. A change in demand is caused by a change in the conditions of demand and means that either more or less of a commodity is demanded at each and every price. Figure 4.3 is used as a basis for illustration.

Demand for this commodity is initially represented by DD. A movement, or shift in demand to the right, to $D_1 D_1$ is referred to as an **increase in demand** because a greater amount is demanded at any given price than previously. Conversely, a movement, or a shift in demand to the left, from DD to D_2D_2, is referred to as a **decrease in demand** because a smaller amount is demanded at any given price than previously.

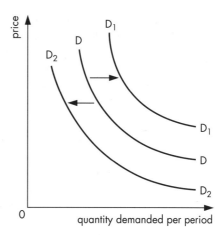

Fig. 4.3 A change in the conditions
of demand

Causes of changes in demand

A change in demand is always caused by a change in at least one of the conditions of demand:

Reasons why demand
curves do shift

■ **Changes in disposable income** This is one of the most important determinants of demand. An increase in disposable income, i.e. income available for spending will lead to an increase in demand for most goods and services. There are exceptions (see below and p. 68) but rising income is undoubtedly the most important reason why demand for most goods and services increases (an outward shift of the demand curve) over time.

■ **Changes in the price of substitutes** Many goods are substitutes for one another. For example, a glance round the shelves of any supermarket will show that, for most foodstuffs, there are many competing brands. In this situation, a rise in the price of one good will lead to a contraction in the quantity of that good demanded and an increase in the demand for its substitutes. The relationship between substitute goods is referred to as **competitive demand**.

■ **Changes in the price of complements** Certain goods are jointly demanded. Fish and chips, bread and butter, and gin and tonic, are all examples of complements. In these cases, a rise in the price of one good will lead to a contraction in the quantity of that good demanded and a decrease in the demand (inward shift of the demand curve) for the complement.

■ **Changes in the weather** Some goods are demanded seasonally and at certain times of the year demand for these goods will increase. Christmas cards, fireworks and Easter eggs are obvious examples, but more generally there is greater demand for ice-cream in the summer than in winter, while there is greater demand for overcoats in winter than in summer. Changes in seasons thus cause changes in demand for certain goods and services.

■ **Changes in tastes and fashions** For certain products, such as clothes, changes in fashions can bring about marked changes in demand. The more fashionable a good becomes, the more demand for it will increase, and vice versa.

■ **Changes in population** Changes in the size of a country's population bring about changes in the demand for most goods and services. However, changes in the structure of the population, such as the age and sex profiles, will also lead to quite substantial changes in demand for most goods and services.

■ **Advertising** An increase in a firm's effective advertising will cause an increase in demand for the product being advertised.

EXCEPTIONAL DEMAND CURVES

It is sometimes suggested that in some cases demand might vary *directly* with price:

■ **Giffen's Paradox** The English economist, Giffen, is credited with the idea of suggesting that in subsistence economies, if the price of basic foodstuffs such as

66 Some unusual demand curves 99

bread and potatoes increases, quantity demanded will also increase. One possible reason for this is that as price rises the higher price makes it impossible for consumers to purchase better quality foodstuffs. They therefore substitute the poorer quality foodstuffs despite the fact that the price of these has increased! Despite its appealing logic, there is no empirical evidence to support this hypothesis and indeed it is uncertain why it is referred to as Giffen's paradox since there is no evidence that he even suggested the idea!

■ **Veblen goods** In this case, it is argued that the attractiveness of some goods increases as their price increase. It is argued that some goods are purchased for ostentatious purposes and as their price rises so does their attractiveness because they provide a means of displaying superior wealth. Alternatively, it is possible to argue that if consumers believe that the price of a good reflects its quality then quantity demanded might increase as price increases. In other words, consumer ignorance might provide an explanation for exceptional demand curves.

SUPPLY

The total market supply of any commodity at a particular price is equal to the total amount that all individual firms which produce that commodity will supply at that price. The market supply curve is therefore the horizontal summation of all individual firms' supply curves. In other words, we simply add the amount that every firm supplies at each and every price. Like demand curves, supply curves are drawn on the assumption that all factors that affect supply, except price, are constant.

A CHANGE IN QUANTITY SUPPLIED

Economic theory indicates that market supply and price vary directly. In other words, that a greater amount is supplied at higher prices than at lower prices. There are two main reasons for this:

■ It is assumed that firms produce for profit, and, other things being equal, at higher prices it becomes more profitable to expand output.

■ At higher prices, it becomes possible for marginal firms, i.e. firms which cannot cover their costs at lower prices, to undertake production. As price rises, more firms enter the industry and market supply rises.

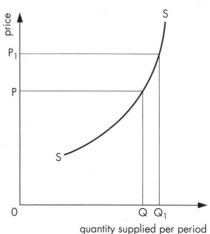

Fig. 4.4 A normal supply curve showing an extension or expansion of supply when price rises and a contraction of supply when price falls

66 Movements along a given supply curve 99

A normal supply curve is illustrated in Fig. 4.4. It is important to stress that the same rules used when describing demand apply when describing both movements along a supply curve and shifts in a supply curve. Thus when price rises in Fig. 4.4 from OP to OP_1, there is an **expansion** or extension in the quantity supplied from OQ to OQ_1. Conversely, a fall in price from OP_1 to OP leads to a **contraction** in quantity supplied from OQ_1 to OQ.

A CHANGE IN SUPPLY

66 Shifts in the entire
supply curve 99

A change in supply implies a complete shift of an existing supply curve. When more is supplied at any given price than previously we refer to an **increase in supply**. This is illustrated in Fig. 4.5 by a movement of the supply curve to the right from SS to S_1S_1.

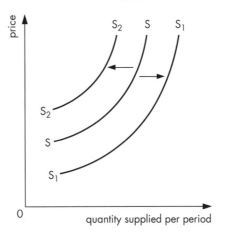

Fig. 4.5 A change in the conditions of supply.

When less is supplied at any given price than previously, we refer to a **decrease in supply**. This is illustrated by a movement of the supply curve to the left, from SS to S_2S_2 in Fig. 4.5.

Causes of changes in supply

Changes in supply such as those illustrated in Fig. 4.5 can only be caused by a change in at least one of the conditions of supply. The most important causes of a change in supply are considered below.

- **Changes in costs of production** If all other things remain equal, a change in costs will change the level of profit available from producing any particular commodity.

66 Reasons why supply
curves do shift 99

  - Specifically, a rise in costs will reduce profits and lead some firms to cut back on output, while other firms will cease production altogether. So, if all other things remain equal, a rise in costs of production will lead to a decrease in supply.

  - Conversely, a fall in costs will lead to higher profits at any given price and so will lead to an increase in supply.

  - Despite this, it is possible to pay a higher reward to any factor of production and yet leave costs of production unchanged. For example, a five per cent increase in wages which is accompanied by a five per cent increase in productivity will leave average labour costs unchanged and therefore the supply curve will not move. However, when costs rise by more than productivity, this will lead to a decrease in supply, and when costs rise by less than productivity there will be an increase in supply.

- **Changes in the prices of other commodities** Some goods such as beef and hides are jointly supplied. This simply means that it is impossible to supply one good without also supplying the other good. In these circumstances, a rise in the price of one good will lead to an increase in the supply of the other.

  For example, if the price of beef rises, there will be an expansion in the quantity of beef supplied. This in turn will lead to an increase in the supply of hides since, at any given price for hides, more hides are now being supplied.

- **Changes in the weather** This can have important repercussions on the supply of certain agricultural commodities.

  - Favourable weather conditions can produce a bumper harvest of certain commodities and a consequent increase in supply.

  - Conversely, unfavourable weather conditions will lead to a poor harvest and a decrease in supply.

■ Changes in indirect taxation and subsidies

- A rise in indirect taxation such as a higher rate of VAT, will have the same effect on producers as a rise in costs of production. It will reduce the profit available to producers at any given price, and will consequently lead to a decrease in supply. In fact, the effect will be to shift the entire supply curve vertically upwards by the full amount of the tax.

  The following example illustrates this, and for simplicity we assume the imposition of a lump sum tax of £1 per unit.

PRICE (£)	QUANTITY SUPPLIED BEFORE TAX	QUANTITY SUPPLIED AFTER TAX
7	145	125
6	125	105
5	105	90
4	90	

After the tax is imposed, producers receive £1 less than previously at any given price. They will therefore supply at each price the amount they would have previously supplied at a price of £1 less. For example, when producers receive £4 per unit, they will supply 90 units. After the tax is imposed, producers actually receive £4 per unit when the market price is £5. They will therefore only supply, at a market price of £5, what would previously have been supplied at a market price of £4.

- A subsidy has exactly the opposite effect. It represents a payment to suppliers in addition to any revenue received from sales and therefore raises the amount of profit obtained from supplying any given level of output. In the case of a specific subsidy such as £1 per unit, the effect will be to shift the supply curve vertically downwards by the full amount of the subsidy.

THE DETERMINATION OF MARKET PRICE

In free markets, prices are determined by the interaction of demand and supply. With given demand and supply functions only one price is sustainable. This is the **equilibrium price**, and it is the only price at which demand and supply are equal. This is illustrated in Fig. 4.6.

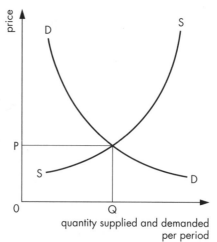

Fig. 4.6 Market equilibrium

> 66 Equilibrium means a state of rest 99

With demand and supply given by DD and SS respectively the equilibrium price is OP, because it is the only price at which supply and demand are equal. At prices above OP, supply exceeds demand and there is a market surplus of this commodity. The existence of this surplus will cause the price to fall. As the price falls producers will cut back production (supply contracts) and consumers will purchase more (demand expands) until supply and demand are equal at quantity OQ. Conversely, at prices below OP there is a market shortage and this shortage will cause the price to rise. The higher price will persuade producers to expand output (supply expands) and consumers will purchase less (demand contracts). Only when the price is OP is there equilibrium in the market, with no tendency for producers or consumers to revise their decisions.

CHANGES IN MARKET PRICE

We have seen that prices are determined by demand and supply. It follows that once equilibrium has been established, prices can only change if there is a change in the conditions of demand and/or supply. This is fairly straightforward. However, it is essential to be clear about the causes of changes in price, otherwise it is impossible to predict the effects.

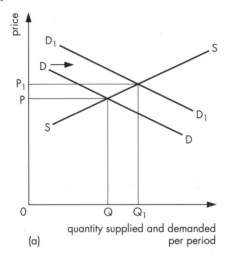
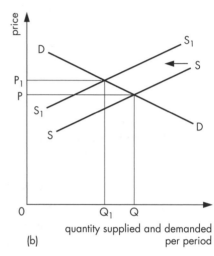

Fig. 4.7 The effect of (a) An increase in demand and (b) A decrease in supply

(a)

(b)

Figure 4.7 shows that it is possible for different causes of a rise in price to have different effects.

- Figure 4.7(a) shows the effect of an increase in demand from DD to D_1D_1. The price rises from its original equilibrium of OP to OP_1 and there is a rise in the equilibrium quantity demanded and supplied from OQ to OQ_1.

- Figure 4.7(b), on the other hand, shows the effect of a decrease in supply from SS to S_1S_1. Again, there is a rise in price from OP to OP_1 but this time there is a fall in the equilibrium quantity supplied and demanded from OQ to OQ_1.

Clearly, the effect of a rise in price on equilibrium output depends on the cause.

PRICE ELASTICITY OF DEMAND (PED)

This is usually referred to simply as **elasticity of demand**. It measures the responsiveness of quantity demanded to changes in price. Elasticity of demand can be measured in several ways but it is most commonly measured as:

$$PED = \frac{\text{percentage change in quantity demanded}}{\text{percentage change in price}}$$

$$= \frac{(\Delta Q/Q) \times 100}{(\Delta P/P) \times 100}$$

$$= \frac{\Delta Q}{Q} \div \frac{\Delta P}{P}$$

$$= \frac{\Delta Q}{Q} \times \frac{P}{\Delta P}$$

$$= \frac{P}{Q} \times \frac{\Delta Q}{\Delta P}$$

where Δ indicates the amount of change of a quantity.

Where the elasticity of demand is less than 1, demand is said to be **inelastic** and where it is more than 1, demand is said to be **elastic**. The larger the value of elasticity, the more responsive is quantity demanded to changes in price.

In most cases, a given demand curve does not possess a constant elasticity. In fact, the value of elasticity associated with a given price change varies all the way along a given demand curve. This is illustrated in Fig. 4.8.

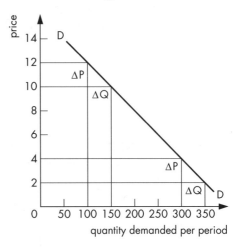

Fig. 4.8 The changing value of elasticity of demand

For the straight line demand curve $\Delta Q/\Delta P$ is a constant $= {}^{50}\!/_2 = 25$

When P = 2, PED = ${}^2\!/_{350} \times 25 = {}^1\!/_7$
When P = 4, PED = ${}^4\!/_{300} \times 25 = {}^1\!/_3$

So even if the demand curve is a straight line, price elasticity of demand varies along its entire length, since the ratio P/Q varies; in fact P/Q rises as price rises, so that elasticity of demand rises as we move up the demand curve. If the demand curve is not a straight line, the ratio $\Delta Q/\Delta P$ will vary as well!

Elasticity can vary along the demand curve

Note: strictly speaking price elasticity of demand is negative for all normal demand curves because a rise in price leads to a fall in quantity demanded and vice versa. However, the negative sign is usually omitted and this convention is followed here.

ELASTICITY: THE LIMITING CASES

There are three exceptions to the general rule that the value of elasticity varies along the length of a demand curve: all three are illustrated in Figure 4.9.

- In Fig. 4.9(a) a change in price has no effect on quantity demanded and, therefore, demand is **perfectly inelastic**.
- In Fig. 4.9(b) an infinitely small change in price leads to an infinitely large change in quantity demanded and therefore, demand is said to be **perfectly** or **infinitely elastic**.
- In Fig. 4.9(c) the proportionate change in quantity demanded is exactly equal to the proportionate change in price that brings it about along the entire length of the demand curve. Elasticity of demand is therefore equal to unity at all points along the entire length of the demand curve and demand is said to be **unit elastic**.

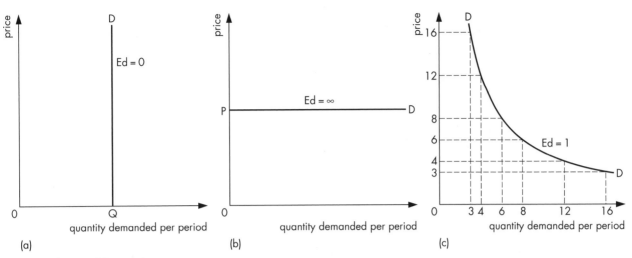

Fig. 4.9 Elasticity of demand: the limiting cases

ELASTICITY OF DEMAND AND TOTAL REVENUE

Elasticity of demand has a crucial bearing on the way total revenue is affected by a change in price. The following relationships exist:

> **Price elasticity of demand will affect total revenue**

- When demand is inelastic (PED<1), a rise in price leads to a rise in total revenue and a fall in price leads to a fall in total revenue.
- When demand is elastic (PED>1), a rise in price leads to a fall in total revenue and a fall in price leads to a rise in total revenue.
- When demand has unit elasticity (PED=1), a rise or fall in price has no effect on total revenue.

DETERMINANTS OF PRICE ELASTICITY OF DEMAND

There are several factors which influence the value of price elasticity of demand for any particular product. The most important of these are summarised below.

The availability of substitutes
This is probably the most important determinant of elasticity of demand for any particular product. When there are few close substitutes available for any particular product, demand will tend to be less elastic and therefore less responsive to changes in price. For example, demand for petrol in total is less elastic than demand for any particular brand of petrol.

> **Factors affecting price elasticity of demand**

The proportion of income spent on the commodity
When the cost of a commodity is a relatively small proportion of total expenditure, demand will tend to be less elastic. For example, spending on pencils accounts for a very small part of total expenditure. Consequently a rise in the price of pencils would have little impact on total expenditure, and we would therefore expect demand for pencils to be little affected by a change in their price – i.e. demand to be relatively inelastic.

The number of uses the commodity has
When a commodity has several uses, demand will tend to be less elastic. For some of these uses a change in price is likely to have little or no effect on quantity demanded. For example, electricity has many uses and this is one reason why demand for electricity tends to be inelastic.

Whether the commodity is a necessity or a luxury
It is difficult to define what is meant by the terms necessity and luxury. However, if a good is considered a necessity, demand for it will tend to be inelastic. Demand for luxuries will be more elastic.

Whether the commodity is habit-forming

Some goods, such as cigarettes, are habit-forming and in these cases demand will tend to be less elastic.

Time period

For most goods demand is less elastic in the short run than in the long run. For example, a rise in the price of domestic gas is likely to have only a minor effect on consumption in the short run. In the longer run, economies can be made by wearing warmer clothing around the house, by better insulation, by switching to electricity for cooking and heating, etc. so that demand may then become more responsive to change in price.

WHO REQUIRES KNOWLEDGE OF PRICE ELASTICITY OF DEMAND?

Because price elasticity of demand determines the effect of price changes on quantity demanded it is an extremely useful concept. So who requires knowledge of price elasticity of demand?

The Government

66 Benefits from a knowledge of price elasticity of demand 99

- Knowledge of price elasticity of demand would be useful to the government and the policy-making authorities in general. It might be useful to the government in assessing the cost or likely effectiveness of price support schemes such as those common in agriculture.

- Similarly, knowledge of price elasticity of demand would be useful if it was decided to influence consumption through the use of taxes or subsidies. For example, taxes might be used to discourage the consumption of certain demerit goods, while subsidies might be used to encourage the consumption of merit goods. Again, knowledge of price elasticity of demand would provide an indication of how successful the policy is likely to be and, in the case of subsidies, it would be useful in providing an estimate of the likely cost of the subsidy.

- For any government considering devaluation/revaluation (see Ch. 15) of its currency, knowledge of price elasticity of demand is essential in order to predict the changes in import expenditure and export revenue following devaluation/revaluation.

The Business Sector

Those involved in the business sector would find knowledge of price elasticity of demand useful if they were considering a price change for their product. If demand is inelastic, a price rise will lead to a rise in profits because revenue will rise and, with less being sold, output will be reduced and costs will fall. In other situations such as a price fall, the effect on profitability depends on the proportionate change in costs and revenue following a price change. Note, however, that if the aim of a price fall is to increase sales revenue, it is important that demand is elastic. Firms might wish to increase sales so as to increase their market share or to enable them to reap important economies of scale. (Knowledge of income elasticity of demand, which is discussed on p. 68, is also useful in planning future investment decisions.)

Trade Unions

Trade unions would find it useful to have an estimate of price elasticity of demand for the products their members produce because this is an important determinant of changes in demand for labour following a rise in wages.

PRICE ELASTICITY OF SUPPLY (PES)

Just as elasticity of demand measures the responsiveness of a change in quantity demanded to a change in price, so **elasticity of supply** measures the responsiveness of a change in quantity supplied to a change in price. Elasticity of supply is measured in the same basic way as elasticity of demand, except, of course, we measure changes in quantity supplied, i.e.

$$PES = \frac{\text{percentage change in quantity supplied}}{\text{percentage change in price}}$$

$$= \frac{P}{Q} \times \frac{\Delta Q}{\Delta P}$$

Again, there are three exceptions to the general rule that elasticity of supply varies along the entire length of the supply curve. These are illustrated in Fig. 4.10.

- In Fig. 4.10(a) elasticity of supply is zero because any change in price has no effect on the quantity supplied. This is often called **perfectly inelastic supply**.

- In Fig. 4.10(b) elasticity of supply is infinite because an infinitely small change in price leads to an infinitely large change in quantity supplied. This is often called **perfectly elastic supply**.

- In Fig. 4.10(c) elasticity of supply is unity because any change in price leads to an equi-proportionate change in quantity supplied. (This is true of any straight line supply curve passing through the origin.) This is often called **unit elastic supply**.

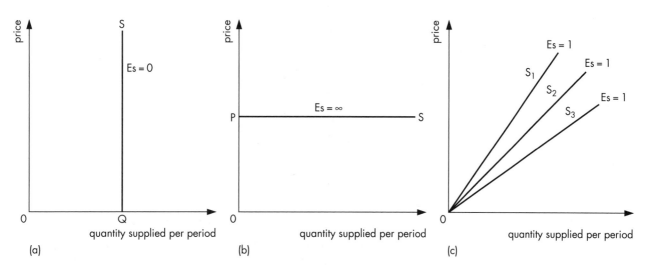

Fig. 4.10 Elasticity of supply: the limiting cases

DETERMINANTS OF ELASTICITY OF SUPPLY

The main determinants of elasticity of supply are briefly summarised below.

The time period

This is an important factor and, in general, supply is more elastic in the long run than in the short run. In fact, economists identify three time periods:

- The **momentary period** This is so short that it is impossible to expand supply. Supply is completely inelastic in the momentary period as when a trawler lands its catch at the quay.

- The **short period** During this it is possible to expand supply by using more of the variable factors. For example, trawlers might stay at sea longer and take on additional crew members. However, the existence of fixed factors limits the scope for increased output. Supply is, therefore, relatively less elastic during the short run.

- The **long period** During this all factors are variable and supply is therefore more elastic than in either of the previous situations. Here it is possible to have more trawlers as well as additional crew members and so on.

`❝ Factors affecting elasticity of supply ❞`

Factor mobility

Although supply is more elastic in the long run, the degree of elasticity will still partly depend on factor mobility. The greater the mobility of the factors of production, the greater the elasticity of supply. For instance, a rise in the price of a good, due, say, to an increase in demand, raises the producer's profits. If he/she can easily attract land, labour and capital from other uses by offering higher rewards (i.e. factors are mobile) then he/she will be more able to expand supply in response to the higher price.

Availability of stocks

Where a product can be stored without loss of quality or undue expense, supply will tend to be elastic, at least while stocks last. This explains why the supply of processed food will tend to be more elastic than the supply of fresh food.

Behaviour of costs as output changes

When firms are subject to relatively small increases in average costs as output expands, supply will tend to be more elastic. However, if firms experience diminishing returns or diseconomies of scale which are severe enough, costs will rise steeply as output expands and, in these circumstances, supply will tend to be less elastic.

The existence of surplus capacity

Even if average costs do increase by small amounts as output increases, supply might be relatively inelastic if firms do not have surplus, or unused, capacity. If they are operating at full capacity, it will be impossible to bring about significant changes in output in the short run.

Barriers to entry

In certain cases, it might be difficult for additional firms to enter an industry and undertake production. These barriers might take a variety of forms (see pp. 00–00) but their existence will tend to make supply less elastic than otherwise.

INCOME ELASTICITY OF DEMAND

This measures the responsiveness of demand to changes in income.

$$\text{Income E of D} = \frac{\text{percentage change in quantity demanded}}{\text{percentage change in income}}$$

❝ Inferior goods have negative income elasticities ❞

For most goods income elasticity of demand will be positive, i.e. a rise in income will lead to an increase in demand. However, there are exceptions to this rule, and for some goods a rise in income leads to a decrease in demand. Such goods are referred to as **inferior goods** or **Giffen goods** (see p. 59). By and large inferior goods consist of cheaper but poorer quality goods that lower income groups purchase. Bread is one of the most often quoted examples of an inferior good, being regarded in the UK as a poor quality substitute compared with other staple items such as meat, fish, etc. The consumption of bread has declined markedly in the western world as incomes have increased and this supports the view that bread is regarded as an inferior good in the western world.

❝ Giffen goods and inferior goods are different ❞

Note: all Giffen goods have a negative income elasticity of demand so they are inferior goods. However, Giffen goods also have positive price elasticity of demand.

CROSS ELASTICITY OF DEMAND

This is a measure of the responsiveness of demand for one good to a change in the price of another.

$$\text{Cross E of D} = \frac{\text{percentage change in quantity demanded of good X}}{\text{percentage change in price of good Y}}$$

❝ The sign of cross elasticity of demand is important ❞

- If the cross elasticity of demand between two goods is positive, the goods are **substitutes**; a rise in the price of say, good Y, leads to an increase in the demand for good X. Moreover, the greater the positive value of cross elasticity between two goods, the greater the degree of substitutability between them.
- If the cross elasticity of demand between two goods is negative, the goods are **complements**; a rise in the price of, say, good Y leads to a decrease in demand

for good X. Again, the higher the negative value of cross elasticity between two goods, the greater the degree of complementarity between them.

THE COBWEB THEOREM

The cobweb theorem is useful in explaining the circumstances when disequilibrium in a free market might be temporary or permanent. Figure 4.11 is used to illustrate this point. In Figs 4.11(a) and 4.11(b) SS and DD represent the long-run supply and demand conditions for a particular commodity. Let us consider the effect, in both cases, of an increase in price above the long-run equilibrium price caused by a temporary reduction in supply, perhaps because of an unusually poor harvest. We begin at point A. The higher price encourages increased production of size AB. However, since there is no change in demand the excess supply will force price down and we move to point C. This represents a lower price than anticipated and consequently producers will cut back on production and we move to point E. The reduction in the amount supplied implies a market shortage at the lower price and so price rises. We move to point F and so on. Note that Fig. 4.11(a) shows a **converging (stable) cobweb** so that each change in production results in a move closer to long-run equilibrium while Fig. 4.11(b) shows an **explosive (unstable) cobweb** where each change results in a move further away from equilibrium. You must explain the causes of this in terms of differences in the elasticities of demand and supply in each case. If the supply curve is sleeper (less elastic) than the demand curve, then we are more likely to have a convergent (stable) cobweb; and vice versa.

You could also mention the conditions which would give rise to a cobweb process. In cases where there are many buyers and many sellers of a product and it is easy for producers to increase or reduce production as in perfect competition (see Chapter 5) we might expect to find adjustment to long-run equilibrium following this sort of pattern.

Another factor that might give rise to market disequilibrium is government intervention in the economy. For example, price controls in many Eastern bloc countries has led to disequilibrium in many markets for food. This is illustrated by the existence of shortages, long queues and even physical rationing in some cases! Such disequilibrium will continue until the price mechanism is allowed to function more freely.

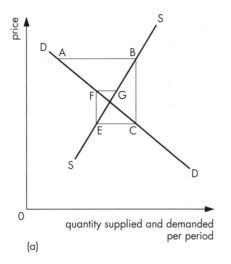

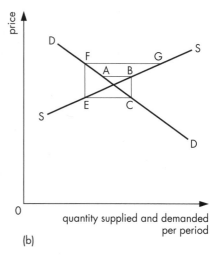

Fig. 4.11(a) A converging cobweb and (b) An explosive cobweb

(a)

(b)

APPLIED MATERIALS

COMMON AGRICULTURAL POLICY (CAP)

A widely documented case study on the use of **minimum prices** is the Common Agricultural Policy (CAP) operated by the EU. Basically, minimum prices are established for agricultural commodities. If prices fall below the minimum level, farmers sell to **intervention agencies** which buy up the surplus at the guaranteed minimum price. In other words, demand is perfectly elastic at the guaranteed minimum price! This is illustrated in Fig. 4.12.

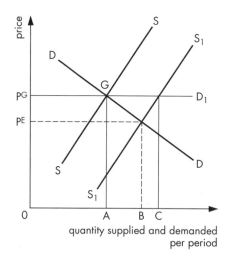

Fig. 4.12 The operation of a guaranteed price support scheme

In Fig. 4.12, the free market supply and demand curves are represented by DD and SS respectively and the equilibrium price in a free market would be P^G. However, suppose P^G is also the minimum price guaranteed to producers by the authorities, and, in order to maintain this minimum price, the authorities are prepared to purchase any excess supply. The demand curve for this product therefore becomes DGD_1. For example, if a bumper harvest results in a shift in supply to S_1S_1, in a free market, price would fall to P^E. To prevent this the authorities purchase the excess supply AC at the guaranteed minimum price. In the real world, such purchases by the intervention agencies has led to the notorious beef, butter and grain mountains as well as the milk and wine lakes.

In practice, it is difficult to distinguish between a shift in a demand curve and a movement along a demand curve, since the latter occurs when all factors which affect demand, other than price, are constant. In the real world, this is an impossible condition to achieve. Consequently, when more of any commodity is sold this could imply an increase in demand, an expansion (extension) of demand, or, indeed, a combination of both. In the latter case it is extremely difficult to quantify the relative effect of each.

THE ELASTICITY OF DEMAND FOR PETROL

An article in *The Economic Review* of February 1993, entitled 'Price and Income Elasticities: Petrol', provides an example of how to measure the price and income elasticity of demand for petrol. The data in Table 4.3 are used as the basis for the calculations.

Date	Petrol consumption (1,000 tonnes)	Gross domestic product (£ million 1980 Prices)	Relative price (Index)
1970	14,234	190,295	100
1971	14,963	195,424	95
1972	15,898	199,879	93
1973	16,926	215,178	86
1974	16,483	213,126	88
1975	16,125	211,882	123
1976	16,925	219,881	112
1977	17,383	222,221	101
1978	18,394	230,168	89
1979	18,729	235,018	82
1980	19,185	230,091	106
1981	18,750	227,400	105
1982	19,274	229,892	116
1983	19,593	237,952	116
1984	20,255	242,806	122
1985	20,379	251,840	119
1986	21,477	259,155	115
1987	22,182	268,608	103
1988	23,252	280,550	95

Table 4.3

Source: EuroStat, Digest of UK Energy Statistics.

Gross domestic product (GDP) (see Ch. 8) is taken as a measure of real income and the relative price of petrol is measured as an index (see Ch. 13). We start with a value of the petrol price index of 100 and express changes in the relative price of petrol as percentage changes on this initial value. So, for example, if the petrol price index rises to 123 this implies a 23 per cent increase in the price of petrol on its initial price.

The main problem with calculating elasticities is that we cannot hold all other relevant variables constant. Our problem is therefore to separate the effects of price and income changes on the demand for petrol. Taking income elasticity of demand first, Table 4.3 shows that the *relative price* of petrol in 1988 was the same as in 1971. This implies that any change in the consumption of petrol between those two dates must be the result of a change in real income. Using the formula:

$$\text{Income elasticity of demand} = \frac{\text{percentage } \Delta Q}{\text{percentage } \Delta Y}$$

we can estimate income elasticity of demand as follows:

% $\Delta Q = 100 \times (23{,}252 - 14{,}963)/14{,}963 = 55.4\%$
% $\Delta Y = 100 \times (280{,}550 - 195{,}424)/195{,}424 = 43.56\%$
Income elasticity of demand for petrol = 55.4/43.56 = 1.27

This implies that for the period under consideration, demand for petrol was income elastic and a 1 per cent rise in income led to a 1.27 per cent rise in demand for petrol.

This estimate of income elasticity of demand can be used to help us estimate price elasticity of demand. The first step is to select a period when there was a significant change in the price of oil. The period chosen is 1973–75 when OPEC forced up a substantial increase in the price of oil. The relevant calculations are set out in Table 4.4.

Table 4.4 Calculation of the price elasticity of demand, 1973–75

1	% Change in petrol consumption	–4.73
2	% Change in GDP	–1.53
3	% Change in relative price	43.02
4	Change in petrol consumption due to change in income	1.27×–1.53=–1.94
5	Change in petrol consumption to be explained by rise in price	–4.73–(–1.94)=–2.79
6	Price elasticity of demand	2.79/43.02=0.06

Source: Paul Turner, Price and Income Elasticities, *The Economic Review*, January 1993.

The estimate of price elasticity of demand is relatively low and indicates that demand for petrol is not very sensitive to changes in the price of petrol. This is not surprising since, for most car users, petrol is a relatively small part of the total cost of running a car. However, it is worth noting that the estimate of price elasticity of demand given here is computed only over a two-year period. Over a longer period, it is likely that elasticity of demand would tend to be greater than 0.06. (Unfortunately the available data do not permit this hypothesis to be tested!)

EXAMINATION QUESTIONS

1 A bus operator understands that the elasticities of demand for coach travel are as follows:
   (i) income elasticity of demand is –0.4;
   (ii) price elasticity of demand is –1.2;
   (iii) cross elasticity of demand in respect to rail fares is +2.1.
   (a) Discuss how the above information might be expected to influence the bus operator in determining whether to continue with the service.   *(70)*
   (b) What other factors might also be relevant to this decision?   *(30)*
                                                          (ULEAC June 1992)

2 Explain why the prices of primary products such as agricultural produce, raw materials and energy are often unstable.

(AEB November 1992)

3 (a) Explain why, with no government regulation, the prices of agricultural products might be very unstable. *(10)*
  (b) Discuss what measures may be taken to correct instability in agricultural prices.
  (15)

(UCLES Nov 1992)

4 (a) Using supply and demand diagrams, examine two factors that might explain the change in 4* petrol prices between mid-1985 and mid-1986 (see Fig. 4.13). *(6)*
  (b) (i) What proportion of the retail price of Shell 4* petrol was accounted for by taxation at the beginning of 1983? Show your calculations. *(2)*
    (ii) Analyse the likely reason why the government has imposed high indirect taxes on petrol consumption. *(3)*
    (iii) With reference to Fig. 4.14, suggest a reason for the difference in tax rates on leaded and unleaded petrol. *(3)*
  (c) (i) With reference to Fig. 4.15, comment on the market structure of the petrol retailing industry. *(3)*
    (ii) Suggest reasons why oil companies own a significant percentage of service station outlets. *(3)*

(ULEAC, June 1992)

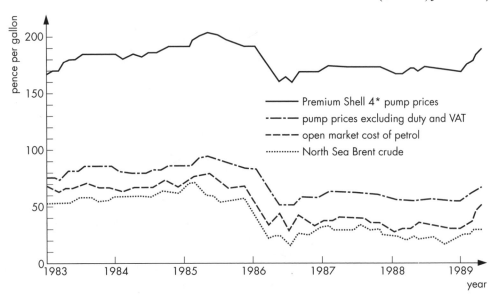

Fig. 4.13

DUTY ON PETROL IN THE UK (as as March 1990 Budget)		
Duty on leaded petrol	Duty on unleaded petrol	
102.3p	88.7p	

Fig. 4.14

NAME OF OIL COMPANY	ESTIMATED MARKET SHARE OF PETROL SALES (%)	NUMBER OF SERVICE STATION OUTLETS	% OF ITS OUTLETS WHICH COMPANY OWNS	COMPANY OUTLETS AS % OF TOTAL OUTLETS (20,016)
Q8	2	1,078	5.7	5.4
Fina	3	795	28.4	4.0
Total	4	612	77.9	3.1
Mobil	7	878	60.8	4.4
Jet	9	1,051	25.1	5.3
Burmah	10	1,403	14.0	7.0
Texaco	10	1,364	53.7	6.8
BP	14	2,119	42.0	10.6
Esso	19	2,685	40.7	13.4
Shell	19	2,886	41.3	14.4
All of the above	97	14,871	–	74.4
All other companies	3	5,145	–	25.6
All oil companies	100	20,016	–	100.0

(*Source*: Institute of Petroleum data for 1986, quoted in *Which?* magazine January 1990)

Fig. 4.15

ANSWERS TO EXAMINATION QUESTIONS

TUTOR'S ANSWER TO QUESTION 1

(a) From the information given it is not clear whether the bus operator should continue or discontinue the service. In the long run, an important factor is the relatively low income elasticity of demand for bus travel.

Income elasticity of demand is a measure of the responsiveness of demand to changes in income and in this example its value is –0.4. This implies that a 10 per cent rise in income will lead to a 4 per cent fall in demand for bus travel. In other words, bus travel is an inferior good. Given the tendency of income to rise over time, if all things remain equal, the long-term prospects of the bus route becoming profitable are not good.

The estimate of price elasticity of demand given is more encouraging for the bus operator. At –1.2, demand for bus travel is price elastic, i.e. relatively responsive to changes in price. In fact, since demand is elastic, it follows that a reduction in bus fares will lead to an increase in the bus operator's revenue because the percentage increase in the demand for bus travel will be greater than the percentage reduction in the price of bus travel. However, this does not necessarily imply that the bus operator's profits will increase because this also depends on how costs change as bus fares are reduced. If the reduction in bus fares attracts additional customers onto existing services, profits will almost certainly rise. After all, most of the costs, such as the wages of the bus driver and the bus itself are fixed costs which will already have been met. Carrying more passengers might lead to a slight increase in petrol consumption but the increase in revenue will almost certainly be greater than any increase in costs. A cut in bus fares, in these circumstances, will almost certainly lead to an increase in profits.

The situation is different if the bus operator has to put on additional services to cater for extra passengers. Then, it is not so clear that profits will increase as a result of a reduction in bus fares. To provide additional services will raise costs and might even require a reduction in other services offered by the bus operator as passengers are attracted to other routes.

The estimate of cross elasticity of demand for bus travel with respect to rail fares is +2.1. This implies that a 1 per cent increase in the cost of rail fares will increase demand for bus travel by 2.1 per cent. Bus travel and rail travel are therefore considered as substitutes by commuters. This is important for the bus operator because, if there is any impending change in rail fares, this will have implications for the demand for bus travel and will have a considerable impact on the bus operator's profitability. On the other hand, if the bus operator does decide to reduce bus fares, commuters will switch from rail travel to bus travel and this might provoke some sort of retaliation from BR (or a franchised operator) in an attempt to retain its passengers. Remember, the estimate of price elasticity of demand at –1.2 is based on the assumption that all other things remain equal. If they do not, and BR retaliates to any cut in bus fares, reducing the price of bus travel might actually lead to a fall in profitability!

(b) There are many other factors the bus operator would need to take into consideration before making a final decision on whether to continue or discontinue the service. One important factor is whether the rail service is likely to continue in the long run. If it is part of a loss-making route, the long-term prospect is that the rail line will be closed and this will increase the profitability of the bus route – perhaps sufficiently to make it a viable proposition.

Future government policy is another factor the bus operator would need to consider. If the central government raises the cost of private motoring, perhaps by raising the duty on petrol, or local authorities restrict the availability of parking spaces and/or ban cars from city centres, this again will increase the demand for bus travel.

We are given no information on whether there are any alternatives available to the bus operator. For example, it may be possible for the bus operator to make economies, perhaps by cutting the frequency of the service, or by extending the route to pick up other passengers. The bus operator would need to explore these options before deciding whether to continue or discontinue the bus service.

Another important factor for the bus operator to consider is whether other changes in the economy are imminent which will affect the profitability of the bus route. For example, if the economy is moving into recession so that incomes are expected to fall, the bus route might become more profitable. The estimate of income elasticity of demand we are given implies that for each 1 per cent fall in income, demand for bus travel will rise by 0.4 per cent.

Another consideration about which no information is given is whether there are any other bus operators competing on the route in question. If there are, are they likely to continue competing in the long run or are they also finding the route unprofitable? How would they react to a cut in bus fares by the operator we are considering? The likely reaction of rival firms to a change in bus fares is therefore an important factor to consider before any changes are implemented.

STUDENT'S ANSWER TO QUESTION 2

In free markets, prices are determined by the interaction of supply and demand. Once the equilibrium price, i.e. the price which equates supply with demand, is established, there will be no tendency for price to change unless conditions in the market change. In other words, for any good or service, once equilibrium is established, a change in price can only occur if there is a change in demand and/or a change in supply.

The concept of equilibrium is illustrated in Fig. 4.16.

66 Good to present diagrams where appropriate 99

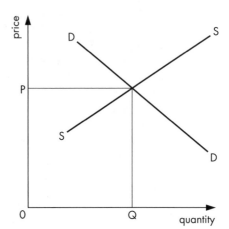

Fig. 4.16 Equilibrium in a free market

66 Good; you have referred closely to your diagram in the text 99

66 Good point 99

66 Well explained 99

In this market SS and DD represent the conditions of supply and demand. P is the equilibrium price and Q is the equilibrium quantity supplied and demanded. At any price above P, quantity supplied exceeds quantity demanded and price will tend to fall as the market adjusts to the excess supply. At any price below P, quantity demanded exceeds quantity supplied and price will tend to rise as the market adjusts to the excess demand. Only when price P is established is the market stable and free from further adjustment.

In the case of primary products such as agricultural produce, demand is normally inelastic, i.e. relatively unresponsive to changes in price. The main reason for this is that there are usually few substitutes for them. This is certainly true of agricultural produce in general, for while it is true that people cannot live by bread alone, it is equally true that they cannot live without it! The demand for other primary products such as raw materials and energy is also likely to be relatively inelastic because there are few substitutes available, at least in the short run. In addition, the demand for primary products is a derived demand and, in many cases, energy and raw materials will form only a small proportion of total costs. The combined effect of these factors will tend to reduce their elasticity of demand. After all, if input costs are a small proportion of total costs, even a relatively large change in input prices will have a relatively small effect on the price of the final product. Consequently sales will be little affected and therefore there will be little effect on the demand for inputs.

Typically, the supply curve of many primary products is also relatively inelastic. In the case of oil, for example, there are few extractable deposits in the world and it can take many years to develop and extract oil from new fields. In the case of agricultural produce, it will take at least several months to increase the output of a particular crop and even here we are assuming the availability of suitable land. Because of this the supply curve for primary products is often relatively inelastic.

Where demand and supply are inelastic, a change in the conditions of demand or supply will cause relatively large changes in price and relatively small changes in quantity. Figure 4.17 is used as a basis for explanation.

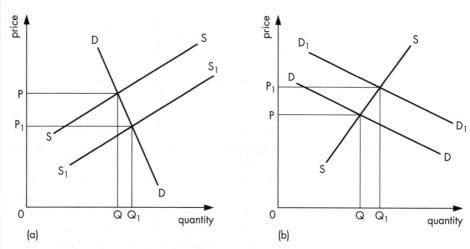

Fig. 4.17 The effect of change in (a) supply and (b) demand, on the equilibrium price and quantity

66 Again, good use made of your diagram 99

>   Demand and supply are initially represented by SS and
> DD. In Fig. 4.17(a) there is a subsequent increase in
> supply to S_1S_1. This causes a relatively large fall in the
> equilibrium price to P_1 but a relatively small increase in
> the equilibrium quantity to Q_1. In Fig. 4.17(b), there is a
> subsequent increase in demand to D_1D_1. As a result, there
> is a relatively large increase in price to P_1, but again a
> relatively small increase in the equilibrium quantity to
> Q_1.
>   For some commodities such as agricultural produce,
> there is a relatively low income elasticity of demand so
> that changes in income have very little effect on demand
> from one year to the next. However, changes in the weather
> can have a very profound effect on supply and produce poor
> or bumper harvests depending on the conditions. However,
> once the market moves into disequilibrium, there might be
> wide fluctuations in price and output before equilibrium is
> re-established. For example, in the market illustrated in
> Fig. 4.17(a) the equilibrium price is initially P and the
> equilibrium quantity is initially Q. Now, if weather
> conditions produce a bumper harvest so that the new
> equilibrium price falls to P1, this will depress farm
> incomes and discourage farmers from producing that crop. In
> a free market, farmers would tend to cut back the amount
> they produce. The implied reduction in supply might shift
> the equilibrium price above P, which will encourage farmers
> to increase the amount of this crop they produce. In this
> way, an initial change in supply can set up a series of
> fluctuations in price and output.

66 You could introduce the elasticity conditions for a stable or unstable cobweb 99

66 This really is a very good effort, as far as it goes. However you have confined yourself to an analysis of agricultural price fluctuations. You should also have considered fluctuations in raw material prices and/or energy prices, and the principles underlying the stable/unstable cobweb. 99

OUTLINE ANSWERS TO QUESTIONS 3 AND 4

Question 3
(a) This part of the question is well covered in the 'Student's Answer to Question 2' above and the examiner comments and so the discussion is not repeated here.
(b) One widely used measure to stabilise agricultural prices is to establish **buffer stocks**. In such cases, the government's agency purchases agricultural produce when harvests are good, places it in store and releases it onto the market in years when harvests are poor. You should illustrate this using a supply and demand diagram to show that the potential effect on price of an increase in supply, implied by a bumper harvest, is neutralised by an off-setting increase in demand as the agency purchases the increased supply. In times of poor harvests, the implied reduction in supply is supplemented as the agency releases food from its stores and again prevents disruption to prices. Again, you should illustrate this using a supply and demand diagram.

A slightly different approach is to establish a minimum price for agricultural output. If this is set above the free market equilibrium, supply will have a tendency to rise and again the excess supply will need to be stored or else destroyed. This is how the CAP operates and to reduce the long-run increase in supply the authorities have introduced a 'set aside scheme' whereby farmers are compensated for leaving land idle rather than growing certain crops.

Alternatively, to encourage continued production so as to prevent agricultural prices from rising, the government could offer farmers a subsidy or tax relief.

Question 4

(a) Between mid-1985 and mid-1986 the price of 4* petrol fell by about £0.40 per gallon. One possible reason for this is that there was a glut of oil on the world market. (The fact that the price of crude oil also fell during the same period is consistent with this view.) You should illustrate this possibility, and its effect on price, in a diagram showing an outward shift of the supply schedule.

A different possibility is that the fall in the price of 4* petrol was caused by a fall in demand. (Again if the demand for petrol fell, demand for crude oil would fall and, in consequence, the price of crude oil would fall.) You should illustrate the effect on the price of 4* petrol in a diagram showing an inward shift of the demand schedule.

(b) (i) In 1983, the pump price of petrol excluding excise duty and VAT was approximately £0.76 per gallon, while the pump price including duty and VAT was approximately £1.68 per gallon. The tax on petrol was therefore equal to about £0.92 per gallon. The percentage of the retail price of a gallon of 4* petrol which was made up of taxation was therefore $((92/76) \times 100) = 121\%$

(ii) One reason the government might have imposed high indirect taxation on petrol consumption is to raise revenue. The relatively inelastic demand for 4* petrol makes it eminently suitable for this purpose. In the longer term, high indirect taxation might encourage the development of lean burn engines which would conserve oil supplies. Again, in the longer term, high indirect taxation might encourage a reduction in consumption of petrol which implies a reduction in environmental pollution from exhaust fumes.

(iii) The difference in tax rates on leaded and unleaded petrol is undoubtedly to encourage a shift in consumption away from leaded petrol in favour of unleaded petrol. The reason for this is that the latter makes a smaller contribution to environmental pollution. These are important considerations with the increase in global warming and acid rain.

(c) (i) The ten largest oil companies account for 97 per cent of total sales of petrol. Petrol retailing is therefore an oligopoly (see pp. 105–106). Vast economies of scale (see pp. 36–38) are available in petrol retailing and therefore it is inevitable that petrol retailers will be relatively large firms.

(ii) There are several possible reasons you might discuss here. One reason might be to restrict the entry of new firms into the oil market. If the oil companies own the service stations, then any firm wishing to begin oil refining faces the cost of entry into that market plus the additional cost of purchasing retail outlets to market the product. This is a powerful deterrent to entry. Firms might wish to discourage entry so as to protect market share or profit levels. Another reason might be to enable firms to market other products they produce such as engine oil. The aim here would be to increase company profitability.

Further reading

Begg, Fischer and Dornbusch, *Economics* (3rd edn), McGraw-Hill 1991. Ch. 3, Demand, Supply and the Market; Ch. 4, The Effect of Price and Income on Demand Quantities; Ch. 5, The Theory of Consumers Choice.

Harrison et al, *Introductory Economics*, Macmillan 1992; Ch. 3, Demand Supply and Market Price; Ch. 4, The Price Mechanism and Market Failure; Ch. 5, Some Applications of Price Theory; Ch. 6, The Basis of Demand.

Maunder et al, *Economics Explained* (2nd edn), Collins 1991: Ch. 5, Demand and supply; Ch. 7, Demand and supply elasticity.

REVIEW SHEET

1 State the condition under which consumers will maximise total utility.

2 Use this condition to show why a lower price will mean greater consumption of a product.

_____

_____

_____

3 Suggest six reasons why a demand curve for good X might shift to the right (increase).

(a) _____

(b) _____

(c) _____

(d) _____

(e) _____

(f) _____

4 Explain why a demand curve might, unusually, slope upwards from left to right.

_____

_____

_____

5 Suggest four reasons why a supply curve for good X might shift to the left (decrease).

(a) _____

(b) _____

(c) _____

(d) _____

6 Draw diagrams to show the impact of each of the following on equilibrium price and output.

<u>Increase in demand</u>   <u>Decrease in demand</u>

7 Use your diagram to explain the mechanism by which the new equilibrium is reached in each of the following cases.

The increase in demand causes: _____

because: _____

The decrease in demand causes: _____

because: _____

8 Define price elasticity of demand (PED).

_____

_____

_____

9 List six factors which influence PED, briefly explaining each one.

(a) _____

(b) _____

(c) _____

(d) _____

(e) _____

(f) _____

10 Under what elasticity conditions will each of the following occur?

A fall in price raises total revenue: _____

A rise in price raises total revenue: _____

A fall in price leaves total revenue unchanged: _____

11 How might a knowledge of price elasticity of demand benefit the government?

_____

_____

_____

_____

12 Define price elasticity of supply (PES). _____

_____

_____

13 List five factors which influence the value of PES.

(a) _____

(b) _____

(c) _____

(d) _____

(e) _____

14 Draw a diagram showing each of the following:

A stable cobweb   An unstable cobweb

15 Explain what makes the difference between a stable and unstable cobweb.

_____

_____

_____

_____

5

PERFECT COMPETITION AND MONOPOLY

GETTING STARTED

Before embarking on this chapter you should ensure that you fully understand the operation of market forces as explained in Chapter 4. You should also understand the behaviour of costs as output changes, the distinction between fixed and variable costs and the relationship between average, marginal and total values as explained in Chapter 3.

We have already seen, in Chapter 4, that in free markets prices are determined by supply and demand. However, this generalisation does not imply that price determination is completely beyond the influence of all firms (or consumers). If firms are able to influence supply and/or demand conditions for their product, they can clearly influence the price at which that product is sold. In fact, we shall see that the influence of any particular firm on the price of its product depends largely on the number of competing firms in the industry and the type of product sold. Differences in these two factors give rise to different market forms and these are usually categorised as **perfect competition**, **monopoly**, **monopolistic competition** and **oligopoly**. The latter three are classed as *imperfect* markets because firms are able to exercise some degree of control over price. The former market is classed as *perfect* in the sense that any individual seller or buyer is powerless to influence the price of its product.

Perhaps the major reason why economists are interested in market structure is not so much to understand the behaviour or firms, important though this is, but rather the fact that different market structures lead to differences in the allocation of resources. The pattern of resource allocation in one market structure might be considered preferable in certain ways to the pattern in a different market structure. With this in mind we proceed to an analysis of perfect competition and monopoly. Other forms of imperfect competition are considered in Chapter 6.

ESSENTIAL PRINCIPLES

PERFECT COMPETITION

CONDITIONS FOR A PERFECTLY COMPETITIVE MARKET

A market is said to be **perfectly competitive** when buyers and sellers believe that individually their own behaviour has no influence on market price. The conditions which give rise to this particular market structure may be summarised as follows:

- There are *large numbers* of both buyers and sellers in the market, each buying or selling such a small amount of the product that individually they are powerless to influence market demand or market supply.

- *Consumers are indifferent from whom they make purchases* because all units of the commodity are homogeneous. In other words, they regard the product that an individual firm supplies as a perfect substitute for the product that any other firm in the same market supplies.

66 **The assumptions of perfect competition** 99

- There is *perfect knowledge* of market conditions among buyers and sellers so that each is fully informed about the prices that producers in different parts of the market are charging for their product.

- Buyers are *able to act* on the information available to them and will always purchase the commodity from the seller offering the lowest price.

- There are *no long-run barriers* to the entry of firms into the market, or their exit from the market.

These conditions are never fully satisfied in the real world but some markets display many of the characteristic features of perfect competition. For example, an individual farmer has little influence on the price of potatoes. (Buyers are well informed about prices, the product is homogeneous and the individual farmer produces only a small proportion of the total market supply.)

THE MARKET AND THE FIRM

These conditions ensure that, in perfectly competitive markets, all firms charge an identical price for their product. Any firm attempting to charge a price above that of its competitors will face a total loss of sales. This will occur because consumers are aware of the higher price the firm is attempting to charge and, since the product is homogeneous, they will have no particular preference for the firm's product.

On the other hand, perfectly competitive firms have no incentive to lower the price of their product since they can sell their entire output at the existing market price. The firm in perfect competition is therefore a **price taker**, i.e. it accepts the market price as beyond its control. Because of this, all firms in perfectly competitive markets perceive their own demand curves, and the demand curves of their competitors, to be perfectly elastic at the ruling market price. Figure 5.1 shows the determination of market price in a perfectly competitive market and the individual firm's demand curve at this price. Market supply and market demand are represented by SS and DD respectively. Given these supply and demand conditions the ruling market price is OP, and the firm perceives its own demand curve to be perfectly elastic at this price.

66 **The firm in perfect competition is a price-taker** 99

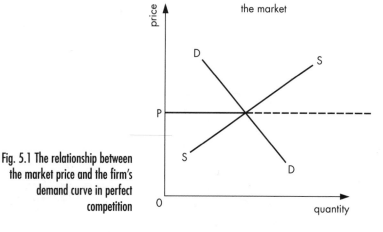
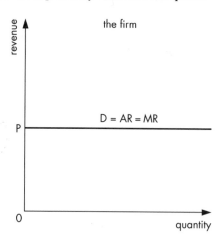

Fig. 5.1 The relationship between the market price and the firm's demand curve in perfect competition

AVERAGE AND MARGINAL REVENUE

Because the firm sells its entire output at the ruling market price, each additional unit of output sold adds exactly the same amount to total revenue as each preceding unit sold. Therefore, for the firm in perfect competition, marginal revenue is constant at all levels of output and equal to market price. We shall see later that this relationship between price and marginal revenue, which is usually expressed in the form Price (AR) = Marginal Revenue (MR), is peculiar to firms in perfectly competitive markets.

66 Here AR = MR 99

COMPETITIVE EQUILIBRIUM

SHORT-RUN EQUILIBRIUM 1: SUPERNORMAL PROFIT

Profit maximisation

Since the firm is powerless to change the price of its product, it maximises profit by adjusting output to the point where marginal revenue equals marginal cost. Figure 5.2 shows the market equilibrium, and the short-run equilibrium position of the individual firm in perfect competition.

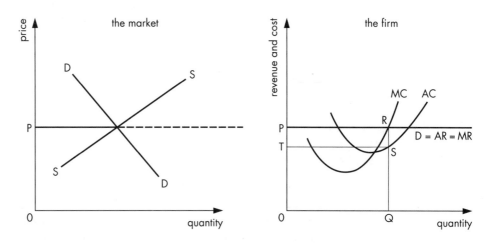

Figure 5.2 Short-run equilibrium: supernormal profit

Given the price and costs shown in Fig. 5.2, the firm's equilibrium (i.e. profit maximising) output is OQ, because this is the output level which equates marginal revenue (MR) with marginal cost (MC). At levels of output below OQ, MR > MC, so that an expansion of output adds more to total revenue than it does to total cost. In these circumstances, total profit can be increased by expanding output. Conversely, at output levels greater than OQ, MR < MC and a reduction in output will reduce total costs by more than it reduces total revenue so that total profit will rise. It follows that profit can only be maximised when MR = MC, and this simple rule applies whatever market structure we are considering.

66 MR = MC for maximum profit 99

Details of marginal revenue and marginal cost enable us to determine the firm's profit maximising output, but it is *total* revenue and *total* cost which tell us the *actual* level of profit earned. With details as shown in Fig. 5.2, price OP and output OQ

> total revenue = OP × OQ = OPRQ
> while
> total cost = OT × OQ = OTSQ
> total revenue − total cost = total profit = PRST

66 Normal profit can be regarded as a 'cost' of producing 99

Alternatively, we can say that average revenue (OP) minus average cost (OT) equals average profit (RS) and this multiplied by output (OQ) gives total profit of PRST. It is usual to include an element of **normal profit** in the firm's average cost of production because normal profit is the minimum level of profit required to keep the firm in the industry in the long run. It can therefore be regarded as a cost which must be met if the firm is to stay in production in the long run.

Effects of supernormal profit

In this case, it is clear that the firm is earning **supernormal profit** because AR > AC. The existence of supernormal profit will, in the long run, attract other firms into the industry. Perfect knowledge of market conditions will ensure that firms outside the industry are aware of the level of profits earned, and the absence of long-run barriers to entry will ensure they are able to enter the industry and undertake production.

Transition

While changes in the output of an individual firm in perfect competition will have no perceptible effect on market supply, the influx of many new producers into the industry will clearly have a marked impact. If market demand for the industry's product is constant, the increased market supply will pull down price. Nevertheless, firms will still be attracted into the industry so long as supernormal profits exist. Only when these have been competed away, with all firms earning only normal profit, will the industry be in equilibrium. The adjustment from short-run equilibrium to long-run equilibrium is shown in Fig. 5.3.

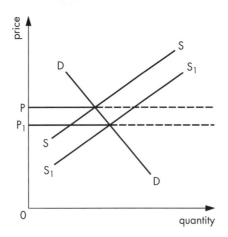
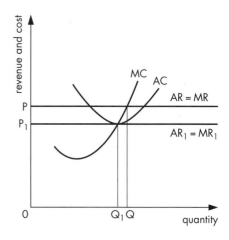

Fig. 5.3 The adjustment from supernormal profit to long-run equilibrium

Market supply and market demand are initially given by SS and DD respectively, and the initial market price is OP. Given this price, the firm produces its equilibrium output, OQ. The existence of short-run supernormal profit attracts other firms into the industry so that, in the long run, market supply increases to S_1S_1 and market price falls to OP_1. The individual firm is powerless to resist the reduction in market price and is forced to adjust its output so as to preserve equality between marginal revenue and marginal cost.

Long-run equilibrium

> **❝ Only normal profits are made in the long run ❞**

The industry is in long-run equilibrium when price has fallen to the extent that all firms in the industry earn only normal profit, or at least potential entrants to the industry see no prospect of earning anything other than normal profit. Normal profit is insufficient to attract additional firms into the industry, but just sufficient to dissuade those firms already in the industry from leaving. In terms of Fig. 5.3, long-run equilibrium is established when market price has fallen to OP_1 and the firm produces OQ_1 units. Given this price and output combination the firm's total revenue ($OP_1 \times OQ_1$) is exactly equal to its total cost ($OP_1 \times OQ_1$) including normal profit, and since the firm equates marginal revenue with marginal cost this is the maximum attainable profit given the ruling market price OP_1.

SHORT-RUN EQUILIBRIUM 2: SUBNORMAL PROFIT

For all firms, irrespective of market structure, production can only continue in the long run if at least normal profit is earned. However, in the short run, firms may be prepared to accept a return below normal profit. For instance, a firm might be willing to continue producing in the short run as long as total revenue from production is at least equal to the firm's total variable costs of production, i.e. as long as AR ≥ AVC. The reason for this is simple. In the short run, firms are obliged to meet their fixed costs whether they undertake production or not.

■ If total revenue from production is only just sufficient to cover the total variable costs, it follows that the firm is making no contribution towards covering its fixed costs. It is therefore neither better off nor worse off, if it remains in the industry.

■ If total revenue is greater than total variable costs, then by continuing in production, the firm makes at least some contribution towards covering the fixed costs already incurred. To cease production would leave the firm with a loss equal to its fixed costs, whereas if the firm undertakes production it will at least have some surplus over variable costs to set against its fixed costs.

■ If total revenue is less than total variable cost, the firm will be better off by ceasing production altogether. If it produces nothing, the firm's total loss is equal to its fixed cost. This compares with a loss equal to the deficit on variable costs added to the fixed costs if it undertakes production.

> Price must exceed AVC in the short run

It is clear, because of this, that in the short run, the *minimum* acceptable price, if the firm is to undertake production, is that price which exactly equals the minimum short-run average variable costs of production. It is for this reason that the minimum average variable cost is sometimes referred to as the **shut down price**.

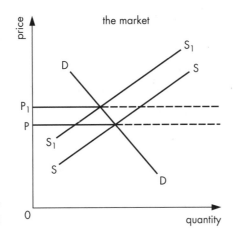
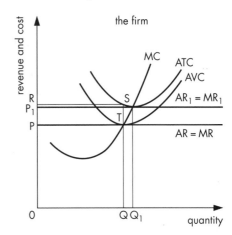

Fig. 5.4 The adjustment from short-run loss to long-run equilibrium

Loss situation

The loss situation is analysed diagrammatically in Fig. 5.4.

The *minimum* acceptable *short-run price* is OP. This price equals the minimum average variable cost, and the firm's loss equals its fixed costs whether it undertakes production or not. Thus, with price OP, the firm's equilibrium output is OQ and

total revenue = total variable cost = OPTQ
total cost = ORSQ
total revenue – total cost = –PRST

This is a negative value, representing the loss made by the firm, which in this case just equals the firm's fixed cost.

Effects of loss situation

> Price must exceed ATC in the long run

However, such losses cannot be sustained indefinitely and, in the long run, some firms will be forced to leave the industry. This will shift market supply to $S_1 S_1$ and raise market price to OP_1. Given this market price, the firm's profit maximising output is OQ_1 and the firm just earns normal profit, since total revenue is $OP_1 \times OQ_1$, which equals total cost. So, the *minimum* acceptable *long-run price* is that price which equals the minimum average total cost of production including normal profit.

LONG-RUN EQUILIBRIUM

We have seen that, in the long run, neither supernormal profit nor subnormal profit can continue to exist. While either is possible in the short run, their very existence will lead to changes in the number of firms in the industry, and hence in market supply, causing changes in the market price of the product. The industry is in long-run equilibrium when there is no longer any tendency for firms to enter or leave, and this occurs when all firms in the industry are making normal profit.

SHORT-RUN AND LONG-RUN SUPPLY IN PERFECT COMPETITION

> 66 The MC curve is the supply curve under perfect competition, but distinguish short-run supply from long-run supply 99

We have seen that firms in perfectly competitive markets are powerless to resist price changes and can only preserve equality between marginal cost and marginal revenue by adjusting *output*. However, since price is equal to marginal revenue for the firm in perfect competition, it follows that the firm adjusts its output so as to equate marginal cost with price. Thus, the **short-run supply curve** of the firm in perfect competition is that part of its marginal cost curve which lies above its average variable cost curve. If price falls below minimum average variable cost, the firm will cease production altogether, since total revenue will no longer cover the total variable costs of production. The firm would then be making no contribution to fixed costs; quite the reverse, it would be making still greater losses by continuing to produce. However, at all prices above the minimum average variable cost, the firm will undertake production in the short run, although it will only continue production, in the long run, if price is at least equal to average total cost.

Figure 5.5 illustrates the firm's short-run supply curve. Suppose that OP is the minimum price at which the firm will undertake production in the short run. At this price, the firm will supply OQ units. If market price rises to OP_1 the firm will increase output to OQ_1, and so on. The short-run supply curve of the *firm* is therefore that part of its marginal cost curve which lies above the average variable cost curve. The short-run supply curve of the *industry* is clearly the sum of each individual firm's short-run supply curve.

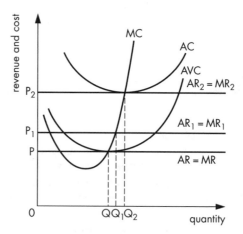

Fig. 5.5 The supply curve of the firm under perfect competition

However, the **long-run supply curve** of the industry is more complex because of the entry or exit of firms. In fact, the very absence of barriers to entry or exit of firms ensures that the long-run supply curve of a perfectly competitive industry is perfectly elastic at the market price which just enables firms to earn normal profit, i.e. OP_2 in Fig. 5.5. The reasoning behind this assertion is illustrated in Fig. 5.6.

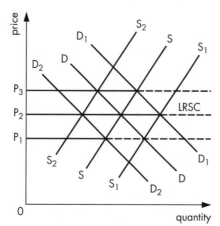
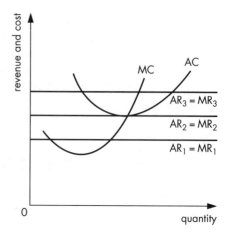

Fig. 5.6 The long-run supply curve of the industry in perfect competition

If, initially, market supply and market demand are represented by SS and DD respectively, then market price is OP_2 and the firm and industry are in long-run equilibrium because only normal profits are earned. An increase in demand to D_1D_1 raises market price to OP_3 enabling existing firms to earn supernormal profit. In the long run, this attracts other firms into the industry, market supply shifts to S_1S_1, market price falls to OP_2 and all firms in the industry are again in long-run equilibrium, since normal profits are earned and there is no longer any tendency for firms to enter the industry.

The opposite would occur if market demand fell to D_2D_2 and market price fell to OP_1. In the long run, losses would force some firms out of the industry, market supply would fall to S_2S_2 and long-run equilibrium would be restored. The industry's long-run supply curve is therefore shown as LRSC, which is perfectly elastic at OP_2, the market price which just enables firms to earn normal profit.

PERFECT COMPETITION AND THE ALLOCATION OF RESOURCES

The most important feature of perfect competition is its impact on the allocation of resources. It is clear from the discussion above that, under perfect competition, price equals marginal costs. This is a fundamental feature of perfectly competitive markets, and it is suggested that it implies an optimum allocation of resources in perfect competition. If price measures the value consumers place on an extra unit of the commodity, and marginal cost measures the cost of attracting resources away from alternative uses, then it follows that the price of the last unit of the commodity produced is equal to its opportunity cost of production. This is an optimum allocation of resources because, if price is greater than marginal cost, society desires more of this commodity in preference to alternatives since they are prepared to pay an amount greater than the cost of attracting resources away from alternatives. Conversely, if marginal cost is greater than price, society values alternatives more highly since they are not prepared to pay an amount equivalent to the cost of attracting resources away from these alternatives. Only under perfect competition is this optimum allocation of resources achieved.

> Price equals MC is an optimum allocation of resources

It is also clear from our discussion that, in the long run, the firm in perfect competition is forced to the point of maximum technical efficiency. In other words, given the existing level of capacity the firm is forced to produce at the point of minimum average cost. Again, this is not true of any other market structure.

MONOPOLY

A **pure monopoly** exists when supply of a particular good or service is in the hands of a single supplier. For convenience, we usually analyse a monopoly in terms of a single firm, but a monopoly can also exist when a small group of firms jointly co-ordinate their marketing policies and so act as a single supplier. The latter situation which is examined more fully later in this section is referred to as a **cartel**.

Because market supply is in the hands of a single supplier, a monopoly has great power to influence the price of its product. However, this does not imply that it has total power to fix price, since it cannot control consumer demand. In effect, the monopolist has two choices:

> Choices of the monopolist

- to fix price and allow demand to determine supply (output); or
- to fix supply (output) and allow demand to determine price.

The inability to *control* market demand makes it impossible for a monopolist to simultaneously fix both price and output.

Average and marginal revenues

Unlike the firm in perfect competition, the monopolist's average and marginal revenues will be different. This is because the monopolist faces a downward sloping demand curve and is forced to reduce price in order to expand sales. Table 5.1 is used as a basis for illustration.

OUTPUT/SALES	AVERAGE REVENUE (£)	TOTAL REVENUE (£)	MARGINAL REVENUE (£)
0	–	–	–
1	10	10	10
2	9	18	8
3	8	24	6

Table 5.1

In order to expand sales from 1 unit to 2 units, it is necessary to reduce the price of both units. Hence, price falls from £10 per unit to £9 per unit and the marginal revenue, i.e. the change in total revenue, is £8. Similarly, when price is reduced from £9 per unit to £8 per unit, marginal revenue falls to £6. Hence marginal revenue will always be less than price (average revenue) under monopoly.

The monopolist's equilibrium price and output

We have already seen that, for *all* producers, profits are maximised when marginal cost equals marginal revenue. Based on this principle, Fig. 5.7 illustrates the monopolist's equilibrium output.

The monopolist maximises profit when price is OP and output OQ because at this price and output combination marginal revenue equals marginal cost. Total revenue (OPRQ) minus total cost (OTSQ) gives a profit equal to PRST.

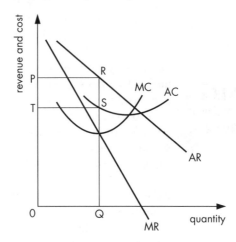

Fig. 5.7 Equilibrium under monopoly

> 66 **The monopolist can retain supernormal profits in the long run** 99

Note: the monopolist is earning supernormal profit, and one of the characteristic features of monopoly is that it is possible to earn this level of profit even in the long run. If supernormal profits continue in the long run, this implies the existence of barriers which restrict the entry of additional firms into the industry. These barriers are therefore the very essence of monopoly power and their nature is examined in the next section.

BARRIERS TO ENTRY

Barriers to entry of firms into a market might take a variety of forms and indeed entry into any particular market might be restricted by the existence of several barriers. These might include any of the following:

TECHNICAL BARRIERS

In certain industries, there is a natural tendency towards monopoly in so far as supply is most efficiently undertaken by a single firm. This is especially true of those industries where technical economies of scale make the minimum efficient scale of operation very large indeed. For example, because of indivisibilities, some organisations have relatively high fixed costs so that average total costs continue to fall as output expands over relatively large ranges. This is true in the production of industrial gases, where it has been repeatedly argued that the British Oxygen Corporation's almost total domination of the UK market is at least partly based on the existence of substantial economies of scale in production. It is also true of the public utilities supplying gas, water, electricity, and so on, through a grid system. Such industries are referred to as **natural monopolies** because distribution is most efficiently undertaken by a single supplier.

> 66 **Barriers to entry are vital to monopoly power** 99

The existence of substantial economies of scale provides some justification for the existence of large firms but not necessarily for the existence of monopoly as such. Indeed, it is increasingly the case that a great deal of manufacturing industry is dominated by a few large-scale producers (**oligopoly**) rather than by a single large-scale producer. For example, in chemicals, petroleum, tyres and motor vehicle production, a small number of firms satisfy the entire market. Nevertheless, it is true that progressively falling average costs as output increases confers enormous advantages on large-scale producers. These cost advantages might well prevent the emergence of competition and lead to monopoly, whether of the 'pure' or 'dominant firm' variety. Not only would a firm attempting entry into the industry have to match the capacity of existing producers, it would also need to consider the effect on market price of a substantial increase in market supply. While it may be possible for a single large firm to earn supernormal profit, if two large firms were to supply the market they might both makes losses!

LEGAL BARRIERS

In certain markets, legal regulations might prevent the emergence of competition. In the UK, the nationalised industries have been granted the sole rights to supply particular goods or services. Additionally, patent rights might ensure a monopoly position by preventing other firms from producing identical products. However, this barrier is only temporary and lasts only as long as the life of the patent (usually 16 years). In any case, it is often possible to circumvent this safeguard by producing similar products.

CONTROL OF FACTOR INPUTS OR RETAIL OUTLETS

If a firm has complete control over the supply of a factor of production, it may be able to exercise monopoly power over the products produced by that factor. An obvious example might be the ownership of land containing the only known deposits of a specific mineral. An equally effective monopoly might result from a single firm owning the key retail outlets for a product. Both the major petrol producers and the breweries have made active efforts to acquire retail outlets for their respective products.

AGREEMENTS BETWEEN SUPPLIERS

An effective monopoly can exist when firms in an industry agree to co-operate rather than compete. The most formal type of agreement between producers is known as a **cartel** and this exists when a single agency organises the marketing of a product supplied by several firms. The aim of the cartel is often to restrict market supply of the product, thereby forcing up price and increasing profits for the members of the cartel.

These are largely illegal in the UK with just a few cartel-type organisations operating within the law. The most obvious examples are the agricultural marketing boards. Where cartels do exist, both in the UK, and abroad, they present a formidable barrier to entry into the market. Any potential entrant must either join the cartel or compete with it. Existing members may not allow the newcomers to join the cartel and effective competition may be uneconomic because of the need to produce on a large scale, or uneconomic because of the effect on market price of a sizeable increase in industry output.

PRICE DISCRIMINATION

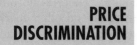

66 Price discrimination defined 99

Price discrimination occurs when a supplier charges different consumers different prices for the *same* product. Such price differences are not based on differences in the cost of supplying each consumer. Instead, they are a means of increasing the supplier's profit, taking advantage of the fact that some consumers are prepared to pay higher prices than others.

Price discrimination must not be confused with the situation that exists when a firm supplies different products. Thus, first and second class travel on trains or in the air are different products and although they are sold at different prices, this is *not* price discrimination. Neither is it price discrimination if prices are based on different transport costs or service charges. Some examples of price discrimination are given later, but first it is necessary to consider the conditions that make price discrimination possible and profitable.

One condition necessary for price discrimination is that there must be at least two distinct markets for the good or service, and there must be no seepage between these markets. This means that it must be impossible or uneconomic for consumers to purchase in the lower priced market and resell in the higher priced market. For this to be the case, there must be barriers which *prevent resale*. Sometimes these exist because the nature of the product makes *storage and resale impossible*. This is particularly true of services, and lower priced haircuts for senior citizens or half-priced travel for minors are examples of this. In some cases, markets might be separated because of *mutual advantage*. For example, motor car manufacturers charge different prices for spares to their service agencies than to independent stockists. Similarly in food processing, large discounts are available to the supermarket chains as compared with small independent grocers.

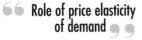
Some necessary conditions

Another condition necessary for price discrimination is that supply must be in the hands of a monopolist so that competing firms are unable to undertake production and undercut the monopolist in the higher priced markets.

Role of price elasticity of demand

These conditions make price discrimination possible, but they do not make it profitable. For this to be the case, elasticity of demand must be different in at least two of the markets. If it were not, there could be no additional profit to the monopolist from price discrimination, and, since the aim of the monopolist is to maximise profit, price discrimination would not occur. The importance of different elasticities of demand can be explained diagrammatically in Fig. 5.8.

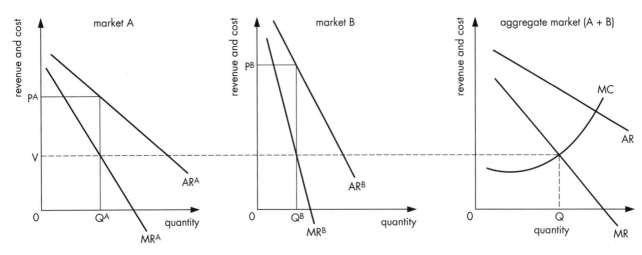

Fig. 5.8 Price discrimination

Markets A and B are two distinct markets separated in some way so that seepage between them is impossible. Figure 5.8 also shows the combined or aggregate market, i.e. the summation of the AR and MR in the two separate markets. If we assume that, in all three diagrams, the scales on the axes are the same, it is clear that the elasticity of demand at any given price is different in markets A and B. This is crucial in deciding what price to charge in each market so as to maximise profit.

To do this, the monopolist simply applies the profit-maximising rule that marginal cost equals marginal revenue to the aggregate of the demand curves for markets A and B. This gives the profit-maximising output OQ, but not the profit-maximising price. To obtain this, the monopolist must equate marginal cost with marginal revenue in each individual market. This gives a profit-maximising price in market A of OP^A and of OP^B in market B, i.e. a higher price in the market with the less elastic demand. The sum of the sales in each market is equal to the total amount produced. There is no other distribution of output OQ between the two markets (and therefore no other market prices) which could increase total profit. For instance, selling one unit less in market A and one more unit in market B would lead to a loss of revenue because it is clear that marginal revenue in market B would rise by less than it would fall in market A. Total revenue would therefore fall, and, with marginal costs unchanged, profit would fall. Profit is therefore maximised when $MR^A = MR^B = MC$.

Existence of an industry and price discrimination

The desirability of price discrimination is debatable, although consumers in the lower priced market clearly benefit compared with those in the higher priced market! However, the main way in which consumers might benefit is when price discrimination enables a monopolist to earn a profit from some activity that might not otherwise be possible. Figure 5.9 (p. 91) is used as a basis for explanation.

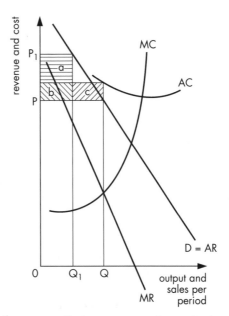

Fig. 5.9 Existence of industry depending on price discrimination

AR and MR depict the monopolist's average and marginal revenue curves while AC and MC depict average and marginal cost. It is clear that, if the monopolist charged all consumers the same uniform price, there is no level of output at which a profit could be earned. Indeed the loss minimising price would be OP, giving a loss equal to area 'b' plus area 'c'. Even if the monopolist were prepared to accept a short-run loss, such losses could not be accepted in the long run and production would eventually cease. However, if the monopolist is able to price discriminate and charge some consumers (OQ$_1$) a price of OP$_1$ while charging others (Q$_1$ – Q) only OP, it becomes profitable for the monopolist to undertake supply of this commodity. This is easily verified since the increase in revenue is equal to area 'a' plus area 'b'; which is greater than the loss which is made (area 'b' + area 'c') when a single price OP is charged (area 'a' > area 'c').

The fact that price discrimination makes production profitable does not necessarily imply that society benefits from discrimination. However, if we consider the case of a doctor providing medical services to an isolated community, it is possible to argue that society can benefit from discrimination. For example, in the terms of Fig. 5.9, by charging wealthier patients a higher price, the whole community benefits because the alternative is no doctor at all!

Despite the fact that it is possible for the community to benefit from price discrimination, the general conclusion is that such discrimination serves only to increase monopoly profits at the expense of consumers. It is therefore usually condemned as an undesirable practice. Nevertheless, the increased profits might still benefit the community if they are used to finance research and development into the creation of new or improved products, or improvements in productive efficiency. There is no general rule and whether price discrimination benefits society can therefore only be judged by examining each individual case.

PERFECT COMPETITION AND MONOPOLY – A COMPARISON

ALLOCATIVE EFFICIENCY

It is often argued that the allocation of resources under perfect competition is superior to that achieved under monopoly. This is because under perfect competition output is pushed to the point at which marginal cost equals marginal revenue. This, as explained on pp. 87–88, implies the value society places on the last unit of output consumed equals the opportunity cost to society of producing that unit. The same is not true under monopoly since, in order to maximise profits, the monopolist *always* charges a price greater than marginal cost. Under monopoly there is, therefore, an efficiency loss in terms of the allocation of resources and the extent of this loss for a particular product is illustrated in Fig. 5.10.

66 Price exceeds MC in monopoly 99

AR is the market demand curve; it shows the quantity demanded at any given price. MR is the monopolist's marginal revenue curve but has no relevance for perfect competition since it is the MR curve for a single supplier supplying the whole market. In perfect competition, the market is supplied by many firms. MC is the marginal cost

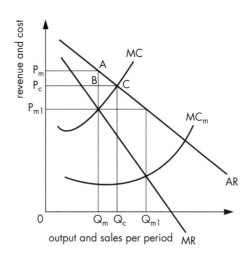

Fig. 5.10 Price and output under monopoly and perfect competition

curve facing the monopolist and it is assumed that this is identical to the sum of all the individual firms' marginal cost curves in perfect competition. In equilibrium, the monopolist charges a price of OP_m and produces OQ_m. The perfectly competitive industry, on the other hand, is in equilibrium when MC = AR (since each firm in perfect competition equates MC with price, AR, the firms' MC curve is its supply curve and the industry MC curve is the competitive industry supply curve). Under perfect competition price is therefore OP_c and output is OQ_c. The efficiency loss to society is therefore equal to the area ABC.

In addition, it is sometimes suggested that price is greater and output lower under monopoly than under perfect competition. However, this is not necessarily true. If economies of scale exist, these will be exploited by the monopolist but will not be available to firms under perfect competition because of their relatively small scale of production. In this case, the monopolist's marginal cost curve will be given by MC_m and price and output for the monopolist will now be OP_{m1} and OQ_{m1} respectively. Society's resources are not used to greatest possible efficiency because price does not equal MC, but price is still lower and output greater under monopoly than under perfect competition!

> Economies of scale are an important consideration

PRODUCTIVE EFFICIENCY

It was argued on page 00 that under perfect competition output is pushed to the point of maximum technical efficiency, i.e. minimum average cost. In fact, in the long run under perfect competition, technical efficiency and economic efficiency (price = MC) coincide. Under monopoly, this is not the case as shown in Fig. 5.7 earlier. The monopolist restricts output to the profit-maximising level and, at this point, average cost is still falling. The monopolist therefore operates with excess capacity and does not exploit all potential economies of scale. Here again, as Fig. 5.10 demonstrates, this might simply mean that monopoly is not as efficient as possible, but society still gains in terms of lower prices and greater output than would exist under perfect competition.

RESEARCH AND DEVELOPMENT

It is sometimes suggested that monopoly might lead to more rapid technological progress which in turn could lead to more inventions, improved techniques and the introduction of new and improved products than would be achieved by perfectly competitive markets. The higher level of profit earned under monopoly facilitates the finance of costly research and development programmes. Furthermore, a greater incentive to undertake such programmes exists since any reduction in cost that results will increase the monopolist's profit, while any improvement in the quality or range of goods produced will strengthen barriers to entry. The lower level of profit earned by firms in perfect competition, together with the certain knowledge that any benefits arising from research and development will quickly be diffused among competing firms, will inhibit research and development expenditures in such markets.

The empirical evidence to support the view that monopoly is associated with relatively high expenditures on research and development and rapid technological advance is inconclusive. Some large firms invest heavily in this type of expenditure but others do not. It might be true that there is no incentive to invest in research and development under perfect competition but this does not imply that there is no incentive under different forms of imperfect competition. In particular, as Table 5.2 illustrates, when there are a small number of competing firms, research and development expenditure might be relatively high. However, this is not always the case!

INDUSTRY	CONCENTRATION %	R & D EXPENDITURE %
Aerospace	79	16
Computers and office machinery	67	11.9
Insulated wires and cables	83	1.5
Motor vehicles and parts	67	1.7
Pharmaceutical products	34	11.3
Shipbuilding and repairs	79	0.3

Table 5.2 Concentration and research and development (shares of largest five firms)

Source: Business Monitor

STABILITY AND RATIONALISATION

One way in which monopoly will almost certainly be preferable to perfect competition is when markets are unstable because of sudden changes in demand or supply. A single firm is able to respond to these changes in a more orderly way than a group of firms whose activities are uncoordinated.

APPLIED MATERIALS

Although no market is perfectly competitive in the textbook sense of the term, some markets are very much more competitive than others. Tables 5.2 and 5.3 give some idea of the extent of concentration in certain markets and on the correlation in certain markets between concentration and R and D expenditure (Table 5.2).

INDUSTRY	NET OUTPUT %	EMPLOYMENT %
Tobacco	99	98
Cement, lime and plaster	89	85
Aerospace equipment, manufacture and repair	77	72
Glass and glassware	53	46
Pharmaceutical products	48	35
Footwear	40	38
Printing and publishing	19	14
Leather goods	13	11

Table 5.3 Concentration, output and employment (shares of largest five firms)

Source: Business Monitor

MONOPOLIES AND MERGERS COMMISSION

There are many situations where a market is dominated by a single firm and several have been investigated by the Monopolies and Mergers Commission. A significant number of these investigations have revealed the existence of excessive profit in certain situations. A well-known example is that of Hoffman la Roche, a manufacturer of drugs, which, through its subsidiary Roche Products, had a monopoly in the supply of chlorodiazepoxide and diazepam from which librium and valium are made. The Commission reported that Roche Products had used its monopoly position to charge excessive prices for its products and had consequently earned an excessive rate of return of 70 per cent on capital employed. This must be judged against the current government target of 21 per cent profit for pharmaceutical companies supplying the NHS.

Despite this the Commission has not always condemned firms which earn a relatively high rate of return on capital employed. For example, in its report on the

'Supply of Cat and Dog Foods in the United Kingdom' the Commission noted that although Pedigree Petfoods had earned an impressive rate of return of 44 per cent on capital employed, this was due to its relative efficiency. The Commission commented that: 'Pedigree Petfoods derives great advantage from its use of capital and financial control of a kind exceptional among large companies in this country.'

PRICE DISCRIMINATION AND AIRLINE TICKETS

An article entitled *Price Discrimination and Airline Tickets* in the *Economic Review* Vol 6 No 1 Sept 1988, provides an interesting case study on price discrimination. In this article, it is alleged that on any transatlantic flight carrying up to 390 passengers there might be as many as 100 different prices for the same journey! Clearly, this comes very close to achieving perfect price discrimination where every consumer pays a different price for the same good. The article highlights the importance of different elasticities of demand in the creation of different prices. Different elasticities of demand arise partly because of differences in the ability of individuals to finalise their travel plans. Those with greatest flexibility have a lower elasticity of demand for any given flight and might only be encouraged to make a booking by the offer of stand-by tickets with a relatively low price. The question of market segmentation is also addressed. After all, a seat on a flight is potentially transferable so why do consumers not buy at the lower price and resell at a higher price? In fact, each ticket has the purchaser's name printed on it, and, since a passport needs to be produced at the time of departure, this prevents the resale of tickets.

EXAMINATION QUESTIONS

1 (a) 'Mergers lead to less competition and a greater degree of monopoly power.' Discuss. *(50)*
  (b) In what circumstances are consumers likely to (i) gain and (ii) lose from company mergers? *(50)*

2 (a) Discuss the factors which give rise to a firm being dominant in a market. *(50)*
  (b) Explain how such a firm might be expected to behave if it wishes to preserve its market domination. *(50)*

(ULEAC June 1992)

3 Why do economists lay stress on the marginal, rather than the average, costs and revenues in explaining a firm's price and output decisions? Discuss how the costs of measures to improve the quality and supply of water in Britain might affect its future price.

(JMB 1991)

4 (a) Explain why firms in a certain industry might wish to collude with each other in setting prices in a cartel arrangement. *(10)*
  (b) Why might collusion between firms be held to be against the 'public interest'? *(10)*
  (c) For what reasons has it been asserted that collusive agreements often tend to break down in the long run? *(5)*

(WJEC 1992)

ANSWERS TO EXAMINATION QUESTIONS

TUTOR'S ANSWER TO QUESTION 1

(a) A merger occurs when the shareholders of two firms agree to combine their equity capital to form a new single company. A merger clearly leads to the creation of a larger firm than either of the two individual firms which merge, and in some cases there will undoubtedly be a reduction in competition and an increase in monopoly power as a consequence. However, this outcome cannot be guaranteed. In some cases, a merger might have little effect on the extent of competition or the degree of monopoly power, while in others a merger might actually increase the degree of competition in the industry.

To begin with, it is important to distinguish between conglomerate mergers, vertical mergers and horizontal mergers. A **conglomerate merger** occurs when two firms in *different* industries merge. The paramount reason for such mergers is the desire to diversify and so avoid the possibility of a firm being forced to close because of a reduction in demand for its product. Such mergers are unlikely to have any discernable effect on the degree of competition in the industry or the extent of monopoly power.

A **vertical merger** exists when firms in the same industry, but at *different stages* in the production process, combine into a single firm. The merger between Hall Ham River Ltd, the sand and gravel quarry company, and Ready Mix Concrete Ltd, is an example of a vertical merger. Here again, since firms are at different stages in the production process, such mergers are unlikely to have any effect on the extent of monopoly power or the degree of competition in the industry – though it might if the merger gives one firm control of the supply of vital inputs. The same is not always true of horizontal mergers.

Horizontal mergers occur when firms in the same industry, and at the *same stage* of the production process, merge. For example, if two chains which sell hi-fi equipment merge, this would be a horizontal merger. Now, it is clear that if two relatively small firms merge, or if an already dominant firm merges with a relatively small firm, there will be little effect on the level of competition or the degree of monopoly power in the industry. However, if two relatively large firms merge, the opposite might conceivably be true and there could easily be a reduction in competition and an increase in monopoly power. Not only would a relatively large firm be created but one of the major motives for horizontal mergers is the greater scope for economies of scale that become available after the merger. This confers significant cost advantages on larger firms and would clearly make it difficult for smaller firms to compete.

Despite this we cannot assume that horizontal mergers always reduce competition and increase monopoly power. It is possible that a merger will create a firm large enough to rival an already dominant firm. If this is the case the merger will lead to an increase in competition and a reduction in monopoly power.

(b) (i) One way in which consumers might gain from vertical company mergers is when a manufacturing firm merges with a chain of retail outlets and the former uses its resources to improve the retail outlets for the product. A merger in the opposite direction might also benefit consumers. For example, when a manufacturing firm merges with a supplier of raw materials and in consequence there is greater security over price and delivery of raw materials. This would avoid any disruption to production and prices.

Consumers might also gain from horizontal company mergers when greater economies of scale become available after the merger. If these cost reductions are passed on to consumers in the form of lower prices there is an obvious benefit. However, consumers might also benefit in other ways. A larger firm might be able to devote more resources to research and development which might lead to economies of scale and lower prices in the future. It might also lead to improvements in existing products and the development of new products.

(ii) On the other hand, consumers might be disadvantaged as a result of a merger. Horizontal mergers which create or strengthen a monopoly and reduce competition would almost certainly work to the disadvantage of consumers. Monopolies are rarely benign and where a merger creates or strengthens a monopoly, the result might well be higher prices for the consumer. This would be particularly likely where demand for the product was inelastic. In the absence of competition, the monopolist could restrict supply to force up prices.

The absence of competition might also induce a reduction in the quality of the product. In a competitive environment, firms have a powerful incentive to ensure that the price and quality of the product match or better the standard set by other firms in the industry. If they do not, sales will be lost and profits will fall. Less competition in the industry might remove this incentive and in this way work to the detriment of consumers.

Similarly, where a merger creates significant barriers to entry, this strengthens a monopoly and might remove the incentive to invest in research and development. The absence of competition leaves consumers little choice if they wish to consume the product. In a competitive environment, firms have an incentive to ensure a continuous flow of new products, but in a monopolistic environment this incentive might be weakened.

STUDENT'S ANSWER TO QUESTION 2

2 (a) **Market dominance** usually implies that a single firm supplies a considerably larger share of the market than any other firm in the industry. In such circumstances, firms can only dominate a market when there are barriers which prevent the entry of competing firms. However, before we examine the barriers which prevent the emergence of competition, we examine a different kind of market dominance.

A single firm can dominate a market when it is the **price leader**. Often the price leader will be the largest firm in the industry but this will not necessarily always be the case. **Barometric price leadership** exists when it is generally acknowledged by all firms in an industry that a particular firm most accurately assesses changes in the pressure of demand in the market. This firm initiates changes in the price of the product and other firms in the industry simply follow suit. It is possible that the barometric price leader will also be the largest firm in the industry, but it is equally possible that it is a smaller firm. In this case, there are no restrictions to prevent the emergence of competition and the barometric price leader dominates the industry only so long as it remains the firm which most accurately assesses changes in market demand.

In many cases, the emergence of a dominant firm reflects the availability of significant economies of scale. In some cases, such as telecommunications, technological progress has made economies of scale possible. In such circumstances, the natural outcome of competition is the emergence of a dominant firm as economies of scale are exploited. Once economies of scale are exploited, an important barrier to the emergence of competition will have been established because the largest firm will have a significant cost advantage over any new entrant to the industry. In other cases, such as chemical and oil production, the fixed costs of production are disproportionately high so that production is only viable when a relatively large output is produced. In such cases, the optimum size of the firm is very large and it is often the case that the market is most efficiently supplied by a single firm. Again, the growth of competition is

" Good point "

" A good introduction, setting the scene "

" Types of price leadership well defined "

" Good practical example "

stifled because of the fixed costs the firm must meet before production can begin, and because the effect on price of a relatively large increase in output might be such as to make production unprofitable for all firms in the industry!

Firms might achieve market domination because they exercise a major influence on the supply of some input. This is true in the case of China clay, for example. In such circumstances, unless alternative sources of supply can be found, a firm's dominance in the market is assured. At the other end of the supply chain, a firm's dominance might be established and maintained if the product requires a particular type of retail outlet and one firm is able to acquire control of a significant number of these. In such cases, the cost of entry for a new firm is significantly increased because of the need to acquire a sufficient number of retail outlets to enable it to market the product.

(b) Once a dominant position is established in the market, the firm will adopt policies designed to preserve its dominance. One approach might be to use non-price methods to restrict the emergence of competition. In particular, a firm might protect its particular brand of a product by heavy advertising. Unless the market is growing, such advertising is unlikely to lead to greater sales. Instead, its aim is to reduce the elasticity of demand for the dominant firm's product and raise the cost of entry to potential newcomers. The lower the elasticity of demand for a firm's product, the greater the amount of advertising necessary to effect entry into the industry. This represents a formidable deterrent to any firm thinking of entering the industry. The necessity to undertake heavy advertising represents an increase in fixed costs and adds significantly to the risks of production since such expenditure must be undertaken *in anticipation* of future sales.

A different argument is that where economies of scale confer significant cost advantages on the dominant firm, these savings will be reflected in lower prices for the consumer. In other words, instead of adopting a strategy of profit maximisation, the dominant firm might offer a lower price and aim at sales maximisation. The diagram is used as a basis for explanation.

66 Good illustration **99**

66 Can you give examples here? **99**

66 Good point **99**

66 Good point **99**

66 Diagram presented and well-used in text **99**

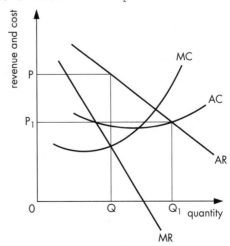

Fig. 5.11 The firm's profit-maximising price and output and break-even price and output

> **Good explanation of creating a barrier to entry**

If the firm represented in the diagram aims to maximise profit, it will equate MC with MR and produce an output of OQ which it will sell for OP. However, if it aims at a greater level of sales, it can produce up to the point where AR = AC;, i.e. the break-even point where the firm earns only normal profit. At this point, the firm charges a price of OP_1 and produces OQ_1. The firm cannot produce beyond this point, except in the short run, since it would be involved in a loss.

Charging a price less than OP might appeal to a dominant firm because it increases its market share and makes entry into the market difficult for any potential newcomer. This is because the newcomer will need to attract consumers away from the dominant firm, which will be particularly difficult unless they can at least match the price offered by the dominant firm. This will not be easy given that the dominant firm has exploited the available economies of scale and charges a price below the profit-maximising price. Similarly, other firms already in the industry will find it difficult to grow and to challenge the dominant firm's position.

> **Another barrier to entry well expressed**

Another strategy a dominant firm might pursue in order to preserve its dominance is to proliferate the number of brands on the market. A dominant firm might adopt such a strategy in order to increase or preserve its aggregate volume of sales and thus maintain its position of dominance. However, by proliferating the number of brands available to consumers, new firms will be discouraged from entering the industry. When consumers have a wide variety of brands to choose from, a new entrant to the industry is unlikely to gain more than a small proportion of the total market since its brand will face competition from a large number of close substitutes. In other words, proliferating the number of brands might deter the emergence of competition in a market dominated by a single firm.

Where firms have a dominant position in the market, there seems little doubt that they will adopt policies designed to enhance or preserve their dominant position. This implies that their marketing efforts are at least partly directed towards restricting the emergence of competition.

> **Some very good analysis presented here. Points made are relevant to the question and well expressed. One or two extra facts and figures could have re-inforced some of your points!**

OUTLINE ANSWERS

Question 3

You could begin your answer to this question by defining the terms **marginal cost**, **marginal revenue**, **average cost** and **average revenue**. It would be helpful to illustrate the concept of the **margin** and the **average** with a numerical example.

You could then go on to explain that a major assumption of conventional theories of the firm is their emphasis on **profit maximisation**. It is easy to prove mathematically that for all firms profit is maximised when marginal cost equals marginal revenue.

However, a simple intuitive explanation will suffice. If marginal cost is greater than marginal revenue, the firm adds more to costs than to revenue from producing and selling the last unit. Conversely when marginal cost is less than marginal revenue, the firm adds more to revenue than to costs from producing and selling the last unit. It follows that profits are maximised when production is pushed to the point at which marginal cost equals marginal revenue. This rule is *always* true, regardless of the values of average cost or average revenue. This point could usefully be illustrated diagrammatically.

Having explained the importance of marginal cost and marginal revenue, you must go on to explain that the firm can make a profit only if average revenue is at least sufficient to cover average total cost. If average revenue is at least sufficient to cover average total cost, this tells the firm that it is profitable to undertake production but it is marginal cost and marginal revenue that tell the firm where to produce and what price to charge in order to *maximise* profit.

Measures to improve the *quality* of water in Britain will raise the cost of supply to consumers. After all, the water authorities, like all other suppliers, must cover their costs if they are to earn a profit. Also, it is unlikely that the water authorities will absorb rising costs and accept lower profit margins. You could usefully illustrate diagrammatically the effect on supply of an increase in costs (see pp. 61–62). Of course, such an analysis is based on the assumption that all other things remain equal. They might not. There are vast economies of scale to suppliers of water and if measures to increase the supply of water enable these to be exploited, this will lead to an increase in supply as productivity rises (rather than a decrease in supply as costs rise). You must explain this fully and again the effect of an increase in supply on price and output can be illustrated diagrammatically. The final effect of measures to improve quality and increase supply depend on the amount spent, the extent to which economies of scale are exploited and demand factors (e.g. size and price elasticity).

Question 4

(a) A **cartel** is an agreement between suppliers of a particular good or service to co-ordinate their marketing activities. In practice, this means suppliers simply agree to charge a common price and to accept output quotas so as to maintain the uniform market price. The incentive to collude is to eliminate competition so that firms in the industry effectively form a monopoly and earn monopoly profit. You could present a diagram to show the (unique) industry output and price at which profits will be a maximum (MC=MR).

(b) Collusion might be against the public interest for several reasons. Clearly, it eliminates competition between firms and drives up prices. The absence of competition might also reduce the incentive to invest in research and development and so improve productivity, product quality and so on. Since each firm retains its own identity, there is little scope for economies of scale from production but, because output is restricted, the cartel will result in an inferior allocation of resources.

(c) The main reason collusive agreements tend to break down is that, because the output of each firm is restricted, firms in the cartel operate with excess capacity. They have the capacity to produce more output and, by secretly under-cutting the cartel, will be able to increase their profits. However, this adversely affects the market price of the product and so destabilises the cartel. Another reason cartels might be unstable is that some members will inevitably feel that their output quota is disproportionately small.

Further reading

Begg, Dornbusch and Fischer, *Economics* (3rd edn), McGraw-Hill 1991: Ch. 9, Perfect competition and pure monopoly: The limiting cases of market structure.

Galt, *Competition, Monopoly and Public Policy*, Longman 1989: Ch. 1, Competition and monopoly; Ch. 5, Monopoly and restrictive trade practice's policy in operation.

Harrison, *Pricing and Competition in the Private Sector*, Longman 1983: Ch. 2, Pricing, Competition and Market Structure.

Harrison et al, *Introductory Economics*, Macmillan 1992: Ch. 11, Perfect Competition; Ch. 11, Monopoly, Ch. 12, Price Discrimination.

Sloman, *Economics*, Harvester Wheatsheaf 1994: Ch. 6, Profit maximizing under Perfect Competition and Monopoly.

REVIEW SHEET

1 State five conditions necessary for perfect competition.
   (a) _____
   (b) _____
   (c) _____
   (d) _____
   (e) _____

2 Draw diagrams showing the short-run equilibrium for the market (industry) and the firm.
   Market   **Firm**

3 Write down an explanation of your diagram, i.e. briefly explain why this is the short-run equilibrium.
   _____
   _____
   _____
   _____
   _____
   _____

4 Draw diagrams showing the long-run equilibrium for the market (industry) and the firm.
   Market   **Firm**

5 Briefly explain why this is the long-run equilibrium.
   _____
   _____
   _____
   _____
   _____
   _____

6 Explain why the marginal cost curve of the industry is the supply curve of the industry under perfect competition. Use a diagram to illustrate your answer if you can.

Explanation:

_____

_____

_____

_____

_____

_____

7 Draw a diagram to show why a perfectly competitive industry taken over by a monopoly might have a higher price and a lower output.

8 Explain why monopoly may not always have a higher price and lower output than perfect competition.

_____

_____

_____

_____

9 What is price discrimination?

_____

_____

10 Under what conditions might price discrimination occur?

_____

_____

_____

11 Draw diagrams to show price discrimination occurring between two separate markets

Market A   **Market B**   **Aggregate Market (A+B)**

GETTING STARTED

In Chapter 5, we looked at two market structures, perfect competition and monopoly. These are extremes and while some markets might possess some of the characteristics of perfect competition and monopoly, neither is particularly common in the real world. Indeed, most market structures in the real world contain many imperfections but fall short of pure monopoly. It is these markets which we consider in this chapter.

Also, we have so far assumed that the firm always seeks to maximise profit. In fact, the firm may have other objectives, especially since the rise of limited liability companies has meant that *ownership* of firms is not necessarily the same as *control* of firms. The owners are the shareholders, who may indeed want profits (at least distributed profits – dividends) to be maximised. The controllers are the directors, who may or may not be major shareholders and who may have different objectives from those of shareholders.

MONOPOLISTIC COMPETITION

ESSENTIAL PRINCIPLES

The market structure, **monopolistic competition**, has features of both perfect competition and monopoly. In particular, there are no barriers to entry into the industry, but each firm produces a product which is *differentiated* in some way from the products of its rivals. Such product differentiation is often achieved or reinforced by branding and advertising. Because each product is differentiated, each firm has a monopoly over the supply of its own product. It therefore faces a downward sloping demand curve for its product with respect to price. This, in turn, implies that its marginal revenue curve lies beneath its average revenue curve.

66 The products are different 99

EQUILIBRIUM: THE SHORT RUN AND THE LONG RUN

The short run

As with other market structures, we assume that the firm aims to maximise profit. It therefore produces that level of output at which MC = MR. The firm's short-run equilibrium position is shown in Fig. 6.1(a).

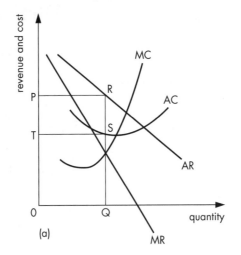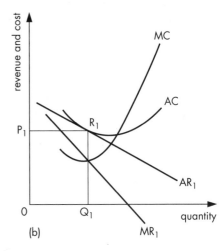

Fig. 6.1 Equilibrium (a) in the short run and (b) in the long run

The firm is in equilibrium when it produces OQ units and charges a price of OP per unit. At this price and output combination, it earns supernormal profit of PRST. However, this cannot represent a long-run equilibrium position because the existence of supernormal profit will attract more firms into the industry. Indeed, firms will continue to enter the industry until supernormal profits have been competed away and each firm earns only normal profit. The firm's long-run equilibrium position is shown in Fig. 6.1(b). The extra firms attract some, but not all, of the firm's customers. This can be shown as a leftward shift of the firm's demand (AR) curve, until it just touches its AC curve.

66 There is freedom of entry in monopolistic competition 99

The long-run

In the long run, total revenue equals total cost ($=OP_1R_1Q_1$). Each firm, although maximising profit (MC = MR) earns only normal profit since, at output OQ_1, price equals average cost. Consequently, there is no tendency for firms to enter or leave the industry. However, this does not imply that monopolistic competition confers the same benefits on society as perfect competition. In particular, we can identify two important ways in which society is worse off:

- In the long run, equilibrium output is not pushed to the point of maximum technical efficiency, i.e. minimum average cost. The firm in monopolistic competition therefore operates with excess capacity in the long run. This under-utilisation of capacity leads both to higher average costs than would exist if output were expanded and consequently to higher consumer prices.

- In the long run, equilibrium output is not pushed to the point at which resources are allocated in the most efficient manner, i.e. a **Pareto optimal resource allocation**. This requires price to equal marginal cost, yet here price is greater than marginal cost. This means that if output were expanded until price equals marginal cost, resource allocation could be improved, but this will not happen because the firm will make a loss.

OLIGOPOLY

66 **Here a few large producers dominate** 99

66 **Firms need to take into account the actions and reactions of each other** 99

A market is oligopolistic when a few large-scale producers dominate the industry. For this reason, **oligopoly** is sometimes referred to as 'competition among the few'. Firms supply competing brands of a product and any 'action' in terms of price and non-price strategies by one firm would almost certainly be matched by the firm's rivals. Because of this, the distinguishing feature of oligopolistic markets is that there is a high degree of interdependence between each firm in the industry. This implies that individual firms will be obliged to consider the effect of their actions on rival producers, and the possible course of action they in turn might pursue.

THE KINKED DEMAND CURVE

The existence of interdependence provides a possible explanation for the relative price stability that sometimes characterises oligopolistic markets. The suggestion is that an individual firm in oligopoly fears that if it raises price, other firms will not follow suit. Instead, they will be content to hold their own price constant and attract consumers away from the firm which has raised the price. Because of this, the individual firm perceives demand for its product to be relatively elastic (DD) if it raises price. On the other hand, if an individual firm lowers price its competitors in the market will be compelled to match the price cut, otherwise they will lose a disproportionate amount of sales. The individual firm therefore perceives demand for its product to be relatively inelastic (D_1D_1) if it lowers price. The implications of this are illustrated in Fig. 6.2

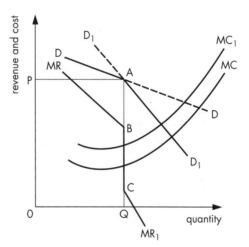

Fig. 6.2 The kinked demand curve
DAD_1

66 **Reasons for the linked demand curve** 99

Because the firm perceives demand to be relatively elastic if it raises price and relatively inelastic if it reduces price, it perceives its demand curve (DAD_1) to be kinked at the ruling market price (OP). It therefore has little incentive to alter price from OP. This can be seen from Fig. 6.2 which shows that because the firm perceives its demand curve to be kinked, it has a discontinuous marginal revenue curve. In fact, when price is OP, marginal revenue is indeterminate because the firm is currently operating at a common point (A) on what is effectively two separate demand curves $(DD$ and $D_1D_1)$, with associated marginal revenue curves. The region BC is therefore referred to as the **region of indeterminacy**. It implies that even when costs are changing, so long as marginal cost remains within the region of indeterminacy, changes in costs will have no effect on the profit-maximising price and output combination, because the firm will still be producing where MC equals MR. For example, in Fig. 6.2 when marginal cost rises from MC to MC_1, this has no effect on the price the firm charges or on the output it produces.

PRICE LEADERSHIP

Another possible reason for relative price stability in oligopolistic markets is that there might be an accepted **price leader**. Price changes are initiated by the leader and other firms in the industry simply follow suit. The role of price leader might be acquired because a firm is the largest producer in the industry, in which case we refer to **dominant firm** leadership. Alternatively, the price leader might be the firm which most accurately perceives changes in market demand for the product. In this case we refer to **barometric price leadership**. Whatever the basis of leadership, its existence would explain price stability because price changes will only be initiated by a single firm. This firm would not be confronted with price cutting by other firms and therefore price would tend to be relatively stable.

PRICE WARFARE

Whilst prices in oligopolistic markets sometimes appear relatively stable, at other times they can be highly unstable. This is particularly common when demand for the industry's product is falling, because, as sales fall, average fixed costs will rise. Individual firms are prevented from raising price because they would lose sales to competitors, and this would simply exacerbate their problems. Because of this, falling sales imply falling profits, and in these circumstances, the temptation for a firm to cut its price in an attempt to prevent further loss of sales is sometimes overwhelming. However, when demand for the product is falling, an individual firm can only increase sales by attracting consumers away from rival firms. To prevent this, rival firms may well retaliate if faced with a price cut, so that profits fall still further. This may then lead to a further round of price cutting, i.e. a **price war** will be under way.

NON-PRICE COMPETITION

The existence of price wars is evidence of competition in oligopolostic markets. However, even when prices are stable, non-price competition between rival producers is often intense. This can take a variety of forms:

Competitive advertising
This is common in oligopolostic markets. Advertising is used to reinforce product differentiation and harden brand loyalty.

Promotional offers
 Types of non-price competition

These are common in some oligopolistic markets, such as household detergents and toothpaste. Such offers frequently take the form of veiled price reductions such as 'two for the price of one' offers or '25 per cent extra free'. In the case of petrol, a common technique is to offer 'free gifts'.

Extended guarantees
This is an increasingly common technique in many of the markets for consumer durables. By offering free parts and labour guarantees for longer periods than their competitors, firms aim to increase the attractiveness of their product.

ALTERNATIVES TO PROFIT MAXIMISATION

This chapter has stressed profit maximisation as the goal of firms. However, in practice, it is doubtful whether firms pursue this goal to the exclusion of all other goals. This is especially true in modern corporations where ownership is in the hands of shareholders, but day-to-day control is exercised by salaried managers. Profit maximisation is likely to appeal to shareholders, because it will lead to higher dividends, but salaried managers might be more interested in pursuing other goals. Two alternatives are considered below.

THE SALES-MAXIMISATION MODEL

66 Firms may have various objectives 99

Rather than maximising profit, it has been suggested that salaried managers might attempt to maximise sales revenue, subject to achieving a target rate of profit. Managers have good reason for maximising sales revenue, since it often affects their salaries and their security of tenure. In general, a higher level of sales revenue is rewarded with a higher salary. In addition, as Fig. 6.3 shows, maximising sales revenue implies a greater level of output, and therefore a greater market share, than is achieved when profit is maximised. The profit-maximising price and output are OP_P and OQ_P respectively, whereas the sales revenue maximising price and output are OP_S and OQ_S respectively.

Note: price is lower and output greater when sales revenue is maximised than when profit is maximised. When MR = 0, total (i.e. sales) revenue is a maximum.

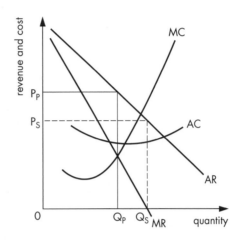

Fig. 6.3 Comparing sales revenue maximisation with profit maximisation

The lower price and greater market share might offer greater protection against the emergence of competitors and, in this sense, might offer better prospects of long-term survival. Profit maximisation, on the other hand, by showing the level of profit that can be achieved, might encourage competitors to enter the industry and threaten the long-term survival of those firms already in the industry. Because of this, it is sometimes argued that maximising sales is, in effect, maximising long-run profits.

Another reason firms might prefer sales maximisation as the major goal is that, for many firms, fixed costs are relatively high. The larger the output, the smaller the average fixed cost. Here again this might give greater protection against the emergence of competition and might maximise long-run profits.

BEHAVIOURAL MODELS

Behavioural theories stress that firms might pursue several goals simultaneously. Each goal is set as a result of bargaining between the various groups involved, such as managers, shareholders, trade unions, and so on. Where goals are in conflict with one another they must be ranked in order of importance, and priority given to one rather than the other. For example, the level of output which maximises sales revenue is likely to be greater than the level of output which maximises profit. If, as a result of bargaining, profit maximisation is given priority, output will be cut back. Bargaining within the firm can clearly lead to different priorities at different times, so that behavioural models stress that no single goal can be assumed to be consistently followed by the firm.

An extension of the behavioural model is that of **satisficing**. This approach stresses that firms seek a satisfactory minimum level of achievement for various goals rather than a maximum level for any single goal. This means that many possible outcomes of price and quantity could then be regarded as situations of equilibrium for the firm.

APPLIED MATERIALS

An article in *British Economy Survey*, Vol 22, No 1, Autumn 1992, discusses four case studies of restrictive trade agreements. Such agreements are designed to restrict competition between firms and the result is usually higher prices for consumers and higher profits for firms.

In 1986, the Restrictive Practices Court investigated 35 agreements among several betting shop owners. It transpired that two or more bookmakers had agreed to reciprocal closure of betting shops in particular localities so that no bookmaker would gain an advantage over another in that area. There were also agreements between bookmakers already dominant in a particular locality to give mutual support against any rival bookmaker attempting to establish a betting office in that locality. The Court ruled that this agreement was against the public interest.

In 1991, the Court found that senior representatives of three manufacturers of steel purlins, Ayrshire Metal Products (Daventry) Ltd, Metal Sections Ltd and Ward Building Systems Ltd, had been meeting for several years to share major customers in an agreed order. This clearly reduced competition in the purlin market and the Court ruled that such agreements were against the public interest.

In 1991, the Court found that G.K. Kinch and Midland Fox Ltd, both Midland bus companies, had reached an agreement covering fare fixing and bus routes in parts of Leicestershire. Again, the Court ruled that this agreement operated against the public interest and both companies gave assurances that the agreement would be terminated.

Again in 1991, the Court gave its judgement on the North East Fuel Oil cartel. This was an agreement between 17 suppliers of various fuel oils who had agreed to fix the prices of domestic fuel oils between August and December 1989. The Court ruled that the agreement operated against the public interest but this was an interesting case in that a customer sued one of the suppliers for not registering the agreement with the OFT and claimed damages. The case was settled out of court.

THE WORLD OIL MARKET

An article entitled *The World Oil Market: An Example of Oligopoly* is published in *The Economic Review*, Vol 5, No 2, Nov 1987. This article focuses on the way price is set in this industry which consists of a few large-scale suppliers of an homogeneous product. It is pointed out that, in the early days of OPEC, no formal mechanism existed for setting price and dominant firm price leadership provides the best explanation of the way prices were set. Saudi Arabia, by far the largest producer of oil, functioned as the dominant firm and adjusted its output so as to maintain the market price that met its objectives. In more recent years however, OPEC has operated more as a cartel and has aimed to reduce uncertainty over the way rivals might react to price changes and to increase the total profit of cartel members by assigning quotas to each member. The problem with all cartels is that, once quotas have been agreed, the temptation for an individual is, secretly, to increase the amount it sells thereby raising its own profit. This is the main reason why cartels tend to be unstable and, in the article, Nigeria and the United Arab Emirates are cited as two countries who exceeded their quotas. This prompted Saudi Arabia and its ally Kuwait to increase production and thus depress the price of oil in order to punish those countries who exceeded their quotas and by so doing threatened the stability of the OPEC cartel. The result of their actions was the dramatic reduction in the price of oil in 1986. This undoubtedly provided a measure of discipline in respect of quotas and thus stabilised the cartel, but another motive for Saudi Arabia's actions seems to have been to safeguard its market share. The success of the OPEC cartel in raising oil prices has led to a sustained reduction in the amount of oil demanded. By effectively committing OPEC to smaller price rises Saudi Arabia hoped to slow down the reduction in demand for oil and thus safeguard its revenue from oil.

THE MONOPOLIES AND MERGERS COMMISSION

The investigations of the Monopolies and Mergers Commission are again relevant because many of the markets investigated by the Commission more closely resemble the model of oligopoly rather than monopoly. There is no doubt that, in these markets, the rival producers recognise the high degree of interdependence which exists between them. Evidence of this interdependence is clear in the following extract from the Commission's report into the supply of ceramic sanitary ware:

There are four major producers in the industry and on two occasions, in 1975 and 1976, individual companies increased their list prices in the expectation that their competitors would do so to the same extent, but were quickly forced to rescind or reduce their increases when they found that their competitors did not raise their prices as expected.

EXAMINATION QUESTIONS

1 Discuss the various factors which a firm operating in an oligopolistic market is likely to take into account when deciding on the price to charge for its product.
(AEB June 1993)

2 (a) How might the profits (or losses) of a firm as reckoned by economists not always correspond to profits as reckoned by accountants? *(5)*
(b) What factors might explain the existence of abnormal profits in a market economy? *(10)*
(c) Why is it argued that profits (and losses) are essential to the workings of a market economy? *(10)*
(WJEC 1991)

3 (a) 'Product differentiation is the crucial dimension that distinguishes monopolistic competition from perfect competition.' Explain this statement. *(70)*
(b) Is product differentiation undesirable? *(30)*
(ULEAC January 1992)

4 Why are there different levels of profits in perfect and imperfect markets?
(UCLES November 1992)

5 Do you agree that successful advertising benefits both the advertiser and society? Explain your answer.

ANSWERS TO EXAMINATION QUESTIONS

TUTOR'S ANSWER TO QUESTION 1

An **oligopolistic market** is one in which there are a few large-scale producers of a particular product. In such a market, there are several factors a firm will take into account when deciding on the price to charge for its product. Any decision the firm takes will, of course, be influenced by its objectives.

For any firm which aims at **profit maximisation**, the rule is to equate marginal cost with marginal revenue. In this case, the firm will simply adjust price whenever a change in demand and/or costs results in a change in marginal revenue and/or marginal cost. On the other hand, firms might aim at maximising their market share. There are many reasons for such a strategy including security (larger firms are less likely to be forced into liquidation) and the fact that managerial salaries are often linked to the firm's size. In this case, the firm is likely to charge the lowest price consistent with its aim, so long as profits are high enough to appease shareholders.

Whatever the firm's ultimate aim, it must earn a satisfactory rate of profit if it is to survive, in the long run. A major influence on the price a firm charges for its product is therefore the cost of producing the product. However, while it is true that firms must cover their costs in the long run, it is not necessarily true that a rise in costs will result in a rise in the product's price. For small changes in costs, firms might be reluctant to alter prices because this will necessitate producing new price lists and frequent price changes might alienate consumers.

However, there is another factor to consider. Because all firms in oligopolistic markets are large-scale producers, an oligopolistic market is characterised by a high degree of interdependence. In other words, the actions of one firm have repercussions on other firms in the industry. An important factor to consider in deciding what price to charge for a product is the way in which rival firms will react. One possibility is that firms in oligopolistic markets perceive their demand curve to be kinked at the ruling market price. Once the market price is established any increase in price by a single firm will be unmatched by rival firms, whereas a price cut will be swiftly matched. To the extent that this is correct, oligopolists will perceive their demand curve above the market price to be relatively elastic and below the market price to be relatively inelastic. At the kink in the demand curve, the marginal revenue curve will be discontinuous. Figure 6.4 is used to illustrate the importance of this.

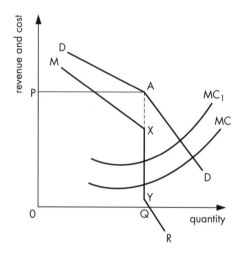

Fig. 6.4 The oligopolist's kinked demand curve. P and Q remain the profit-maximising price and output combination so long as marginal cost fluctuates within the region of indeterminacy.

In Fig. 6.4, DAD shows the kinked demand curve as perceived by the oligopolist. MXYR is the marginal revenue curve. Below the kink the marginal revenue curve is discontinuous and marginal cost can fluctuate anywhere within the discontinuous region without breaking the profit-maximising rule. Again, we see that changes in costs might not affect the price of the product though, of course, if they go on rising then at some point prices will also rise. However, the crucial point is that the kinked demand curve shows that the reaction of rival firms is an important consideration for oligopolists when deciding on the price to charge for their product. The kinked demand curve is therefore one possible explanation of relative price stability in oligopolistic markets.

Oligopolistic markets might be characterised by **price leadership** where one firm, the price leader, initiates price changes and other firms simply follow suit. The price leader might be the dominant firm in which case other firms accept its leadership because they are powerless to challenge it. However, economists also refer to **barometric price leadership** where the price leader is the firm which most accurately measures changes in the pressure of demand and initiates price changes accordingly. In this case, other firms accept the ability of the price leader to interpret market changes and simply follow suit. Where a price leader exists, oligopolists will consider the price set by the leader in setting their own price.

A different approach which oligopolists might use is **limit pricing**. Here, price is set with the objective of preventing the entry of new firms into the industry. Oligopolists will have more freedom in setting prices when there are barriers which prevent the entry of new firms into the industry, such as the existence of significant economies of scale. When there are significant economies of scale, limit pricing implies setting price just below the long-run average cost of the most efficient potential entrant. Such a price is referred to as the **maximum entry forestalling price**.

Oligopolistic markets are often characterised by a high degree of product differentiation and non-price competition. Product differentiation, reinforced by heavy advertising, is designed to create and enhance brand loyalty. When brand loyalty exists, oligopolists have more freedom in setting price since demand for their product will be less elastic than otherwise. This is an important consideration because, when demand is inelastic, an increase in price will lead to a less than proportional reduction in sales and hence total revenue will increase. In these circumstances, profits will rise as a result of an increase in price because total revenue rises and total costs fall (because sales and output will fall). This is an important factor which firms will take into consideration when setting the price of their product.

It is often suggested that oligopolists use **cost-plus** as a basis for setting price. This simply means they add a mark-up to the average cost of production. This is a relatively straightforward approach to pricing but it is not inconsistent with the analysis above. For example, the mark-up could be varied depending on whether oligopolists wish to implement limit pricing, maximise profits or maximise market share.

Clearly there are many factors oligopolists will take into account when setting price. However, except in the case of a price leader, the interdependent nature of oligopolistic markets implies that no oligopolist will have an entirely free hand in setting price; each firm is bound to consider the effect on rival firms of any decision taken to initiate a price change.

STUDENT'S ANSWER TO QUESTION 2

66 Good – but normal profit could be explained a little more here 99

66 Diagram here perhaps! 99

66 Good 99

66 More explanation 99

66 Good – but explain further 99

66 Good point 99

(a) An accountant's view of profit is simply the difference between total costs and total revenue. If total revenue is greater than total cost then a profit is earned, and if total revenue is less than total cost the firm makes a loss. An economist's view is that the entrepreneur has an opportunity cost and this is considered as a cost of production. To the economist, if total revenue is just sufficient to cover total cost, then the firm earns **normal profit**.

(b) Abnormal profits are anything in excess of normal profit. Abnormal profit can only exist when there are barriers to prevent the entry of firms into the industry. Barriers might take several different forms but, in the modern world, economies of scale are particularly important.

Economies of scale are defined as 'the advantages of increasing size which lead to falling average costs'. Because of this, large firms have a major advantage over smaller firms which makes it difficult for smaller firms to enter the industry.

Abnormal profits might also stem from a domestic firm having a comparative advantage over firms in different countries. This might be because the domestic firm is more efficient than overseas producers, but it might also result from a rate of exchange which favours the domestic firm.

Sometimes abnormal profits have little to do with efficiency or barriers to entry. In financial markets, windfall gains can be earned by banks and building societies when the government raises interest rates. When this happens, banks and building societies earn extra revenue from lending to customers purely as a result of government policy.

(c) A market economy exists when there is little government interference in the allocation of resources. In market economies, resources are allocated through the price mechanism. Here, changes in demand and supply cause price changes which provide signals to producers. For example, when consumers demand more of a product, the price of this product rises. It will therefore become

66 Good – diagram to illustrate perhaps 99

> more profitable for firms to increase the amount of
> this product which they produce. When they do this,
> they will compete resources away from other products
> and therefore an increase in demand for a product will
> cause a reallocation of resources.
>
> Exactly the opposite happens when there is a fall
> in demand for a product. Here, consumers are signalling
> that they require less of a product. Because of this,
> the price of the product will fall and, as profits
> fall, producers will cut back on the amount they
> produce. When this happens resources are released and
> are then available for the production of other goods
> and services.

66 Again, a well-used diagram could help here 99

66 Many good points raised but often these need to be taken a little further. Look for opportunities to present relevant diagrams and then to *use* these in the text 99

OUTLINE ANSWERS

Question 3

(a) You could begin your answer to this question by outlining the conditions necessary for **monopolistic competition** and the conditions necessary for **perfect competition**. The major difference is that in the former the market is characterised by product differentiation whereas in the latter market a homogeneous product is sold. You should stress that because of this, firms in the different markets face different demand curves.

You could then go on to analyse the implications of product differentiation for long-run equilibrium of the firm in both markets. The important point to stress is that although in both cases the firm earns only normal profit in the long run, there are important differences in the allocation of resources. Whereas, in perfect competition, resources are allocated to their most efficient uses because consumers pay an amount for the last unit consumed which is exactly equal to its marginal cost of production, in monopolistic competition there is an inferior allocation of resources because price is always above marginal cost. You should also explain that, in perfect competition, the firm is forced to the point of minimum average cost in the long run whereas, in monopolistic competition, the firm operates with excess capacity in the long run.

(b) Product differentiation is not necessarily undesirable. It gives consumers increased choice and, because of increased competition between firms, might result in lower prices for the consumer. Greater competition might also provide a spur to invest in research and development which might lead to advances in techniques of production and through this to lower prices. It might also lead to product development.

Question 4

You could begin your answer to this question by explaining the distinction between *normal* profit and *supernormal* profit. You could then explain that it is possible for any firm to earn supernormal profit in the short run. However, the assumptions of perfect competition and monopolistic competition ensure that, in the long run, supernormal profits are competed away. You should discuss this in some detail and illustrate your points with appropriate diagrams.

The main reason that supernormal profits are competed away in perfectly competitive markets and in monopolistically competitive markets, is that there are no barriers which prevent the entry of new firms into the industry. The existence of supernormal profits in the long run implies the existence of barriers which prevent the entry of new firms into the industry. Having explained this point you could go on to discuss the different barriers which might prevent entry into the industry.

66 **Very clear definitions** 99

You might complete your answer by explaining that supernormal profits will be greater the lower the elasticity of demand for the monopolist's product and the greater the efficiency with which the monopolist utilises resources. Remember, the greater the degree of efficiency, the lower the cost of producing any given level of output.

STUDENT'S ANSWER TO QUESTION 5

There are two types of advertising: informative and persuasive. **Informative advertising**, as its name suggests, simply aims to provide consumers with information on which to make decisions about their purchases. **Persuasive advertising**, on the other hand, aims to persuade consumers that one product is in some way superior to competing products.

Whether advertising is successful or not must be judged in terms of its aims. No one would argue that, if informative advertising is successful, the consumer benefits. The more information consumers have at their disposal, the more rational their choices will be. In addition, since there is no attempt to persuade consumers that one product is superior to others, consumers are not provided with false information. The judgement they exercise when making choices will therefore be based on a full understanding of the facts.

However, persuasive advertising is a different matter. Here the aim is to persuade consumers to purchase one product in preference to rival products. To do this, it is necessary to highlight differences between products and if no real differences exist they must be created in the minds of consumers. This is done by advertising and since it highlights imaginary differences between products, it seems that there is no benefit to society from this type of advertising. Indeed, if consumers are provided with misleading information, they will make decisions which do not maximise their welfare because they are based on an incorrect interpretation of information. In the case of imaginary differences, consumers believe they are buying something that in reality does not actually exist!

However, the advertiser might derive great benefits from advertising. One possible benefit is that successful advertising will have a favourable effect on demand for the firm's product. This might imply that the firm experiences an increase in demand for the product it has advertised. It might also reduce the elasticity of demand for its product. These are the aims of persuasive advertising and both possibilities might enable the firm to charge a higher price for its product and increase its profits. However, if profits increase because a firm is able to charge higher prices for its product, this might be considered a disadvantage from society's point of view. On the other hand, there are possible gains which might partly offset this disadvantage. Increased profits will lead to higher tax payments and this money might be spent in ways which benefit society. Higher profits might also finance research and development and lead to cost reductions in the future as well as the development of new and improved products. Again, society benefits from this.

Despite these advantages, there are other factors to consider. In particular, advertising can be used as a means of restricting the entry of new firms into an industry.

66 **Good** 99

66 **But there is still an opportunity cost involved in gathering and disseminating information** 99

66 **Even persuasive advertising gives consumers information** 99

66 **An excellent paragraph** 99

❝ Very good ❞

Where existing producers spend relatively large sums of money advertising their products, a potential new entrant to the industry must at least match the advertising expenditures of existing producers if it is to effect entry into the market. This represents a considerable barrier to entry because existing producers finance current advertising from current sales receipts. However, a potential new entrant cannot do this and must finance advertising expenditures in anticipation of sales receipts. This not only involves heavy expenditure which firms must have the ability to finance, it also involves considerable risk because there is no guarantee that, having financed advertising expenditures, firms will be successful in breaking into a new market. Because of this, persuasive advertising might discourage the growth of competition and although this might work to the advantage of the advertiser, it is doubtful that it will work to the advantage of society as a whole.

Another important factor to consider is the effect of advertising expenditure on a firm's costs and the way in which this affects the price paid by consumers. Any expenditure on advertising adds directly to a firm's costs of production and might therefore lead to higher prices. As previously argued, these higher prices might not benefit society. However, it is often argued that advertising actually lowers the price which consumers pay. If advertising is successful in increasing demand for a firm's product and the firm gains economies of scale as it expands production, then average costs of production will fall. If these cost reductions are passed on to consumers in the form of lower prices, then both the firm and society gain from advertising. This is usually suggested as the main way in which society gains from advertising. However, whether there is any gain in practice depends on whether firms gain economies of scale and whether the benefits of these are passed on to society.

Successful advertising might benefit society and the advertiser but it does not necessarily do so. Clearly, if advertising is successful, the advertiser must benefit otherwise advertising would be unsuccessful. Whether society also benefits depends on whether the gains of successful advertising are passed on to society or whether they are simply used to increase the advertiser's profit.

❝ Advertising revenues also make independent television and radio, along with the production of provincial newspapers, possible. An important point is that if one believes in competition one must believe in persuasive advertising – it is the main instrument of competition! An encouraging answer, which is perceptive and clear ❞

Further reading

Begg, Fischer and Dornbusch, *Economics* (3rd edn), McGraw-Hill 1991: Ch. 10, Market structure and imperfect competition.

Harrison et al, *Introductory Economics*, Macmillan 1992: Ch. 13, Imperfect Competition.

Maunder et al, *Economics Explained*, Collins Educational 1987: Pricing and output decisions in monopolistic competition and oligopoly.

REVIEW SHEET

1 List the key features of monopolistic competition.

_____

_____

_____

_____

2 Draw diagrams to show both the short-run and long-run equilibrium situations under monopolistic competition.

3 Explain how the market moves from the short-run to the long-run equilibrium, referring to your diagram wherever possible.

_____

_____

_____

_____

_____

_____

4 Suggest two reasons why the long-run equilibrium solution under monopolistic competition may be less satisfactory than that under perfection competition.

(a) _____

_____

(b) _____

_____

_____

5 List the key features of oligopoly.

_____

_____

_____

6 Draw a diagram showing a solution involving the kinked demand curve.

7 Use your diagram to explain why prices might be 'sticky' (rigid) under the kinked demand curve.

_____

_____

_____

_____

_____

_____

8 Suggest any other reasons for price stability in oligopoly markets.

_____

_____

_____

_____

_____

_____

9 List some types of non-price competition found in oligopoly markets.

_____

_____

_____

_____

_____

_____

10 Explain why managers might be interested in sales (revenue) maximisation?

_____

_____

_____

_____

_____

_____

11 Draw a diagram to compare profit maximisation with sales (revenue) maximisation.

12 Explain the consequences for price and output under each objective, referring to your diagram wherever possible.

_____

_____

_____

_____

_____

_____

_____

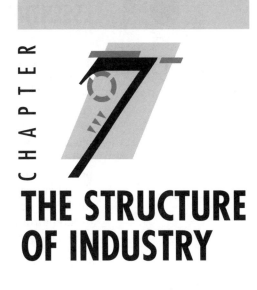

CHAPTER 7

THE STRUCTURE OF INDUSTRY

GETTING STARTED

This chapter examines the reasons for the continued existence of small firms and the different methods by which firms grow. The motives for growth are also examined in some detail.

We have already seen, in Chapter 3, that large firms sometimes gain economies of scale and so have cost advantages over small firms. Despite this, small firms continue to survive and are very common in some sectors, such as retailing. This is very important since the government has repeatedly stressed its aim of encouraging an expansion of the small firm sector as an integral part of its economic strategy.

We also look at the methods by which firms can grow into medium/large size firms, and the advantages/disadvantages of such methods.

Before you proceed with this chapter, an important point to bear in mind is that although it is brief in comparison with some other chapters, this does not imply that it is comparatively unimportant. Examination questions on this topic are still fairly frequent!

SMALL FIRMS

THE GROWTH OF FIRMS

APPLIED MATERIALS

ESSENTIAL PRINCIPLES

SMALL FIRMS

There is no uniform measure of size and, therefore, no single criterion against which a firm can be judged small or large. Statistically, the most widely used measures are in terms of employment or turnover (i.e. total revenue) per year. However, capital employed is also sometimes used as a measure of size.

The difficulties of deriving a single, simple definition of a small firm were amply illustrated in the Bolton Committee Report (1971). The committee's terms of reference had defined small firms as broadly those with not more than 200 employees, but in practice it found this definition to be totally inadequate. Instead, it suggested that a definition was needed which emphasised those characteristics of small firms which might be expected to make their performance and their problems significantly different from those of large firms. They concluded that three main characteristics had to be taken into account:

66 **Key features of the small firm** 99

1. A small firm is one that has a relatively small share of its market.
2. It is managed by its owners or part-owners in a personalised way, and not through the medium of a formalised management structure.
3. It is independent, in the sense that it does not form part of a large enterprise, so that its owner-managers are free from outside control when taking their principal decisions.

These characteristics formed the 'economic' definition of the small firm. However, to make this operational, the committee needed a statistical definition, although it recognised that no single quantifiable definition could be entirely satisfactory. In attempting to reflect the three characteristics above, the committee found that for statistical purposes the criteria of a small firm would have to vary from sector to sector. For manufacturing, it retained the usual '200 employees or less' definition, though in construction and mining the upper limit for small firms was reduced to '25 employees or less'. In the motor trades, retailing and miscellaneous services, the statistical definition was based not on the number of employees, but on a specified upper limit for annual turnover, e.g. £200,000 for the motor trades, and £50,000 for retailing and miscellaneous services. For road transport, the definition adopted was based on the number of vehicles operated (less than five), whereas in catering all enterprises were to be included except multiples and brewery-managed public houses.

Problems of defining the small firm are not confined to the UK. The definition often used for small firms varies widely, from less than 50 employees in the Netherlands, to less than 1,000 employees in the USA! Whether within a single country, or between countries, there will inevitably be a strong element of arbitrariness in the statistical definition used for the small firm.

REASONS FOR SURVIVAL

Despite the advantages of economies of scale which are experienced by large firms, small firms continue to survive. There may be many reasons for this:

- Many people prefer to be self-employed and so set up their own business. However, not all people classed as self-employed would also be classed as owning a firm, e.g. window cleaners. Those that do own a firm often remain 'small' out of choice.

66 **Why the small firm survives** 99

- Small firms have limited access to finance. Many rely on their own savings and that of other family members. This severely restricts growth and is a reason why many firms remain small.

- Small firms often supply small markets. This is true of small independent retailers which often serve neighbourhood communities. Some firms produce specialist goods which cannot be mass produced. In other words, small firms flourish where consumers demand variety.

- Sometimes the nature of production is such that size gives no advantage. This is true of repair and window cleaning, for example.

- Firms supplying personal services are often small because the nature of the product means that growth does not confer the same advantages on producers as growth of a manufacturing firm does. This is true of hairdressing, for example.
- Small firms often supply a small part of a much larger market that is of no interest to larger firms. For example, Wimpey and Barrett build housing estates but have no interest in barn conversions or house extensions. These are carried out by small jobbing builders. The two groups survive alongside each other but neither competes directly.
- Large firms often subcontract work to smaller firms. It is often cheaper for larger firms to do so because they can accept a greater volume of work without incurring an increase in overheads. In this sense, they act as agents, providing work for smaller firms and charging a fee for their services. (It is doubtful that the clients know the work is subcontracted or they would contact the firms doing the work direct!)
- In recent years, the government has actively encouraged the growth of smaller firms. In particular, measures have been introduced to encourage the unemployed to set up their own businesses and VAT regulations have been changed to ease the cash flow situation of small firms. There is also a Business Start-up Scheme which pays unemployed people up to £90 per week for a year while they set up their own business. As a result the numbers of self-employed have increased by over 40 per cent to about 1.88 million. Furthermore, the Enterprise Investment Scheme (EIS) provides tax relief on investment by individuals in unquoted public companies, i.e. those companies without a stock exchange quotation. There is no doubt that these measures have had a powerful impact on the growth of small firms.

THE ROLE OF SMALL FIRMS IN THE ECONOMY

Since the government has done so much to help the growth of the small firm sector, it is reasonable to ask why they are considered important. One reason is that, if individuals can be encouraged to set up in business rather than remain unemployed, this reduces the unemployment figures and might also improve the allocation of resources. After all, if workers are unemployed the opportunity cost of this is the output they might otherwise have produced. It is also possible that as unemployment falls and therefore social security payments fall, the government will be able to reduce taxation. This is important because it is frequently alleged that a lower burden of taxation will increase incentives (see Ch. 16). Small firms might also promote employment because they tend to be more labour intensive than larger firms, so having a proportionately larger effect on employment as they grow.

However, there are other ways in which the growth of the small firm sector might be important to the economy. In particular, they are important in providing training and it is generally argued that they can respond more flexibly to changes in market conditions because of their ability to vary output more quickly than larger firms.

THE GROWTH OF FIRMS

There are many reasons why any individual firm might grow but the major factors are probably a desire to achieve increased profits and/or a desire to achieve greater security. Of course, larger firms are not always the most profitable or the most secure, but because they often experience economies of scale they have clear advantages in both of these areas over smaller firms.

The methods by which firms grow can be classified as internal or external:

66 Internal and external growth 99

- **Internal growth** occurs when firms plough back profits into additional fixed assets and so expand their productive capacity.
- **External growth** occurs when one firm combines its existing assets with the assets of at least one other firm.

ACQUISITIONS AND MERGERS

An **acquisition** occurs when one firm purchases another firm from its shareholders. This is often referred to as a **take-over** of one firm by another firm. A **merger**, on the other hand, is a voluntary agreement between two or more firms to combine their assets into a single firm. While the techniques used to achieve external growth might differ, the motives are often the same.

Reasons for amalgamation

Firms might prefer external growth for a variety of reasons. There might be specific reasons depending on the type of amalgamation or integration which takes place. These are discussed in the following section. Here we focus on some of the more general factors that might explain why firms amalgamate.

❝ Some reasons why firms seek external growth ❞

- External growth can mean the immediate transfer of existing brand loyalty and goodwill which takes time to build up and is not immediately available when a firm grows internally. In other words, when one firm acquires another firm it also acquires whatever consumer loyalty exists for the acquired firm's brands. The advantage of this is that if a firm grows internally it has to persuade additional customers to consume its products.

- External growth is sometimes used as a means of diversifying. **Diversification** is important because it increases security for a firm. A firm that produces only a single product, or a small number of related products is vulnerable to changes in demand for its product. Diversification increases the chances of long-run survival. Here again it might be considered more expedient to acquire an existing firm already in the market than to attempt entry into the market as an outsider. In such cases, the costs of entry can sometimes be high and when an additional producer undertakes supply it usually means an increased number of firms competing for the same fixed market. This can be a dangerous strategy!

- Sometimes external growth offers the prospect of better locations. This is particularly important in retailing.

- Amalgamation might be a mean of pooling expertise and sharing the costs of research and development (R&D) expenditure as in the case of electronics where the R&D expenditures are high. This is particularly appealing when an industry is dominated by an existing producer or where there is a threat of increased competition from abroad.

- A possible motive for an acquisition is **asset stripping**. This occurs when one firm takes over another firm with the intention of breaking the firm up into smaller units which are then resold. This is likely to happen when the price of a firm's equity on the stock market does not reflect the real values of its assets. One reason for this is that management of the firm is incompetent so that profits and dividends have been relatively low. If this were the only reason for asset stripping, it might seem that it performed a useful role and the threat of being taken over would most likely encourage efficient management. However, the threat of being taken over might actually encourage inefficiency rather than a long-run perspective. They might therefore prefer to recommend higher dividends to shareholders rather than ploughing back profits into long-run growth and projects likely to increase long-run efficiency. This is a very real possibility. Corporate raiders are always on the look-out for possible gains from asset stripping regardless of why these possible gains exist. For example, a firm might find the value of its equity is reduced if it has embarked on an expansion programme using ploughed-back profits. It therefore could be vulnerable to the threat of a take-over before the benefits of its policies materialise.

HORIZONTAL AND VERTICAL INTEGRATION

Horizontal integration

Horizontal integration occurs when firms in the same industry and at the same stage of the production process amalgamate. There are many motives for horizontal integration:

- Sometimes firms integrate in order to **rationalise production**, i.e. to concentrate production in the most profitable units. Such a policy, by reducing capacity in he industry, might reduce fixed costs and also result in higher prices. The combined effect might be to raise the overall profitability of firms in the industry.

Reasons for horizontal integration

■ Another motive might be to take advantage of **economies of scale**, especially technical economies in the case of manufacturing firms. Since firms are at the same stage of production the desire to reap economies of scale is a particularly important motive for horizontal integration.

■ It is possible that horizontal integration might be motivated by the desire to **create a monopoly** in the industry. Whatever the motive, since firms are at the same stage of production, it is easy to see that horizontal integration could lead to the formation of a monopoly. For example, if a firm is able to gain control of the retail outlets or of the supply of a particular input, it could effectively restrict the growth of competition and exercise monopoly power.

Vertical integration

Vertical integration occurs when firms in the same industry but at different stages of the production process amalgamate. We can identify two forms of this:

Reasons for vertical integration

■ **Vertical integration backwards** This occurs when firms amalgamate with other firms in a way which brings them closer to their raw material suppliers. For example, if a newspaper publisher took over a paper mill this would be vertical integration backwards.

■ **Vertical integration forwards** This brings a firm closer to its retail outlets. For example, if a brewery took over a chain of public houses, this would be vertical integration forwards.

There are several possible reasons for vertical integration:

■ Firms might integrate vertically for **strategic reasons**. In the case of backward integration, the aim might be to safeguard the delivery or quality of raw material. The aim of forward integration might be to ensure that the firm has a chain of retail outlets through which its products can be distributed.

■ Firms might improve and control the **image** of the retail outlets through which the product is distributed with the aim of increasing sales.

■ Firms might gain **economies of scale** from either forwards or backwards integration. The increased size of the firm might make financial or managerial economies possible, for example. There might also be economies from linked processes (see p. 37).

■ Integration might lead to a **reduction in costs**. For example, when a firm acquires control of raw materials supplies, inspection costs and reject rates might fall. In addition, having a reliable source of raw materials might enable firms to operate with lower stocks. Similarly, if firms acquire retail outlets they might be better able to predict market demand or respond more quickly to any increase in market demand. Here again, firms will be able to operate with lower stocks than previously.

APPLIED MATERIALS

An article in the *Department of Employment Gazette*, February 1992, provides information on the small firm sector. Table 7.1 provides a comparison between 1979 and 1989.

		Share of total (per cent)			Cumulative (per cent)		
Employment size band	Number of businesses (thousand)	Businesses	Employment	Turnover	Businesses	Employment	Turnover
1979							
1–2	1,099	61.4	6.6	3.4	61.4	6.6	3.4
3–5	319	17.8	5.9	2.4	79.2	12.4	5.8
6–10	179	10.0	6.7	3.3	89.1	19.1	9.1
11–19	109	6.1	7.6	3.6	95.2	26.7	12.6
20–49	46	2.6	6.9	5.3	97.8	33.6	17.9
50–99	16	0.9	5.3	7.9	98.7	38.9	25.8
100–199	15	0.8	10.2	16.4	99.5	49.1	42.2
200–499	5	0.3	8.1	8.2	99.8	57.3	50.4
500–999	2	0.1	7.5	10.2	99.9	64.7	60.6
1,000+	2	0.1	35.3	39.4	100.0	100.0	100.0
All	1,791						
1989							
1–2	2,025	67.8	12.3	4.2	67.8	12.3	4.2
3–5	596	19.9	10.0	4.7	87.7	22.4	8.9
6–10	181	6.1	6.3	4.1	93.8	28.7	13.0
11–19	92	3.1	6.0	4.3	96.9	34.6	17.3
20–49	57	1.9	7.7	6.0	98.8	42.3	23.3
50–99	18	0.6	5.8	3.7	99.4	48.1	27.0
100–199	9	0.3	7.2	13.6	99.7	55.2	40.6
200–499	6	0.2	10.6	17.9	99.9	65.8	58.4
500–999	2	0.1	6.7	11.2	100.0	72.5	69.6
1,000+	1	0.0	27.5	30.4	100.0	100.0	100.0
All	2,988						

Number of businesses, employment and turnover share by size band, UK

Table 7.1 Information on the changes in the contribution of firms of different sizes, end of 1979 to end of 1989.

Source: Department of Employment Gazette, Feb. 1992.

At the end of 1989, there were almost 3 million businesses in the United Kingdom. Of these, almost 94 per cent employed fewer than 11 people and almost 97 per cent employed fewer than 20 people. This represents quite a considerable change on the position in 1979 when there were fewer than 1.8 million businesses in the UK. Of these, fewer than 90 per cent employed fewer than 11 people and just over 95 per cent employed fewer than 20 people.

Over the decade 1979–89, the total number of businesses in the UK increased by almost 67 per cent – an average of almost 500 firms every working day! This was mainly due to growth of very small firms. Whereas in 1979, there were almost 1.1. million firms employing fewer than three people, this number had increased to over 2 million by 1989, a percentage increase of over 84 per cent. This contrasts with only a small increase in the number of firms employing 6–10 people and a decline in the number of firms employing 11–19 people.

Despite these impressive statistics, which give some credibility to notions of an enterprise economy, some caution is necessary in interpreting the statistics. Employment levels in the different size bands are regarded as a fairly reliable indicator of firm size, but less reliance can be placed on turnover which includes a whole series of imperfections due to the way turnover is measured. However, there are other problems which more directly reflect the shortcomings of turnover as a measure of size. In particular, the turnover of a business includes all of the variable costs of production (as well as a contribution to fixed costs) such as the costs of materials and intermediate goods purchased as inputs. Because of this, a firm which assembles components into finished goods will have a considerably higher turnover than a firm which manufactures the components. Data on turnover are therefore subject to far greater uncertainty than data on employment.

While employment is undoubtedly a superior measure of size than turnover, it is not a perfect measure of size. Some businesses might be capital intensive and employ relatively few people while others might be labour intensive and employ relatively large numbers of people. Nevertheless employment is regarded as the most reliable guide to firm size.

SMALL FIRMS AND FINANCE

Sources of finance for UK industry vary with the size of company. Smaller firms rely on personal savings at the start-up stage but then obtain some 60 per cent of external financing from banks, although very small firms also use hire purchase and leasing arrangements. The relationship between smaller firms and banks is therefore of vital importance for this sector of UK industry. The rate of interest for the smallest firms employing less than 30 employees is between 3 per cent and 5 per cent above base rates and this is often doubled if the overdraft is exceeded, even if only briefly. International comparisons of interest rate charges paid by small firms in 1994 did not show significant differences but it should be noted that in France small businesses of under 20 employees could obtain soft loans at 2 per cent below base rates, whilst in Germany, the Kreditanstalt für Wiederaufbau refinances commercial loans to smaller firms at reduced rates.

Another problem for UK small firms is the *debt structure*. As can be seen in Table 7.2 the debt structure of the UK smaller firms differs significantly from elsewhere in the European Union. The most obvious difference is in the high proportion of UK overdraft finance and the low proportion of term loans in the UK as compared with the others. The major disadvantage of overdrafts is that they are payable on demand and therefore restrict the ability of smaller firms to take a long term view. Term loans on the other hand mean that both the company and the bank have a longer term commitment to the relationship. There is a rather belated move in the UK towards longer term loans. For example, the National Westminster Bank now provides 52 per cent of its finance to smaller firms on a medium or long-term basis.

	OVERDRAFT	SHORT TERM LOANS	LONG TERM LOANS	SUBSIDISED LOANS	LEASE & HIRE PURCHASE
UK	58	18	11	3	10
Germany	14	36	31	8	11
France	31	26	23	1	19
Italy	35	26	18	15	6
* Up to five years					

Table 7.2 Debt structure of smaller firms (% of total debt) 1991

Source: House of Commons, 1994.

Another major issue regarding the relationship between UK banks and small firms concerns the basis on which loans were provided. A detailed study in 1992 of financing arrangements in the Netherlands, Germany and the UK found that UK bank officials who were assessing company risk were more dependent on a narrow range of financial information and on the potential of the entrepreneur. Again, the Bank of England has noticed some 'improvement' in the UK in that the commercial banks now appear to be taking lending decisions based less on security and more on cash flow and business plans.

A final problem is that UK banks have been criticised for not providing small firms with sufficient *liquidity* to avert bankruptcy, unlike the German banking system which is more flexible in such situations. This seems to indicate that there may be failures of understanding among UK banks of how to help small businesses in both growth and recession periods. In contrast with Germany and Japan, the UK has no regional banks which are likely to have greater knowledge of local industry and can develop mutual trust between bank and small firms. Also the big UK commercial banks often lack a strong local or regional career structure, so that managers are often shifted across country and find it difficult to get to know their locality before they are moved on. However, the National Westminster Bank have recently begun a scheme whereby managers are moved only *within* each of their 19 regions.

EXAMINATION QUESTIONS

1 If economies of scale are so significant, why are there so many small firms in the economy?

(AEB November 1992)

2 (a) Explain the trend towards increasing size of firms selling in national and international markets. *(13)*
  (b) Discuss the costs and benefits for consumers and employees resulting from the trend described in (a). *(12)*

(Total 25 marks)
(Scottish Higher, 1989)

3 (a) How would you compare the sizes of firms? *(5)*
  (b) Account for the simultaneous existence of firms of different size within the same industry. *(7)*
  (c) Is an increase in industrial concentration necessarily undesirable for the economy? *(8)*

(Total 20 marks)
(Cambridge, June 1988)

4 'Only large firms can exploit economies of scale.
  Economies of scale lead to lower costs.
  Lower costs lead to lower prices.
  Therefore, large firms are good for society.'
  Discuss.

5 Explain what the economist means by a 'firm' and why organisations as diverse as ICI and a corner shop can be said to possess the same essential characteristics from the economic viewpoint. Consider the possible reason why approximately 90 per cent of firms in the UK are 'small'.

(NEAB, 1987)

ANSWERS TO EXAMINATION QUESTIONS

OUTLINE ANSWERS

Question 1
You could begin your answer to this question by explaining what economies of scale are, why they are important and how firms experience them. The important point to stress is that economies of scale give large firms significant cost advantages over smaller firms. There is no doubt that in some industries economies of scale are highly significant (see Ch. 3). Despite this, small firms continue to survive. The reasons for their survival are discussed on pages 118–119.

Question 2
(a) The main reason for the trend towards large firms is undoubtedly the availability of significant economies of scale particularly in manufacturing but also in the provision of certain services such as financial services. Economies of scale are discussed on pages 36–38.

  However, another factor is that governments now adopt a more lenient attitude towards the growth of large firms and even when a merger threatens to create a monopoly situation there is no automatic referral to the Monopolies and Mergers Commission for investigation. Even when an investigation by the MMC produces an unfavourable report on the desirability of a merger, the government sometimes allows the merger to proceed.

The most likely reason for this is that economies of scale lead to larger firms abroad as well as in the UK. These firms seek further expansion by increasing international sales and have been encouraged by a reduction in certain barriers to trade. For example, membership of the EU has encouraged the growth of large European firms.

(b) One benefit to consumers from selling in international markets is that choice is increased. There is a greater range of goods from which to choose. This also implies an increase in competition which is likely to have a favourable impact on prices. You could usefully illustrate and discuss this in terms of a standard supply and demand diagram.

Greater competition might also produce longer run advantages by stimulating investment in research and development. It is also possible that the increased size of the market will make it possible for firms to reap economies of scale and again prices might fall as a result. This is good news for consumers but might be bad news for employees. If foreign firms increase sales at the expense of domestic firms, then domestic employers will require fewer workers. If the situation is reversed and domestic firms increase sales, then wages and employment in the domestic economy might well rise.

On the other hand, increased competition might eventually lead to some firms being driven out of the industry and the emergence of a monopoly. Similarly, the existence of economies of scale might promote the emergence of monopoly. This might adversely affect the interests of consumers because monopolists have the power to drive up market prices by restricting supply. Again, you could illustrate this diagrammatically. Note also that, if it is an overseas firm which emerges as the dominant firm, then this will adversely affect employment in the domestic economy. However, if a domestic firm gains the advantage then domestic employment and wages might rise.

Question 3

(a) Firm size can be measured in various ways, such as numbers employed, value of capital employed, value of turnover, etc. Remember that the same criterion must be used when comparing the sizes of firms in the same industry.

(b) Industries can consist of firms of differing size for many reasons. The main reason for the existence of larger firms is, of course, economies of scale. However, large firms might not compete as aggressively against smaller firms as they could, so as to avoid their own emergence as a monopoly. Smaller firms can offer more personal attention, which is important when consumers demand variety, as in clothing for example. In addition, they can often respond more quickly to changes in demand by consumers than larger firms. In some cases, smaller firms supply part of the market which is of no interest to larger firms. In building for example, there are large firms such as Wimpey and Barrett who have no interest in tendering for house extensions because they have expensive pieces of capital equipment which can only be used economically on large projects. Jobbing builders on the other hand have no such overheads. In retailing, large firms offer lower prices but smaller corner shops offer convenience and personal service since they are often prepared to deliver groceries and in some cases to extend credit to regular customers. Sometimes they might also offer competitive prices because they organise themselves into a large buying chain, for example, Happy Shopper.

(c) Increasing size and concentration of production in fewer hands is traditionally thought to reduce competition within an industry. However, an oligopolistic market is highly concentrated and yet competition in such a market is often fierce! You could discuss the different types of competition that might exist in oligopolistic markets (see p. 110). However, increasing concentration often implies a reduction in competition. When there are many firms and a low degree of concentration, there is greater consumer choice and therefore a high degree of competition.

It is also possible that increasing concentration will result in barriers to entry and it is possible that firms in a protected market will slow down the process of innovation because they have less incentive to invest in research and development. There might also be diseconomies of scale from increasing concentration especially the lack of managerial expertise required to control and co-ordinate larger firms.

Question 4

Again you could begin your answer to this question by explaining economies of scale. It is not strictly correct that only large firms can exploit economies of scale. They are available as firms grow! However, it is certainly correct that when firms exploit economies of scale their average costs of production fall. It would be useful to explain why this is so, perhaps including a numerical example to show that economies of scale imply that total output rises by a proportionately greater amount than total costs, i.e. average costs fall. However, there is no guarantee that lower costs will lead to lower prices! They might do and you could argue that if costs are falling these will be passed on to consumers so that firms restrict the emergence of competition or increase their profit if demand is elastic and costs fall faster than prices.

However, it is also possible that falling average costs will simply lead to higher profit per unit for firms who make no adjustment to the price of their product. This is more likely to happen when economies of scale are significant and lead to a single firm dominating the market. If a firm exploits its monopoly position, this will almost certainly be to the detriment of society. The possible abuses of monopoly power are discussed on p. 91. Even if a monopoly situation is not created, when markets consist of a few large firms, there will be a sub-optimal allocation of resources and again this will be to the detriment of society.

Question 5

Economists define a firm as a unit of ownership through which decisions are taken to transform inputs into outputs. Note that a firm might control any number of establishments where part of the production process takes place.

ICI and independent corner shops possess some similar characteristics and you are asked to identify and discuss these. One obvious similarity is that they both exist to generate a profit for their owner(s). They do this by combining the factors of production to satisfy consumer demand. In both cases, decisions about what to produce and how it is to be produced are taken by the entrepreneur. In a small independent corner shop this role might be performed by one person; it is shared between salaried managers and shareholders in joint stock companies such as ICI. In answering this part of the question you should therefore consider the functions of the entrepreneur (see p. 32).

The latter part of the question asks about the reasons for the survival of small firms. The relevant points are discussed on page 118 but you should also try to include examples to illustrate these points. The retail trade, the professions, repair work, photography, bespoke tailoring and building are examples where small firms are common.

Further reading

Griffiths and Wall (eds), *Applied Economics: An Introductory Course* (6th edn), Longman 1995: Ch. 4, The small firm; Ch. 5, Mergers and acquisitions in the growth of the firm.

REVIEW SHEET

1 List three key characteristics of a small firm.

(a) _____

(b) _____

(c) _____

2 Explain why it is difficult to use data to compare small firms in the UK with small firms in other countries.

_____

_____

_____

_____

3 Suggest eight main reasons why small firms continue to exist.

(a) _____

(b) _____

(c) _____

(d) _____

(e) _____

(f) _____

(g) _____

(h) _____

4 Why have governments taken such an interest in small firms?

_____

_____

_____

_____

5 Distinguish between an acquisition (take-over) and a merger.

_____

_____

_____

_____

6 Why do firms seek to grow by amalgamation (acquisition or merger)?

_____

_____

_____

_____

7 What is horizontal integration? Give an example.

_____

_____

_____

8 List three motives for horizontal integration.

(a) _____

(b) _____

(c) _____

9 What is vertical integration? Give an example.

_____

_____

_____

_____

_____

10 List three motives for vertical integration.

(a) _____

_____

(b) _____

_____

(c) _____

_____

11 Turn back to Table 7.1 (p. 122). Comment on the changing contribution of firms with 1–5 employees between 1979 and 1989.

_____

_____

_____

_____

_____

_____

12 Why might a firm seek to grow by a conglomerate merger (i.e. diversification)? Give an example.

_____

_____

_____

_____

_____

_____

_____

_____

_____

_____

_____

GETTING STARTED

National income is a measure of the value of the output of the goods and services produced by an economy over a period of time. Since national income measures production per period of time it is referred to as a flow concept. There is often considerable confusion between stocks and flows. A **stock** is the total accumulated quantity of any item existing at a particular time. A **flow**, on the other hand, measures the rate at which that stock is changing. When we are running a bath, for example, the quantity of water in the bath itself is the total stock of water, whereas the rate at which we are adding to that stock of water is the flow of water. Similarly, when we measure national income, we are measuring the flow of output over a period of time, and this period is invariably one year.

National income is defined as a flow of output; however, it is the money value of that flow of output which is usually measured. It is not really practical to measure it as so many houses, so many cars, so many washing machines and so on, produced annually because we have no way of adding these together except in terms of their money value. Nevertheless, one reason for computing national income figures is to provide an accurate estimate of changes in the volume of output produced during one year, which can then be compared with other years. It would be misleading to simply compare the money value of output produced in two separate years because inflation will lead to a higher money value in later years irrespective of whether the volume of output has increased. In order to see what has happened to *real* national income when two years are compared, we must remove the effect of inflation on prices from data. In other words, we must measure national income at constant prices. An example will illustrate how this is done.

	National income (£m)	Index of prices
Year 1	50,000	100
Year 2	55,000	105

Between Year 1 and Year 2, the money value of national income has increased by 10 per cent. However, prices have increased by 5 per cent over the same period, so that the value of national income in Year 2 in terms of Year 1 prices is:

$$£55,000 \times \frac{100}{105} = £52,381\text{m (approx)}$$

Because we have measured national income at constant prices we can say that the volume of output or real national income, has increased by approximately 4.8 per cent compared with a rise in money national income of 10 per cent.

CHAPTER 8

NATIONAL INCOME ACCOUNTING

THE CIRCULAR FLOW OF INCOME

GROSS DOMESTIC PRODUCT AND GROSS NATIONAL PRODUCT

GROSS NATIONAL PRODUCT AND NET NATIONAL PRODUCT

MEASURING THE NATIONAL INCOME

NATIONAL INCOME AND THE STANDARD OF LIVING

INTERNATIONAL COMPARISONS OF THE STANDARD OF LIVING

USES OF NATIONAL INCOME STATISTICS

APPLIED MATERIALS

ESSENTIAL PRINCIPLES

IN THEORY

We have seen that national income is the value of output produced by a country over a period of time. However, the factors of production which create this output will receive rewards in the form of wages, interest, rent and profit. For the economy as a whole the value of output produced must equal the gross income paid to the factors of production. This is unlikely to be true for any individual firm in the economy because, in addition to paying factor rewards, firms will use part of the revenue from selling their output to cover other costs of production in respect of raw material purchases, power to drive machinery, and so on. Nevertheless, for all firms in the economy, the aggregate value of final output produced must equal the value of gross factor incomes. Hence national output equals national income.

> 66 National output =
> national income 99

IN PRACTICE

In practice, indirect taxes and subsidies may distort this identity. Indirect taxes are collected by the Customs and Excise Department; they are placed on goods and services and are paid by firms during the process of production. The most widely known indirect tax is VAT. Indirect taxes will raise the market prices of the goods or services above those which are necessary to cover all factor rewards. We must therefore *subtract* indirect taxes from the value of output if we are to arrive at our identity. Subsidies will have the opposite effect, reducing market prices below factor cost, so that these must be *added* to the value of output, if the identity is to be maintained.

ADDITIONS TO STOCK AND WORK IN PROGRESS

It is possible to look at national income in yet another way. Incomes received by the factors of production over any given period of time must equal the total expenditure on national output over the same period of time. However, at any moment in time this will not necessarily be true. Some output will only be partially complete, while some will be complete but not yet sold. In both cases, labour will have been paid, with the result that gross factor incomes will exceed aggregate expenditure. The official statistics refer to incomplete or unsold output as additions to stock and work in progress. Over time, as additions to stock and work in progress are sold, the flow of expenditure will equal the flow of gross incomes paid to the factors of production. However, statistics are compiled at the end of some accounting period when there will always be unsold output and work in progress. For accounting purposes, it is therefore convenient to treat the item 'additions to stock and work in progress' as output which has been purchased by firms. In other words, it is regarded as investment by firms and as such is counted as expenditure.

BASIS OF THE CIRCULAR FLOW OF INCOME

> 66 We can use income,
> output and expenditure as
> methods of
> measurement 99

By adopting the procedures outlined above, we establish the basic accounting identity:

national income ≡ national output ≡ national expenditure

This accounting identity is the basis of the circular flow of income illustrated in Fig. 8.1 As it stands, this diagram is highly unrealistic. It neglects the fact that saving and investment take place in the economy; it neglects the role of government in the economy and also the fact that, in the real world, international trade takes place. However, the diagram does illustrate the very important principle of the circular flow of income, and we shall see in Chapter 9 that it forms the basis of an understanding of the actual flows of income in the economy.

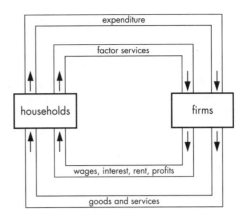

Fig. 8.1 The circular flow of income

GROSS DOMESTIC PRODUCT AND GROSS NATIONAL PRODUCT

66 Know the difference between domestic and national 99

Gross Domestic Product (GDP) is the value of output produced by factors of production located *within* the UK. In other words, it is the sum total of all incomes earned by UK residents when producing goods and services with resources located inside the UK. However, the main official measure of total output is **Gross National Product (GNP)**. This measures the total value of output produced, and incomes received, by UK residents from the ownership of resources, wherever these happen to be located. GNP therefore takes account of the fact that some UK residents earn incomes such as rent and profit from owning resources abroad.

FLOW OF INCOME FROM ABROAD

The flow of income from abroad mainly arises because foreign subsidiaries remit payments to the UK parent company. These are referred to as *property income received from abroad*. Similarly, foreign subsidiaries located in the UK remit payments abroad and these are referred to as *property income paid abroad*. The difference between these two flows of *property income* is referred to as net property income from abroad. It may be positive or negative, depending on whether there is a net inflow or net outflow of funds, i.e.

GDP + net property income from abroad = GNP

GROSS NATIONAL PRODUCT AND NET NATIONAL PRODUCT

66 Distinguish gross from net 99

Gross National Product is the total value of incomes received by UK residents in the course of a year. It therefore includes the full value of plant and equipment produced during the course of the year (i.e. gross domestic fixed capital formation). However, over this period existing plant and equipment will have **depreciated**, i.e. declined in value due to wear and tear and obsolescence. In order to obtain a true measure of national income an appropriate deduction for capital depreciation must be made, i.e.

GNP – depreciation = **Net National Product (NNP)**

NNP is the aggregate that is most usually taken to mean national income.

WHY IS GNP THE OFFICIAL MEASURE?

This raises the very interesting question that if net national product is national income, then why is GNP the main official measure of the value of incomes received? The answer is simple. Net national product is *conceptually* the better measure, but in practice it is impossible to estimate the value of depreciation. How can we measure the value of wear and tear over the course of a year, or assess the rate of obsolescence? In fact, estimates of depreciation tend to be influenced more by the technicalities of income tax than by other considerations. It is far easier to measure investment gross than net. It is therefore GNP rather than NNP which is more likely to give values of output and income which can be meaningfully compared overtime, and between countries.

MARKET PRICES AND FACTOR COST

Before considering the problems involved in actually measuring income, we must distinguish between national income at market prices and national income at factor cost. National income at **market prices** simply means that the value of output and expenditure has not been adjusted to take account of the effect of indirect taxes and subsidies. As we noted above, this must be done if we are to obtain an accurate estimate of the incomes paid to the factors of production. Deducting that part of expenditure paid in taxes, and adding on any subsidies received by firms, leaves us with national income at **factor cost**, i.e.

NNP at market prices − indirect taxes + subsidies = NNP at factor cost

OUTPUT[1]	£m
Agriculture, hunting, forestry and fishing	9309
Mining and quarrying including oil and gas extraction	9842
Manufacturing	114698
Electricity, gas and water supply	13717
Construction	32002
Wholesale and retail trade including hotels, repairs and restaurants	72549
Transport, storage and communication	41613
Financial intermediation, real estate, renting and business activities	121704
Public administration, national defence and compulsory social security	36605
Education, health and social work	52509
Other services including sewage and refuse collection	32892
Less Adjustment for financial services[2]	−23058
Statistical discrepancy[3]	212
Gross Pomestic product at factor cost	514594
Net property income from abroad	87348
Gross National Product at factor cost	601942
Less Capital consumption	−63984
National Income	537958

INCOME	£m
Income from employment	341009
Income from self-employment	58060
Gross profit and interest	89534
Rent	46846
Imputed charge for capital consumption	4207
Less Stock appreciation	−2216
Less Adjustment for financial services	−23058
Statistical discrepancy	212
Gross Domestic Product at factor cost	514594
Net property income from abroad	87348
Gross National Product at factor cost	601942
Less Capital consumption	−63984
National income	537958

EXPENDITURE	£m
Consumers' expenditure	382696
General government final consumption of which:	
Central government	82477
Local authorities	49901
Gross Domestic Fixed Capital Formation	92892
Less Value of physical increase in stocks and work in progress	−1992
Total Domestic Expenditure at market price	605974
Exports	139827
Less Imports	−149164
Statistical discrepancy	−472
Gross Domestic Product at market prices	596165
Net property income from abroad	87348
Taxes on expenditure	−87679
Subsidies	6108
Gross National Product at factor cost	601942
Less Capital consumption	−63984
National Income	537958

1 *The contribution of each industry to GDP after providing for stock appreciation.*
2 *To avoid some double counting of interest paid on loans, and interest received by financial institutions.*

3 *The statistical discrepancy includes all errors and omissions. It has a different value in the expenditure estimates than in the estimates for output and income because estimates of GDP are built up from independent data on incomes expenditure. The statistical discrepancy is the difference between these estimates, but there is no implication that expenditure estimates are superior in accuracy.*

Source: National Income and Expenditure, HMSO 1993.

Table 8.1 United Kingdom national income in 1992 (£ million)

MEASURING THE NATIONAL INCOME

National income can be measured in any one of the three ways (see Table 8.1). In theory because they all purport to measure the same aggregate, they should all give exactly the same total. However, in practice this is unlikely to be the case. We are dealing with extremely large aggregates arising out of tens of millions of transactions of varying amounts paid over varying time periods. In these circumstances, it would be miraculous indeed if all three measures gave exactly the same result. Additionally, we shall see below that some transactions are recorded in one measure of national income (namely expenditure), but because of illegal dealings there is no counterpart in other measures. The existence of this so-called *Black Economy* also makes it unlikely that all three aggregates will balance.

In discussing the three methods of measuring national income, we shall frequently illustrate out points with reference to Table 8.1.

THE OUTPUT METHOD

A country's national income can be calculated from the **output** figures of all firms in the economy. However, this does not mean that we simply add together the value of each firm's output. To do so would give us an aggregate many times greater than the national income because of *double counting*. The point is that the outputs of some firms are the inputs of other firms. For example, the output of the steel industry is partly the factor input for the automobile industry, and so on. Clearly, to include the total value of each industry's output in national income calculations would mean counting the value of the steel used in automobile production twice. Double counting can be avoided by summing the **value added** at each stage of production, *or* by adding together the **final value** of output produced.

> Summing value added avoids double counting

Whichever method is used to obtain the value of output produced, we must ensure that both additions to stock and work in progress are included in the output figures for each sector. These output figures are shown in the first column of Table 8.1. Given this, certain adjustments to the output figures are needed in order to obtain the value of the national income.

Public goods and merit goods
We have already seen, in Chapter 2, that the government provides many goods and services through the non-market sector, such as education, medical care, defence, and so on. Such goods and services are clearly part of the nation's output, but since they are not sold through the market sector, strictly they do not have a market price. In such cases, the value of the output is measured at resource cost or **factor cost**. In other words, the value of the service is assumed to be equivalent to the cost of the resources used to provide it. For instance, the value of education, health and social work was estimated to be £52,509m in 1992, but most of this was the cost of purchasing equipment and the cost of hiring teachers, doctors, nurses and administrators in providing that output, and only a small proportion of these services were sold on the market.

Self-provided commodities
A similar problem arises in the case of self-provided commodities, such as vegetables grown in the domestic garden, car repairs and home improvements done on a do-it-yourself basis, etc. Again, these represent output produced, but there is no market value of such output. The vast majority of self-provided commodities are omitted from the national income statistics.

Exports and imports
Not all of the nation's output is consumed domestically. Part is sold abroad as exports. Nevertheless, GDP is the value of domestically produced output and so export earnings must be included in this figure. If exports were omitted, the value of output produced would be less than the value of incomes received from producing that output. Table 8.1 shows that in 1992 export earnings accounted for over 23 per cent of GDP.

> Remember to deduct imports

On the other hand, a great deal of domestically produced output incorporates imported raw materials and there is a considerable amount of consumer expenditure on imported goods and services. Expenditure on imports results in a flow of factor incomes abroad. Hence the value of the import content of the final output must be *deducted* from the output figures if GDP is to be accurately measured. Failure to do this would result in the value of total output exceeding the value of incomes received from producing that output. Table 8.1 shows that import expenditure was equivalent to just over 25 per cent of GDP in 1992.

Net property income from abroad

This source of income to domestic residents will not be included in the output figures of firms. We have already noted that the net inflow (+) or outflow (–) of funds must be added to GDP when calculating the value of domestically owned output, i.e. GNP. This gives a figure of £601,942m for GNP in 1992. When we subtract depreciation of capital (capital consumption) we are left with a national income (NNP) of £537,958m.

THE INCOME METHOD

> 66 Gross values of income are summed 99

When calculating national product as a flow of incomes, it is important to ensure that only **factor rewards** are included. In other words, only those incomes paid in return for some productive activity and for which there is a corresponding output, are included in national income. Of course, it is the *gross value* of these factor rewards which must be aggregated, since this represents the value of output produced. Levying taxes on factor incomes reduces the amount factors receive, but it does not reduce the value of output produced! Income from employment (£341,009m) and from self-employment (£58,060m) together make up over 66 per cent of GNP in 1992. When calculating the aggregate value of factor incomes, adjustments might also be necessary for other reasons.

Transfer payments

> 66 Exclude transfer payments 99

The sum of all factor incomes is not the same as the sum of all *personal* incomes, since the latter includes transfer payments. These are simply transfers of income within the community, and they are not made in respect of any productive activity. Indeed, the bulk of all transfer payments within the UK are made by the government for social reasons. Examples include social security payments, pensions, child allowances, and so on. Since no output is produced in respect of these payments they must not be included in the aggregate of factor incomes.

Undistributed surpluses

Another problem in aggregating factor incomes arises because not all factor incomes are distributed to the factors of production. Firms might retain part or all of their profits to finance future investment. Similarly, the profits of public bodies, such as nationalised industries, accrue to the government rather than to private individuals. Care must be taken to include these *undistributed surpluses* as factor incomes. The gross value of profits and undistributed surpluses was equal to £64,251m in 1992.

Stock appreciation

Care must be taken to deduct changes in the money value of stock caused by inflation. These are windfall gains, and do not represent a real increase in the value of output.

Net property income from abroad

When measuring either gross national product or net national product we have seen that it is necessary to add net property income from abroad to the aggregate of domestic incomes.

THE EXPENDITURE METHOD

> 66 Only expenditure on final output is added 99

The final method of calculating national income is as a flow of expenditure on domestic output. However, it is only expenditure on *final output* which must be aggregated, otherwise there is again a danger of double counting, with intermediate expenditure such as raw materials being counted twice. Additionally, it is only expenditure on *current output* which is relevant. Second-hand goods are not part of the current flow of output, and factors of production have already received payment for these goods at the time they were produced. We should note, however, that any income earned by a salesman employed in the second-hand trade, or the profits of second-hand dealers, are included in the national income statistics. The service these occupations render is part of current production!

Like the output and income totals, the value of expenditure in the economy must be adjusted if it is to measure national income accurately.

Consumers' expenditure

At £382,696m this is the major element in exenditure in 1992 accounting for over 63 per cent of total domestic expenditure.

General government final consumption

Since only domestic expenditure on goods and services is relevant, care must be taken to deduct any expenditure on transfer payments by the government or other public authorities. Such expenditures do not contribute directly to the current flow of output and, therefore, we must only include that part of public authorities' current expenditure which is spent directly on goods and services. In 1992, public authorities' expenditure on goods and services was £132,378m, i.e. just over 20 per cent of total domestic expenditure.

Gross investment

Expenditure on fixed capital, such as plant and machinery, must obviously be included in calculations of total expenditure. **Gross Domestic Fixed Capital Formation** incorporates this item and, at £92,892m, was 18 per cent of Total Domestic Expenditure. What is not so obvious is that *additions to stock and work in progress* also represent investment. The factors of production which have produced this, as yet, unsold output, will still have received factor payments. To ignore additions to stock and work in progress would therefore create an imbalance between the three aggregates of output, income and expenditure. Additions to stock and work in progress are therefore treated as though they have been purchased by firms. Care must be taken to include them in the aggregate of total expenditure. In 1992 the figure for this item came to –£1,992m, the negative figure indicating a run-down in the value of stock held and work in progress.

Exports and imports

We have already see that it is important to include exports and exclude imports from our calculation of national income. Care must again be taken to ensure this when aggregating total expenditures.

Net property income from abroad

As before, when moving from *domestic* to *national* income, it is important to include net property income from abroad when aggregating total expenditures.

Taxes and subsidies

In measuring the value of expenditure, we are attempting to measure the value of payments made to the factors of production which have produced that output. Indirect taxes raise total expenditure on goods and services relative to the amount received by the factors of production. Subsidies have the opposite effect. In order to avoid a discrepancy between the income and expenditure totals, it is necessary to remove the effects of taxes and subsidies from the latter. The expenditure total is adjusted to *factor cost* by deducting indirect taxes and adding subsidies.

NATIONAL INCOME AND THE STANDARD OF LIVING

66 An important measure of standard of living 99

The most widely used statistic for measuring changes in a country's standard of living is **per capita income**. This is GNP divided by total population and provides a measure of the average amount of output available per head per year. For comparisons to be accurate, it is necessary to ensure that GNP is measured at constant prices from one year to the next, otherwise per capita income would probably rise because of inflation but this would not necessarily imply that living standards had increased. Even measuring per capita income at constant prices does not provide an unambiguous measure of changes in living standards. The reasons for this are considered below.

66 Problems with per capita income measure 99

Changes in the number of hours worked

Changes in GNP might be influenced by changes in the number of hours worked. A reduction in the size of the working week or an increase in the number of annual days' holiday will have a positive effect on economic welfare even though GNP might be adversely affected. Comparisons of economic welfare should therefore include a measure of the increased value of leisure.

Qualitative changes in output

Another factor to consider is that, over time, there will be qualitative changes in the goods society consumes. Accurate comparisons of economic welfare must make some allowance for the additional satisfaction this improvement in quality confers on consumers.

Valuing public services

The government's privatisation programme might also reduce the reliability of GNP as an indicator of economic welfare, at least when comparing years in which changes are taking place. Public services, such as education, are valued at *resource cost*, but since the consumer has no choice about whether or not to purchase these commodities, this estimate of their 'worth' is arbitrary. Indeed, if it *over estimates* their worth for a particular commodity it is possible that a shift from public sector provision of services to private sector provision would reduce the recorded size of GNP without (at least initially) markedly affecting the level of economic welfare.

Non-market activities

Problems also arise because many services are performed neither by the government nor the market and therefore do not appear in the national income figures. The services of housewives are the biggest omission here, though gardening and home repairs are often done by members of the family. It is difficult to estimate the value of these but there is no doubt that their omission reduces the reliability of GNP as a measure of economic welfare. Despite this, their value is unlikely to change significantly from year to year and it is not thought that their exclusion seriously impairs the reliability of using GNP as a basis for comparing changes in economic welfare in the short term.

Military expenditure

Military expenditure is another important factor to consider. A great deal of such expenditure is undertaken simply to avoid giving a military advantage to potential aggressors. However, economic welfare only grows to the extent that higher military expenditure confers a greater sense of security on society. Where society values the additional security at an amount less than total military expenditure, GNP will overestimate the real value of output by that excess.

Environmental factors

Environmental considerations are an increasingly important factor in assessing economic welfare. One consequence of modern production is the pollution of air, soil and water, as well as the degradation of the environment. Such environmental 'costs' are unrecorded but reduce the real value of GNP below the official figures. As a consequence, the reliability of measured GNP is reduced.

Capital depreciation

Another reason why GNP might not be entirely accurate as a measure of economic welfare is that no allowance is made for capital depreciation. Over time, part of the nation's capital stock comes to the end of its working life and is scrapped. In calculating GNP, that part of output which simply replaces obsolete equipment is included and to this extent GNP inaccurately indicates the true value of economic welfare. Similarly, part of the nation's expenditure on education is necessary to maintain the stock of 'human capital' intact. It simply ensures continued availability of skills as people leave the labour force through retirement, and so on. Part of expenditure on education therefore simply covers 'depreciation' and its inclusion over estimates the real value of GNP.

INTERNATIONAL COMPARISONS OF THE STANDARD OF LIVING

Despite its shortcomings as a measure of living standards, per capita income is also used to compare the standard of living in different countries. However, there are several problems involved in such comparisons:

- Countries sometimes differ in the way they compute GNP. For example, unlike the UK, the Commonwealth of Independent States (former Soviet Union) does not include bus journeys made to or from work. The reason is that such journeys do not represent output that becomes available for consumption. They simply enable people to undertake production of goods and services for consumption by others. When GNP is computed differently, per capita income will be an unreliable guide to international living standards.

Problems with
international
comparisons

- There may be substantial differences in the composition of GNP. For example, some countries spend very large amounts on defence compared with other countries. It could be argued that devoting resources to defence preserves liberty and in this way adds to the standard of living. However, it is equally true that the opportunity cost of defence expenditure is a lower output of goods for domestic consumption. Again, some countries might devote considerably more resources to the accumulation of capital than others. This might make possible a higher level of output in the future, but only because consumption is foregone in the present. In such cases, international comparisons of GNP per head might give a misleading indication of *current* living standards.

- There are other natural or climatic factors that might give rise to differences in the composition of output. Therefore some countries will devote more resources to the production of heat and light than is the case in countries where these are provided freely by nature. In the latter countries, resources that are not needed to provide heat and light are available for the production of other goods and services. Again, per capita income might not be very different in two countries, yet there might be marked differences in actual living standards when one country benefits relative to the other from goods provided freely by nature.

- In some countries, per capita income might be relatively high in relation to domestic consumption. This is another important factor that might reduce the credibility of per capita income as a measure of living standards. Many OPEC countries, for example, have relatively high per capita incomes, but these are derived mainly from export earnings from the sale of oil unmatched by equivalent expenditure on imports. The true standard of living for most people in these countries is therefore relatively low, since domestic income per capita is well above domestic consumption per capita. The converse is also true. It is possible for countries to raise their standard of living in the short term by importing more than they export, i.e. by running a balance of payments deficit. In this case, domestic consumption is raised above its usual proportion of domestic income by increasing imports relative to exports.

  Clearly, variations between countries in the ratio of per capita income to per capita consumption can complicate the use of national income statistics in assessing standards of living.

- Even if countries do have similar per capita incomes and similar per capita levels of consumption, they may still have different standards of living for the majority of their respective populations. This would happen where the distribution of income was more equal in one country than in the other. It might also happen where taxation was significantly higher for the majority of the population in one country than in the other.

- Another factor to consider is the role of the 'black', or informal economy, i.e. those transactions which add to GNP but which are not recorded in the official statistics in different countries. If the black economy were equally significant in all countries, then per capita income would still be useful in comparing relative living standards. However, IMF estimates of the black economy put it as low as 2 per cent of GNP in some countries, and as high as 40 per cent in others. Additionally, living standards are influenced by the availability of leisure time, and the extent to which social costs are imposed on the population as a result of production and consumption. These factors clearly affect overall economic welfare and may vary considerably between countries, but they are not recorded in GNP. Because of this, differences in the standard of living between countries are quite consistent with similar per capita incomes.

- For purposes of international comparisons, there is the problem of converting per capita incomes into a common unit of account. In practice, this involves converting all per capita incomes into a single currency ($ USA) by using purchasing **power parities** (see below). Any inaccuracies in converting domestic currencies to dollars using purchasing power parities will impair the reliability of comparative per capita statistics.

USES OF NATIONAL INCOME STATISTICS

66 Reasons for calculating national income 99

Governments collect national income statistics for a variety of reasons:

■ National income statistics are important in the formulation and assessment of macro economic policy. It is clearly important to know current levels of output and patterns of expenditure when formulating policies to combat unemployment, inflation, balance of payments deficits, and so on.

■ National income statistics are used to monitor changes in real income. This is important because changes in real income have an important bearing on changes in living standards.

■ National income statistics are used to make international comparisons between the home country's economic performance and that of other countries. A relatively slow growth of real income is a strong indication that the economy is doing less well than it might, and often leads to a detailed scrutiny of the reasons for this 'shortfall'.

■ Per capita income statistics provide a guide to the standard of living in different countries and are used as a basis for allocating aid to third world countries.

APPLIED MATERIALS

INITIAL RESIDUAL DIFFERENCE

Table 8.1 shows how the national income accounts for 1992 were built up at current prices to give gross domestic product, gross national product and national income. Despite efforts to ensure accuracy in the compilation of these statistics, there is a great deal of economic activity which is unrecorded. Such activity is usually referred to as the **black economy**. It is alleged that, in the UK, the size of the black economy casts serious doubts on the credibility of official statistics and deprives the government of substantial income tax revenue.

One way in which the size of the black economy can be estimated is by taking the difference between total expenditure and total factor income. This assumes that individuals and organisations have less incentive and opportunity to conceal expenditures than receipts of income. The difference between these two aggregates (known as the **initial residual difference**) is estimated by the Central Statistical Office at 3 Qw per cent of GDP for the UK.

COMPARISON OF INTERNATIONAL LIVING STANDARDS

Despite the problems of measurement, GNP per capita is still the most widely used estimate of comparative living standards. Table 8.2 shows a recent comparison of international living standards in certain countries, converted into dollars using purchasing power parities.

Purchasing Power Parities (PPP) measure how many units of one country's currency are needed to buy exactly the same basket of goods as can be bought with a given amount of another country's currency. For example, how many pounds are required to buy what can be bought in the USA with a given amount of dollars. This is used as the basis for converting one currency into another currency for purposes of comparing certain aggregates such as GNP and GDP per head.

COUNTRY	GNP per head in 1992 (PPP $)
Ethiopia	310
Mozambique	620
Uganda	800
India	1150
Nigeria	1420
Philippines	2320
Indonesia	2350
Brazil	4780
Greece	7340
Saudi Arabia	8820
Singapore	14920
UK	14960
Finland	15620
Germany	16290
Japan	16950
USA	21360
Switzerland	21690

Table 8.2 International living standards in 1992.

Sources: Adapted from *Human Development Report,* UN, 1992; *World Development Report 1992*, World Bank.

EXAMINATION QUESTIONS

1 (a) Explain the differences between the income and expenditure methods of measuring national income. *(10)*
   (b) Discuss the value and limitations of national income statistics as a means of making international comparisons of living standards. *(15)*

   (UCLES November 1992)

2 (a) Distinguish between the cost of living and the standard of living. *(30)*
   (b) Examine the factors likely to improve the standard of living *either* in the UK or in a country of your choice over the next ten years. *(70)*

   (ULEAC January 1992)

3 (a) Distinguish between income and wealth. Indicate which of the two is more evenly distributed at present in the United Kingdom and suggest why this is the case. *(7)*
   (b) Outline the main components of the expenditure approach to measuring the national income. *(10)*
   (c) 'When attempting to measure economic welfare, knowledge of the distribution of national income is just as important as knowledge of its total size.' Discuss *(8)*

   (NICCEA June 1992)

4 Consider why each of the following items affecting a country's 'true' national income is difficult to measure and may cause the published statistics to be an inaccurate reflection of 'true' national income.
   (a) Capital consumption *(7)*
   (b) Services derived from owner-occupied housing *(6)*
   (c) The value of educational services provided by the government *(6)*
   (d) The time spent on 'do it yourself' car maintenance *(6)*

   (WJEC 1992)

5 (a) Distinguish between a country's gross domestic product and its gross national product.

(b) To what extent will these two measures differ for:
(i) a developed economy?
(ii) a developing economy?

ANSWERS TO EXAMINATION QUESTIONS

TUTOR'S ANSWER TO QUESTION 1

(a) National income is the flow of output that is produced during the course of a year. **Gross Domestic Product (GDP)** is the flow of output which is produced using resources located within a nation's frontiers. **Gross National Product (GNP)**, on the other hand, measures the flow of output produced with resources which are owned by the nation, wherever they might be located. The difference between the two flows is net property income from abroad. The word 'gross' in both of these measures of national income indicates that no account has been taken of depreciation, i.e. no account has been taken of the loss in value of resources that has occurred during the year.

GNP – depreciation = Net National Product (NNP)

and it is this measure which is usually taken to refer to national income.

Since national income is a flow of output, it can be measured as the value of income received, the value of expenditure incurred or the value of output produced. Using the income method, we calculate the value of incomes received from production, i.e. gross factor incomes. By far the most important factor income in terms of its contribution to national income is wages from employment. To this, we must add earnings of the self-employed, rent and profits. The rationale for computing the value of incomes received is that, by definition, they must be equal to the value of output produced.

A major problem with measuring national income by the income method is that care must be taken to avoid including *transfer payments*. Examples of transfer incomes are retirement pensions and sickness benefits. These are simply transfers of income within the community. They are not payments made in return for a factor input and are therefore unrelated to national income.

Summing the value of factor incomes in this way will give us GDP. To this, we must add net property income from abroad and subtract depreciation to yield net national income.

National income can also be measured as a **flow of expenditures**. It is necessary to include expenditure on domestic output net of any taxes or subsidies. It is also necessary to aggregate only final expenditures otherwise the value of inputs would be counted twice. We must therefore include consumer's expenditure, investment, public sector expenditure on goods and services, export expenditure and net property income from abroad. From this, we must deduct import expenditure and depreciation.

The rationale for summing the value of expenditures is that, by definition, the value of expenditure on output must be equal to the value of output produced.

(b) The most commonly used measure of the standard of living is **per capita income**. This is simply GNP divided by total population. To compare the standard of living in different countries, we need to convert GNP per capita in each case into a common currency. For convenience, the dollar is the most widely used currency for this purpose.

The rationale for using GNP per capita is that, to a large extent, the standard of living depends on income. If all other things remain equal, the higher the average level of income, the higher the average standard of living. GNP per capita is a measure of average income in a country and, by comparing GNP per capita in different countries, we have an indication of relative living standards.

GNP per capita has another advantage as a means of comparing living standards: since all countries compute data on GNP and population, it is relatively easy to derive an estimate of GNP per capita.

Despite this, there are several problems with using GNP per capita to make international comparisons of the standard of living. One important point to stress is that GNP per capita is simply an *average*. Where there are vast differences in the distribution of income between countries, comparing GNP per capita will give a misleading indication of relative living standards in each country.

There might also be substantial differences in the *composition* of GNP between countries. This is important because not all output makes an identifiable contribution to current living standards. For example, two countries might have similar levels of GNP per capita but one country might spend more on defence or investment than the other. It might be argued that defence expenditure helps preserve freedom, which affects the standard of living, and investment makes possible a higher level of output in the future. However, both imply a cut in the production of consumer goods and therefore a reduction in current living standards. Because of this, GNP per capita might be a misleading basis for comparing the standard of living between different countries.

Similarly, in some countries, *exports* constitute a relatively large proportion of GNP compared with other countries. If all other things are equal, the larger the volume of exports, the lower the current standard of living. Even when countries have similar levels of GDP per capita there might be considerable differences in volume of output available to the population for consumption.

Climatic factors will influence the amount of resources devoted to the production of heating. In some countries with warm climates, it will not be necessary to devote so much to the production of heating compared with countries, such as Russia, where the climate is colder. In such cases, resources will be available for other uses. Again, similar levels of GNP per capita will not necessarily imply a similar standard of living.

Another factor limiting the usefulness of GNP per capita to compare living standards in different countries is the *size of the black economy*. In some countries, such as Italy and many less developed countries, this might be relatively large. In such cases, GNP per capita will provide a misleading indicator of the true magnitude of GNP and will give erroneous results if per capita income is used to compare the standard of living in different countries.

There are many other factors that have an important influence on the standard of living but which are *unrecorded* in GNP statistics. These include the extent to which negative externalities are imposed on the community, life expectancy, the number of doctors per head of population, the extent of political freedom and so on. Where these differ substantially between countries, GNP per capita will not provide an accurate basis for comparing the standard of living.

There are clearly many factors which limit the value of GNP per capita for comparing the standard of living in different countries (remember also the problem of exchange rates and the need for using purchasing power parities to obtain meaningful comparisons). Despite these problems GNP per capita is the most widely used statistic for this purpose and, when used in conjunction with other indicators of the standard of living such as the number of doctors per head, it provides a useful guide.

STUDENT'S ANSWER TO QUESTION 2

(a) The **cost of living** is measured by the amount that has to be paid to purchase a given, representative, basket of goods and services. When the prices of those goods and services in the basket increase, it costs more to purchase them and therefore the cost of living has increased. Conversely, when the prices of goods and services in the basket fall, the cost of living falls.

> **Other aspects, such as quality of life might be mentioned here**

The **standard of living** is more difficult to define because it is influenced by many factors which cannot be measured accurately. In practice, the standard of living is most commonly measured by per capita income or GNP per head of population. This gives a guide to the average level of income per head but not to the amount the average individual can purchase because it tells us nothing of the price level or the distribution of income.

(b) Many factors will influence the standard of living in the UK over the next ten years. One important factor is the change in the total population. In fact, the population of the UK is expected to grow by about 4.2 per cent or just over 4 million over the next ten years. Another important factor is, of course, the growth in GNP. If this grows faster than total population, then per capita income in the UK will rise over the next ten years. Because of this it is important to identify the factors that will influence the rate of growth of GNP.

> **Good use of factual data**

> **Changes in age structure of population also important**

One very important factor is the amount firms devote to investment. The main reason real GNP has grown rapidly by historical standards in post-war years is the substitution of capital for labour. Capital is many times more efficient than labour. If interest rates remain at relatively low levels so that it is cheap for firms to borrow and finance investment, it is likely that real GNP will rise.

Government economic policy will also have an important bearing on changes in the standard of living over the next ten years. If governments can deal with the problems of recession so that aggregate demand in the economy is rising, firms will be persuaded to invest more. In times of recession, firms do not invest and this will have an unfavourable effect on the future standard of living.

> **Idea of accelerator theory, etc., might be mentioned**

Another factor that will have an important bearing on the standard of living over the next ten years is the growth of international trade. This has grown rapidly in post-war years and countries have tended to specialise in the production of those goods and services in which they are relatively efficient as compared with other countries. It is well known that specialisation leads to vast increases in productivity and, as productivity increases, so the standard of living rises. Considerable progress was made in reaching a solution to the Uruguay Round of the GATT talks and, if fully implemented, there will be a reduction in restrictions on international trade. This will encourage the growth of international trade and, since the UK is a major trading nation, the standard of living will be favourably influenced.

> **Single Market of EU relevant here; scale economies etc.**

There are many factors that will influence the standard of living in the UK over the next ten years. It is not certain that the standard of living will increase but, if historical experience is anything to go by, it is likely that this will happen.

> **Many good points raised, but sometimes these need to be taken further. Try to use established economic theories and empirical facts/studies to support your ideas.**

OUTLINE ANSWERS

Question 3

(a) **Income** is usually defined as the flow of output produced over a given period of time. **Wealth**, on the other hand, is usually taken to imply marketable wealth. For the nation as a whole, *marketable wealth* is defined as the stock of physical assets which have a market value.

In the UK, wealth is less equally distributed than income. For example, the top 10 per cent own 38 per cent of total wealth but receive only about 24 per cent of income. At the other end of the scale, the bottom 50 per cent own only 17 per cent of wealth, but receive about 25 per cent of income. The main reason that wealth is less evenly distributed than income is that a great deal of wealth is inherited. Income, by definition, cannot be inherited. Another factor is that income is subject to progressive taxation whereas wealth is untaxed except when ownership is transferred from one person or organisation to another person or organisation. You should, of course, explain what is meant by **progressive taxation** (see p. 313) and why this will redistribute income more evenly.

(b) This is explained on pp. 134–135.

(c) Welfare is usually measured in terms of *per capita income*, i.e. GNP per head. The rationale for measuring economic welfare in this way is that income is the main determinant of consumption and this is the most important determinant of **economic welfare**. However, per capita income is an average measure and when income is unevenly distributed it will give a misleading indication of the standard of living enjoyed by most people. In severe cases, such as those which exist in many less developed countries, the top income earners enjoy a relatively high standard of living but the majority of the people live in abject poverty. In such cases, per capita income must be considered alongside other measures of economic welfare such as life expectancy, adult literacy rates and so on.

Question 4

(a) It is impossible to measure the true level of **depreciation** over time since wear and tear on an asset cannot be measured. Neither can we estimate the rate of technological progress which would enable us to guess at the expected life of an asset before technology renders it redundant. Nevertheless, depreciation is an important cost of production and firms must make provision for the replacement of assets. The rate of depreciation used for assessing national income is derived from current tax legislation which is unrelated to the true rate of depreciation.

(b) The services provided by **owner-occupied housing** are included in the national income statistics so as to prevent any distortion of the estimates caused by a movement away from rented accommodation into owner-occupied housing or vice versa. In fact, the services provided by owner-occupation are not sold on the market and all the statisticians can do is impute a rent as an estimate of their value.

(c) The true value of **education services** are impossible to measure since education is an investment in human capital which benefits the individual but, because of the externalities associated with education, also benefits society. The value of these externalities is unpriced by market forces and therefore statisticians value education at resource cost, i.e. the cost of the resources used to provide education.

(d) The value of **do-it-yourself activities**, such as car maintenance, are unrecorded and impossible to estimate. Partly such activities will be aimed at repairing cars, but they will also be aimed at improving the appearance and performance of cars. The value added is indeterminate but might also have an opportunity cost. When a car breaks down, repairing it is likely to take precedence over other do-it-yourself activities.

STUDENT'S ANSWER TO QUESTION 5

(a) **Gross domestic product** is the value of output produced within a nation's borders during the course of a year. However, not all of the resources used to produce this output will be owned by the country within which that output is produced. Some will be owned by residents of other countries. These resources will receive payment and will generate a flow of income overseas. This flow of income is referred to as property income paid abroad. Any corresponding flow from overseas is referred to as property income received from abroad. The difference between these flows of income is referred to as net property income paid abroad. Adding net property income from abroad to gross domestic product gives **gross national product**.

66 Good – clear definitions 99

(b) A developed economy is likely to have invested funds abroad. To do this, it will be necessary to save. If all funds are spent on consumer goods, none will be available for investment and only in a developed economy are residents likely to be able to save. In a developing economy, the people are very poor and need to spend all their income on the basic necessities of life, such as food. In such countries there is very little saving and therefore *very little opportunity for investment overseas*. For developing countries property income received from abroad is therefore likely to be relatively small. On the other hand, because developed countries invest in developing countries, property income paid abroad is likely to be relatively high. For developing countries, net property income from abroad is likely to be negative. For a developed country, it might be positive or negative depending on how much that country has invested abroad and how much investment it has attracted from abroad. Similarly an important part of output produced in a developed country will be capital goods. However, a developing country will produce fewer capital goods as a proportion of both GNP and GDP. As previously explained, the bulk of its output will be consumer goods and there will be little opportunity to release resources for the production of capital goods.

66 Not necessarily. There will be overseas investment if there is a current account surplus in the balance of payments (see pp. 280–282) 99

66 Unclear 99

66 Although for some developing countries migrant workers send much income back home 99

Typically, a developing country will have a large primary sector. In many cases, agriculture is the largest industry but in some cases commodities, such as copper in Zambia, are particularly important. Developing countries tend to have small manufacturing sectors and even smaller tertiary sectors. This contrasts markedly with developed countries which have large manufacturing and tertiary sectors but a relatively small primary sector. Even in the UK, where we often read of deindustrialisation, the manufacturing sector is large compared with developing countries. It is not surprising that developing countries have small manufacturing and tertiary sectors. Lack of investment restricts the growth of manufacturing and the tertiary sector produces an output that largely consists of 'luxury' goods. It might make us feel better to have our hair trimmed properly by a hairdresser but it is hardly a necessity. In a developing country, few people could afford such a luxury.

66 Some developing countries have very large tertiary sectors 99

> 66 Sometimes the fraction of GNP devoted to these activities is very high 99

In developed countries, governments typically devote a great deal of exenditure to education and health care. In the UK, for example, about 9 per cent of GNP is devoted to education and health care. This is not true of developing countries, which only devote a tiny fraction of GNP to these activities.

> 66 What kind of differences? 99

There is far more equality in the distribution of income in developed than less developed economies. Indeed, in many less developed countries there are extremes of poverty while, at the other end of the scale, a few individuals are fabulously rich. This creates differences in the composition of GDP and GNP between developed and less developed countries.

These are the main reasons for differences in GNP and GDP in developed and less developed countries. The poverty of less developed countries makes it impossible for them to produce the same type of output as developed countries and in particular there is little scope for diverting resources away from the production of goods for current consumption to the production of capital goods which would increase production in the future.

66 A good understanding of the basic points is shown here. However, there will also be considerable differences in the state of the balance of payments – many developing countries are heavily in debt. The accuracy with which statistics are compiled might also explain differences. Developing country statistics are usually less accurate and these countries may well have a larger 'black economy'. 99

Further reading

Begg, Dornbusch and Fisher, *Economics* (3rd edn), McGraw-Hill 1991: Ch. 20, Introduction to Macroeconomics and National Income Accounting.

Harrison et al, *Introductory Economics*, Macmillan 1992: Ch. 18, National Income and its Measurement.

1 What is meant by real national income?

REVIEW SHEET

2 Draw a diagram to show the circular flow of income.

3 Distinguish between Gross Domestic Product (GDP) and Gross National Product (GNP).

4 Distinguish between
   (a) Gross National Product (GNP) and Net National Product (NNP): _____

   (b) Market prices and factor cost: _____

5 Describe the output method for measuring national income, noting any problems with this method.

6 What are transfer payments? How are these dealt with in the income method for measuring national income.

7 Real national income per head is a widely used measure of standard of living. Identify six problems associated with using this measure for recording changes in the true standard of living in a given country.

(a) _____

_____

(b) _____

_____

(c) _____

_____

(d) _____

_____

(e) _____

_____

(f) _____

_____

8 Now identify six problems with using this measure for comparing the true standard of living across different countries.

(a) _____

_____

(b) _____

_____

(c) _____

_____

(d) _____

_____

(e) _____

_____

(f) _____

_____

9 Why do governments collect income statistics? _____

_____

_____

10 Look back to Table 8.1. Comment on each of the following, *using* the data in the table wherever possible.

(a) Comment on the contribution of the various sectors to the *output* measure of National Income.

_____

_____

(b) Comment on the contribution of the various elements to the *income* measure.

_____

_____

(c) Comment on the contribution of the various elements to the *expenditure* measure.

_____

_____

GETTING STARTED

We have seen in Chapter 8 how national income is measured. We now analyse the forces which determine the size of national income. This is of major importance to an economy, since national income affects both living standards and the level of employment.

In the short term, the relationship between real national income and employment is simple: a higher level of output requires the input of more workers, and vice versa. This must be so, because in the short term *all* factors are constant. There is therefore no possibility of substituting capital for labour. Neither is there any possibility of technological advance leading to the substitution of more efficient capital for less efficient capital. Thus, an increase in real national income leads to more employment, and a fall in real national income leads to less employment.

The model of income determination analysed here is a simple version of the model developed by Keynes, who wrote in his *General Theory of Employment, Interest and Money*, "The economic system in which we live ... seems capable of remaining in a chronic condition of sub-normal activity for a considerable period without any marked tendency towards recovery or towards complete collapse. Moreover ... full or even approximately full employment is of rare and short-lived occurrence." Keynes therefore advocated direct manipulation of the forces which determine national income so as to achieve full employment. In the discussion which follows, it is assumed that prices are constant, so that any change in the money value of national income implies an equivalent change in real national income.

Throughout this chapter, the following conventional notation is used. Where appropriate, definitions of these terms are given in the text.

Y	=	national income
Yd	=	disposable income
C	=	consumption
S	=	saving
I	=	investment
G	=	government current expenditure on goods and services
T	=	taxation (direct and indirect)
X	=	exports
M	=	imports
AD	=	aggregate demand
AS	=	aggregate supply
MRT	=	marginal rate of taxation
MPM	=	marginal propensity to import
APC	=	average propensity to consume
APS	=	average propensity to save
MPS	=	marginal propensity to save
Δ	=	'a change in', e.g. ΔS = a change in savings
k	=	the multiplier

ESSENTIAL PRINCIPLES

The term **aggregate demand** refers to the total of planned expenditure for the economy as a whole; **aggregate supply**, on the other hand, refers to the total output of all firms in the economy. Aggregate supply is therefore the same as real national income, which has already been defined as the total value of output produced at constant prices.

THE COMPONENTS OF AGGREGATE DEMAND

For purposes of analysis, the components of aggregate demand can be grouped into planned expenditures by the various sectors of the economy. There are four sectors:

- the household sector
- the firm sector
- the government sector
- the international sector.

Corresponding to this classification, there are four types of expenditure in the economy:

- consumption spending by households
- investment by firms
- government expenditure
- sales of exports abroad.

Each type of expenditure is now examined in turn. It should be noted that aggregate demand refers to expenditures on the output produced by domestic firms, and does not therefore include expenditures on imports.

Consumption (C)

In the macro sense, consumption refers to the total spending of households on goods and services for their own private use. It is termed **consumer's expenditure** in the national income accounts. Table 8.1 (p.132) shows that consumer's expenditure is by far the largest component of aggregate expenditure, comprising 60 per cent of the total. However, care must be taken when analysing the contribution expenditure adds to national income. Part of consumer expenditure is on imports, and this represents spending by domestic residents on goods and services produced abroad. Only that part of consumer expenditure which is spent on *domestically produced* output adds to national income.

Investment (I)

Investment is the creation of any output that is *not* for immediate consumption. It consists of capital goods, such as factory buildings and machinery, as well as additions to the stock of raw materials, semi-finished goods or finished goods. Total investment is shown in Table 8.1 (p. 132) as **gross domestic fixed capital formation**, plus the value of the physical **increase in stocks and work in progress**. Although fixed investment is only about 20 per cent of GNP, it is highly variable. This gives investment an important role in the determination of national income. Again, we should note that imports of capital are excluded from total investment since they do not add directly to national income.

Clearly, in practice, investment will not only help determine the level of national income, but will in part be determined by the level of national income. A higher level of national income, and therefore output, will induce a higher level of investment. However, for simplicity, investment is usually assumed to be an *autonomous* or *exogenous* variable, that is one which does not vary with national income. Put another way, investment is assumed constant at all levels of national income.

Government expenditure (G)

The government is an extremely large spender in the economy; for example, in 1994 total (central + local) government expenditure on goods and services was equal to 25 per cent of GNP. However, not all government expenditure adds directly to aggregate demand. For example, in 1994–95 some 38 per cent of government spending is expected to consist of **transfer payments**, such as social security payments, family income supplement, and so on. These are not payments to the factors of production in return for services rendered; they are simply transfers of income within the community. Similarly, government spending on imports adds nothing to national income. However, the remainder of government expenditure represents spending on real domestic output and contributes directly to national income.

Sales of exports (X)

The sale of exports represents expenditure by foreigners on domestically produced output. Exports therefore make a direct contribution to national income, although this is only true of exports *net of import content*.

Summary of aggregate demand

In summary, using the notation established earlier, we can say that:

$$AD = C + I + G + X - M$$

THE CONSUMPTION FUNCTION

66 Know how to calculate these propensities 99

The main determinant of consumer spending, in the short run, is the level of **disposable income**, i.e. gross factor income plus transfer payments minus direct taxation. Of course, other variables, such as the distribution of income, the cost and availability of credit, and expectations of future income will also affect consumer spending, but these are only likely to change in the longer term.

The relationship between consumption and disposable income is known as the **propensity to consume**.

■ The *marginal propensity to consume* is the rate of change of consumption with respect to disposable income, i.e.

$$MPC = \frac{\Delta C}{\Delta Yd}$$

■ The *average propensity to consume* is the proportion of total disposable income spent on consumption, i.e.

$$APC = \frac{C}{Yd}$$

A **consumption function** shows the different levels of consumption at different levels of income, and is usually presented in the form $C = a + bY$, where a and b are constants. A consumption function of this type produces a straight-line graph (and is therefore called a *linear* or *straight-line* consumption function) as illustrated in Table 9.1 and Fig. 9.1 which also includes the corresponding savings function. Initially, we assume that any income not consumed is saved; in other words, that we have a closed economy with no government so that there is no import spending and no taxation, with saving the only withdrawal.

For simplicity, we assume that there is no direct taxation, and that a = £1,000m and b = 0.75. A certain amount of consumption expenditure will always be undertaken, no matter what the level of income. Thus, a is *exogenous* at £1,000m, since it does not vary with income. However, as income rises this will induce a higher level of consumption spending, the extent of which will depend on the size of b, the marginal propensity to consume. In Table 9.1, we note that each time national income rises by £1,000m, consumption rises by £750m, since b = 0.75.

It might seem puzzling that when income is less than £4,000m, consumption is greater than income. The reason for this is that consumption is partly financed by drawing on savings accumulated in previous periods. Since we are running down our previous savings to finance current consumption, the net change in savings is negative. We call this *dis-saving* by the community.

INCOME (£m)	CONSUMPTION (£m)	SAVINGS (£m)
0	1,000	−1,000
1,000	1,750	−750
2,000	2,500	−500
3,000	3,250	−250
4,000	4,000	0
5,000	4,750	250
6,000	5,500	500
7,000	6,250	750
8,000	7,000	1,000

Table 9.1

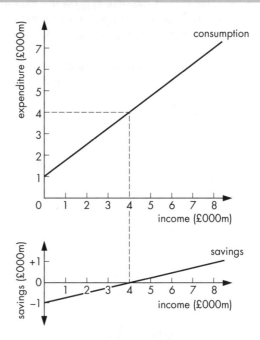

Fig. 9.1 The consumption function and the savings function

PLANNED AND REALISED VALUES

66 Distinguish planned from realised values 99

It is important to distinguish between planned and realised values (some textbooks refer to these as ex-ante and ex-post values, respectively). For example, **planned expenditure** in the economy is simply the aggregate spending each sector plans to undertake in the next accounting period; **realised expenditure**, on the other hand, is the *actual* level of spending achieved by each sector over that accounting period.

Planned and realised values have most significance in relation to investment because any excess of spending over output (or of output over spending) manifests itself in *unplanned changes in stock*. Since additions to stock are recorded as investment in the official statistics, it follows that any unplanned increase in stocks is referred to as *unplanned investment*. The importance of unplanned investment and unplanned disinvestment is that since they are unanticipated, they lead producers to revise their planned levels of output in the following period. In this way, unplanned investment or unplanned disinvestment will initiate *changes in national income*.

THE EQUILIBRIUM LEVEL OF INCOME

Equilibrium exists when there is no tendency to change. It follows that the national income can only be in equilibrium when there is no tendency for it to rise or fall. This can only occur when planned expenditure in one period exactly equals the planned output for that period. When this is the case, producers are receiving back in expenditure on their output an amount which equals the amount they have paid out to the factors of production for producing that output.

We can easily establish that planned expenditure must equal planned output for equilibrium to be achieved:

- If planned expenditure *exceeds* planned output, then firms will experience unplanned disinvestment as their stocks are depleted. Their response to this will be to raise output in the following period, so that national income will rise.

- If planned expenditure is *less than* planned output, then firms experience unplanned investment as their stock levels increase. Their response to this will be to reduce output in the following period, so that national income will fall.

It is clear that, in equilibrium, planned expenditure in the form of aggregate demand (AD) must equal planned output in the form of aggregate supply (AS). This can be explained in terms of the notation established earlier.

Finding the equilibrium condition

$$AD = C + I + G + X - M$$
$$AS = Y$$
$$AD = AS \text{ in equilibrium}$$
$$C + I + G + X - M = Y \text{ in equilibrium}$$

NATIONAL INCOME (£m)	AGGREGATE DEMAND (£m)	UNPLANNED CHANGE IN STOCKS (£m)	TENDENCY OF CHANGE IN NATIONAL INCOME
1,000	3,500	−2,500	Increase
2,000	4,000	−2,000	Increase
3,000	4,500	−1,500	Increase
4,000	5,000	−1,000	Increase
5,000	5,500	−500	Increase
6,000	6,000	0	No change
7,000	6,500	500	Decrease
8,000	7,000	1,000	Decrease

Table 9.2

Table 9.2 provides a numerical example for the determination of equilibrium national income. It is derived from the following planned values (in £m).

$$C = \pounds1,000m + 0.75Yd$$
$$I = \pounds600m$$
$$G = \pounds900m$$
$$X = \pounds500m$$
$$T = 0.2Y$$
$$Yd = Y - T$$
$$M = 0.125Yd$$
$$C + I + G + X - M = Y \text{ in equilibrium}$$

i.e.
$$1,000 + 0.75Yd + 600 + 900 + 500 - 0.125Yd = Y$$
$$1,000 + 0.75(Y - 0.2Y) + 2,000 - 0.125(Y - 0.2Y) = Y$$
$$3,000 + 0.6Y - 0.1Y = Y$$
$$3,000 + 0.5Y = Y$$
$$3,000 = 0.5Y$$
$$6,000 = Y$$

Equilibrium means at rest

- If aggregate demand were *greater than* £6,000m, then the value of output, Y, must rise.

- If aggregate demand were *less than* £6,000m, then the value of output, Y, must fall.

It is more usual to illustrate equilibrium diagrammatically and this is done in Fig. 9.2. Since both axes have the same scale, the 45° line which bisects them gives the path of all points of equality between planned expenditure and planned output (national income). It therefore shows all the possible equilibrium levels of national income within the range illustrated. It is clear that given the aggregate demand schedule shown, £6,000m is the equilibrium level of output (income). At levels of output (income) below this, aggregate demand exceeds the value of national output and the tendency will be for the value of national output to rise. At levels of output (income) above this, aggregate demand is less than national output (i.e. aggregate demand is insufficient to purchase the existing level of output) and the tendency will be for the value of national output to fall. Only when Y = £6,000m is there no tendency for national output (income) to change, because aggregate demand is just sufficient to purchase the existing level of output.

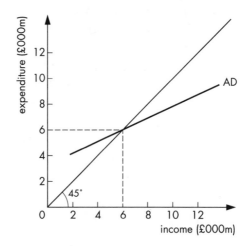

Fig. 9.2 The equilibrium level of national income

LEAKAGES AND INJECTIONS

National income equilibrium can be looked at in another way, in terms of leakages and injections.

LEAKAGES

A leakage is a withdrawal of potential spending from the circular flow of income. A leakage occurs when any part of the income which results from the production of domestic goods and services is not used to purchase other domestic goods and services. We can identify three leakages from the circular flow of income:

> ❝ The types of leakage from the circular flow ❞

■ savings

■ taxation

■ import expenditure.

Savings (S)
Savings are any part of income received by domestic households which is not spent. By definition, therefore, savings are a leakage from the circular flow of income, and we can write

$$S = Yd - C$$

Taxation (T)
There are two types of taxation, direct and indirect. Both are leakages from the circular flow of income. **Direct taxes**, such as income tax, reduce potential spending, since they reduce disposable income in relation to gross factor income. Part of the value of output produced is therefore not received by the factors of production, but is withdrawn from the circular flow by the government. On the other hand, **indirect taxes** such as VAT, reduce the receipts of producers in relation to total expenditure. In this case, part of the total spending undertaken by the community is not received by the factors of production since it is paid to the government in indirect taxes. The total tax leak from the circular flow of income is therefore the amount paid in direct taxes plus the amount paid in indirect taxes.

Imports (M)
Import expenditure represents the purchase by domestic residents of output produced abroad. Imports are therefore a leakage, since part of the income received by domestic residents is not returned to the circular flow as expenditures on domestic goods and services.

Summary of total leakages

Summarising, we can write:

Total leakages from the circular flow of income = S + T + M

INJECTIONS

An injection is an addition of spending to the circular flow of income. It consists of any expenditure on domestic goods and services which does not arise from the spending of domestic households. An injection is therefore spending other than consumption expenditure. There are three injections into the circular flow of income. They are:

66 The types of injection into the circular flow 99

- investment (I)
- direct government expenditure on goods and services (G)
- exports (X).

Each of these was discussed earlier.

Summary of total injections

We can write:

Total injections into the circular flow of income = I + G + X

AN ALTERNATIVE VIEW OF EQUILIBRIUM

Realised injections must always equal *realised* leakages, but the economy can only be in equilibrium when *planned* injections equal *planned* leakages.

- If planned injections into the circular flow of income are greater than planned leakages from it, then national income will tend to rise. This is because planned spending will exceed national output (income) so producers will experience unplanned disinvestment in stocks and will expand output in the following period.

- Conversely, if planned injections are less than planned leakages, then national income will tend to fall. Planned spending will now be less than national output (income) so there will be insufficient demand to purchase existing output. Producers will experience unplanned investment in stock and will reduce output in the following period.

It follows that national income can only be in equilibrium when *planned injections* equal *planned leakages*. The equilibrium condition may therefore be stated as:

I + G + X = S + T + M

This is clearly shown in Table 9.3 which extends Table 9.2 to include the various injections and leakages discussed above.

Note: planned injections are assumed to be exogenous and thus do not vary with income.

The appropriate values (in £m) are:

$$
\begin{aligned}
C &= £1{,}000m + 0.75Yd \\
I &= £600m \\
G &= £900m \\
X &= £500m \\
S &= -£1{,}000m + 0.25Yd \\
Yd &= Y - T \\
T &= 0.2Y \\
M &= 0.125Yd
\end{aligned}
$$

National Income Y	Aggregate demand AD	Planned savings S	Planned taxation T	Planned expenditure on imports M	Planned government expenditure G	Planned export sales X	Planned investment I	Realised investment	Tendency to change in National Income
0	3,000	−1,000	0	0	900	500	600	−2,400	Increase
1,000	3,500	−800	200	100	900	500	600	−1,900	Increase
2,000	4,000	−600	400	200	900	500	600	−1,400	Increase
3,000	4,500	−400	600	300	900	500	600	−900	Increase
4,000	5,000	−200	800	400	900	500	600	−400	Increase
5,000	5,500	0	1,000	500	900	500	600	100	Increase
6,000	6,000	200	1,200	600	900	500	600	600	No Change
7,000	6,500	400	1,400	700	900	500	600	1,100	Decrease
8,000	7,000	600	1,600	800	900	500	600	1,600	Decrease

Table 9.3

The equilibrium level of income is £6,000m, because this is the only level of income at which planned injections equal planned leakages. (See also the solution on p. 153.) Since planned spending exactly equals national output (income), producers will experience no unplanned investment in stock, i.e. planned investment equals realised investment. There will be no incentive for producers to change output in the following period. If income is at any other level, it will have a tendency to increase or decrease.

Again, equilibrium can be represented diagrammatically, this time using the injections and leakages approach. This can be seen in the lower part of Fig. 9.3 which uses the values of Table 9.3. The upper part of the diagram reproduces Fig. 9.2 in order to help us compare the two approaches. Planned injections (I + G + X) are constant at £2,000m. Planned leakages (S + T + M) vary with national income. To plot the leakages curve, we can add together the various values of S, T and M in Table 9.3 at each level of national income. Alternatively, we can derive the leakages function by adding together the separate functions for S, T and M.

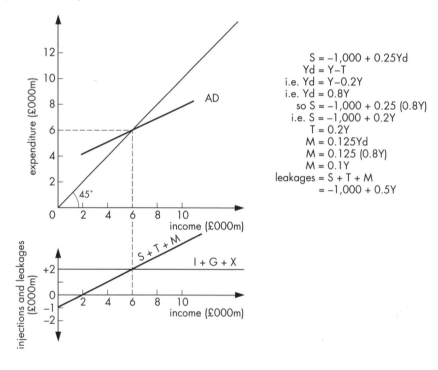

$$S = -1,000 + 0.25Yd$$
$$Yd = Y - T$$
i.e. $Yd = Y - 0.2Y$
i.e. $Yd = 0.8Y$
so $S = -1,000 + 0.25(0.8Y)$
i.e. $S = -1,000 + 0.2Y$
$$T = 0.2Y$$
$$M = 0.125Yd$$
$$M = 0.125(0.8Y)$$
$$M = 0.1Y$$
leakages $= S + T + M$
$$= -1,000 + 0.5Y$$

Fig. 9.3 The equilibrium level of income

THE MULTIPLIER

One of the most important features of the Keynesian model is that it shows how any change in injections or leakages can lead to a more than proportional change in national income. This is known as the **multiplier effect**. It arises because an initial change in injections or leakages leads to a series of changes in national income, the cumulative effect of which exceeds the initial change which brought it about. For example, if firms increase their investment in plant and equipment, and all other things remain equal, national income will initially rise by the same amount as the increase in investment. If we assume an absence of taxation, the increased expenditure on plant

66 Be familiar with the multiplier 99

and equipment will in turn be received as rewards by the factors which have produced this output. Part of this (depending on the size of the MPC) will be spent, generating a further increase in income, part of which will also be spent, and so on. However, this process does not go on indefinitely. With each rise in income, a smaller amount will be passed on, and this will generate successively smaller changes in income.

A NUMERICAL EXAMPLE

A numerical example will help to clarify this. For simplicity we assume there is only one injection, i.e. investment, and one leakage, i.e. savings. Assume further than nine-tenths of any increase in income is spent on consumption and that investment in plant and equipment rises by £100m. The letter k is used to denote the multiplier. The increase in investment initially raised income by £100m, £90m of which is subsequently spent on consumption, so that output and income rise by a further £90m. Nine-tenths of this £90m is also spent on consumption, so that output and income rises by a further £81m, and so on. We can see that income goes on rising as a geometric progression diminishing to infinity. The first few terms of this series, together with the final value (in £m) are set out below.

$$\Delta I = £100m$$
$$\Delta Y = £100m + £90m + £81m + £72.9m + ...$$
$$\text{i.e.} \quad \Delta Y = £1,000m$$
$$k = \frac{\Delta Y}{\Delta I} = \frac{£1,000m}{£100m} = 10$$

This implies that an increase in injections causes an eventual increase in income which is ten times greater than the initial increase in injections.

Effect on savings

It is equally interesting to look at what happens to savings following the increase in investment. We have seen that for each increase in income there is an increase in consumption. But since not all of the increase in income is passed on, there must also be an increase in savings. In fact, since in this discussion savings is the only leakage from the circular flow, it follows that

$$\Delta Y = \Delta C + \Delta S$$

In other words, savings also rises as a geometric progression diminishing to infinity, and the first few terms of this series, together with the final value (in £m), are:

$$\Delta S = £10m + £9m + £8.1m + ...$$
$$\text{i.e.} \quad \Delta S = £100m$$

The significant point is that, following an increase in investment of £100m, income goes on rising until households wish to save a further £100m. This is because equilibrium can only exist when planned injections equal planned leakages. Following an increase in planned investment, these two items are brought into equality by an increase in income which encourages the households to revise their savings plans upwards.

THE VALUE OF THE MULTIPLIER

The value of the multiplier can be obtained by using the formula:

$$k = \frac{1}{(1 - \text{common ratio})}$$

This can be applied to the example above. Thus

$$k = \frac{1}{1 - \text{MPC}} = \frac{1}{1 - 0.9} = 10$$

However, when there are other leakages from the circular flow of income, it is more usual to express the multiplier as:

" Calculating the multiplier ""

$$k = \frac{1}{\text{marginal rate of leakage from gross income}}$$

In the four-sector economy, this can be written as:

$$k = \frac{1}{MPS + MRT + MPM}$$

For example, using the values from which Table 9.3 was derived (i.e. MPS = 0.25Yd, MRT = 0.2Y, and MPM = 0.125Yd) we can calculate:

$$k = \frac{1}{0.25(0.8) + 0.2 + 0.125(0.8)}$$
$$= \frac{1}{0.5}$$
$$= 2$$

THE BALANCED BUDGET MULTIPLIER

The balanced budget multiplier shows the effect on income of equal changes in government expenditure and taxation. It might be expected that the net effect would be zero and that income would remain unchanged. In fact, the following example illustrates that this is not the case.

Suppose there is an increase in government current expenditure of £100m, financed entirely by an increase in taxation of £100m, with MPC = 0.8Y and MPS = 0.2Y.

- The increase in government spending will lead to a diminishing series of *increases in income*. The first few terms and the eventual sum of this series (in £m) are:

$$\Delta Y = £100m + £80m + £64m + ... = £500m$$

- The increase in taxation will lead to a similar series of *reductions in income*.
- The change in tax, however, is not so straightforward as the change in government expenditure; part of any increase in taxation will be financed by a reduction in the amount saved. To the extent that this is the case, the increase in one leakage from the circular flow of income (tax) is in part compensated for by the reduction of another. In other words, the net change in leakages is less than the change in taxation. Thus, only that part of any increase in taxation which is financed by a *reduction in consumption*, rather than by a reduction in savings, has any effect on income.

In our example, the net increase in leakages is equal to 0.8T, because one-fifth of the increase in taxation is financed by a cut in savings. Only that part of any increase in taxation which leads to a reduction in consumption has any effect on national income. It follows that the increase in taxation of £100m will lead to a diminishing series of reductions in income. In this case the first few terms (in £m) and the eventual sum of the series are:

$$\Delta Y = \frac{-0.8\Delta T}{1 - 0.8}$$

$$\Delta Y = -(£80m + £64m + £51.2m + ...) = -£400m$$

Thus, the *net* result of an equivalent increase in G and T is that income rises by £100m, i.e. by the increase in government expenditure. The *balanced budget multiplier* therefore has a value of one.

THE MULTIPLIER IN PRACTICE

We have seen that the size of the multiplier is given by the formula:

$$k = \frac{1}{MPS + MRT + MPM} = \frac{1}{MRL}$$

- The size of the multiplier is determined by the marginal rate of leakage (MRL). One important factor which affects the MRL is the distribution of income. Since higher income groups have a higher MPS than low income groups, a less than equal distribution of income implies a lower value for the multiplier. The tax system can have an important effect here. Where taxation bears more heavily on lower income groups this will also reduce the value of the multiplier because these groups tend to have a higher MPC (i.e. lower MPS). For the same reason, a general increase in taxation will reduce the value of the multiplier. Some countries are heavily dependent on imports and have a relatively high MPM. In such cases, the size of the multiplier will be lower than otherwise.

- A related factor is the overall level of economic activity in the economy. When the economy is close to full employment, there will be supply inelasticities or supply bottlenecks. Firms will therefore find it difficult to recruit additional workers, to obtain additional supplies of raw materials, etc. in response to an increase in investment. This will limit any increase in output and, if the increase in investment is large enough, might generate inflation because the higher level of demand for resources would pull up their prices. Such bottlenecks will also encourage the consumption of imports. An economy which is experiencing supply inelasticities will therefore tend to have a lower value for the multiplier.

- Another factor that will affect the size of the multiplier is the response of firms to an increase in demand. When firms currently have high stock levels they might choose to run down stocks rather than increase output in response to an increase in demand. Moreover, when an increase in demand is not considered to be permanent, firms might simply lengthen their waiting lists, or allow the higher level of demand to bid up the price of their products. In all these cases, the value of the multiplier will be lower than otherwise.

- The size of the multiplier will also be lower if 'crowding out' takes place. **Crowding out** is the term used to describe the effect of an increase in public sector investment on private sector investment. In particular, it is argued that an increase in public sector investment crowds out, i.e. reduces, private sector investment. When crowding out does take place an increase in public sector investment will have a smaller multiplier effect than an increase in private sector investment.

THE PARADOX OF THRIFT

66 Attempts to save more can be self defeating 99

We have already seen that in a two-sector economy realised savings must always equal realised investment. However this does not imply that an increase in planned savings will always lead to an equivalent increase in investment. Indeed the *paradox of thrift* indicates that in some circumstances an attempt by the community to increase aggregate savings actually leads to a fall in aggregate savings and investment.

TWO-SECTOR MODELS

In two-sector models of the economy, the equality between savings and investment is often illustrated using symbols:

$$Y = C + I$$
$$Y = C + S$$
$$\therefore I \equiv S$$

It seems, on the basis of this, that an increase in savings must indeed lead to an increase in investment. However, the identity refers to realised savings and realised investment. If planned savings and planned investment are not equal, then income will be changing so as to ensure that planned and realised savings equals planned and realised investment. Now, if the economy is initially in equilibrium and the community attempts to increase its savings when there is no simultaneous increase in planned investment by firms, firms will experience an *unplanned increase in stocks*. This is because they will be receiving back from the community an amount which is less than the value of output produced. This increase in stocks will ensure that realised investment equals the higher value of realised savings, but the change in investment was unplanned and will not therefore continue.

In fact, firms will react to an unplanned increase in stocks by cutting back on the amount of output they produce. As output falls, incomes will fall, and this will reduce the ability of the community to save. In other words, an attempt by the community to save more, actually leads to a reduction in savings. This is referred to as the paradox of thrift and it is illustrated in Fig. 9.4.

The economy is initially in equilibrium at OY with planned investment equalling planned savings (= OX). An increase in the propensity to save at all levels of income shifts the savings function from SS to S_1S_1. This causes the equilibrium level of income to fall from OY to OY_1. The equilibrium level of savings and investment is now OX_1. In other words, the community's attempt to save more has actually resulted in a reduction in the amount saved (and a reduction in the level of investment).

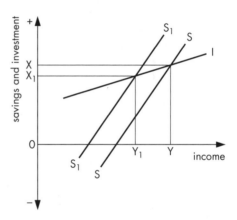

Fig. 9.4 The paradox of thrift

EQUILIBRIUM WITH UNEMPLOYMENT

THE DEFLATIONARY GAP

We have seen that with a given level of aggregate demand, i.e. given values for planned leakages and planned injections, there is only one possible equilibrium level of national income. Any other level will be unstable and the economy will be tending to move towards the equilibrium level. The main problem which concerned Keynes was unemployment, and he pointed out that it will only be by pure chance that the equilibrium level of national income and the full employment level of national income coincide. In fact, the economy can be in equilibrium with large numbers of the workforce unemployed. Keynes regarded the great depression of the 1920s and 1930s as just such a case.

In terms of the Keynesian model, we can say that unemployment exists when aggregate demand falls short of the level necessary to achieve full employment at the current price level. Keynes argued that, in cases such as this, the government should pursue expansionary policies to raise aggregate demand and so reduce unemployment. This is analysed in Fig. 9.5.

With aggregate demand given by AD, the equilibrium level of income is OY. However, if OY_F is the full employment level of income, we can say that BC is the deficiency of aggregate demand compared with the level necessary to generate full employment. In fact, BC is referred to as the **deflationary gap**, and a government wishing to achieve full employment must pursue policies to close the deflationary gap, such as raising the level of G or reducing the level of T. Policies aimed at managing the level of aggregate demand so as to achieve various economic aims are discussed more fully in Chapter 17. Reducing the level of T would raise disposable income, and therefore increase C at any given level of gross income. This would be shown as an upward shift of the aggregate demand function:

66 Closing the deflationary gap 99

$$AD = C + I + G + X - M$$

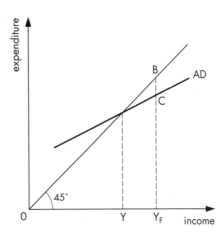

Fig. 9.5 The deflationary gap

THE INFLATIONARY GAP: OVERFULL EMPLOYMENT

It is possible for the level of aggregate demand to exceed the level necessary to achieve full employment at the current price level. This case is analysed in Fig. 9.6.

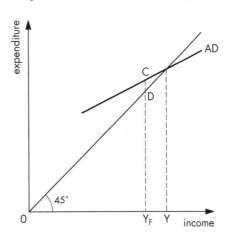

Fig. 9.6 The inflationary gap

In terms of Fig. 9.6, OY_F represents the full employment level of income. With aggregate demand AD, the equilibrium level of income is OY. However, it is impossible to achieve an equilibrium level of real income greater than the level achieved at full employment, because physical output cannot be increased beyond that achieved at full employment.

In this case, OY is an unattainable level of real income. Once the economy reaches the full employment level of output, OY_F, any excess of aggregate demand over the level necessary to achieve full employment, i.e. CD in Fig. 9.6, is therefore referred to

> 66 Closing the inflationary gap 99

as the **inflationary gap**. The government must pursue contractionary policies in order to close the inflationary gap and so stop prices rising. This implies the pursuit of policies to reduce aggregate demand by CD, such as reducing the level of G or raising the level of T.

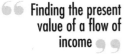

INVESTMENT

DISCOUNTING TO PRESENT VALUE

In the real world, an important determinant of investment is the expected net rate of return on additional capacity. This can be estimated by subtracting the estimated operating costs over the life of the asset from the expected revenue through additional sales. However, since cash today can be invested and so earn interest, it is worth more than cash in the future. Because of this, the future stream of net returns expected from

> 66 Finding the present value of a flow of income 99

the asset must be **discounted** to a present value (PV) equivalent which can then be compared with the current cost of the asset. The most obvious discount rate to use is the *current rate of interest*, since this represents the return foregone if cash is used to purchase fixed assets instead of being loaned. If the present value (PV) of this future stream of net returns is greater than the current cost of the asset (its *supply price*), then additional investment will be profitable. Put another way:

Net present value (NPV) = PV – supply price

If NPV is positive, then additional investment will be profitable.

A numerical example

Assume a firm is contemplating the purchase of an additional machine with an expected life of five years and a current cost (supply price) of £10,000. Assume further that expected annual net returns (i.e. expected revenue minus expected operating costs) are £5,000, £5,000, £3,500, £2,000 and £1,000 respectively. If the machine has no scrap value after five years and the current rate of interest is 10 per cent, then the present value of the future stream of earnings from buying the machine can be set out as follows:

$$PV = \frac{£5,000}{1.1} + \frac{£5,000}{(1.1)^2} + \frac{£3,500}{(1.1)^3} + \frac{£2,000}{(1.1)^4} + \frac{£1,000}{(1.1)^5} = £13,294$$

Thus, purchasing the machine is expected to yield a profit of approximately £13,294 at current prices. Subtracting the current cost of the machine, i.e. £10,000, still yields a positive net return of £3,294.

In other words:

NPV = PV – supply price = +£3,294

Since NPV is positive, additional investment will be profitable.

THE MARGINAL EFFICIENCY OF CAPITAL

> ❝ MEC is a rate of discount ❞

The preceding calculation is more important in explaining investment by individual firms than in explaining aggregate investment. Nevertheless, it forms the basis of the Keynesian approach to investment. The only difference is that instead of discounting to present value, we obtain the *rate at which future earnings must be discounted* in order to bring their present value into equality with the current cost of the capital asset (the supply price). Keynes referred to the rate of discount which brings a stream of future earnings into equality with current capital costs as the **marginal efficiency of capital** (MEC).

■ If the MEC is greater than the current cost of borrowing funds to finance the investment, i.e. the rate of interest (R), then additional investment will be expected to yield a profit.

■ If MEC = R then there is neither a gain nor loss from the investment.

■ If MEC < R then the investment will be unprofitable.

MEC schedule

At any moment in time, different investment projects will have a different marginal efficiency of capital, but if these are aggregated then we can obtain a marginal efficiency of capital schedule. Assuming that firms aim to maximise profit, the marginal efficiency of capital schedule will show the demand for capital at various rates of interest. This is shown in Fig. 9.7. When the rate of interest is OR, the aggregate demand for capital is OM.

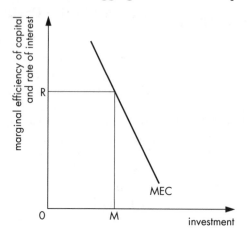

Fig. 9.7 The determination of investment

One important feature illustrated by the diagram is that the demand ¡
inversely with the rate of interest. There are two main reasons for this:

- As investment increases, the return on additional investment, i.e.
  revenue productivity of capital (see Ch. 10), is likely to fall because:
  - greater investment will increase the amount of goods or services available,
    and this will tend to depress their prices, reducing the expected revenue from
    extra investment projects, and therefore reducing MEC; and
  - as investment increases beyond some point, firms will experience
    diminishing returns to capital – a fall in the productivity of capital will also
    reduce the expected revenue from extra investment projects, and therefore
    reduce MEC.
- Greater investment demand might pull up the cost of the capital asset, i.e. the
  supply price of capital, and therefore reduce MEC.

> 66 Investment varies inversely with the rate of interest 99

The combined effect of these factors will be to reduce the return on additional
investment, giving a downward sloping MEC schedule. Thus a reduction in the rate of
interest will raise the demand for capital because it will make it profitable to undertake
investment projects that were unprofitable at a higher rate.

Investment decision making

Although there is no doubt that changes in the rate of interest influence investment
decisions, the relationship is unlikely to be as precise as Fig. 9.7 implies. There are
many reasons for this:

- A great deal of investment in the public sector is undertaken for social reasons.
  Economic considerations have far less influence on such investment.
- In practice, it is extremely difficult to estimate the marginal efficiency of capital.
- The investment plans of large firms often stretch over several years and changes
  in the rate of interest are unlikely to persuade them to revise their plans once they
  have embarked upon them.
- Unplanned investment in stocks is unlikely to be affected by changes in the rate
  of interest.
- In times when the government is exercising tight control over the availability of
  credit, it might not be possible to obtain funds for investment, even when such
  funds can be used profitably.
- The volatility of expectations which will cause the MEC schedule to shift wildly to
  left or right.

> 66 Why investment also depends on factors other than the rate of interest 99

Let us consider this last reason more fully. The current rate of interest is only one factor
influencing the decision to invest. The *expectations* of people in the business world is
another important consideration. Expectations often change rapidly, so the whole MEC
schedule will be highly unstable. If expectations about future economic conditions
decline, the expected revenues from investment projects will fall and the whole MEC
schedule will shift to the left. The opposite will happen if expectations about the future
improve. The fact that investment may therefore change substantially even when the
interest rate is unchanged, means that there will be a poor statistical fit between the
interest rate and the level of investment.

THE ACCELERATOR

It is also possible for *changes in the level of income* to exert a powerful effect on the level
of investment, independently of the rate of interest. In other words, changes in the level
of income might induce substantial changes in investment. This is usually referred to
as the **accelerator principle**, and it is most clearly understood by reference to Table
9.4 which shows how an individual firm's investment decisions are influenced by
changes in demand for its product. We assume a capital/output ratio of 2:1, i.e. two
units of capital are required to produce one unit of output per period, that each unit of
capital has an economic life of five years and that the firm has built up its capital stock
by regular additions of 2,000 units each year.

YEAR	SALES	EXISTING CAPITAL	REQUIRED CAPITAL	REPLACEMENT INVESTMENT	NET INVESTMENT	GROSS INVESTMENT
1	5,000	10,000	10,000	2,000	0	2,000
2	6,000	10,000	12,000	2,000	2,000	4,000
3	7,500	12,000	15,000	2,000	3,000	5,000
4	8,000	15,000	16,000	2,000	1,000	3,000
5	7,750	16,000	15,500	2,000	−500	1,500

Table 9.4

Table 9.4 clearly shows the impact of changes in demand on investment. During Year 2 sales rise by 20 per cent, but this induces a rise in gross investment, i.e. net investment plus replacement investment, of 100 per cent! The proportionate change in investment is not so spectacular in Year 3, with gross investment rising by only 25 per cent despite the greater (25 per cent) increase in sales. However, during Year 4 there is a smaller proportionate increase in sales than in previous years, and this causes a decline in the *absolute* level of investment. A simple increase in sales is not therefore sufficient to induce an increase in investment. The level of investment will only go on rising when sales are rising at an *increasing rate*. The table also shows the effect of a reduction in sales on investment.

> The accelerator theory relates net investment to the rate of change of sales

Effect of sales on investment

From Table 9.4 we can see that $In = a\Delta Y$, where In is net investment, 'a' is the capital/output ratio (2), and ΔY is the absolute change in sales. In practice, it is unlikely that investment will vary with sales as precisely as implied in the table because:

- firms might meet increased demand out of stocks or might choose to lengthen waiting lists rather than increase investment;

- firms might consider the increase in demand is only temporary, and will not therefore raise their investment;

- rather than increasing investment to meet the extra demand it is more likely that firms will, initially at least, introduce overtime working, etc.

- there are likely to be technological advances which will raise the productivity of capital and so reduce the need for additional investment to meet increased demand for output; and

- firms might currently have excess capacity from which they can meet any increase in demand.

Despite these qualifications there is no doubt that changes in income can exert a powerful influence on investment decisions. While the accelerator is not a precise model, it may, nevertheless, help to explain the instability of investment demand.

AGGREGATE DEMAND AND AGGREGATE SUPPLY

A major assumption of the Keynesian model discussed in this chapter is that the price level is constant. Hence any change in national income implies a change in real national income, i.e. a change in the *volume* of output. Of course, changes in *nominal* national income might imply a change in real income, a change in nominal income caused entirely by a change in the price level or a change in nominal income caused by a combination of the two. In fact, a more modern treatment of aggregate demand and aggregate supply focuses on the latter two possibilities.

THE AGGREGATE DEMAND CURVE

An **aggregate demand curve** shows total expenditure in an economy over some period of time. The aggregate demand curve shows an inverse relationship between the price level, i.e. the average of all prices in the economy, and the total quantity of all goods and services demanded. A typical aggregate demand curve is illustrated in Fig. 9.8.

There are three basic reasons why aggregate demand might be expected to vary *inversely* with the price level: changes in real money balances, exports and imports, and the rate of interest.

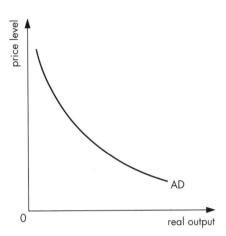

Fig. 9.8 A typical aggregate demand curve

Changes in real money balances

When the price level changes this will change the purchasing power of money balances. For example, a *fall* in the price level implies a rise in real money balances, i.e. a given quantity of money now exchanges for a greater volume of goods and services. In consequence, firms and consumers will increase their expenditures. The opposite occurs when the price level rises.

Exports and imports

Changes in the price level have important effects on the price of exports and the relative price of imports. Thus, as the price level *falls*, exports become more competitive in world markets and imports become less competitive in the domestic market. Because of this, it is likely that the quantity of exports consumed will increase and the quantity of imports will fall as domestic consumers switch to the now cheaper domestic substitutes. This implies an increase in aggregate demand as the price level falls. Conversely, as the price level rises, aggregate demand will fall as demand for exports falls and demand for imports rises.

The rate of interest

When the price level rises, individuals and firms will be encouraged to carry larger money balances with which to finance their expenditures. However, since the supply of money is constant (remember, demand curves are drawn on the assumption that all other things remain the same) it is impossible for all economic agents to simultaneously increase their holdings of cash. Any attempt to do so will simply create a shortage of funds at the existing price level. To alleviate this shortage, economic agents will run down their savings and this will force up the rate of interest. As the rate of interest rises, firms will cut down on investment, consumers will cut down their purchases of durable goods and, if the exchange rate is floating, appreciation of the exchange rate will cause a fall in demand for exports and an increase in demand for imports (see pp. 282–285). The reverse situation occurs when the price level falls. So again a fall in the price level will tend to be associated with a cut in interest rates and an increase in aggregate demand.

THE AGGREGATE SUPPLY CURVE

In the Keynesian model, the assumption of a constant price level implies that the **aggregate supply curve** is perfectly elastic up to the full employment level. Once we relax the assumption of a constant price level, we can construct a more realistic aggregate supply curve. In fact, it is now customary to argue that we must distinguish between aggregate supply in the *short run* and aggregate supply in the *long run*.

Aggregate Supply in the Short Run

The *short-run* aggregate supply curve shows a direct relationship between aggregate supply and the price level. This is because costs are incurred in anticipation of sales. Now if the actual price level exceeds the anticipated price level, this will encourage firms to increase output because it implies a higher level of profit from production. In other words, as the price level rises, aggregate supply rises – at least up to the point at which resources are fully employed. Once the point at which resources are fully employed is reached, the short-run aggregate supply curve becomes vertical.

Aggregate Supply in the Long Run

In the short run, aggregate supply varies directly with the price level because the expected price level differs from the actual price level. However, in the *long run*, firms and individuals adjust their expectations and will accurately predict changes in the price level. In other words, in the long run, there will be *no* discrepancy between the actual price level and the expected price level. This has important implications for the behaviour of aggregate supply in the long run.

To understand why, let us assume initially that the actual price level and the expected price level coincide. Now assume that there is an unanticipated rise in the price level which encourages an increase in aggregate supply. However, as economic agents adjust to the higher price level costs will rise, for example as wage rates are renegotiated. This rise in costs will wipe out the higher level of profit associated with the initial increase in the price level. Because of this, the incentive to produce a higher level of output disappears and output will therefore return to its original level. In fact, the original level of output is referred to as the *natural rate of output* because it is that rate to which the economy tends in the long run. Any deviation from the natural rate of output is transitory, i.e. it is a short-run phenomenon only. The short-run and long-run aggregate supply curves are shown in Fig. 9.9.

> ❝ The natural rate of output ❞

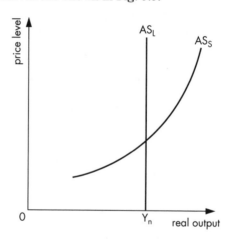

Fig. 9.9 Aggregate supply in the short run (AS$_S$) and the long run (AS$_L$)

- In Fig. 9.9, AS$_S$ is the short-run aggregate supply curve and AS$_L$ is the long-run aggregate supply curve. Y$_n$ is the natural rate of output. It is determined by such factors as the capital stock, the rate of technological progress, the size of the labour force, the skills possessed by the labour force, the mobility of labour, and so on. It is these factors that set the upper limit on production in the long run and it is important to note in particular that, in the long run, changes in the price level have no effect on the level of output. The long-run aggregate supply curve is therefore vertical at the natural rate of output.

LONG-RUN EQUILIBRIUM

In the long run, the economy will settle at the natural rate of output. This is therefore the equilibrium level of output. In Fig. 9.10, AS$_S$ is the short-run aggregate supply curve, AS$_L$ is the long-run aggregate supply curve and AD is the aggregate demand curve. The economy is in equilibrium with output at the natural rate Y$_n$ and the price level at P. Note that when the economy is at the natural rate there are unemployed resources in the economy shown by the fact that in the short run aggregate supply can increase above Y$_n$.

FACTORS CAUSING A CHANGE IN AGGREGATE DEMAND

Many factors might cause a change in aggregate demand, i.e. an increase or decrease in the amount demanded at any given price level. Some of the more important factors are summarised below.

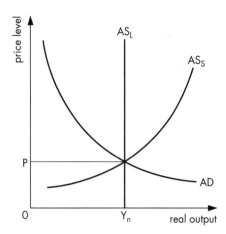

Fig. 9.10 Long-run equilibrium

- **Technological progress** Over time, technological progress will increase the long-run aggregate supply of the economy. This will shift the long-run aggregate supply curve to the right. However, an increase in aggregate supply implies an increase in real income. As real income rises, aggregate demand will rise. This implies a rightward shift in the aggregate demand curve.

- **A change in the exchange rate** When the exchange rate *depreciates* this reduces the foreign price of exports and raises the domestic price of imports (see p. 283). Because of this, demand for exports will rise and demand for imports will fall. Because there has been no change in the domestic price level, this implies an outward movement of the aggregate demand curve. Exchange rate *appreciation* has the opposite effect.

- **Changes in the expected rate of inflation** Changes in the expected rate of inflation will encourage changes in expenditure. For example, if all other things remain the same, an increase in the expected rate of inflation will encourage firms and individuals to bring their anticipated expenditures forward to avoid paying a higher price later. A fall in the expected rate of inflation will have the opposite effect. Note that because expenditure is changing in response to expected changes in the price level, aggregate demand changes at any given price level.

- **Changes in business confidence** Changes in business confidence can exert a powerful effect on aggregate demand because of its effect on the rate of investment. When entrepreneurs feel confident of buoyant sales they will be encouraged to increase their investment and this implies an outward movement of the aggregate demand curve. Conversely, when they are pessimistic about future sales they will cut back on investment and this implies an inward movement of the aggregate demand curve.

- **Government policy** If all other things remain the same, an increase in government expenditure and/or a reduction in taxation will cause an increase in aggregate demand. A reduction in government expenditure and/or an increase in taxation will have the opposite effect.

> Reasons for shifts in the aggregate demand curve

FACTORS CAUSING A CHANGE IN AGGREGATE SUPPLY

Many factors might cause a change in aggregate supply, i.e. an increase or decrease in the amount supplied at any given price level. Some of the more important factors are summarised below.

- **A change in costs of production** The short-run aggregate supply curve shows the planned level of output at different price levels, assuming the cost of producing any given level of output does not change. In other words, each level of output is associated with its own particular cost of production. Now if these costs change, e.g. because trade unions negotiate higher wage rates, this will reduce the amount firms are willing to supply at any given price level. In other words, the aggregate supply curve will shift inwards. A reduction in costs has the opposite effect.

- **Supply shocks** A supply shock causes an unanticipated but temporary shift in the short-run aggregate supply curve. Examples of supply shocks are bumper

> Reasons for shifts in the aggregate supply curve

harvests, or natural disasters like the severe flooding which affected parts of America in 1993 and seriously reduced agricultural output in many areas. The former implies an increase in aggregate supply and the latter a decrease.

- **Incentives** In recent years, greater emphasis has been placed on the importance of incentives in influencing aggregate supply. The importance of incentives is discussed more fully in Ch. 17 but it is important to note here that if greater incentives lead to increased productivity, this will shift both the long-run and the short-run aggregate supply curves to the right.

- **Investment and technological progress** Changes in investment and technological progress have important implications for productivity and aggregate supply. Again, as productivity rises the long-run and the short-run aggregate supply curves shift to the right.

THE EFFECT OF A CHANGE IN AGGREGATE DEMAND

We have already argued that, in the long run, aggregate supply is fixed at the natural rate. Because of this, a change in aggregate demand will, in the long run, only affect the *price level*. However, it will have a short-run effect on real income. To understand why, consider Fig. 9.11.

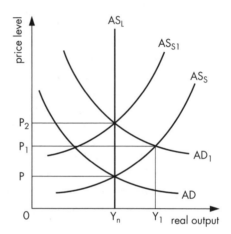

Fig. 9.11 The effect of an increase in aggregate demand in the short run and the long run

In Fig. 9.11, AD is the original aggregate demand curve, AS_S is the original short-run aggregate supply curve and AS_L is the long-run aggregate supply curve. Initially, the economy is in equilibrium with the price level at P and income at the natural rate OY_n. Now, suppose aggregate demand increases to AD_1. The economy moves up the short-run aggregate supply curve and, as a result, the price level rises to P_1 and real output increases to Y_1. However, the higher price level will lead to higher wages when contracts are renegotiated and, if there is no corresponding increase in productivity, the implied increase in costs shifts the aggregate supply curve to AS_{S1}. The economy is back in long-run equilibrium but, although output has returned to the natural rate, note that the price level has increased to P_2. (To understand more fully the process of adjustment back to long-run equilibrium, see Ch. 13.) The opposite sequence of events occurs when there is a fall in aggregate demand.

THE EFFECT OF A CHANGE IN AGGREGATE SUPPLY

To understand the effect of a change in aggregate supply let us consider Fig. 9.12. Again, we begin with AD as the original aggregate demand curve, AS_S as the original short-run aggregate supply curve and AS_L as the long-run aggregate supply curve. P is the price level and OY_n the level of real output. Now, if there is an exogenous increase in wage rates unmatched by an increase in productivity, the aggregate supply curve will shift to AS_{S1}, the price level will rise to P_1 and real output will fall to Y_1. However, the higher wage rates will shift the aggregate demand curve to AD_1 and long-run equilibrium will be restored when output has returned to the natural rate. Note that in long-run equilibrium, the price level has increased to P_2.

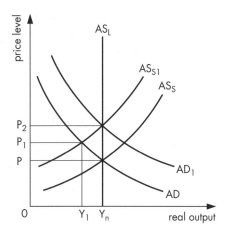

Fig 9.12 The effect of an exogenous increase in costs in the short run and the long run

APPLIED
MATERIALS

THE UK ECONOMY

One of the important concepts used in the Keynesian theory of income determination is the **multiplier**. However, in practice it is difficult to estimate the value of the multiplier. Nevertheless, it is unlikely that the marginal rate of leakage from changes in income will equal one. We can therefore be fairly certain that any change in injections will lead to a change in income that is larger than the change in injections. One estimate of the multiplier in the UK by M. Kennedy puts its value at 1.35. Other studies quoted by Kennedy, in *The UK Economy*, Artis (ed) produce a different value for the multiplier (mainly because they are based on different assumptions), but they are not vastly different from the estimate given here and it seems there is general agreement that the multiplier has a relatively low value in the UK.

There may be several reasons for the relatively low value of the multiplier. There is no doubt that the UK has a relatively high propensity to import. Kennedy estimates its value at 0.24 of GDP at factor cost. Additionally, the rise in the savings ratio in the UK to relatively high levels in recent years implies a relatively high marginal propensity to save. However, there is general agreement that tax levels in the UK are not disproportionately high compared with other countries. It follows that the value of the multiplier in the UK is likely to be relatively low, mainly because of the relatively high marginal propensities to import and save.

CONSUMPTION AND SAVING

An article in the *National Westminster Bank Quarterly Review* of February 1992 analyses the changing nature of the savings ratio in the UK. The savings ratio is of personal savings to personal income. Personal income is simply income from employment and self-employment plus personal receipts of rent, interest and profit plus transfer payments. Figure 9.13 shows the behaviour of the savings ratio in recent years.

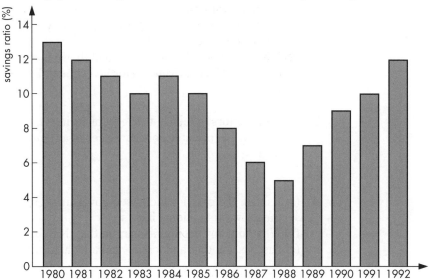

Fig. 9.13 The savings ratio in the UK, 1980–1992.
Source: HMSO, *Financial Statistics.*

Economists are very interested in the behaviour of the savings ratio because changes in it imply changes in consumption and this has a powerful effect on such economic aggregates as national income and employment. However, the savings ratio is clearly a very unstable statistic and, in recent years, several factors are thought to have influenced its behaviour:

■ **Inflation** Economists are not in agreement on the way inflation affects savings. However, it is often argued that as the rate of inflation increases, economic agents might be persuaded to increase the amount saved in order to preserve the real value of their savings. There is some support from the UK that there is a positive link between the rate of inflation and the rate of saving.

■ **The Business Cycle** Again economists are not completely in agreement on the way the business cycle affects savings, but there is some evidence that as unemployment rises, savings rise. One reason for this might be that the threat of redundancy encourages saving as a kind of insurance against the possibility of lower earnings in the future.

■ **Demographic changes** The UK has an ageing population which has affected the savings ratio. Older people tend to be major savers, whereas younger people tend to be major spenders as homes and families are established. However, in the UK there are clearly other factors involved because demographic changes cannot account for the sharp rise in the savings ratio after 1988.

■ **Financial innovation and deregulation** Financial innovation in the form of many new types of securities during the 1980s reduced the costs of borrowing for the financial sector while deregulation led to an increase in competition, e.g. between banks and building societies. This led to a substantial increase in borrowing; as more individuals and institutions become net borrowers, there will be fewer net savers.

EXAMINATION QUESTIONS

1 (a) Examine the factors which influence the size of the national income multiplier.
                                                                          (40)
   (b) Distinguish between the different multiplier effects of:
      (i) an increase in social security payments;   *(30)*
      (ii) a cut in the top rate of income tax.   *(30)*
                                                     (ULEAC January 1992)

2 (a) What is meant by the 'equilibrium level of national income'?   *(3)*
   (b) What are the main determinants of the level of national income in a closed economy with no government sector?   *(9)*
   (c) How can the government use fiscal policy to influence the equilibrium level of the national income?   *(7)*
   (d) It is sometimes claimed that too high levels of government spending will 'crowd out', i.e. reduce, private sector investment. Explain why this may be so.   *(6)*
                                                       (NICCEA June 1992)

3 (a) What factors influence the level of savings in an economy?   *(14)*
   (b) Discuss the possible consequences of a significant increase in the proportion of income saved.   *(11)*
                                                     (AEB November 1991)

4 (a) Explain the case for increased government spending as a means of stimulating the growth of national income.   *(9)*
   (b) Why do many economists argue that this policy would not work?   *(9)*
   (c) Discuss whether an increase in national income would benefit the UK economy.
                                                                          (7)

ANSWERS TO EXAMINATION QUESTIONS

TUTOR'S ANSWER TO QUESTION 1

(a) It is well known that a change in injections will lead to an ultimate change in income which is more than proportional to the change in injections. This is caused by the **multiplier effect**. The multiplier can therefore be defined as the ratio of the change in income to the change in injections that brought it about.

In symbols, the multiplier is usually written as:

$$k = \frac{1}{MRL}$$

where k is the multiplier and MRL is the marginal rate of leakage from the circular flow of income. Thus if the marginal propensity to save (MPS) is 0.25Yd, the marginal rate of tax (MRT) is 0.2Y and the marginal propensity to import (MPM) is 0.125Yd, where Y is gross income and Yd is disposable income, the value of the multiplier will be

$$\frac{1}{0.25(0.8) + 0.2 + 0.125(0.8)} = \frac{1}{0.2 + 0.2 + 0.1}$$

$$= \frac{1}{0.5}$$

$$= 2$$

Now, since the value of the multiplier is determined by the marginal rate of leakage, it follows that anything which changes the marginal rate of leakage will change the value of the multiplier. Perhaps the most obvious factor which influences the size of the multiplier is the marginal rate of taxation. Changes in the rate of taxation will affect the marginal rate of leakage directly, but also indirectly because it will change the amount individuals and organisations are able to save or spend on imports.

However, there are other, less obvious factors, which influence the size of the multiplier. Changes in the *level of income* will cause changes in the *marginal rate of leakage* from income. In general, as income rises we might expect the marginal rate of tax to increase, not only because rising incomes attract higher rates of taxation, but also because firms and individuals spend more on goods and services on which VAT is levied. We might also expect the marginal propensity to save and the marginal propensity to import to increase as income rises.

The size of the multiplier is also influenced by the *distribution of income*. If all other things are unchanged, the more uniform the distribution of income, the higher the value of the multiplier. In countries where distribution of income is not uniform, the marginal propensity to save might be relatively high as wealthy individuals and organisations save while the vast majority of people live in abject poverty. Where the distribution of income is more uniform, the marginal propensity to save is likely to be lower and the value of the multiplier will therefore be greater. Similarly, a change in the age structure of the population will influence the size of the multiplier. Where the population is ageing, the value of the multiplier will tend to fall because, in general, older people have a higher marginal propensity to save.

(b) (i) An increase in social security payments will tend to have a relatively large multiplier effect since they are received by those on relatively low incomes. Because of this, it is unlikely that an increase in social security payments will significantly affect the income tax liability of their recipients. Furthermore, those on low incomes will generally purchase more goods which are either zero rated, or completely exempt, of VAT. For any increase in social security payments therefore, the marginal rate of tax will be relatively low.

In addition, those who receive social security payments will tend to have a higher marginal propensity to consume, i.e. a lower marginal propensity to save, than those on higher incomes. The majority of any increase in social security payments will therefore be spent rather than saved or paid in taxation. Furthermore, the majority of expenditure generated by increased social security payments is likely to be spent on domestic output (except in so far as domestic output contains imports of raw materials) since imports tend to consist of relatively expensive consumer durables.

The implication is that an increase in social security payments will be associated with a relatively low marginal rate of leakage and therefore a relatively large multiplier effect.

(ii) A cut in the top rate of income tax will tend to have the opposite effect of an increase in social security payments. Top rate income tax payers are, by definition, relatively wealthy members of the community and they will therefore tend to have a higher marginal propensity to save. A larger proportion of the increase in disposable income which results from a cut in the top rate of income tax will therefore be saved, compared with an increase in disposable income which results from an increase in social security payments.

In addition, higher income earners will consume relatively more of those goods on which VAT is levied and therefore, to some extent, the effect on the marginal rate of leakage of a cut in the marginal rate of tax will be neutralised by an increase in VAT payments. Moreover, they will almost certainly consume more imported goods and services than those on lower incomes.

A cut in the top rate of income tax will therefore generate a smaller increase in expenditure on domestic output than an equivalent increase in social security payments. This implies that an increase in social security payments will have a larger multiplier effect than a cut in the top rate of income tax.

STUDENT'S ANSWER TO QUESTION 2

<table>
<tr>
<td>

Good

</td>
<td>

(a) An economy is in equilibrium when planned expenditure equals planned output. If planned expenditure exceeds planned output then national income will rise, and vice versa.

</td>
</tr>
<tr>
<td>

Define a closed economy

</td>
<td>

(b) In a closed economy, national income is equal to consumer's expenditure plus investment including additions to stock. In symbols, we can write Y = C + I, where Y is national income, C is consumer's expenditure and I is investment. The way in which equilibrium is determined in a two-sector economy can be illustrated diagramatically as in Figure 9.14.

</td>
</tr>
</table>

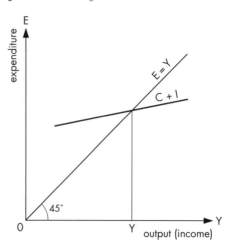

Fig. 9.14 The equilibrium level of income in a two-sector economy

Good; a diagram is presented and used in the text

In Figure 9.14 C + I represents total planned expenditure at different levels of national income and

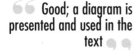

the 45° line represents all points of equality between planned expenditure and planned output. At any level of income below OY, total planned expenditure is greater than planned output. Firms will therefore experience an unplanned reduction in stocks and they will respond by increasing their output. Conversely, at any level of output above OY, planned expenditure will be less than planned output and firms will experience an unplanned increase in stocks. They will respond by reducing their output. Only when output is at OY, will planned expenditure equal planned output and in these circumstances there will be no tendency for output to change. OY is therefore the equilibrium level of output.

(c) In an economy which includes a government sector, national income is equal to consumer's expenditure, plus investment, plus direct government expenditure on goods and services (G). Thus we can write Y = C + I + G. It is important to stress that G is equal to direct government expenditure on goods and services rather than total government expenditure. Part of government expenditure includes transfer payments. These are simply transfers of income within the community and do not contribute directly to national income.

A change in G will lead to a direct change in national income. The magnitude of the change in national income depends on the magnitude of the change in G and on the value of the multiplier. In an economy with a government sector but no international trade, the value of the multiplier is equal to 1/(MPS + MRT) where MPS is the marginal propensity to save and MRT is the marginal rate of taxation. The smaller the marginal rate of leakage, the greater the value of the multiplier and therefore the greater the change in national income following a change in government expenditure.

(d) **Crowding out** is the term used to describe the effect of an increase in public sector expenditure on private sector investment. Basically, it is argued that an increase in public expenditure will, after a time lag, crowd out, i.e. lead to an equivalent reduction in, private sector investment.

It is argued that crowding out occurs because an increase in public sector expenditure leads to an increase in interest rates. This raises the cost of borrowing funds and because of this, firms revise their investment plans downwards.

OUTLINE ANSWERS

Question 3
This is quite a straightforward question but take care: you are asked for a discussion in part (b), rather than a list of the factors that influence the level of savings.
(a) The most obvious factor that influences the level of savings is the level of income.

If all other things remain the same, as income rises we might expect the average propensity to save to rise. Paradoxically there is some evidence that a fall in income might encourage a rise in the average propensity to save. One possible explanation is that, as the economy moves into recession, individuals attempt to save more to provide a cushion in the event of redundancy.

Another important determinant of aggregate savings is the state of the public sector accounts. This consists largely of the central government's budget and, if all other things remain the same, when there is a budget surplus the average propensity to save will be greater than when there is a budget deficit.

The extent to which the financial services sector is developed influences the aggregate level of savings. The availability of a banking sector in which people have confidence and of contractual savings schemes such as insurance policies and pension schemes will exert a powerful influence on the average propensity to save.

The rate of interest might exert some influence on the aggregate level of savings. It might be expected that as the rate of interest rises, firms and individuals will be persuaded to increase the proportion of income saved since the opportunity cost of expenditure will have increased. However, this is not necessarily the case. If firms and individuals are saving for a particular purpose, an increase in the rate of interest might lead to a fall in the amount saved. In addition, public sector saving and contractual saving are unaffected by changes in the rate of interest.

Expectations of future inflation might also affect the aggregate level of savings. When inflation is expected to rise, firms and individuals might be encouraged to bring forward their purchases and, in so doing, will reduce the amount they save.

Another important factor that influences the average propensity to save is the structure of the population. An ageing population tends to be associated with a relatively high average propensity to save.

(b) A significant increase in the proportion of income saved will make possible an increase in the rate of investment which, in turn, will make possible an increase in GNP and a rise in the standard of living. However, this result cannot be guaranteed. An increase in savings makes possible an increase in investment. It does not guarantee it.

Another possibility is that an increase in the proportion of income saved will throw the economy into recession because of the implied reduction in consumer's expenditure. If this is the case, unemployment will rise. However, the recession might also encourage a reduction in the rate of inflation and an improvement in the current account of the balance of payments.

Question 4

(a) You could begin your answer to this part of the question by explaining the Keynesian view of national income equilibrium. You could then explain why an increase in government spending will lead to a multiplied increase in national income.

(b) It is now argued by many economists that there is a natural rate of national income which is unaffected, in the long run, by government spending on goods and services. Indeed, it is argued that increased spending by governments on goods and services simply leads to a higher rate of inflation in the long run. (This approach is discussed on pp. 166–169.)

(c) It would be useful to begin your answer to this part of the question by explaining the distinction between *nominal* national income and *real* national income. Only an increase in the latter will benefit the economy because it implies an increase in the volume of output produced. If all other things remain the same, this implies a higher standard of living and a reduction in unemployment.

Further reading

Begg, Dornbusch and Fischer, *Economics* (3rd edn), McGraw-Hill 1991: Ch. 21, The determination of national income; Ch. 22, Aggregate demand, fiscal policy and foreign trade.

Harrison et al, *Introductory Economics*, Macmillan 1992: Ch. 19, The Determination of National Income: the four-sector Economy; Ch. 21, Investment; Ch. 22, Aggregate Demand and Aggregate Supply.

REVIEW SHEET

1 Identify, and briefly outline, four key components of aggregate demand.

(a) _____

(b) _____

(c) _____

(d) _____

2 Draw a diagram of the consumption function.

3 Briefly explain the key features of this consumption function.

_____

_____

_____

4 State the equilibrium condition for national income.

_____

5 Draw a 45° diagram to show how the equilibrium level of national income is determined.

6 Explain, using your diagram, why only one (unique) level of national income can be said to be the equilibrium.

_____

_____

_____

_____

7 List three leakages/withdrawals from the circular flow of income.

(a) _____

(b) _____

(c) _____

8 List three injections into the circular flow of income.

(a) _____

(b) _____

(c) _____

9 Draw a diagram with leakages and injections on it, showing how the equilibrium level of national income is determined.

10 Explain why using your diagram, there is only one (unique) level of national income which could be said to be the equilibrium.

_____

_____

_____

11 Write down a formula for the national income multiplier.

_____

12 List three factors which might cause the multiplier to increase.

(a) _____

(b) _____

(c) _____

13 Draw diagrams to show the following:

Deflationary gap   **Inflationary gap**

14 Briefly explain, referring to your diagrams, how the government could remove each gap.

Deflationary gap: _____

_____

Inflationary gap: _____

_____

15 Explain the process of discounting to present value.

_____

_____

_____

16 Explain why investment is likely to rise as the rate of interest falls.

_____

_____

_____

WAGES

GETTING STARTED

We have seen, in Chapter 8, that the value of all factor incomes received in a particular year is equal to a country's gross national product. In this chapter, we are concerned with the share of national income that goes to labour in the form of wages. Reference to Table 8.1 (p. 132) shows that approximately 70 per cent of all incomes earned are wages.

With the exception of profit, the reward that any factor of production receives is clearly equal to the price which is paid to hire it. As with all prices in competitive markets, the price of any factor of production is determined by supply and demand. However, the factors of production are not demanded in order to obtain ownership, as is the case with consumer goods, but rather because of the stream of services they offer. For example, the demand for labour implies a demand for the mental and physical effort of workers involved in production. Because of this, the demand for labour (and indeed for any factor of production) is referred to as a **derived demand** rather than a direct demand. It is derived from the demand for the product which labour (and all other factors) produces.

The classical theory of income distribution is the **marginal productivity theory**. According to this theory, firms will continue to employ factors of production until the employment of the marginal unit of each factor adds as much to revenue as it does to costs. For simplicity, it is sometimes assumed that there is perfect competition in the market in which the product is sold so that firms sell their entire output at the *ruling market price*. In these circumstances, the contribution of the marginal unit of any factor of production, i.e. its *marginal revenue product*, is equal to the factor's *marginal physical product* multiplied by the price at which the product is sold.

In markets which are *not* perfect, firms will be compelled to reduce price in order to sell more units. Because of this, marginal revenue product can only be measured as the change in total revenue when the additional output of the marginal factor is sold.

THE MARGINAL PRODUCTIVITY THEORY

66 MRP is the employers' concern 99

ESSENTIAL PRINCIPLES

We have seen in Chapter 3 that the marginal physical product of labour is the addition to total output from the employment of the marginal worker. The **law of variable proportions** predicts that marginal physical product at first rises but subsequently falls as the employment of workers increases. However, employers are not so concerned with marginal physical product as with marginal revenue product (MRP) and profit maximising firms will continue to employ workers until the last person employed adds exactly the same to revenue as to costs, i.e. until MRP = MC.

This is the basic prediction of the marginal productivity theory, and it is possible to consider the implications of this in different market structures.

PERFECT COMPETITION IN THE FACTOR AND PRODUCT MARKETS

If we assume perfect competition in the product market, so that the firm sells its entire output at the ruling market price, and perfect competition in the labour market, so that the firm recruits workers at a constant wage rate, the profit-maximising condition is easily demonstrated.

NO. OF WORKERS	TOTAL PRODUCT	MARGINAL PHYSICAL PRODUCT	MARGINAL REVENUE PRODUCT	MARGINAL COST	TOTAL REVENUE PRODUCT	TOTAL COST	TOTAL PROFIT
1	12	12	60	100	60	100	−40
2	26	14	70	100	130	200	−70
3	50	24	120	100	250	300	−50
4	90	40	200	100	450	400	50
5	140	50	250	100	700	500	200
6	200	60	300	100	1,000	600	400
7	254	54	270	100	1,270	700	570
8	304	50	250	100	1,520	800	720
9	340	36	180	100	1,700	900	800
10	358	18	90	100	1,790	1,000	790
11	374	16	80	100	1,870	1,100	770
12	378	4	20	100	1,890	1,200	690

Table 10.1

Table 10.1 assumes a constant market price for the product of £5 per unit and a constant wage rate of £100 per worker per week. It is clear that after the employment of the second person and up to the employment of the ninth person, each worker adds more to revenue than to cost. After the employment of the ninth worker, the situation is reversed and each additional employee adds more to costs than to revenue. It follows that profit is maximised when nine people are employed.

The individual firm's demand for labour

The general relationship between MRP, ARP and the number of workers employed at a constant wage rate is set out diagrammatically in Fig. 10.1. At a constant wage (when MC = AC) of OW, the profit-maximising firm will employ OM workers, where MRP = MC. If the market wage rate increases to OW_1, the number of workers employed will fall to OM_1. It follows that when there is perfect competition in the factor and product markets, the firm's demand for labour curve is that part of its MRP curve which lies below its ARP curve. At wage rates above ARP, the firm is making a loss and will not undertake production.

66 The firm's demand curve for labour, under perfect competition 99

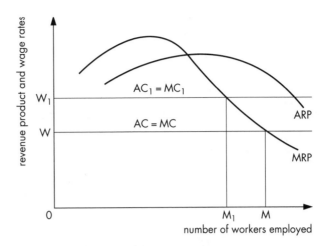

Fig. 10.1 Wage rates and
employment in perfect competition

IMPERFECT COMPETITION IN THE PRODUCT MARKET

The fundamentals of the analysis are unchanged if we relax the assumption of perfect
competition in the *product market*. There will still be a tendency for marginal revenue
product at first to rise and to pull up average revenue product because of increasing
returns. Subsequently, the onset of diminishing returns will mean that MRP will fall as
successive workers are employed, and this will eventually pull down the ARP. However,
with *imperfect product markets* there are now two reasons why marginal revenue
product declines as employment expands beyond a certain point:

- the onset of diminishing returns;
- firms with imperfect product markets must now reduce the price of all units in
  order to increase sales (see Chapters 5 and 6).

In imperfect markets then, marginal revenue product is determined both by marginal
physical product and by the effect on market price of an increase in output. Because
price will always fall in imperfect markets as output increases, the effect is to make the

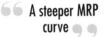

A steeper MRP
curve

MRP curve fall more steeply than for firms in perfect competition. Nevertheless, where
the firm recruits additional workers at a constant wage rate, its demand for labour is
still given by its (now steeper) marginal revenue product curve.

IMPERFECT COMPETITION IN THE FACTOR MARKET

When there is imperfect competition in the *factor market*, the firm will be unable to
recruit as many workers as it wishes at the ruling wage rate. Instead, it will be
compelled to increase wage rates in order to attract more workers. The marginal cost
of employing additional workers will therefore rise as employment increases, so that
the marginal cost curve will now lie above the average cost curve. Figure 10.2 shows
the equilibrium position of the firm when there is imperfect competition in the factor
market. The intersection of MC with MRP determines the *number of workers employed*
and the average cost curve determines the *wage rate* at this level of employment. In

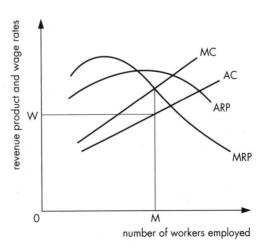

Fig 10.2 Wage rates and
competition in imperfect
competition

other words, because the marginal cost and average cost of employing additional workers are no longer the same, the firm's marginal revenue product curve no longer shows the demand for labour at any given wage rate.

INDUSTRY'S DEMAND FOR LABOUR

It is clear that the marginal revenue productivity theory is not a theory of wage determination. It simply enables us to identify the number of workers that will be employed at a given wage rate and in certain situations. In fact for most workers, wage rates are fixed at any moment in time. For many workers, wages are negotiated collectively by their union, while many other workers receive the rate negotiated by unions even though they are not union members. Nevertheless, as a theory of the firm's *demand for labour*, the marginal productivity theory still has some relevance.

ELASTICITY OF DEMAND FOR LABOUR

However, a theory of wage determination in competitive markets involves an understanding of the *market demand* and *market supply* conditions which relate to any particular occupation. If we know the number of workers each firm demands at any given wage rate, then we can derive the *industry's* demand for labour by adding together the *individual firm's* demand curves. Because each individual firm's demand for labour varies inversely with the wage rate, the industry's demand for labour will also vary inversely with the wage rate. In other words, market demand for labour will expand as the wage rate falls. The *elasticity* of an industry's demand for labour will, as with any factor of production, vary directly with:

66 Factors affecting elasticity of demand for labour 99

- the elasticity of demand for the product produced by the industry;
- the proportion of total costs of production accounted for by labour; and
- the elasticity of substitution between labour and other factors of production, i.e. the ease with which labour can be substituted by other factors.

The demand for labour will therefore be less elastic:

- the less elastic is the demand for the product it produces;
- the smaller the proportion of total costs accounted for by labour input; and
- the less easy it is to substitute labour by capital or by other factors.

SUPPLY OF LABOUR AND THE WAGE RATE

The supply of labour to any particular occupation will vary directly with the wage rate. At higher wage rates, more workers will be available for employment in the occupation and vice versa. however, in certain cases, the supply of labour to an occupation might be relatively inelastic in the short run. For example, where the nature of work is highly skilled and requires considerable training, the supply of labour to the occupation will *not* rise substantially as wage rates increase. This is true of doctors and barristers, for example. Nevertheless, the supply of labour to *all* occupations will be more elastic in the long run than in the short run. Where wages increase in particular occupations, more people will be encouraged to undertake the necessary training, so increasing the amount of labour available. In the case of unskilled labour, supply will tend to be relatively elastic in both the short run and the long run, since little, if any, training is required.

DETERMINATION OF WAGES

In competitive labour markets, wage rates are determined by the forces of supply and demand for labour. In these circumstances, different wage rates between occupations will reflect differences in the respective conditions of supply and demand conditions in two hypothetical labour markets (see Fig. 10.3).

The higher wage rate in one labour market is due entirely to the fact that *at any given wage rate* demand for labour is greater and supply of labour is lower than in the other labour market. However, you should also note that in this labour market, demand for, and supply of labour are relatively inelastic compared to the labour market with the

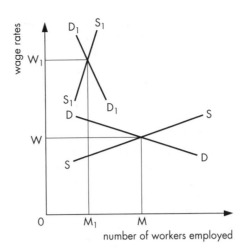

Fig. 10.3 Wage rates in different labour markets

lower wage rate. The higher wage rate is therefore likely to reflect conditions in a market for skilled labour and the lower wage rate is likely to reflect conditions in a market for unskilled labour. The different elasticity conditions will be an important factor in preserving the wage differential between these labour markets.

Given a free market and a particular set of supply and demand conditions for labour, only one wage rate is sustainable: that which equates supply of labour with demand for labour. It follows that wages in a particular occupation can only change if there is a prior change in the conditions of supply, or in the conditions of demand, or in both. Furthermore, differences in wage rates between occupations will reflect differences in the conditions of supply and demand for different types of workers.

THE EFFECT OF A TRADE UNION

A trade union is usually defined as a group of workers who band together to pursue certain common aims, especially the achievement of wage increases for their members. A trade union can therefore influence the supply of labour to an industry depending on the extent to which the workforce are members of the union. Their ability to obtain such increases depends on several factors and, in particular, on the elasticity of demand for labour as discussed on p. 180. If all other things remain the same, a union's ability to obtain higher wages is greater, the *less elastic* the demand for labour.

There are several areas to consider: restricting supply, productivity, profit-financed wage increases and reducing supply.

RESTRICTING SUPPLY

A union might refuse to supply workers below a particular wage rate. The implications of this are examined in Fig. 10.4.

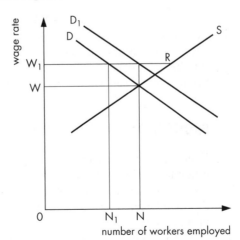

Fig. 10.4 The effect of a trade union on wage rates and employment in an industry

Supply and demand for labour in this industry are initially represented by S and D respectively and the equilibrium wage rate is OW with ON workers employed. If a trade union now demands a pay rise of WW_1 and refuses to supply labour below OW_1, then the effective supply curve of labour to this industry becomes W_1RS. If all other things remain the same, the higher wage rate implies a reduction in the number of workers employed to ON_1. However, if demand for the product is rising, perhaps because of a general rise in incomes, it might be possible for the firm to finance the increase in wages by raising the price of the product. The effect of this will be to raise the demand for labour (MRP = MPP × price) at each and every wage rate. In this case, the demand increases to D_1, with the result that the higher wage rate OW_1 does *not* lead to any reduction in the number of workers employed.

In practice, this is often what happens as a result of an increase in wages. Firms are able to pass on the costs of wage increases in the form of higher prices, helped by the fact that incomes in the economy as a whole rise over time. However, when firms are unable to pass on the full effect of higher costs to consumers because demand is relatively price elastic and income inelastic, the higher wage increase might lead to some workers losing their jobs.

HIGHER PRODUCTIVITY

Another way in which a trade union might obtain a higher wage rate for its members is by increasing productivity. If all other things remain the same, it is possible to increase wage rates by the same percentage as an increase in productivity without increasing average costs of production. Of course, because of increased productivity, the firm will have a larger output to sell. Provided price remains constant this again implies an increase in the demand for labour as each worker's marginal revenue product increases. Figure 10.5 illustrates that, in these circumstances, it is possible for a firm to pay higher wages without necessarily reducing the number of workers employed.

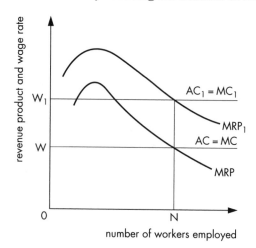

Fig. 10.5 The effect of an increase in productivity where there is perfect competition in the product market

Initially, the wage rate is OW and ON workers are employed, because profits are maximised here (MRP = MC). If an increase in productivity shifts the MRP curve to MRP_1, it is possible to increase wages to OW_1 without there being any reduction in the number of workers employed. This explains why so much emphasis is attached to productivity deals when wage increases are negotiated.

PROFIT-FINANCED WAGE INCREASES

Even without an increase in marginal revenue productivity, it might be possible for a union to obtain a substantial wage increase for its members. This would be possible if it could persuade employers to accept a cut in profits. Figure 10.6 is used to illustrate this point and refers to a firm operating with perfect competition in the factor and product markets.

If ARP and MRP represent the net returns to labour, it follows that at the profit-maximising level of employment (OM), employers earn a surplus of XY per worker. If unions can persuade employers to accept a smaller surplus, it is possible to negotiate a higher wage rate above the existing level OW, without reducing the number of workers

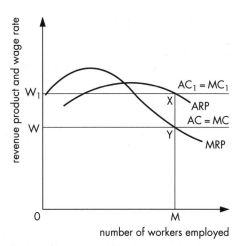

Fig.10.6 The net contribution of labour to profit

employed. For example, employers might be willing to offer a wage of OW_1 rather than risk the union taking industrial action with a consequent loss of output. If the union took this course, profits might be seriously affected and, in these circumstances, offering the higher wage rate might still leave the firm earning the highest attainable profit.

REDUCING SUPPLY

In the long run, unions might be able to reduce the supply of labour to the industry without any of its members becoming unemployed. The most obvious way in which this can be achieved is to reduce the number of workers taken on annually. A trade union can do this by restricting the number of trainees or apprentices taken on annually or by insisting on a reduction in the number of part-time workers. Over time, as workers leave the industry through retirement and job-changing, this will bring about a reduction in the supply of workers to the industry. The effect of this is illustrated in Fig. 10.7. In the long run, a reduction in the number of employees taken on annually shifts the supply curve of labour from SS to S_1S_1. As a result, wages rise from OW to OW_1 and although employment in the industry falls from OM to OM_1, higher wages have not led to union members becoming unemployed. In this sense, wage increases might be self-financing, because although the wage rate has increased, the total wage bill might actually fall. In recent years, wage bargaining has often been accompanied by moves to increase the early retirement of workers and here again the aim is to offer a wage increase without proportionately increasing the total wage bill. Reducing the supply of labour might be particularly effective when productivity can be increased or when capital is easily substituted for labour.

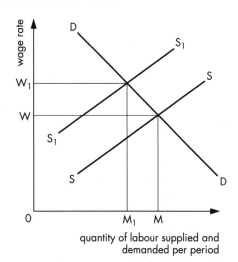

Fig. 10.7 The effect on wage rates of a reduction in the supply of labour to a particular occupation

COLLECTIVE BARGAINING

DEFINITION AND SCOPE

Collective bargaining is the term used to describe arrangements whereby a trade union bargains collectively on behalf of its membership about such matters as pay and conditions, rather than each person negotiating these matters individually with their employer. The aim of bargaining collectively is to strengthen the bargaining power of the workforce. In the UK, a two-tier system of collective bargaining is said to exist with bargains being struck at the 'national level' and the 'local level'. Often minimum levels of pay and conditions are negotiated at the national level, and these are supplemented at the local level so as to reflect different conditions in particular markets. Agreements in the UK normally run for twelve months, but they are not legally binding and either party can terminate them at any time.

ADVANTAGES OF COLLECTIVE BARGAINING

Better pay and conditions
There seems little doubt that on average those workers who are members of a trade union have benefited in terms of obtaining better pay and working conditions than could have been negotiated by individual employees.

Grievance procedure
Agreements reached through collective bargaining cover more than just the pay and conditions of employees. A very important area frequently covered is the establishment of procedures to be followed in the event of a dispute. It is widely agreed that the existence of this has reduced the incidence of industrial action.

DISADVANTAGES OF COLLECTIVE BARGAINING

Labour market imperfections
It has been argued that when unions negotiate the pay of their members they introduce a monopoly element into the labour market which might raise the price of labour but lead to a reduction in the numbers employed. It might also adversely affect the allocation of resources.

Misallocation of resources
It is sometimes suggested that agreements reached nationally have often had little regard to the national interest. In particular, wage awards in certain industries establish minimum acceptable levels for other industries irrespective of supply and demand conditions in different labour markets. This process prevents the price mechanism from functioning efficiently in the labour market. To the extent that this has happened, collective bargaining has led to inefficiency in the allocation of resources and might be a source of inflation. Similarly, if bargains include agreements to maintain employment levels even after the introduction of labour-saving machinery, this will create inefficiency in the allocation of resources and might again raise costs and prices.

MINIMUM WAGES

Low pay is regarded as an economic problem because it means that some people have a low standard of living. Many ideas have been put forward to deal with the problem of low pay. It is often suggested that a **statutory minimum wage** is one of the most effective means of dealing with this problem.

If we consider a single labour market, we can analyse the consequences of establishing a legal minimum wage above the existing equilibrium wage in this labour market. In Fig. 10.8, demand for labour is represented by DD and supply of labour is represented by SS. The equilibrium wage is OW, and OM workers are employed.

If the minimum wage is set above OW, for example at OW_1, those workers who receive the higher wage clearly gain when a minimum wage is established. However, by raising the price of labour, the minimum wage leads to a reduction in the number of workers employed, which now falls to OM_1. In other words, fewer workers are employed at a higher wage. In terms of economic theory, they lose employment

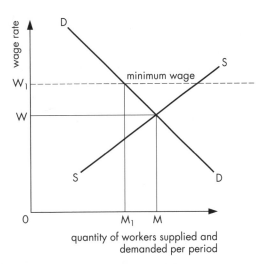

Fig. 10.8

because their marginal revenue productivity is less than the statutory minimum wage. If we add together all the labour markets affected in this way, then this implies an increase in unemployment nationally should a legal minimum wage be established. So, setting a legal minimum wage may raise the earnings of the low paid workers still employed, but make those that become unemployed worse off.

The *extent* to which unemployment rises as a result of the minimum wage depends on the **elasticity of demand for labour**. In fact, the elasticity of demand for labour in each market will depend on:

(i)   the elasticity of demand for the product which that labour produces;
(ii) the ease with which other factors of production can be substituted for labour; and
(iii) the proportion of total costs which are made up of labour costs.

Since low-paid workers are often unskilled, there is likely to be some substitutability between factors. In addition, low-paid workers are often employed in labour intensive occupations, such as local authority ancillaries, cleaners and canteen staff. In these cases, labour costs form a large proportion of total costs. Both of these factors will tend to make demand for low-paid workers relatively elastic. The greater the elasticity of demand for labour, the greater will be the impact of a legal minimum wage on the numbers employed.

Another factor to consider is the effect of school leavers on employment. If the minimum wage applies to *all* workers, this will reduce the incentive of firms to take on and train young workers since their higher wage will represent an effective increase in training costs. This has very serious implications and could lead to major skill shortages in the future and a consequently slower growth of productivity.

Another possible consequence of a statutory minimum wage is a reduction in the mobility of labour. The price mechanism functions in the labour market (as well as in product markets) and discharges its role of allocating workers to the highest bidders. By reducing the differentials available from changing jobs, a statutory minimum wage reduces the incentive of workers to seek better paid alternatives. Here again productivity might be adversely affected in the future, because expanding industries might not be able to offer a wide enough differential to persuade workers to leave their existing jobs.

The establishment of a statutory minimum wage might also lead to wage demands from trade unions in order to safeguard their established differentials. If pay awards are granted in excess of productivity, this will generate inflation and might well leave the real wage of the low paid unchanged, even after the establishment of a legal minimum wage. In fact, the relative position of the low paid might be adversely affected as a result of such pay awards!

If inflation is generated, it is also possible that a statutory minimum wage will adversely affect the position of the low-paid workers in another way. Higher prices in the domestic market will make exports less competitive and imports more competitive. This will lead to unemployment in the domestic economy. To the extent that those workers who become unemployed were previously employed in low-wage occupations, they will be adversely affected by the statutory minimum wage. Furthermore, any lack of competitiveness might encourage employers to offer smaller pay increases to their workers in an attempt to restore competitiveness.

NEW EARNINGS SURVEY

Every year the Department of Employment publishes the *New Earnings Survey* which gives details on earnings and hours worked by all the different occupational groups. Table 10.2 shows average gross weekly earnings of full-time males in selected occupations in April 1992. There are clearly substantial differences in earnings between occupations.

OCCUPATIONAL GROUP	AVERAGE GROSS WEEKLY EARNINGS (£)
Medical practitioner	780
Solicitor	621.9
Electrical engineer	513.7
Accountant	489.3
Architect	479.4
Police officer (sergeant and below)	431.4
Quantity surveyor	385.9
Sales representative	365.9
Ambulanceman	294.7
Motor vehicle mechanic	273.5
Bricklayer	242.0
Roadsweeper	222.3
Chef	217.3
Waiter	188.5
Bar staff	178.9
Hospital porter	173.9

Table 10.2 Average gross weekly earnings of full-time males in selected occupations in April 1992.

Source: New Earnings Survey: Department of Employment, 1993.

A great deal of research has focused on the **union mark-up**, i.e. on the differential in rates of pay between union workers and non-union workers. Estimates of this vary widely. Earlier research in this area put the differential at 30 per cent or so, but more recent estimates put the differential much lower than this at around 10 per cent. No one doubts that a differential exists; the problem lies in accurately measuring it. Realistically, the differential is unlikely to be great. After all, if it was there would be a powerful incentive to join a union, but union membership is falling in the UK! In the peak year of 1979, trade union membership reached 13.289 million. It is currently less than 10 million and accounts for less than 40 per cent of the civilian labour force.

UNIONS AND THEIR MEMBERSHIP

In recent years there has been a decline in the number of unions and in the total membership of unions. A report in the *Department of Employment Gazette*, April 1992, discusses these trends. Figure 10.9 illustrates these trends while Table 10.3 gives information on union numbers and membership in 1990.

NO. OF MEMBERS	NO. OF UNIONS	MEMBERSHIP (000S)	NO. OF UNIONS (%)	MEMBERSHIP OF ALL UNIONS (%)
Under 100	44	2	15.3	0.02
100–499	65	17	22.6	0.2
500–999	22	15	7.7	0.2
1,000–2,499	43	72	15	0.7
2,500–4,999	27	98	9.4	1
5,000–9,999	15	104	5.2	1
10,000–14,999	6	71	2.1	0.7
15,000–24,999	9	167	3.1	1.7
25,000–49,999	25	892	8.7	9
50,000–99,999	7	490	2.4	4.9
100,000–249,999	14	2,233	4.9	22.4
250,000 and more	9	5,785	3.1	58.2
*membership unknown	1		0.3	
All	287	9,947	100	100

Table 10.3 Trade unions: numbers and membership December 1990

*There was one newly formed union in 1990 whose membership is not available.

Source: Department of Employment Gazette, April 1992.

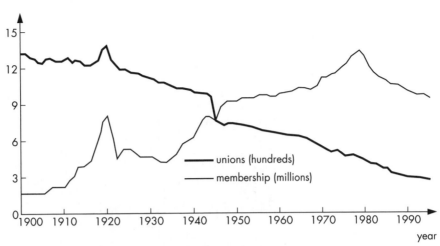

Fig. 10.9 Numbers and membership of trade unions, 1900–1990

Source: Department of Employment Gazette, April 1992

The main conclusions of the report are summarised below.

■ At the end of 1990, there were 287 unions in the United Kingdom with 9.9 million members – the lowest membership since 1961.

■ There were 22 fewer unions and 211,000 less members than in 1989.

■ This was the eleventh consecutive fall in membership from the peak of 13.3 million in 1979, taking it more than 25 per cent below the peak level.

■ The reduction in membership was almost entirely a result of a fall in male membership, although men still accounted for two-thirds of the membership.

■ Union density declined from 38.8 per cent of employees to 38 per cent over the year to spring 1990.

TRENDS IN PAY FLEXIBILITY

During the 1980s, there were radical changes in the conduct of industrial relations in Britain. An article in the *Department of Employment Gazette*, September 1993, looks at one aspect of this: trends in pay flexibility.

Two key developments have profoundly influenced the way in which pay is determined:

(a) the tendency towards greater decentralisation of business activities which has often included a decentralisation of industrial relations arrangements; and

(b) increased managerial emphasis on treating each employee as an individual with a concomitant decline in the role of collective arrangements.

Figure 10.10 provides some relevant information. Figure 10.10 shows data on the proportion of employees whose pay was *directly* affected by collective national agreements. It shows that in the early- to mid-1970s the pay of over half of all full-time employees was affected by one of these agreements. The proportion fell to below 50 per cent in the late 1970s but the most dramatic fall occurred between 1985 and 1990 when the proportion affected by them fell from 47 per cent to 34 per cent.

The downward trend in the importance of collective agreements is not uniform across all industries. Indeed, differences in pay determination tend to reflect differences between the public and private sectors. The vast majority of employees in the public sector, and almost as high a proportion in public sector workplaces, were covered by collective bargaining. This is a completely different institutional pattern from the private sector. In the private sector, collective bargaining was less widespread, especially for non-manual employees. Bargaining structures were also more decentralised, with a good deal of company-, plant- or establishment-level bargaining taking place.

There was also a link between pay determination and workplace size. In establishments with over 500 employees, collective bargaining was very much the norm and, in very large establishments, multi-union/employer agreements were more common. Single union/employer bargaining tended to be more important in workplaces with between 200 and 1,000 employees.

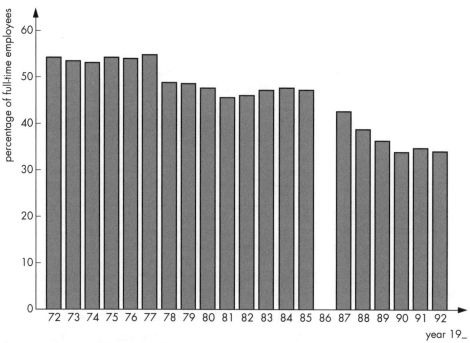

Fig. 10.10 Coverage of major collective agreements: proportion of full-time employees, whose pay was directly affected

Source: Department of Employment Gazette, September 1993

It is also noted in the article that increasing attention has been paid in recent years to the link between pay and performance. Performance-related pay is now widespread and was used in over half of all establishments in 1990. Again, there are differences between the public and private sector and, in 1990, private-sector workplaces were almost twice as likely as public-sector workplaces to use individual or group incentive payments.

EXAMINATION QUESTIONS

1 Do you agree that the higher wages paid in some occupations occur solely because some trade unions have a stronger bargaining position than others?

(UCLES November 1992)

2 (a) How can the differences between positive and normative economics be illustrated by reference to the proposal for a national minimum wage? *(3)*
(b) Examine the likely economic effects of the implementation of a national minimum wage. *(7)*

(ULEAC June 1993)

3 Some occupations, such as nursing, are vital but are paid very little. Others, such as financial advisers, are not so vital but are very highly paid. How can economic theory explain this situation?

(UCLES June 1992)

4 Consider how economic theory might be used to explain the following examples of wage differentials:
(a) the higher than average wages earned by star footballers like Ian Rush; *(7)*
(b) the tendency for unionised workers to earn on average more than non-unionised workers *(6)*
(c) the higher wages of manual workers on North Sea oil rigs compared with manual workers on shore; and *(6)*
(d) the tendency for university graduates to earn on average more than non-graduates. *(6)*

(WJEC 1992)

ANSWERS TO EXAMINATION QUESTIONS

TUTOR'S ANSWER TO QUESTION 1

A trade union is a group of workers who band together to pursue certain common aims. In particular, trade unions bargain for higher wages and better working conditions for their members. How successful they are at gaining higher wages without loss of jobs is a matter of dispute, but there is no doubt that unionised workers, on average, receive higher wages than non-unionised workers.

The demand for labour is derived from the demand for the product which labour produces. Economic theory hypothesises that workers will be employed up to the point at which their marginal revenue product, i.e. the contribution of the last worker employed to total revenue, equals their marginal cost. It is argued that, as more workers are employed, marginal revenue product will at first rise because of the increase in productivity which specialisation makes possible, but will subsequently decline as diminishing returns set in. The rising marginal revenue product will, at first, pull up average revenue product but as soon as marginal revenue product dips below the existing average revenue product, average revenue product will decline. The behaviour of marginal revenue product and average revenue product is important because it enables us to derive a demand curve for labour. Figure 10.11 is used for illustration.

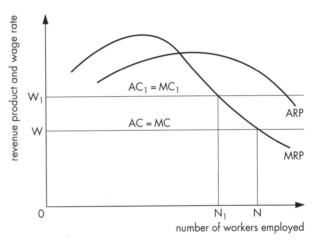

Fig 10.11 Wage rates and employment in perfect competition

If the marginal cost of labour is W, a profit-maximising firm will employ ON workers. If the wage rate is W_1, a profit-maximising firm will employ ON_1 workers. In other words, from the firm's marginal revenue product curve, we can derive the firm's demand for labour at any given wage rate. To do this, we simply equate marginal cost with marginal revenue. By summing the demand curve for labour of all individual firms in the industry, we can derive the industry's demand for labour curve. Since the firm's demand for labour curve slopes down from left to right, it is hypothesised that the industry's demand for labour curve will also slope down from left to right. It is also argued that the supply of labour curve slopes upwards from left to right because it will be necessary to offer workers higher wages in order to attract them away from alternative employment. The determination of wages in a free market is illustrated in Fig. 10.12.

In this labour market, the equilibrium wage is OW. However, if a trade union is formed and demands a wage of W_1 and refuses to supply labour below this wage, then this might be one reason why the existence of a trade union will result in unionised workers receiving higher wages than non-unionised workers. However, if all other things remain the same, fewer workers will be employed at the higher wage.

It is also possible that, by restricting the number of trainees taken on annually, trade unions can exercise some control over the supply of workers so as to gain higher wages. Another possible explanation of wage differentials through the influence of a trade union is when a union negotiates a wage increase financed by a cut in profits. Figure 10.13 is used to explain this possibility.

In Fig. 10.13, the firm is maximising profits when the wage rate is W and the number of workers employed is N. At this wage rate, the firm earns a surplus per worker of XY,

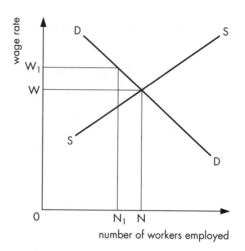

Fig. 10.12 The effect of trade union negotiation

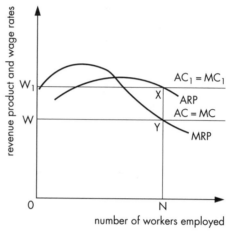

Fig. 10.13 The net contribution of labour to profit

i.e. the difference between the average cost of labour and the average revenue product. If the firm pays a wage of W_1, it is earning normal profit. XY therefore represents the scope for bargaining between a trade union and the employer. Any wage increase granted above W must be financed by a cut in profits. It is most unlikely that an individual worker would be able to persuade a firm to finance a wage rise by a cut in profits, but it is conceivable that a trade union, bargaining collectively on behalf of the workforce, will be able to do so.

In practice, trade unions are not the only factor which influences the amount workers receive. *Elasticity of demand for labour* is an important determinant of wage rates. If all other things remain the same, elasticity of demand for labour will be greater when demand for the product labour produces is inelastic. Another important influence on the elasticity of demand for labour is the elasticity of substitution between capital and labour. If this is low, demand for labour will be less elastic than otherwise. Similarly, if labour costs represent only a small proportion of total costs, elasticity of demand for labour will be lower than otherwise because a wage rise will have relatively little effect on total costs and therefore relatively little effect on the price of the product. Trade unions can exploit a low elasticity of demand for labour to the advantage of their members. However, if all things remain the same, a low elasticity of demand will tend to be associated with a higher wage rate than otherwise – even in the absence of trade-union activity.

With or without trade unions, wage differentials would exist because of differences in supply and demand conditions in different labour markets. The earlier Fig. 10.3 (p. 181) is used as a basis for explanation.

In Fig. 10.3 S_1 is the supply and D_1 is the demand, for *skilled* labour. The supply of skilled labour is relatively inelastic because of the time it takes to train additional workers. Demand is also relatively inelastic because there are no substitutes for skilled workers. S is the supply and D is the demand, for *unskilled* workers. Supply is relatively elastic because there is little or no time involved in training unskilled workers. They already possess the necessary skill requirements. Demand also tends to be relatively elastic because, since work is unskilled, it can often be carried out by individuals for themselves if the price rises too severely. In addition, unskilled work usually has a relatively high degree of substitutability between capital and labour. A rise in the price of labour will therefore result in a relatively large contraction of demand as capital is substituted for labour. In the skilled versus unskilled labour markets, wage differentials exist more because of the differences in the elasticity of demand and supply of labour than because of trade-union influence.

Some occupations, such as deep-sea diving, are relatively dangerous. In such cases, supply is likely to be relatively inelastic. On the other hand, when the services of a deep-sea diver are required, there is no substitute so that demand will be relatively inelastic. Again, inelastic demand and inelastic supply explain wage differentials between labour markets irrespective of any trade-union activity.

In some labour markets, trade unions can exert considerable influence over wage rates. However, their power is constrained by the conditions of supply and demand and in labour markets where supply and demand are relatively inelastic, wage rates will be higher than in labour markets where demand and supply are relatively elastic – irrespective of whether workers are unionised or not.

STUDENT'S ANSWER TO QUESTION 2

(a) **Positive economics** deals with objective statements. The accuracy of such statements can be checked by reference to the facts and proved to be either correct or incorrect. **Normative statements,** on the other hand, are matters of opinion. Such statements cannot be checked by reference to the facts since they are neither correct nor incorrect. With reference to minimum wages, an example of an objective statement is: "In the UK, there is no national minimum wage." An example of a normative statement is "Everyone in employment should receive at least a national minimum wage."

> 66 You might have included a little more detail here. After all, this section carries 30 per cent of the marks! 99

(b) A national minimum wage will have several effects, not all of which will work to the advantage of the labour force. In particular, it is almost certain that a national minimum wage will lead to an increase in unemployment. This possibility is illustrated in Fig. 10.14.

> 66 Not necessarily if productivity increases 99

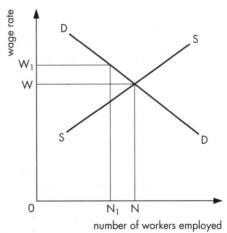

Fig. 10.14 The effect of a minimum wage

In Fig. 10.14, DD and SS represent the demand and supply conditions in the labour market. OW is the equilibrium wage rate and, in equilibrium, ON workers will be employed. However, if a national minimum wage is established at OW_1, the number of workers employed will fall to ON_1. The earnings of those who retain their jobs will increase but those workers who lose

> 66 Good point 99

their jobs will be disadvantaged by the establishment of a minimum wage.

It has also been argued that the establishment of a national minimum wage will have long-term disadvantages for the economy. The main reason for this is that firms would be discouraged from training workers because the national minimum wage would make it relatively expensive to do so. In the long term, this would lead to serious shortages of skilled workers. This would lead to a decline in economic growth and would adversely affect the standard of living in the UK.

A national minimum wage would almost certainly raise firms' costs of production and this would lead to a rise in inflation. This has many disadvantages. One possibility is that as prices rise, the national minimum wage will not rise in proportion to the rise in prices and therefore real income will fall – despite the establishment of a national minimum wage!

A rise in the rate of inflation might also cause the economy to move into recession. As real income falls, demand for output will fall so that fewer workers will be required. However, rising prices in the UK will also make exports less competitive in world markets and imports more competitive in the UK market. This would adversely affect the UK balance of payments but, as demand for exports falls and imports are substituted for domestic output, the economy would move further into recession.

Establishing a national minimum wage will have several consequences. It might lead to an improvement in the earnings of some workers but it will almost certainly also lead to a rise in unemployment. It might also lead to a rise in the rate of inflation and it seems clear that the disadvantages of a national minimum wage outweigh the advantages.

66 **Good point** 99

66 **Yes – could say more here, e.g. more dependent on imports** 99

66 **Good point – monetarists would argue that only increased money supply will cause inflation!** 99

66 **Depends on elasticity of demand for exports and imports!** 99

66 **This is a normative statement!** 99

66 This essay raises many interesting points but does not always discuss them in sufficient detail. Other points that might have been mentioned include the fact that a minimum wage will lead to a misallocation of resources and unemployment will rise if firms substitute capital for labour. 99

OUTLINE ANSWERS

Question 3

You could begin your answer to this question by explaining how wages are determined through the market mechanism, i.e. the operation of supply and demand. In free markets, differences in wages exist because of differences in the conditions of supply and demand. You could then go on to explain why there are differences in supply and demand conditions stressing the determinants of elasticity of demand and supply.

This is not to suggest that a trade union has no power to influence the wages of its members. The way in which a union might do this is explained on p. 181. Despite this, the main reason for wage differentials is different conditions of supply and demand, so you would be well advised to disagree with the statement in the question!

Question 4

Each of the examples of wage differentials quoted in this question must be explained analytically and illustrated using appropriate supply and demand curves.

(a) The demand for star football players is relatively high because fans (and television companies) are willing to pay relatively large sums to see them play. However, as the supply of any individual player is limited and indeed above some minimum reward, the supply of Ian Rush's talents is perfectly inelastic. You could usefully illustrate this diagrammatically and use the diagram as a basis for your explanation.

(b) Unions have the power to restrict entry into an occupation by stipulating minimum entry requirements. They can also influence demand for workers by negotiating increases in productivity. By threatening a strike, they might persuade firms to finance an increase in wages from a cut in profits. If unions are willing to negotiate redundancies, they will be able to raise wages by accepting a reduction in employment.

(c) One reason for the higher earnings is that workers on North Sea oil rigs work longer hours than on-shore workers! However, the major reason is that off-shore work is more dangerous and disrupts family life. Higher wages offer compensation necessary to persuade workers to accept off-shore work.

(d) The skills of university graduates are often valued by society more highly than the skills of non-graduates. Demand is also likely to be relatively inelastic, since there is often no substitute for their skills. This is true of accountants and surgeons, for example. The supply of graduates, on the other hand, is limited and many of their skills cannot be increased until after a relatively long period of time. Again, this is true of accountants and surgeons.

Further Reading

Griffiths and Wall, *Applied Economics: An Introductory Course* (6th edn), Longman 1995: Ch. 22, Trade Unions, Wages and Collective Bargaining.
Harrison et al, *Introductory Economics*, Macmillan 1992: Ch. 17, The Distribution of Factor Incomes.
Lipsey and Harbury, *First Principles in Economics* (2nd edn), Weidenfeld and Nicolson 1992: Ch. 18, Competitive Factor Markets; Ch. 19, Labour and Capital.

REVIEW SHEET

1 Define each of the following:
   Marginal physical product (MPP): _____
   _____
   Marginal revenue product (MRP): _____
   _____
   Average revenue product (ARP): _____
   _____

2 Draw a diagram showing the relationship between MRP and ARP.

   Use this diagram to explain why the MRP curve is the demand curve for labour when there is perfect competition in both factor and product markets.
   _____
   _____
   _____
   _____

3 What difference will be made to your analysis if there is now *imperfect competition in the product market*?
   _____
   _____
   _____
   _____

4 Draw a diagram and use it to explain how we find the equilibrium wage and level of employment when there is *imperfect competition in the factor market*.

   Explanation: _____
   _____
   _____

5 Draw a diagram to explain why the wages of doctors might be expected to be higher than the wages of nurses. Use your diagram to explain this difference in wages.

Explanation: _____

_____

_____

_____

_____

_____

6 Outline three situations which might help a trade union increase the wage rate of its members.

(a) _____

_____

(b) _____

_____

(c) _____

_____

7 Now take one of these situations, and explain in detail how wages might rise and what implications, if any, there might be for employment. Use a diagram to help your analysis.

Explanation: _____

_____

_____

_____

_____

_____

CHAPTER

11

INTEREST, RENT AND PROFIT

INTEREST AND RATES OF INTEREST

THE LOANABLE FUNDS THEORY

THE LIQUIDITY PREFERENCE THEORY

THE TERM STRUCTURE OF INTEREST RATES

RENT AND ECONOMIC RENT

APPLIED MATERIALS

GETTING STARTED

Chapter 10 focused on the return to labour, this chapter is concerned with rewards to other factors of production. In the classical sense, interest is the return to capital, rent is the return to land and profit is the return to the entrepreneur.

Interest rates are an important aspect of saving and investment decisions. We use interest rates in 'discounting' future flows of income, as from possible investment projects. This allows us to find the *present value* of such future flows of income so that a realistic appraisal of return and cost for the project can be made. There are different theories as to how the rate of interest is determined and these are considered in some detail in this chapter.

INTEREST AND RATES OF INTEREST

ESSENTIAL PRINCIPLES

INTEREST AND ITS COMPONENTS

Interest is sometimes treated as the reward for postponing consumption but more often it is viewed as the price that has to be paid for the use of funds. In other words, interest is the amount the borrower pays over and above the original amount borrowed. For convenience, it is usually expressed as an annual rate so that if one person borrows £5,000 for one year at 10 per cent, the total amount repayable in one year's time will be £5,500.

Strictly an interest payment has several components:

■ A payment is necessary to persuade holders of funds to forego current consumption and so release funds for lending. After all, for most of us, current consumption is preferable to future consumption. The payment of interest persuades individuals to overcome their **time preference** for current consumption.

■ A payment is necessary to compensate for **risk**. There is a risk that the borrower will default on repayment of the loan when such repayment falls due. There is also the risk that inflation will reduce the real value of the amount lent so that it will buy less at the time repayment is made.

■ A payment is necessary to cover the costs of **administration** associated with borrowing and lending.

THE RATE OF INTEREST

Economists refer to *the* rate of interest as if there was only one such rate. In fact, there are many different rates of interest, such as those charged on mortgages, bank loans, hire purchase agreements and so on. This is to be expected, and in general, interest rates vary with the creditworthiness of the borrower and with the duration of the loan. Nevertheless, after allowance has been made for these two factors, there still remains a minimum (or net) rate of interest that must be paid by all borrowers.

Where interest rates in particular markets are above this minimum, even after due allowance has been made for the specific circumstances of the loan and the borrower, funds will tend to move to those markets. The increase in supply will **bid down** interest rates in those markets. Conversely, the shortage this creates in other markets will **bid up** interest rates in those markets. Thus, in the long run, the net interest rate in all markets tends to equality, and this provides some justification for the notion of a single rate of interest. Any reference to the rate of interest therefore implies reference to a single, *representative*, rate of interest. When interest rates in general are rising or falling, this will be reflected in appropriate movements in any rate of interest which is monitored.

THE REAL RATE AND THE NOMINAL RATE

The **nominal rate of interest** is the annual amount that must be paid on borrowed funds. It is this rate of interest which is quoted in all financial markets. However, the **real rate of interest** takes account of inflation. In order to calculate the real rate of interest, we simply deduct the rate of inflation from the nominal rate of interest. Thus, if the nominal rate of interest is 12 per cent and the rate of inflation is 8 per cent, the real rate of interest is 4 per cent. In this chapter, we are mainly concerned with the nominal rate of interest.

" Real rates take account of inflation "

BASE RATES

All banks have a **base rate** of interest. This is simply the underlying rate of interest to which all of the other rates of interest are related. For some borrowers, the rate of interest charged might be 2 per cent above base rate; for others it might be 3 per cent above base rate, and so on. When a bank changes its base rate, all the other rates of interest operated by the bank will change.

Economists have long been interested in what determines the rate of interest and, over the years, several theories have evolved which seek to explain how interest rates are determined. Here, we concentrate on only two theories: the **loanable funds theory** and the **liquidity preference theory**.

THE LOANABLE FUNDS THEORY

This is an early theory of how interest rates are determined. Although its significance decreased after the evolution of the liquidity preference theory, it is again gathering respectability as an explanation of how interest rates are determined. The loanable funds theory focuses attention on the demand for, and supply of, loanable funds and the interaction of these in determining the rate of interest.

DEMAND FOR LOANABLE FUNDS

This theory assumes that the *demand* for loanable funds is a derived demand that stems from the demand for capital investment by different sectors of the economy. If firms and individuals wish to invest more than they currently save, they must borrow the excess. However, if all other things remain the same, the quantity of funds demanded will depend on the cost of those funds, i.e. on the rate of interest, because capital equipment will only be purchased if the expected *net* return from its operation is above some minimum acceptable level. The lower the rate of interest, the lower the cost of capital and, if all other things remain the same, the greater the net return from any capital investment. Because of this, the demand for loanable funds will be greater at lower rates of interest, and vice versa, i.e. the demand curve for loanable funds will be normal in shape (varying *inversely* with the rate of interest).

In the real world of course, the demand for loanable funds is not simply determined by the demand for capital investment by firms. In particular, households demand funds for the purchase of housing and many consumer durables. However, there is no doubt that demand for funds for these purposes is inversely related to changes in the rate of interest.

SUPPLY OF LOANABLE FUNDS

The loanable funds theory assumes that the *supply* of loanable funds is determined by the level of savings in the economy. For most individuals, the level of savings depends on such factors as current income, holdings of wealth and the rate of interest. If all other things remain the same, a rise in the rate of interest increases the *opportunity cost of current consumption* because a raise in the rate of interest makes an even higher level of consumption possible in the future. Because of this, it is argued that the supply of loanable funds will vary *directly* with the rate of interest; i.e. savings rise when the rate of interest rises, and vice versa.

Determination of interest rates
Figure 11.1 illustrates the determination of interest rates in terms of the loanable funds theory.

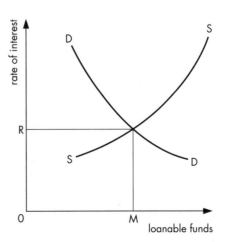

Fig. 11.1 Supply and demand for loanable funds

In Fig. 11.1, DD represents the demand and SS the supply, of loanable funds. The equilibrium rate of interest is R because this is the only rate at which supply of, and demand for, funds are equal. At any rate of interest above R, there is excess supply of funds, and therefore the rate of interest will fall. At any rate below R, there is excess demand, and therefore the rate of interest will rise. Once established at R, the rate of interest will not change, unless there is a change in the conditions of demand and/or the conditions of supply. For example, technological advances might cause an increase in the demand for loanable funds, while a rise in income might cause an increase in the supply of loanable funds. The former would tend to pull the rate of interest up, while the latter would tend to pull it down.

THE LIQUIDITY PREFERENCE THEORY

This theory is sometimes referred to as the **monetary theory** of interest rates or the **Keynesian theory** of interest rates, after its originator, John Maynard Keynes. In this theory, the rate of interest is determined by the demand for money to hold and the supply of money, rather than the demand for and supply of loanable funds. An important feature of the liquidity preference theory is that it focuses attention on the reasons why people prefer to hold money rather than assets, i.e. the reasons why the community has a preference for liquidity.

DEMAND FOR MONEY

Keynes identified three motives for holding money, i.e. three reasons why individuals and organisations demand money. Each is considered in turn.

Transactions demand for money

Everyone needs to hold some money in order to carry out ordinary, everyday transactions such as paying for bus fares and other routine purchases. The sum of all the individual balances held by individuals and institutions for such purposes gives the community's demand for **transactions balances**. Since transactions balances are held with the intention of financing purchases, they are unlikely to be affected by changes in the rate of interest.

One of the main determinants of the demand for transactions balances is the level of income. For most individuals (and certainly for the community as a whole) as income rises, expenditure increases and therefore the higher the demand for transactions balances to hold as a means of financing that (greater) expenditure. However, the frequency with which income is received is also an important factor in determining the transactions demand for money. For example, if an individual receives £140 per week and spends it at the rate of £20 per day. the average weekly holding of money (or the average weekly demand for transactions balances) is £70, and the annual level of expenditure is £7,280. On the other hand, if the same individual were paid on a four-weekly cycle, the income received would be £560 every four weeks. Again if expenditures were spread evenly throughout the period, the average weekly holding of money would be £280 (4 times as high as before!) – but the annual level of expenditure would remain constant at £7,280. In this case, what is true for the individual is true for the nation. Changing the frequency with which income is received will change the community's demand for transactions balances: the less frequently a given annual sum is paid, the higher the demand for transaction balances.

66 Reasons for holding money 99

Precautionary balances

The demand for **precautionary balances** represents money balances held as a precaution against some unforeseen event, such as unanticipated repair work becoming necessary on a car or a reduction in prices offering the prospect of an unanticipated bargain. Again, the major determinant of precautionary balances is likely to be the *level of income*. An individual with an annual income of £30,000 might be expected to hold larger precautionary balances than an individual with an annual income of £5,000! It is normally assumed that the rate of interest has no effect on the precautionary demand for money.

Speculative demand for money

The third motive identified by Keynes for holding money is the **speculative motive** or the **asset motive**. Money that is not required for transactions or precautionary purposes can be held as an asset, or used to provide funds for borrowers. The problem is to identify the circumstances in which an individual or institution will prefer to hold surplus balances in the form of money, in preference to assets that will earn interest.

SECURITIES

In the liquidity preference theory, it is assumed that only one type of asset is available to individuals and institutions, namely **securities**. These are basically IOUs and we shall see in Chapter 12 that when a person makes a loan to the government they receive a government security. These IOUs will usually be redeemed at some stage in the future, but until then the holder of the security receives interest. We therefore have to decide under what circumstances a person or institution will prefer money to securities, and vice versa.

An example: consols

For simplicity let us consider the case of a security with no fixed redemption date, such as a **consol** which is a security, or bond, issued by the UK Government, therefore having no risk of default. The holder of these securities receives an annual interest payment and the rate of interest is fixed in terms of the face value of the security. Thus if the nominal price, i.e. face value, of a security is £100 and the rate of interest is 4 per cent, the holder of this security receives £4 annually. Although consols carry no fixed redemption date, there is an active market in them which simply means that holders of consols can find ready buyers should they wish to sell them. However, as with all market prices, the price of consols will vary with supply and demand so that although the holder of the security receives the same fixed payment annually, the price of the security in the market is *not* fixed.

To see what happens to the market rate of interest, or **yield**, (R) when security prices change, let us consider two examples.

Example 1: It is assumed that when sold the price of the consol is £120. Then,

$$R = \frac{£4}{£120} \times 100\% = 3.33\%$$

Example 2: The sale price of the consol is £80. Then,

$$R = \frac{£4}{£80} \times 100\% = 5\%$$

> ❝ The market price of securities is inversely related to the rate of interest ❞

Notice that as the *price of the security falls*, the *rate of interest rises*, and vice versa. This is because, although the annual interest payment on the security is fixed at £4, in Example 1 the purchaser of the security gives up £120 to receive that annual payment of £4, but in Example 2 the security purchaser only parts with £80 to receive the same annual £4 interest.

This is a very important relationship, because, if an investor expects the price of securities to fall, i.e. the rate of interest to rise, he or she will prefer to hold money rather than securities. This is the case because, if security prices do fall, the investor makes a capital loss. On the other hand, if security prices are expected to rise and the rate of interest to fall, securities will be preferred to money, and an expected capital gain will be made.

Zero and infinite speculative demand

This is easy to understand in the case of an individual investor, but *not all investors have the same expectations* about security prices. At any moment in time, some investors will expect there to be a rise in interest rates, while others will expect a fall. However, the more interest rates rise, the more investors will come to expect the next change in interest rates to be downwards, i.e. the next change in security prices will be upwards.

❝ ❝ Finding the liquidity preference schedule ❞ ❞

Because of this, as interest rates rise and rise, investors will *increasingly prefer* to hold securities rather than money because of the expectation of making a capital gain when interest rates fall. In fact, there must be some rate of interest that is so high that *everyone* expects the next change in interest rates to be downwards; and here the **speculative demand** for money will be *zero*. The converse is also true. As interest rates fall and fall, the more investors will come to expect the next change in interest rates to be upwards, i.e. the next change in security prices to be downwards. Here, money will increasingly be preferred to securities because of the expected capital loss from holding securities. Again, there must be some low rate of interest when *everyone* expects the next change in interest rates to be upwards, i.e. the next change in security prices will be downwards. In this case, there will be an **infinite demand** for speculative money balances, because no one will be willing to purchase securities.

THE LIQUIDITY PREFERENCE CURVE

Since transactions balances and precautionary balances are held with the intention of being used to make purchases as and when required, they are sometimes jointly referred to as the **demand for active balances**. The important point about the demand for active balances is that it is *not* responsive to changes in the rate of interest, i.e. it is interest rate inelastic. The demand for speculative balances, on the other hand, is sometimes referred to as the **demand for idle balances** since it represents money that is demanded because its face value is fixed and there is therefore no risk of capital loss.

Liquidity preference schedule

Figure 11.2 shows that when the demand for active (La) and idle (Li) balances are *added together*, we have the community's total demand for money or liquidity preference schedule (LP).

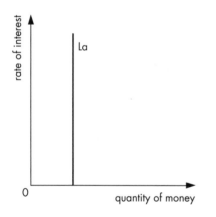
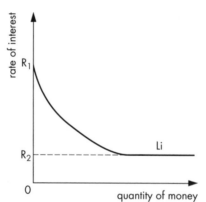
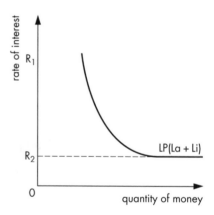

Fig 11.2 Liquidity preference schedule

THE SUPPLY OF MONEY

In the liquidity preference theory, the supply of money is assumed to be determined by the monetary authorities, i.e. the Treasury and the Bank of England. This implies that, on a day-to-day basis, the supply of money is *not* influenced by changes in the rate of interest. In the long term, however, changes in the rate of interest *do* exert considerable influence on the supply of money, but this can be ignored because the liquidity preference theory concentrates on the determination of the rate of interest at a particular point in time when the money supply is fixed.

What determines interest rates?

The interaction of supply and demand for money determines the rate of interest. In Fig. 11.3 the demand for money is given by LP and the supply of money is given by SM. This gives an equilibrium rate of interest of R.

At any rate of interest above R, the supply of money exceeds demand and this will pull down the rate of interest, while at any rate of interest below R the demand for money will exceed supply and this will bid up the rate of interest. Once the rate of

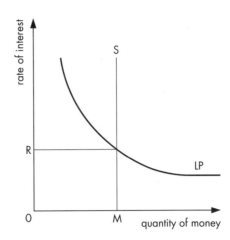

interest is established at R, it will remain at this level until there is a change in the demand for money and/or the supply of money. This implies that the authorities have two choices:

- they can fix the supply of money and allow interest rates to be determined by the demand for money; or
- they can fix the rate of interest and adjust the supply of money to whatever level is appropriate so as to maintain the rate of interest.

THE LIQUIDITY TRAP

We have seen that, in the liquidity preference theory, there is some low rate of interest at which everyone expects the next change in interest rates to be upwards. Here the demand for money is infinitely elastic since no one will be prepared to purchase securities. In this case, a change in the supply of money will not necessarily have any affect on the rate of interest. For example, in Fig. 11.4, if LP shows the demand and SM the supply of money then the equilibrium rate of interest is determined at R_0. Now, if the authorities engineer an increase in the money supply to S_1M_1, there is no change in the rate of interest. The increased money supply is simply absorbed into idle balances because no one can be persuaded to purchase securities. This is referred to as the liquidity trap and the implication is that, because changes in the money supply have no influence on the rate of interest, monetary policy cannot be used to influence other variables such as consumption and investment when the rate of interest is R_0.

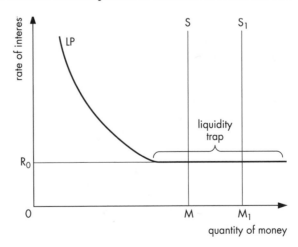

Fig. 11.4 The liquidity trap

THE TERM STRUCTURE OF INTEREST RATES

In practice, the authorities are not only interested in the level of interest rates; they are also interested in the structure. The term **structure** of interest rates refers to the *spread* of interest rates paid on the *same type of assets* with different times to maturity. It relates to securities which carry a fixed rate of interest and have a specified maturity date. In general, the longer the time to maturity, the greater the return on a security. Remember, although the amount received is fixed as a proportion of the nominal value of a security, the rate of interest, or yield will vary because the market price of the security varies.

THE YIELD CURVE

Figure 11.5 shows the general relationship between the yield on a security and the length of time to maturity. This is usually referred to as the **yield curve**.

66 A typical yield curve 99

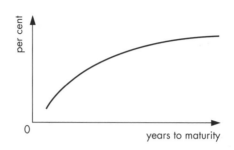

Fig. 11.5 Yield curve

The yield curve in Fig. 11.5 is referred to as *normal* because the yield increases as the length of time to maturity increases. This is to be expected because, if all other things are equal:

■ the risk of default increases over time along with the risk that inflation will erode the real value of interest payments and the initial capital sum when it is repaid; and

■ lenders require compensation for loss of liquidity so the longer they forego current consumption, the greater the amount of compensation required.

Expectations and the yield curve
The normal yield curve is drawn on the assumption that all other things remain equal and in particular that no change is expected in the rate of interest. When such changes *are* expected, the shape of the yield curve will change.

66 Expectations will affect yield curves 99

■ **An expected increase in the rate of interest** In this case, the yield curve will rise more steeply and will reach a higher level than the normal yield curve. This is because *lenders* will seek to avoid being locked into securities which will have a relatively low yield after interest rates increase. They will therefore prefer to hold short-term securities so that when these mature they can re-lend their funds at higher rates of interest. This implies an increase in the demand for short-term securities and a reduction in the demand for long-term securities. On the other hand, *borrowers* will prefer to borrow long term, knowing that when interest rates increase there will be no increase in their borrowing costs. This implies an increase in the supply of long-term securities and a reduction in the supply of short-term securities. These changes in demand and supply will tend to increase the price of short-term securities (depress short-term interest rates) and depress the price of long-term securities (increase long-term interest rates).

Figure 11.6 shows the effect of an expected increase in interest rates on the yield curve with Y representing the normal yield curve and Y_1 the yield curve after the expected increase in interest rates.

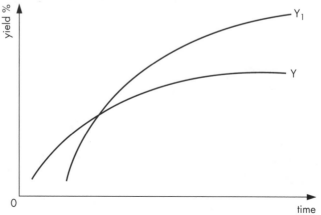

Fig. 11.6 Yield curve after an expected increase in the rate of interest

■ **An unexpected reduction in the rate of interest**   As might be expected, the effect this has on the yield curve is exactly opposite to an expected increase in the rate of interest. Here *lenders* will prefer to hold long-term securities, so locking in the higher rate of interest after interest rates fall. This implies an increase in demand for long-term securities and a fall in demand for short-term securities. On the other hand, *borrowers* will prefer to borrow short term, so enabling them to reduce their interest payments on long-term borrowing after interest rates fall. This implies an increase in the supply of short-term securities and a reduction in the supply of long-term securities. The result is a reduction in the price of short-term securities (increase in short-term interest rates) and an increase in the price of long-term securities (fall in long-term rates).

A shift in the yield curve from Y to Y_1 shows the effect on the yield curve of an expected reduction in the rate of interest; see Fig. 11.7.

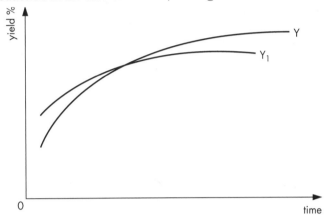

Fig. 11.7 Yield curve after an expected reduction in the rate of interest

In certain circumstances a strong expectation of a fall in interest rates can produce a descending yield curve; see Fig. 11.8 on p. 207.

<table>
<tr><td>**RENT AND ECONOMIC RENT**</td><td>In most cases, a factor of production is assumed to have transfer earnings. **Transfer earnings** are defined as the minimum amount necessary to keep a factor of production in its present occupation. Any excess earnings above transfer earnings are referred to as **economic rent**. Much more is written about economic rent in the Tutor's Answer on p. 208.</td></tr>
</table>

URBAN RENTS AND CITY CENTRE PRICES

It is sometimes alleged that retail prices in outlets occupying city centre locations are higher than they are for the same items sold in outlets located away from the city centre, because city centre rents are higher than elsewhere. It is certainly true that city centre rents are generally higher than elsewhere but it is not always true that retail prices are higher in the city centre. Even in cases where retail prices are higher, this is not necessarily because retailers pay higher rents in the city centre.

Reasons for higher rents

Higher rents stem from the increasing demand for city centre sites which have an inelastic supply. The increasing demand for city centre sites in turn stems from the relatively high demand for the goods and services sold in city centre locations.

So, any higher prices that are observed for goods sold in city centres are as likely to be the result of the greater *demand* existing in such locations as of the higher *cost* factors due to higher rents. Indeed, the *only* reason that costs (rents) are higher is due to the increased demand among retailers for the favourable city centre sites which are in short supply.

SHOULD ECONOMIC RENT BE TAXED?

It is often suggested that economic rent should be taxed. The reasoning behind this is that since economic rent is a *surplus* rather than a *cost of supply*, a tax on economic rent will be borne entirely by the factor of production receiving economic rent. This will leave the supply of that factor, and therefore the output it produces, unchanged. For example, when a monopolist is currently earning supernormal profit and producing at the profit maximising level of output, a tax on the supernormal profit will not lead the monopolist to change the output produced. The tax will certainly lower the amount of profit earned, but it will *not* change the profit maximising level of output.

A tax on economic rent would not affect supply, because the tax has *no* effect on the costs of production. It is simply a tax on the excess earnings of a factor over and above the amount necessary for that factor to be supplied. For example, in the case of urban and development land, landowners frequently do little or nothing to improve the quality of the land and simply benefit from an increasing demand. Taxing the surplus that results from this will have no effect on supply.

Difficulties of implementation

Although the case for taxing economic rent is a powerful one, there are major difficulties with implementing such a tax. In the first place it is extremely difficult to identify economic rent. If a tax *exceeds* the value of the surplus, then the supply of the factor of production will be reduced and its price, along with the price of whatever it produces, will be increased. Another problem is that not all economic rent earned is true economic rent. It might simply be **quasi rent**. This refers to income that is entirely a surplus in the short run, but part of which is a *transfer earning* in the long run. Taxing this will reduce the long-run supply of the factor of production. Here again the result might be rising prices.

APPLIED MATERIALS

INTEREST RATES

An article in the *Accountant's Record*, June 1987, entitled *Interest Rates – Understanding and Forecasting their Movements*, provides considerable insight into the causes of changes in interest rates in the UK. It is argued that a major factor is the expected change in the foreign exchange value of sterling. The principle of **covered interest parity** implies that when account is taken of the various expected exchange rate changes, interest rates around the world would tend to be equal. Remember, it is now very easy for investors to withdraw funds from one country and to invest them in another. So, for example, if sterling is expected to depreciate against the dollar, i.e. exchange for less dollars, sterling interest rates must exceed dollar interest rates by an amount which exactly compensates for the expected fall in the value of sterling against the dollar. This idea is explored in more detail in Chapter 15 but is mentioned here because of its importance in determining interest rates.

The article also emphasises the **role of inflation** in determining interes rates. Inflation causes a fall in the value of money and, in order to compensate lenders for this fall, they require interest payments. Here again there is an international dimension. We shall see in Chapter 15 that a higher rate of inflation in one country will cause a fall in that country's exchange rate and covered interest parity would predict a higher rate of interest to offset this.

Expected changes in the exchange rate are therefore important in determining interest rates, but another important factor is the **government's monetary policy**. When the government restricts the money supply there will be upward pressure on interest rates; see Fig. 11.3. Similarly, if government borrowing increases (and all other things remain the same), the greater demand for loans will result in upward pressure on interest rates.

YIELD CURVES

In its *Quarterly Bulletin*, the Bank of England publishes regular information on yield curves. Figure 11.8 shows some recent yield curves. Can you explain their shape?

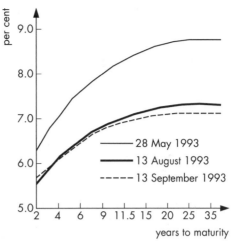

Fig 11.8 Time/yield curves for
British government stocks

Source: Bank of England Quarterly Bulletin November 1993

SOURCES OF FINANCE

Table 11.1 indicates the importance of profit as a source of (internal) finance.

SOURCES OF FINANCE	1992 (%)
Internal	59
Bank borrowing	–4
Ordinary shares	9
Debentures and preference shares	4
Other capital issues	13
Other	19

Table 11.1: Sources of funds for UK
industrial and commercial
companies: percentage shares

Source: Financial Statistics, No. 375, July 1993

EXAMINATION QUESTIONS

1 Why might economic rent be regarded as an unnecessary payment? *(10)*
  If this is so, why are property rents high in city centres? *(10)*

  (ODLE, Summer 1992)

2 (a) Examine the view that the total rental earnings of landowners can be taxed
      without affecting the rents charged to land users or the price of land. (Providing
      the rate of taxation is less than 100%.) *(15)*
  (b) Why might it be appropriate in certain contexts to argue that land rents are
      price-determining rather than price determined? *(10)*

  (WJEC 1991)

3 'It is irrational for people to keep their wealth in the form of money because money
  earns no interest.' Discuss.

  (AEB, Nov 1988)

4 How are interest rates determined?

  (ULEAC, June 1987)

5 Are profits a reward for a useful service?

ANSWERS TO EXAMINATION QUESTIONS

TUTOR'S ANSWER TO QUESTION 1

Economic rent is defined as a surplus earned by any factor of production over and above the minimum price at which that factor would be supplied. The minimum price at which a factor will be supplied is referred to as its supply price, and hence economic rent is a surplus over supply price.

The supply price of a factor of production might also be referred to as a factor's **transfer earnings**. Any factor of production that is offered less than the amount it could receive in its next-best-paid alternative employment will transfer to that alternative. Figure 11.9 illustrates the concepts of economic rent and transfer earnings.

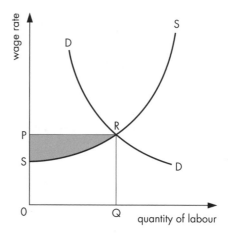

Fig 11.9

In Figure 11.9, S and D represent the relevant supply and demand curves for any factor of production. In this market, the equilibrium price is OP. However, all units except the last unit employed would have been prepared to accept a lower price than OP. In fact, the very first unit would have been supplied at a price of approximately S. All units, except the last unit supplied, therefore receive an amount in excess of their supply price or transfer earnings. Because of this, the area PRS is referred to as **economic rent** and the area OSRQ is referred to as **transfer earnings**.

For any factor of production, economic rent is determined by demand for that factor of production and its supply, which also influences transfer earnings. However, in the case of labour, a small number of individuals receive incomes which are sometimes hundreds of times greater than the average income. In these cases, the transfer earnings of the individual concerned are often relatively low so that the bulk of their earnings consist of economic rent. The most often quoted examples are probably film stars and pop singers. These individuals possess unique *qualities*, the supply of which is inelastic in the sense that their abilities cannot be duplicated.

However, it is not sufficient to possess unique abilities to earn relatively high rewards. After all, everyone has some unique ability! Instead, it is necessary to possess those unique abilities which are demanded by others and for which people are prepared to pay. It is, therefore, demand which accounts for the relatively large earnings of pop singers, film stars and some individuals from the sporting world such as some boxers and footballers. In this sense, economic rent is demand determined. Figure 11.10 is used to illustrate this point.

Above some relatively low rate of pay, the supply of this individual's services become totally inelastic. The actual rate of pay is determined by the intersection of supply and demand at W, but, because of the inelastic supply, the bulk of this person's earnings consist of economic rent, equal to the shaded area WRNS.

Labour is not the only factor of production which can earn economic rent. When firms earn supernormal profits, this is economic rent and when land has only one use, its entire earnings will consist of economic rent! However, whichever factor of production we are considering, the nature of economic rent remains unchanged. It is always a surplus above supply price and for this reason might be considered an

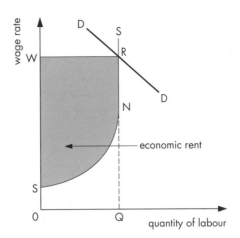

Fig. 11.10

unnecessary payment. Referring to Fig. 11.10, it is clear that the earnings of this individual could fall substantially below their current level without affecting supply.

It is important to distinguish between rent (the payment for property services) and economic rent (any surplus above a factor's supply price). Rent, like any other factor payment, is determined by supply and demand. The supply of city centre sites is, of course, rigidly fixed and therefore elasticity of supply is zero. Demand for city centre sites is derived from demand for the product sold in city centre retail outlets. While the total supply of city centre sites is fixed, a site will have a variety of uses. For example, a shoe shop can quickly be converted into a clothes shop and the use to which any city centre site is put depends on demand for different goods and services. As consumer demand for purchases from city centre retail sites rises, demand for city centre sites rises. Because of this, economic rent earned by such sites rises. Figure 11.11 illustrates this point.

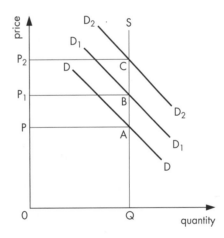

Fig. 11.11 Economic rent earned on city centre sites

In Fig. 11.11, S shows the supply of city centre sites. The initial demand for such sites is shown by D, and D_1 and D_2 show higher levels of demand. City centre sites have few alternative uses. They could provide residential accommodation but in our case, Fig. 11.11 implies that the earnings of city centre sites consists entirely of economic rent. For example, when demand is given by D, the total economic rent earned on the city centre sites illustrated is represented by the area OPAQ. When demand rises to D_1 total economic rent rises to OP_1BQ and when demand rises to D_2, total economic rent rises to OP_2CQ.

Now, it is true that economic rent is a surplus over and above supply price and therefore could be eliminated, without affecting the quantity of city centre sites supplied. In this sense, economic rent is an unnecessary payment but it will always be earned on city centre sites because of the limited supply of such sites coupled with rising demand for them. This also implies that, contrary to what might be expected, high retail prices in city centre retail outlets is not caused by high rents for such sites. It is demand for the products of city centre retail outlets which bids up retail prices and, as a consequence, bids up city centre site rents.

STUDENT'S ANSWER TO QUESTION 2

(a) As a factor of production, land has the unique characteristic of being completely fixed in supply. Because of this, we can say that the price of land is determined entirely by demand. This is illustrated in Fig. 11.12.

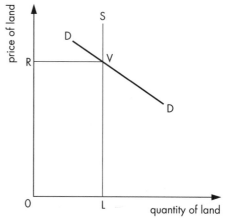

Fig. 11.12 Economic rent earned by land (which has no alternative use!)

66 **No. Total rent is area ORVL** 99

In Fig. 11.12, SL is the supply of and DD is the demand for, land. The equilibrium price, total rent received by landowners, is OR. Economists distinguish between rent and economic rent but, in the case of land, there is no difference. Rent is the total reward earned by landowners for the use of land whereas economic rent is any amount earned over the supply price of a factor of production. The supply price of a factor of production is the minimum amount necessary before the factor of production will be supplied. It is clear from Fig. 11.12 that land has no supply price and therefore its earnings consist entirely of economic rent!

66 **Good** 99

66 **Only in the extreme case where land has no alternative uses** 99

If the government introduced a tax on the earnings of landowners this, as long as the tax was less than the total earnings of land, would have no effect on the amount of land supplied because the entire earnings of land are a surplus. Because the total supply of land is fixed, the earnings of land are in excess of the amount necessary to retain supply. Similarly a tax on land will not affect the demand for, or supply of, land and so will have no effect on the price of land.

(b) The demand for land is derived from the demand for the product that land is used to produce. When demand for the product is high, demand for land will also be high and this will drive up its price. A classic example is land in city centre sites. There is only a limited amount of land available and so supply is perfectly inelastic. Fig. 11.12 shows how the price of land in the city centre is determined in a free market.

In Fig. 11.12 demand for city centre land is shown by DD and the supply of city centre land is shown by SL. Supply is completely inelastic because the supply of city centre sites is strictly limited and cannot be increased in the short run, or the long run. The main point is that city centre sites are highly desirable because of their access to consumers. Many people shop in city centres and because of their demand for goods

> 66 Good point about
> derived demand 9 9

and services which are sold in the city centre, they
drive up the prices of these goods and services.
Because of this, traders demand sites in the city
centre because they will earn higher profits than if
they are located elsewhere. This drives up demand for
city centre sites and forces up rents. But, it is
demand for goods and services by city centre shoppers
that is the main cause of the high city centre rents.
In this case, rents are price determined rather than
price determining.

66 Some good and relevant points made. Diagram presented but an error in its use early on. Perhaps also a non-perfectly inelastic supply curve could be used for a less extreme case where land does have alternative uses. 9 9

OUTLINE ANSWERS

Question 3

One way to begin your answer to this question is to define interest and show that if money is lent, it earns interest for the lender whereas money that is held earns nothing. You could then go on to explain that individuals have a time preference for current consumption and that to overcome this time preference it is necessary to offer interest. It seems that holding money is therefore irrational because it implies individuals forego current consumption without compensation.

However, it is not necessarily irrational to hold money. Money is needed by both individuals and organisations for transactions and precautionary purposes. You must explain these motives for holding money and their determinants in some detail, stressing the convenience of holding money in terms of immediate spending power. In the real world, expenditures and receipts are often irregular and uncertain especially for businesses and in these circumstances holding money is the rational thing to do. You must also discuss the speculative demand for money stressing that it is a desirable store of wealth when its value is more certain than that of other assets, when interest rates are low and the next expected change in bond prices is downwards. In these circumstances, the opportunity cost of holding money is low and the risk associated with holding bonds is high.

In the modern world, many financial institutions have accounts which offer liquidity and interest. These are discussed in Chapter 12 but when they are available it is clearly irrational to hold cash that is surplus to immediate requirements.

Question 4

You could begin your answer by defining the rate of interest and why economists look at a single representative rate. You could then discuss either the loanable funds theory or the liquidity preference theory to explain how interest rates are determined. These theories explain the general level of interest rates but the structure of interest rates depends on the expectations investors hold at any moment in time. You should briefly explain this in terms of the shape of the yield curve. You could also discuss the importance of the exchange rate, the rate of inflation and the government's monetary policy (see Ch. 15).

STUDENT'S ANSWER TO QUESTION 5

> 66 The economist's
> definition is different.
> Remember normal profit is
> regarded as a cost of
> production 9 9

Profits are usually defined as the difference between total
revenue and total cost. If total revenue exceeds total cost
firms make a profit but if it does not they make a loss.
This is the risk entrepreneurs take — their businesses
might make losses and when this happens entrepreneurs lose
the money they have invested in their businesses.

> **But we can still discuss the advantages and disadvantages for society**

> **Profits are only necessary for production in capitalist societies**

> **No. People would still produce for their own consumption**

> **Good paragraph**

> **Depends why profits are rising. You should relate this to changes in demand and the operation of the price mechanism**

> **A weak conclusion**

However, entrepreneurs aim to make profits. In fact, it is usually assumed by economists that entrepreneurs aim to maximise profits and this simply means that they aim to make as much profit as possible from the resources they control. Profits are therefore the entrepreneur's reward and to decide whether profits are the reward for a useful service, we must ask if the entrepreneur provides a useful service. The answer is really a value judgement because we have no way of saying whether something is useful or not. It is a matter of opinion. All that we can do, is to look at the functions of the entrepreneur.

The entrepreneur's first function is that of risk taker. If individuals or groups of individuals are unwilling to bear the risks of production, nothing would be produced. Profit is therefore necessary to persuade the entrepreneur to undertake production and if profits are not earned in the long run, entrepreneurs cease production and leave the industry. This implies that, without profit, society would be worse off because nothing would be produced.

Profit also encourages entrepreneurs to undertake investment in new technology. It encourages research and development along with the adoption of innovations. Entrepreneurs who fail to do this will experience falling sales and consequently falling profits. We must be careful to distinguish between inventions and innovations. Scientists are often responsible for inventions, but it is entrepreneurs who see the commercial uses for new inventions. For example, science was responsible for the creation of micro-electronics but it is entrepreneurs who are responsible for devising commercial uses for them. Without profits, there would be no incentive for entrepreneurs to seek out commercial applications for inventions.

Another function of profit is that it guides entrepreneurs. When profits are rising in one industry and falling in another, this indicates that society desires more of the commodity where profits from production are rising and less of the commodity where profits are falling. Without profits, more especially changes in profits, entrepreneurs would not know what society most desired from its available resources. This implies that, in the absence of profits, there would be an inferior allocation of resources.

Because of all of these factors, my opinion is that profits are a reward for a very useful service and without them society would be worse off.

> **Some good points here but in general the essay is superficial. You could have included a discussion of the entrepreneur as a factor of production and discussed the importance of normal profit.**

Further reading
Harrison et al, *Introductory Economics*, Macmillan 1992; Ch. 17, The Distribution of Factor Incomes; Ch. 26, Interest Rates.

REVIEW SHEET

1 Give three reasons why interest must usually be paid on funds borrowed.

(a) _____

_____

(b) _____

_____

(c) _____

_____

2 Distinguish between real and nominal rates of interest.

_____

_____

_____

3 Use a diagram to explain the loanable funds theory for determining the level of interest.

Explanation: _____

_____

_____

_____

_____

_____

_____

4 Explain briefly each of the following:

The transactions demand for money: _____

_____

_____

The precautionary demand for money: _____

_____

_____

The speculative demand for money: _____

_____

_____

_____

5 Draw the liquidity preference schedule, i.e. the community's total demand for money to hold.

6 Explain in detail the shape of this schedule, including:

Zero speculative demand: _____

_____

_____

_____

Infinite speculative demand (liquidity trap): _____

_____

_____

_____

$> 0 < \infty$ (infinity) speculative demand: _____

_____

_____

_____

7 Use a diagram to show when an increase in the supply of money will have no effect on the equilibrium rate of interest.

8 Draw a yield curve and explain its shape.

Explanation: _____

_____

_____

_____

_____

9 Describe what might happen to the yield curve if there is an expected increase in the rate of interest. _____

_____

_____

_____

MONEY AND BANKING

GETTING STARTED

Despite the fact that we are all familiar with money and use it almost every day of our lives, it is difficult to define exactly what money is. Over the years, a variety of commodities have been accepted as money, ranging from precious metals to shells. In fact, the term **pecuniary** is derived from the word 'cattle' and **salary** from the word 'salt' indicating that, in the past, these commodities have functioned as money. It is because of this that economists say 'money is as money does'. In other words, anything which performs the functions of money, is money.

ESSENTIAL PRINCIPLES

One term frequently used in connection with money is **liquidity**. An asset is more liquid the more swiftly and less costly it can be converted into the means of payment. It follows that money is the most liquid asset of all. In modern economies, money takes two forms: cash, i.e. notes and coin, and bank deposits. There are several kinds of bank deposit with varying degrees of liquidity. For instance, **sight deposits** are immediately spendable, but **time deposits** can only be withdrawn after a period of notice has been given to the institution holding the deposit. Because of this, there are several different official measures of the money supply, each reflecting a different measure of liquidity in the economy. It is important to be familiar with the different measures of the money supply.

In the UK, bank deposits are by far the most important component of the money supply, accounting for about 90 per cent of the total value of all transactions. However, care must be taken to distinguish between the role of the bank deposits and the role of the cheques. Cheques are simply the means of transferring a bank deposit from one person to another. It is the bank deposit which is accepted in settlement of a debt, not the cheque. A cheque that cannot be honoured against a bank deposit is worthless.

FUNCTIONS AND CHARACTERISTICS OF MONEY

FUNCTIONS OF MONEY

There are four functions which money performs:

A medium of exchange or means of payment

Money is unique in performing this function, since it is the only asset which is universally acceptable in exchange for goods and services. In the absence of a medium of exchange, trade could only take place if there was a double coincidence of wants, i.e. only if two people had mutually acceptable commodities to exchange. Trade of this type takes place on a basis of **barter**.

Clearly, barter would restrict the growth of trade. It would also severely limit the extent to which individuals were able to specialise. By acting as a medium of exchange money therefore promotes specialisation. A person can exchange his labour for money, and then use that money to purchase the output produced by others. We have seen in Chapter 4 that specialisation greatly increases the wealth of the community. By acting as a medium of exchange, money is therefore fulfilling a crucial function, enhancing trade, specialisation and wealth creation.

The remaining functions of money stem from its use as a medium of exchange.

A unit of account

By acting as a medium of exchange, money also provides a means of expressing value. The prices quoted for goods and services reflect their relative value and, in this way, money acts as a unit of account.

A store of wealth

66 The functions of money 99

Because money can be exchanged immediately for goods and services, it is a convenient way of holding wealth until goods and services are required. In this sense, money acts as a store of wealth.

A standard for deferred payment

In the modern world, goods are often purchased on credit, with the amount to be repaid being fixed in money terms. It would be impractical to agree repayment in terms of some other commodity; for example, it may not always be easy to predict the future availability or the future requirements for that commodity. It is therefore money which serves as a standard for deferred payments.

CHARACTERISTICS OF MONEY

For any commodity to function as money it must possess certain characteristics:

Acceptability

No asset can function as money unless people are willing to accept it in settlement of a debt.

Durability

To function as money an asset must be durable. After all, during its working life, any unit of currency changes hands many times and an asset which deteriorated quickly would not be acceptable in settlement of a debt.

66 The characteristics of money 99

Divisibility

To function as money, an asset must be capable of division into smaller units to accommodate transactions of differing value.

Portability

Trade often takes place between individuals and organisations located miles from each other and sometimes at opposite sides of the world. To function as money an asset must therefore be portable.

THE CREATION OF BANK DEPOSITS

We have already mentioned the importance of bank deposits as a component of the money supply. But what are bank deposits and how are they created?

Bank deposits come into being in one of three ways:

66 Creating bank deposits increases the money supply 99

- when a bank receives a deposit of cash;
- when a bank buys a security;
- when a bank makes a loan.

We shall look at each of these in turn but it is important to realise that whichever way bank deposits are created, a bank must always ensure that its liabilities and assets are equal. Deposits are the *liabilities* of a bank, since they are bound to honour all demands for cash from individual depositors up to the full amount deposited in each individual's account. In other words, deposits are claims against a bank. The *assets* which banks hold, however, can take a variety of forms, but they always give the bank a claim against someone else. Notes and coin, for example, give commercial banks a claim against the central bank (the Bank of England in the UK) whereas securities and advances give the bank a claim against the borrower.

BANK DEPOSITS AND THE MONEY SUPPLY

One important aspect of bank deposit creation is its effect on the money supply. We can illustrate this by looking at each of the three ways in which bank deposits are created. The examples below record the initial impact of a £100 creation of bank deposits on the bank's assets and liabilities:

- **Cash deposits**   When a bank receives a deposit of £100 cash, the effect on its balance sheet is:

  Liabilities   *Assets*
  Deposits + £100   Notes and coin + £100

  It is clear that a deposit of cash has no initial impact on the money supply. The same amount of money exists, it is simply held in a different form. In this example, an individual has simply exchanged £100 cash for a bank deposit of £100.

- **Buying a security**   When a bank buys a security for £100, the effect on its balance sheet is:

  Liabilities   *Assets*
  Deposits + £100   Securities + £100

  In this case, the bank's purchase of a £100 security increases the money supply by £100. This is because securities, which are not acceptable in exchange for goods and services, have been exchanged for a bank deposit, which is acceptable.

■ **Making a loan**   When a bank grants a loan of £100, the effect on its balance sheet is:

Liabilities   *Assets*
Deposits + £100   Advances + £100

Again, the granting of a £100 loan *increases* the money supply by £100. This must be so because deposits which are immediately acceptable in exchange for goods and services, have been exchanged for a debt (an advance which is repayable at some future date).

THE MULTIPLE EXPANSION OF BANK DEPOSITS

Although the purchase of securities and the granting of loans leads to an increase in the money supply, banks cannot purchase securities or grant loans indefinitely. They are obliged to pay out cash on demand to account holders up to the limit of whatever is held in each individual's account. They must therefore keep sufficient cash to meet all possible demands for it. Nevertheless, on any particular day, only a relatively small portion of the funds held by banks will be withdrawn because of the widespread use of cheques and credit cards. There may well be a very substantial outflow of funds, but there is also likely to be a very substantial inflow. Because of this, the net change in a bank's holdings of cash, on any particular day, is likely to be relatively small. They are therefore able to lend a substantial part of the funds deposited with them. If all banks in the system do this, and we can expect them to do so since lending is their most profitable activity, the effect will be a multiple expansion of credit following an initial deposit of cash. The following hypothetical example is used to illustrate this process.

Example
Assume that, on any particular day, banks wish to maintain a ratio of 10 per cent cash to total deposits. Assume further that there is no absence of willing borrowers so that banks will lend 90 per cent of all cash deposited with them. So, if a bank receives a cash deposit of £1,000 it will lend £900 in the form of advances. The effect of these transactions on the bank's balance sheet is set out below.

Liabilities   *Assets*
Deposits + £1,000   Cash   + £1,000
Deposits + £900   Advances   + £900

We can assume that having been granted loans, borrowers will spend them, with cash being withdrawn from the bank to meet these expenditures. The £900 used by borrowers to finance purchases will flow back into the banking system as someone else's deposits and will be indistinguishable from any other inflows. Thus, 90 per cent of these deposits, i.e. £810, will be re-lent. Again, this will flow back into the banking system with 90 per cent of these deposits, i.e. £729, being re-lent. It is apparent that the *initial* deposit of £1,000 cash leads to an eventual increase in bank deposits *many times greater* than the initial cash deposit.

This process does not, however, go on indefinitely. In fact, the eventual increase in bank deposits is the sum of a geometric progression which reaches an upper limit as the number of terms in the progression rises. In general, the eventual increase in deposits following an initial deposit of cash is equal to:

$$\frac{1}{\text{cash ratio}} \times \text{cash reserves}$$

In this particular case, we have:

$$\frac{1}{10/100} \times £1,000$$

> 66 A multiple expansion of
> bank deposits 99

In other words, an initial cash deposit of £1,000 leads to an eventual increase in bank deposits of £10,000. Since the cash ratio is 10 per cent, this is to be expected. We are simply saying that bank deposits expand until the initial deposit of cash is just sufficient to meet day-to-day demands for cash by depositors. The size of the cash ratio, therefore, sets the *upper limit* on the extent to which bank deposits can be expanded following an initial deposit of cash.

It is important to realise that individual banks do not create credit simply by expanding their deposits by some multiple of their cash reserves. If an individual bank did this it would quickly experience a *net outfow of cash* as it was forced to *honour cheques* drawn on these deposits. In other words, there will be payments into other banks. Clearly such a situation could not continue for long. Instead, each individual bank simply re-lends a part of whatever is deposited with it. However, the effect of this is to create a situation where the combined total level of deposits held by *all* banks is a multiple of their combined cash reserves.

FINANCIAL INTERMEDIATION

Financial intermediation refers to the process whereby funds are channelled from those who wish to lend to those who wish to borrow. Financial intermediaries therefore include banks, building societies, insurance companies, pension funds and so on. Financial intermediation arises because lenders and borrowers have different requirements in terms of risk and time.

- **Maturity transformation** is an important function of financial intermediaries. They borrow short and lend long. They are able to do this by attracting short-term deposits and then attracting other funds to repay the original borrowings when the need arises.

- **Risk reduction** is another important function of financial intermediaries. If one person lends directly to another the entire risk of default is borne by the lender. However, by depositing funds with a financial intermediary, the original lender eliminates the risk of default almost completely. For its part, the financial intermediary is able to spread the risk over many transactions and, through interest charges to all customers, can ensure it is compensated for losses arising out of default. It is also in a better position to estimate the likelihood of default by a borrower than is an individual lender.

In this chapter we will be considering *bank* financial intermediaries; other institutions that participate in the money markets are referred to as *non-bank* financial intermediaries. The distinction between these is a legal one and is not always clear cut. Some of the more important non-bank financial intermediaries include building societies, finance houses, the National Savings Bank, insurance companies and pension funds.

THE STRUCTURE OF BANKING

THE BANK OF ENGLAND

Monetary policy

An important function of the Bank of England is to implement the government's monetary policy. Monetary policy aims to control the cost of credit and therefore to increase or reduce the demand for loans. The Bank does this by buying or selling securities in the money markets so as to achieve the desired rate of interest. For example, it can create a shortage of funds in the money markets by issuing sufficient Treasury bills to ensure the markets are short of funds. It can then relieve the shortage of funds by lending to the discount market at interest rates of its own choosing (see p. 228).

Banker to the Government

The Government maintains two accounts with the Bank of England: the Exchequer Account and the National Loans Fund. The former is the account through which central government revenue and central government expenditure are passed. Thus the Exchequer Account handles receipts from the Inland Revenue Department and from privatisation of assets. It also releases funds to meet the spending commitments of the different government departments. Where there is a shortfall of receipts over expenditure the Bank offers 'overdraft' facilities to the Government via 'ways and means' advances. Such advances are for relatively short periods of time – often overnight – and more permanent government deficits are financed by issuing securities such as Treasury bills. This implies another important function performed by the Bank of England – handling the Government's borrowing; this is conducted through the National Loans Fund. It is this account which administers the National Debt and it is therefore the account through which the Bank issues securities, pays interest to holders of existing securities and repays sums borrowed when securities mature. There is no doubt that such arrangements are more conveniently handled by a single agent such as the Bank of England because it is then easier to select the optimal timing for new issues and redemptions of securities.

Management of the foreign exchange reserves

As agent for the Treasury, the Bank manages the Exchange Equalisation Account. It is through the Exchange Equalisation Account that foreign exchange receipts are converted into sterling and sterling is converted into foreign currency so as to honour overseas commitments, such as payment for goods and services. The Exchange Equalisation Account holds the country's reserves of gold and foreign currency which are used to influence the external value of sterling in line with the Government's foreign exchange rate policy (see p. 288). It does this by adding to the supply of sterling when demand for sterling is rising on the foreign exchanges, and reducing the supply of sterling when demand for sterling is falling on the foreign exchanges.

Banker to the banking system

All banks above a certain size are obliged to hold deposits at the Bank of England. In addition, the London clearing banks hold operational deposits which gives them current account facilities at the Bank of England. It is by transferring these operational deposits that inter-bank settlements are made at the end of each working day as the final stage of the clearing process. They also provide the banks with facilities through which they can obtain additional supplies of notes and coin when necessary.

Functions of the Bank of England

Lender of last resort

An important function of the Bank of England is that it acts as lender of last resort to the banking system. This simply means that if the banking system is short of liquidity, the Bank of England will always be prepared to lend to it. However, as we shall see, it reserves the right to specify what rate of interest it will charge when lending to the banking system. We shall see that in making finance available to the banking system the Bank of England deals only with a group of institutions known as the **discount market**.

Note circulation

The Bank is the sole note issuing authority in England and Wales. In this context, its responsibilities are the printing, issue and withdrawal of bank notes. This is an important function because the note issue is now **fiduciary** and is therefore backed by securities rather than gold. The Bank responds passively to changes in the demand for cash by the public but a persistent over-issue of notes would cause a rise in the rate of inflation (see p. 248). This would quickly result in a loss of confidence in the acceptability of Bank of England notes in settlement of a debt.

THE DISCOUNT MARKET

The London discount market is primarily a market in short-term funds and consists of nine discount houses. Together, these comprise the London Discount Market Association (LDMA). The discount houses borrow at short term, mainly from the commercial banks and use these funds to carry out their primary function, discounting short-term instruments of credit, i.e. short-term securities. Much of the borrowing is at 'call' which means that the bank can ask for repayment at any time. These funds are used by the discount houses to purchase a variety of short-term instruments such as Treasury bills, commercial bills and gilt-edged securities which are close to maturity. (The securities in which the discount market deals are discussed on pages 225–226.) Indeed, the discount houses are the principal market makers in bills, and by borrowing from the commercial banks they provide them with a modest return on short-term loans. Currently, all eligible banks are obliged to maintain at least an average of $2\frac{1}{2}$ per cent of their eligible liabilities in the form of secured money with the discount market.

Discounting and the discount rate

A security is *discounted* when it is purchased for less than its face value. The difference consists of interest which accrues from the date of purchase until the date on which the security matures, i.e. when its face value is paid by the drawee to the holder of the security. For example, if a security due to mature in 91 days' time with a face value of £100,000 is discounted at 10 per cent, the discount is:

❝ Finding the discount rate ❞

$$£100,000 \times \frac{10}{100} \times \frac{91}{365} = £2,493.15$$

The seller of the bill therefore receives £97,506.85 and in this case the discount house charges a rate of interest of:

$$\frac{£2,493.15}{£97,506.85} \times \frac{365}{91} \times 100 = 10.26\%$$

The difference between interest payments on borrowed funds and interest receipts from discounting, is profit (or loss) for the discount houses.

Functions of the discount market

The function of any discount house is to earn a profit from their activities. This is the reason they are in business. However, in carrying out its activities the discount market performs several important economic functions:

- The discount houses are the **primary market makers** in short-term securities. As market makers they are always prepared to buy and sell (make a market) in suitable securities. The securities in which they deal are discussed more fully on pp. 225–226 but are typically those with only a few months to maturity. In buying securities, the discount houses provide a source of short-term credit for those with securities to sell.

- As well as buying securities the discount houses also sell securities to investors. Such investors have differing requirements in terms of the desired maturity date of securities and the amount of funds they wish to invest. The discount houses are able to **arrange portfolios** (groups) of securities to match the requirements of investors thereby reducing 'search costs' for the latter. For example, they purchase Treasury bills at the 'weekly auction' and, if approached, will sell these and other securities when they are closer to maturity.

❝ Functions of the discount market ❞

- The discount houses also peform an important role in financing the government's short-term borrowing. Each week the Bank of England issues Treasury bills by tender, the so-called weekly auction, and the discount houses collectively agree to **cover the tender**. This simply means that they submit a bid for all the bills on offer, thus ensuring that the government is provided with the funds it requires. In practice, the discount market only takes up a portion of the weekly issue, the remainder being allocated to those who submit the highest bids. To ensure that the discount market is always able to carry out this function, uniquely in the UK, it has direct access to the Bank of England as lender of last resort.

- The discount market performs a crucial role in the **implementation of the government's monetary policy**. It is, in effect, the fulcrum through which the Bank of England engineers changes in short-term interest rates. The way in which the Bank does this is discussed on pp. 227–230.

- The discount houses borrow a large proportion of their funds from the commercial banks. Some of this money is at 'call' and repayment can be demanded almost immediately. Other funds are lent overnight. In this way, the discount houses provide the commercial banks with highly liquid, yet profitable, assets.

THE CLEARING BANKS

The clearing banks are so called because they handle the exchange and settlement, i.e. clearing of cheques. One of their main functions is therefore the **provision of a payments mechanism**. A second important function of the clearing banks is in **accepting deposits**.

However, we are mainly concerned with a third function, namely the **provision of finance**. The clearing banks are major providers of short-term finance, and their activities in the money market have an important bearing on the money supply. The eligible liabilities (ELs) of the clearing banks consist mainly of deposits, but their assets are more varied.

The asset side of the balance sheet

- **Notes and coins**   These are the bank's most liquid, but least profitable asset.
- **Balances at the Bank of England**   Of the three assets maintained at the Bank of England only *operational deposits* are a liquid asset. *Cash ratio deposits* are not liquid, since all deposit takers with ELs in excess of £10 million are obliged to maintain such deposits at the Bank of England equal to $\frac{1}{2}$ per cent of the ELs. Equally, *special deposits* are not liquid. More will be said about these later, but they are basically deposits 'frozen' at the Bank of England and repaid only at the Bank's discretion.

> *Assets of the clearing bank*

- **Bills**   The banks hold a variety of bills, but these are grouped in Table 12.1 as Treasury bills, eligible bank bills, eligible local authority bills and other bills. The precise nature of these bills is discussed on pp. 225–226 and we shall see below that they are of fundamental importance in the implementation of the government's monetary policy.
- **Investments**   These consist largely of the banks' holdings of gilt-edged securities, i.e. government bonds of various maturity dates. Company bonds, i.e. debentures, are also within this heading, as are holdings of equity (shares).
- **Advances**   These are the banks' most profitable asset and consist of loans and overdrafts made to private customers.

LIABILITIES (£m)		ASSETS (£m)	
Sterling liabilities		*Sterling assets*	
Notes Outstanding	1,883	Notes and Coin	2,928
Deposits: of which		Balances with the Bank	
Sight deposits	193,012	of England, of which:	
Time deposits	289,265	Cash ratio deposits	1,425
Certificates of deposit[2]	51,720	Operational deposits	205
		Special deposits	–
Other sterling liabilities	77,869	Market loans	
		LDMA, of which:	
Other currency liabilities		Secured	7,732
Deposits, of which:		Unsecured	35
Sight and time deposits	698,698	Other UK bank	80,181
Certificates of deposit[2]	59,663	UK bank CD's	18,875
		Building society CD's and	
Other foreign currency liabilities	46,859	time deposits	4,580
		UK local authorities	1,404
		Overseas	34,857
		Bills, of which:	
		Treasury bills	1,392
		Eligible bank bills	8,233
		Other bills	650
		Advances	383,441
		Investments	44,048
		Other sterling assets	27,577
		Other currency assets	
		Advances	172,271
		Market loans	481,441
		Bills 12,592	
		Investments	106,931
		Other foreign currency assets	28,171
Total liabilities	1,418,969	Total assets	1,418,969

Table 12.1 Banks in the UK: combined balance sheet of monthly reporting institutions[1] as at 30 Sept 1993

1 Generally those with total balance sheet of £100m or more, or eligible liabilities of £10m or more, other than members of the LDMA.
2 and other short-term paper (short-term securities) issued.
Source: Bank of England Quarterly Bulletin, November 1993.

Liquidity and profitability

We have already seen that banks have the ability to create deposits by making loans. Indeed, this is their most profitable activity, and it appears on the asset side of the balance sheet as 'advances'. Unfortunately advances are not easily converted into cash should the need arise, i.e. they are illiquid. Once granted, they cannot be called in unless a customer defaults in some way, such as failing to meet interest payments. Investments are another profitable asset representing as they do long-term loans. However, they can also be risky. While they can easily be sold on the stock exchange, their prices cannot be guaranteed. A bank forced to sell investments might therefore be compelled to do so at unfavourable prices. In general, the least liquid and most risky assets carry the highest rates of return, but banks also require liquidity so as to meet sudden outflows of cash caused by withdrawals from customers. This is why banks make short-term loans such as **money at call** to the discount market, or **overnight loans** to the other money market institutions as well as to the discount market. The problem for banks is to arrange their balance sheets so as to achieve the highest profit consistent with acceptable degrees of risk and liquidity. The main assets of the commercial banks are discussed above.

MERCHANT BANKS

Merchant banks perform a variety of functions in both the capital and money markets.

Acceptance business

This was one of the earliest activities of merchant banks. For a fee, they simply add their name to bills of exchange issued by traders. In this way, they guarantee payment of bills on maturity should the drawee default. Accepted bills of exchange are therefore highly marketable (liquid) securities.

Issuing business

66 Functions of the merchant bank 99

One of the earliest functions of merchant banks was to raise finance for overseas trading activities but during the present century they have become more active in raising finance in the home market. In particular, they now undertake the *issuing* and *underwriting* of share issues by joint stock companies and charge a fee for this service. More recently still they have combined this with financial advice, e.g. advice on the desirability of a merger.

Wholesale banking

Wholesale banking is a term used to describe *large-scale dealing* in deposits and is the most important activity of the London money markets. The sums involved are not less than £$\frac{3}{4}$ million and are placed for terms ranging from overnight to several months and, in some cases, years. The merchant banks have become active participants in the market for wholesale deposits and this is by far their main deposit-taking activity. In this context, they are active participants in the Euro-currency markets (p. 225). Like all banks, they earn income on the difference paid to attract funds and the amount charged when lending funds.

Foreign banks

The number of foreign banks operating in London has grown rapidly in recent years, from 77 in 1960 to around 450 today. In the main, foreign banks are concerned with international banking activities and are active participants in the Euro-currency markets. Indeed, the bulk of their business is concerned with wholesale banking activities and, as yet, retail banking activities account for a small proportion of their activities. However, since deregulation, the retail side of their activities has grown rapidly and they now compete with commercial banks for private customers. Many also compete for wholesale desposits in the domestic money market.

BANKING REGULATIONS

In August 1981, the Bank of England introduced important new measures concerned with the activities of the *monetary sector*. All of the institutions described in this chapter, both bank and non-bank financial intermediaries, are included in the definition of the monetary sector, which currently comprises:

- all recognised banks and licensed deposit-takers;
- the National Savings Bank;
- the Trustee Savings Bank;
- the Banking Department of the Bank of England;
- those institutions in the Channel Islands and the Isle of Man which have opted to adhere to the new arrangements.

The regulations currently in force concerning the monetary sector are as follows:

- All banks and licensed deposit takers with *eligible liabilities* (ELs) in excess of £10m are required to keep non-operational deposits with the Bank of England equal to $\frac{1}{2}$ per cent of total ELs. The purpose of this is to provide the Bank of England with funds and resources rather than to enable it to control the growth of ELs within the monetary sector.

- Special deposits are extended and now apply to all institutions within the monetary sector having ELs greater than £10m.

- All eligible banks, i.e. recognised banks, whose acceptances, i.e. accepted bills, are eligible for rediscount at the Bank of England, are required to hold secured call money with the LDMA. This must equal at least $2\frac{1}{2}$ per cent of their ELs. They are also required to hold an amount equal to a further $2\frac{1}{2}$ per cent of their ELs, with other institutions in the money and gilt-edged markets, making 5 per cent in total. The purpose of this is to ensure an adequate supply of funds to enable the bill and gilt-edged markets to function efficiently. We shall see on p. 227 that this is necessary if the Bank's own open market operations are to be effective.

- The previous reserve assets ratio, in which a minimum of $12\frac{1}{2}$ per cent of selected liquid assets had to be kept against liabilities, was abolished in 1981. The Bank will, however, continue to monitor the liquidity ratios of the banks to ensure that they are adequate.

- In normal circumstances, the Bank will no longer publicly announce its **minimum lending rate** (MLR), i.e. the rate at which it rediscounts first class bills when acting as *lender of last resort*, but will maintain it within an unpublished band. This is to give market forces a more prominent role in determining short-term rates, which will be allowed to fluctuate within the unpublished band without the authorities intervening. This does not mean that MLR can only fluctuate within the limits initially set by the unpublished band. The authorities might vary the position of the band from time to time, and in any case they have reserved the right to make public announcements about MLR in exceptional circumstances.

THE SECONDARY MONEY MARKET

Alongside the primary market described above there has grown a **secondary** or **parallel money market**. This has grown rapidly since the 1960s, mainly because the secondary money market has not been subjected to the same degree of regulation by the authorities as has the primary market. Put simply, willing borrowers who have been unable to obtain funds in the primary market have turned to other institutions. These institutions have therefore grown and now compete for deposits with the primary market. The more deposits they can attract, the more loans they can create and this increases their income.

The principal markets which together make up the secondary market are described below.

THE INTER-BANK MARKET

On any particular day, certain banks will have a shortage of funds, while other banks will have a surplus. Shortages and surpluses are matched as far as possible by borrowing and lending in the inter-bank market. Dealings are normally in sums of £250,000 or more. Money may be lent at call, overnight, or for any period up to about five years. However, the bulk of lending in the inter-bank market is for three months.

THE MARKET FOR STERLING CERTIFICATES OF DEPOSIT

> Components of the secondary money market

The nature of certificates of deposit (CDs) is discussed on p. 226 but it is important to note here that certificates of deposit are a *negotiable* security. In other words, they can be sold on the open market at prices determined by supply and demand. The banks have benefited particularly from the growth of a market in CDs because, by issuing such certificates, i.e. creating claims against themselves, they are able to obtain additional funds which can then be on-lent at a higher interest rate.

THE EURO-CURRENCY MARKET

When an exporter receives payment for goods or services in foreign currency, these can be deposited with a bank or some other licensed deposit taker. The exporter therefore has a foreign currency deposit which will be on-lent to willing borrowers by the institution holding the deposit. It is this on-lending of foreign currency by European institutions that has given rise to the term 'Euro-currency market'.

In terms of the value of deposits held, this is the largest of the parallel money markets. Companies, banks, and even governments, borrow in the Euro-currency market, and although funds can be borrowed for as long as five years, most borrowing is for six months or less.

INSTRUMENTS OF THE LONDON MONEY MARKET

The London money market deals mainly in instruments, i.e. securities, with one year or less to maturity. The main instruments traded are summarised below and any institution dealing in these instruments is therefore a participant in this market.

BILLS OF EXCHANGE

Bills of exchange are IOUs given by one person, usually a buyer of goods, to another person, usually a seller of goods. The drawee promises to pay the drawer a fixed sum of money at a specified future time. The drawer of the bill therefore gives the drawee time to sell the goods before paying for them. In the absence of this credit, buyers might not have sufficient cash to place orders and this would leave manufacturers without markets for their goods. However, bills of exchange are negotiable securites and once accepted are eligible for discounting. This has important implications because, if manufacturers granted trade credit, the reduction in their cash flow might make it impossible to finance further production without borrowing funds and incurring interest charges. In other words, by discounting a bill of exchange, an institution is providing credit to manufacturers or other suppliers, and this enables production and distribution to continue uninterrupted.

TREASURY BILLS

> The various instruments of the London money market

Treasury bills are issued by the Bank of England on behalf of the government and normally mature 91 days after issue. Like bills of exchange, these are a promise to pay a fixed sum of money. The rate of interest the government pays on its short-term borrowing is therefore determined by the price at which Treasury bills can be sold at the weekly tender. The higher the bid price, the lower the rate of interest the government pays on its short-term borrowing.

LOCAL AUTHORITY SECURITIES

Local authorities issue bonds which frequently mature within one year. They also issue bills which conventionally mature within 91 days. Like Treasury bills, these are issued by tender and, as government has issued fewer Treasury bills, so the discount houses have acquired more local authority bills.

CERTIFICATES OF DEPOSIT (CD)

A CD is a document certifying that a deposit has been placed with a bank, and that the deposit is repayable with interest after a stated time. The minimum value of the deposit is usually £50,000 and CDs normally mature in twelve months or less, although they have been issued with a five-year maturity.

SHORT-DATED BONDS

As well as the securities discussed so far, a host of other securities are traded on the money market. As time goes by, any security issued for a fixed number of years will approach its maturity date. The discount market discounts securities with *five years or less* to maturity, but in general it is only when securities have one year or less to maturity that they are traded on the money market.

EURO-CURRENCY CERTIFICATES OF DEPOSIT

These are similar to sterling CDs, but are given as evidence of a *foreign* currency deposit with a UK bank. Dollar certificates of deposit are the most important instrument traded in the Euro-currency deposit market. The most important outlet for Euro-deposits is the interbank Euro-currency market. Although banks might borrow from one another for as long as five years, most borrowing is for six months or less. Indeed, a substantial amount is typically lent overnight. As they approach maturity, certificates of deposit become more attractive to money market institutions because of their higher degree of liquidity.

EURO-BONDS

The Euro-bond market specialises in the provision of medium-term finance. In this market, banks arrange, on behalf of borrowers in the UK, to issue and to underwrite bonds. These bonds are usually taken up, i.e. purchased, by private investors who supply the appropriate amount of foreign currency. Like other securities, as they approach maturity, Euro-bonds become more liquid and so are traded on the London money markets in the same way that other short-term instruments are traded (see above – 'short-dated' bonds).

MEASURES OF THE MONEY SUPPLY

66 Different measures of the money supply 99

Until now we have discussed the general area of money and liquidity without specifically defining the type of money. The fact that there are several measures of the money supply (see Ch. 17 p. 338) appears to make any reference to this concept ambiguous. However, the different measures of the money supply aim to reflect different levels of liquidity within the system. Some measures of the money supply, such as M0, provide an estimate of the level of transactions balances or immediate spending potential in the economy. These are referred to as **narrow money**. Narrow money therefore focuses on the 'medium of exchange' function of money but is not a *leading* indicator, i.e. it does not provide any information on the future growth of GDP. On the other hand, measures of **broad money** such as M4, include a range of assets which vary in their degree of liquidity. Broad money therefore focuses more on the 'store of value' function of money and might be useful as a leading indicator.

One problem for the authorities is that having several measures of the money supply sometimes makes it difficult to assess whether monetary policy is restricting the growth of the money supply or not, because the different measures of the money supply sometimes move in different directions with some aggregates rising when others are falling.

In the UK, the authorities have always taken the view that narrow money is an accurate indicator of current money conditions and, as we shall see in Chapter 17, they have set targets for its rate of growth since 1980. Target rates of growth for broad money ceased to be published after 1986. However, this was more to do with the problems of measuring and controlling broad money growth than because broad money was not considered important. In October 1992, the Chancellor underlined the view that broad money was important when he introduced **monitoring ranges** (see p. 339) for the rate of growth of M4.

<table>
<tr><td>

THE MECHANICS OF MONETARY POLICY

</td><td>

The term **monetary policy** is usually taken to include all the measures which influence the supply of money and/or the price of money, i.e. the rate of interest. In the UK, the Bank of England has overall responsibility for the implementation of monetary policy. It uses a variety of techniques but it is important to be clear that the Bank cannot opt to control *both* the supply of money *and* the rate of interest *simultaneously*. A policy of controlling interest rates implies that the money supply must be allowed to vary so as to meet changes in the public's demand for money at the target rate of interest. If the authorities did not allow the money supply to vary in this way, an increase in demand for money would pull up interest rates and vice versa.

</td></tr>
</table>

More specifically, the implication of an *interest rate target* is that the Bank must allow commercial banks to vary the level of their operational deposits by absorbing cash surpluses which emerge in the money market or by relieving any shortages through its role as **lender of last resort** so as to preserve the existing level of money market rates. A *money supply target*, on the other hand, implies that the Bank must not mop up any surpluses or relieve any shortages of money which develop, irrespective of how far short-term interest rates rise or fall. The techniques available to the authorities to achieve the aims of monetary policy are now considered.

OPEN-MARKET OPERATIONS

This technique involves the sale or purchase of government securities on the open market by the Bank of England. It can be used to reduce or to increase the stock of money, i.e. bank deposits, in circulation with the public.

66 Be familiar with open-market operations 99

- Suppose the Bank of England wishes to *reduce* the money supply by open-market operations. The Bank of England sells securities to the non-bank private sector, i.e. households and firms other than those engaged in banking in the private sector. These securities will be paid for by cheques drawn against deposits with the commercial banks. The Bank of England will settle these claims against banks by deducting the appropriate amount from their operational deposits. If necessary, the banks will be able to replenish their operational deposits at the Bank of England by calling in their loans to the discount market. However, there will still be a reduction in their overall level of liquidity, since loans to the discount market are liquid assets and these have now fallen in total. This reduction in liquidity will compel banks to reduce their lending, i.e. bank deposits, otherwise they risk being unable to honour all the claims that bank lending creates against them.

- If the Bank of England wishes to *increase* the money supply by open market operations, it will purchase securities from the non-bank private sector. In this case, the banks operational deposits increase. Assuming that there are willing borrowers, then this extra liquidity can be used to increase their lending, that is, bank deposits increase.

INTEREST RATE POLICY

In practice, open-market operations have been used less frequently for controlling the money supply in recent years. Instead, the authorities have relied much more on money market intervention to influence interest rates and, in this way, to control the growth of bank lending. A rise in interest rates might be expected to damp down the demand for bank credit, thus restricting growth of the money supply and vice versa.

The techniques of interest rate policy are complex but, under the present arrangements, the clearing banks inform the Bank of England daily about the target they are aiming at for their assets. This information, together with the Bank's estimate of flows between the commercial banks and the public sector, as well as seasonal patterns, etc. enables the Bank to estimate the likely shortage or surplus of funds in the money market. This estimate is announced at about 9.45 a.m. and, if necessary, a revised estimate is announced at noon.

- If the Bank estimates that the market will be short of funds, it informs the discount houses that it is prepared to buy bills from them. However, it does not stipulate a price, and the discount houses must offer bills to the bank at prices of their choosing.

- If the Bank of England considers that the rate of interest implied by these offers (remember the relationship between security prices and the rate of interest) is consistent with the conduct of monetary policy, it will accept the offers, and the shortage of funds will be relieved.

- However, if the Bank considers that the rate of interest implied by these offers is too low, then it will decline to buy the bills and the discount houses will be compelled to make further offers of bills at lower prices (implying higher rates of interest).

- When the Bank wishes to engineer a fall in short-term rates of interest it simply increases the price at which it is prepared to buy bills from the discount houses.

THE STERLING MONEY MARKET

An article in the National Westminster Bank Quarterly Bulletin entitled *The Sterling Money Market and the Determination of Interest Rates* provides an analysis of the Bank's operating procedures in the money market.

The article emphasises that the Bank operates at the short end of the market, i.e. seeks to influence short-term interest rates and, in particular, the 7-day rate. It can do this by buying or selling bills on a sufficient scale so as to create a surplus or shortage of bankers' cash (operational deposits). However, in practice the authorities do not always seek to achieve this. The Bank buys or sells on a modest scale seeking only to make the market aware of its desire to achieve a particular rate of interest. Other money market operators, being aware of the power of the authorities to achieve their aim by coercion, are quick to ensure that interest rates fall into line with the intentions of the authorities once these intentions are known. The Bank's operations in the money market therefore function as a system of communication as well as a mechanism of control.

It is also explained that the Bank's declared current aim is to maintain short-term (7-day) rates within an undisclosed band having an upper limit and a lower limit. The whole bank will shift from time to time in keeping with the changing interest rate targets set by the authorities. The authorities also reserve the right to publish their target rate if circumstances demand it (as happened in 1986 when the authorities disclosed their minimum lending rate as an indication to the market of their intention to see no further reduction in the sterling exchange rate). In practice, however, only the upper end of the band has been relevant for control purposes because over-funding sales of government debt to the non-bank sector has meant a persistent shortage of bankers' cash which the Bank has then been able to relieve on terms of its own choosing by buying bills in the market.

Despite its declared intention it seems that the Bank has been dealing in all maturities up to 3 months. Indeed it reports its dealing rates twice daily in four maturity bands:

Band 1: up to 14 days
Band 2: 15 to 33 days
Band 3: 34 to 63 days
Band 4: 64 to 91 days

and these are taken as the Bank's estimate of the optimum course of the 7-day rate over the next 13 weeks. In other words, they are taken by the market as an attempt by the authorities to give an indication of the expected future course of interest rates. The market has often been ready to accept this indication so that the 3-month rate has adjusted to the Bank's Band 4 rate. On other occasions, the market has taken a different view of the future course of interest rates and the Bank has preferred to alter its Band 4 rate rather than be seen to disagree publicly with the market.

How does the Bank engineer a change in short-term rates?

The question might be asked as to how the Bank will engineer a change in rates when the market is *not* short of funds, and so does not need to deal with. In fact, this is an unlikely occurrence, because the Bank can create short y increasing the weekly Treasury bill issue. Since the LDMA agree to cover the tender, this will create a shortage of funds. Alternatively, the Bank can 'fund' the national debt; see below. To engineer a fall in short-term rates, the Bank simply buys securities thus creating a surplus of funds in the money markets.

Another way in which the Bank can affect short-term rates is provided by the 1981 regulations. Under these, the Bank retains the option, in exceptional circumstances, to reveal in advance the rate at which it will operate in the market for a short period ahead. It has used this option on several occasions and it has proved very effective with all institutions acting quickly to fall into line with the Bank's wishes once it has made these known. The alternative, of course, would be for the Bank to implement measures which would force institutions to comply with its intentions!

Problems of controlling money supply by using interest rates

There are several problems associated with using interest rates to control the money supply:

- Changes in the rate of interest cause changes in the sterling exchange rate which might conflict with the aims of the authorities.
- Sometimes relatively high interest rates are needed to reduce monetary growth. As well as being unpopular with home buyers, this causes the retail price index to rise. High interest rates also reduce the rate of investment in fixed capital and hence reduce future economic growth.
- Changes in interest rates usually work only after a considerable time lag has elapsed. (The relatively low rates of interest during 1993/94 took many months to encourage expenditure and stimulate recovery from recession.)

SPECIAL DEPOSITS

When the Bank of England makes a call for special deposits, it requires banks and licensed deposit takers with ELs in excess of £10m to place funds in a special account at the Bank. Although these funds earn interest, they are effectively 'frozen', since those making the deposits do not have the right to withdraw them. The Bank of England alone decides when special deposits will be repaid. The level of special deposits is fixed as a percentage of ELs and payment is again made by a reduction in operational deposits, i.e. cash reserves at the Bank. A call for special deposits is the most direct means currently available to the Bank for reducing the liquidity position of banks and licensed deposit takers, and is therefore the most direct means of controlling their lending. As the stock of liquid assets falls, banks are again forced to cut their lending. Special deposits can be released when the Bank wishes to see an expansion of the money supply.

No call has been made for special deposits since the 1970s because, as with any selective control mechanism, the result of using them has often been rapid growth of business by those organisations *not* subject to these controls. The authorities take the view that such growth is undesirable because it represents growth of less efficient institutions, i.e. institutions which only grow when other institutions are subjected to controls. This explains the emphasis on control through changes in the rate of interest, which affects *all* institutions indiscriminately and does not therefore encourage the growth of inefficient institutions.

FUNDING

This involves the sale of *more long-term debt*, e.g. bonds, and the issue of less short-term debt, e.g. Treasury bills. Since Treasury bills are short-dated securities, they are highly liquid assets because they can be sold easily and quickly on the money market. By issuing fewer Treasury bills, the authorities can reduce the degree of liquidity in the system, and thereby restrict the ability of the banks to make loans. If a bank's holdings of Treasury bills falls and its holdings of long-term securities increases, it is likely to cut its lending for two main reasons:

- Longer-term securities are not eligible for re-discount at the Bank of England and are therefore less liquid.
- Although longer-term securities can be sold on the capital market, their value is less certain.

These are important considerations, since they imply that if a bank needs to replenish its holdings of cash because of a sudden outflow of funds, it might be forced to sell its securities at unfavourable prices. Rather than risk this, banks would tend to cut their lending.

FISCAL POLICY

The authorities believe that there is a close association between the amount the public sector borrows – the **Public Sector Borrowing Requirement (PSBR)** – and the growth of broad money. This relationship is discussed in detail on pp. 309–311, but it is important to note here that at the present time the authorities believe that unless growth of the PSBR is controlled, it will be difficult to control the growth of broad money without raising interest rates, thereby reducing freedom of manoeuvre in the conduct of monetary policy.

MONETARY BASE CONTROL

This technique of monetary control has not so far been used in the UK but is still favoured by many economists, especially those economists referred to as **monetarists**. The technique is simple enough. Banks would maintain a minimum proportion of their deposits in *base money* (normally defined as notes and coin plus operational deposits at the Bank of England) either because this is mandatory or because it is prudent for them to do so. The authorities can then either:

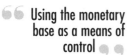
Using the monetary base as a means of control

- control the supply of base money and so control the growth of bank deposits; or
- use divergencies in the growth of base money above the desired trend to trigger interest rate increases – higher interest rates will in turn limit the growth of borrowing and hence correct the divergence.

So far there has been little official support for either technique though the former has received most criticism and the authorities have taken the view that any attempt to limit the growth of deposits by controlling the supply of base money would lead to a distortion in the money supply figures. In other words, it might well control the growth of bank deposits, but might lead to a significant change in the composition of the money supply, with assets not officially included in narrow measures of the money stock, such as commercial bills of exchange, functioning as money.

SUMMARY

Despite the availability of a wide range of techniques for controlling the money supply, recently the authorities have relied most on:

- limiting the growth of the PSBR;
- limiting the extent to which the PSBR is financed through the banking sector; and
- interest rate policy.

APPLIED MATERIALS

MONETARY AGGREGATES

The *Bank of England Quarterly Bulletin* of May 1993 contains an article on **Divisia measures of money**. Traditional measures of money are termed **simple-sum monetary aggregates**, because they assume that all their components are the same.

In other words, £1m in notes and coin is treated as exactly equivalent to £1m in a time deposit.

Divisia indices take account of these differences by *weighting* each component asset according to the extent to which it provides transactions services. Such assets are priced, or measured, by rates of interest foregone when holding them. The benchmark rate of interest is the rate earned on 3-month deposits with local authorities.

Despite the apparent logic of weighting the different assets according to their liquidity there are problems with this approach.

■ By measuring 'user cost' in terms of interest foregone, any other benefits from holding an asset, such as automatic overdraft facilities, are ignored.

■ The credit balances held in many current accounts, and certainly the personal holdings of notes and coin, are below the minimum deposit held by local authorities. Because of this, it is not strictly accurate to simply take the arithmetic difference between two rates of interest.

■ Since the weights in the Divisia index are derived from interest rates, when interest rates in general change, the weights in the Divisia index will change. The problem is that the actual totals of the component assets will be much slower to change as the new rates of interest take effect.

■ There are problems in choosing a benchmark rate of interest. The 3-month local authority rate was chosen because the asset is non-marketable and non-transferable. It is therefore 'non-monetary'. However, local authority rates are not well known.

The article also considers whether Divisia is a leading indicator. The Bank's view is that Divisia *is* a leading indicator and therefore leads changes in nominal GDP. For example, between 1985 and 1987, strong growth in Divisia preceded an upturn in GDP growth in 1986–89. Similarly, the deceleration in Divisia growth preceded the decline in nominal GDP growth as the economy moved into recession in the early 1990s.

One problem with Divisia is that it is compiled only quarterly and this limits its value as a leading indicator. Because of the delay in compiling Divisia, it is difficult to plan policy in light of the information it provides.

EXAMINATION QUESTIONS

1 (a) Explain the role of the commercial banks in a modern economy. *(13)*
   (b) Evaluate the arguments for, and against, the commercial banks in the United Kingdom being more closely controlled. *(12)*

(AEB June 1993)

2 (a) Explain how the commercial banking system can 'create' deposits. *(15)*
   (b) Consider how the Bank of England has attempted to influence the creation of bank deposits in the UK in the period since 1980. *(10)*

(WJEC 1992)

3 (a) Why are there several definitions of money in the UK? *(30)*
   (b) What issues arise for the monetary authorities in controlling the money supply? *(70)*

(ULSEB June 1993)

4 Discuss the case for making the Bank of England completely independent of government.

(JMB 1992)

ANSWERS TO EXAMINATION QUESTIONS

TUTOR'S ANSWER TO QUESTION 1

(a) Commercial banks are profit-seeking enterprises. In the UK, many of the larger commercial banks, such as Lloyds, National Westminster, Barclays and the Midland, are household names. These institutions earn profit by providing services for private individuals, for the business community and for the government.

Banks are financial intermediaries, i.e. they attract funds from depositors and lend funds to borrowers. Broadly, three types of deposits are accepted: sight deposits, notice of withdrawal (NOW) deposits and fixed-term deposits. **Sight deposits**, as we shall see later, can be withdrawn on demand and are used primarily as a means of payment. These accounts are highly liquid and consequently earn only a small rate of interest. **NOW deposits** can only be withdrawn after a period of notice has elapsed. Such accounts earn interest as compensation for loss of liquidity. **Fixed-term deposits**, as their name implies, cannot be withdrawn until their full term has elapsed. This implies a total loss of liquidity during the time in which deposits are placed with the banks and consequently term deposits earn relatively high rates of interest.

Banks compete vigorously with each other for funds which are then on-lent to borrowers. The difference between the amount they pay to attract funds (plus their other costs of production) and the amount they charge for loans is their profit. Bank loans take a variety of forms but lending to most private individuals and businesses is through an *overdraft*. Here an individual or business is able to overdraw his or her current account up to an agreed limit. Interest is paid on the day-to-day amount the account is overdrawn. They also lend longer term to the business community by purchasing certificates of deposit. Commercial banks also lend to central and local government. Here the bank 'purchases' bills or bonds which simply means that fixed amounts are loaned for a specific period of time.

In accepting deposits and making loans, banks function as financial intermediaries. However, this does not imply that banks merely perform the role of 'middlemen'. Instead, they transform the funds which pass through their accounts. For example, an individual might deposit funds with a bank on seven days' notice of withdrawal. However, borrowing is often for much longer periods and **maturity transformation** is a primary function of financial intermediaries. They are able to borrow short and lend long because, over time, inflows tend to match outflows, and because financial intermediaries can source funds by borrowing in the money market if necessary. For the individual lender, financial intermediaries offer **risk reduction**. When funds are lent there is always a possibility of default by the borrower. Since financial intermediaries make loans to many different individuals and organisations, the risk of default by one is not so serious as it would be if an individual lent funds and the borrower subsequently defaulted. The importance of maturity transformation and risk reduction cannot be over-emphasised and in the absence of financial intermediaries, there is no doubt that individuals, industry and government would experience considerably more difficulty in sourcing funds.

Banks also provide a well-developed and highly efficient means of transferring funds between individuals and organisations. By drawing cheques in favour of one person or organisation, funds can be transferred from one sight deposit to another. Movement of bank deposits is the main means of settling financial obligations in a developed economy. The process is highly secure and, on average, cheques take two full working days to clear. Speed and security in the transfer of funds are important advantages of using the banks for this purpose.

Banks also provide a range of other services. They will undertake to make regular payments on behalf of depositors by way of standing orders or direct debits. They provide foreign exchange facilities for individuals and firms. They provide financial advice to customers, for example on taxation and investments and so on.

(b) It is sometimes argued that the activities of commercial banks should be more closely controlled so as to facilitate greater control over growth of the money supply by the authorities.

The major argument in favour of controlling the growth of bank lending is that, if controls are effective, the authorities will be better able to control the growth of the money supply. It is argued that if the authorities *can* control the money supply, they will be able to exercise greater control over the rate of inflation. Maintaining inflation at relatively low rates has emerged as the paramount goal of economic policy and it is now widely accepted that the main determinant of inflation, in the long run, is money growth. Since bank deposits are the main component of money growth, it could be argued that greater control over the banking system would facilitate greater control over the rate of inflation. Control over the rate of inflation would confer a multitude of benefits on the economy. It would facilitate lower interest rates, improve export competitiveness and generally encourage economic growth.

The potential advantages of controlling the banking sector are considerable, but how is control to be exercised? One technique of control, now abandoned in the UK but still used in other countries, is the imposition of **reserve ratios**. Here, the authorities impose a requirement that the banks must maintain some minimum ratio between their total deposits and some specified range of assets. Total control over the lending activities of the banks can be exercised if the authorities are able to exercise total control over the specified range of assets.

A different approach to control of the commercial banks is the imposition of **direct controls**. In the UK, direct controls have taken the form of **special deposits** and supplementary special deposits. The former involved placing a specified level of deposits with the Bank of England. These deposits were then effectively withdrawn from circulation and were only repaid when the Bank considered it expedient to do so. **Supplementary specials deposits**, on the other hand, functioned as a tax on the growth of bank lending above a certain limit and this provided a powerful incentive for banks to cut back on the growth of their lending.

The problem with imposing controls on the commercial banks is that they lead to inefficiency in the allocation of credit. It is an inevitable result of controls that some potential borrowers who can use credit more effectively than other borrowers, will be denied funds. Now it is well known that controls leave some credit-worthy borrowers unable to source funds and therefore governments frequently encourage financial institutions to give priority to certain types of borrower. This implies that decisions by officials overrule market forces and resources are again allocated inefficiently. Inefficiency will be further encouraged because both mechanisms of control outlined above imply the creation of credit shortages which will reduce competition between the commercial banks for business.

A major problem with applying controls to the commercial banks is that such controls would be ineffective if they prevented willing lenders from supplying credit to willing borrowers. In such circumstances, both parties have an incentive to find ways of evading the controls. This implies a misallocation of resources into unproductive activities and a diversion of business to the unregulated, and therefore less efficient (otherwise they would already be supplying credit) providers of credit. Furthermore, controls impose costs on the authorities since they will be obliged to combat evasion, otherwise there would be no point in imposing controls in the first place! The tighter the controls, the greater the problem of evasion and therefore the greater the cost of combatting it. In a world that is increasingly free of capital controls, it would be easy to circumvent regulations imposed on the commercial banks by borrowing from overseas banks.

It is now widely accepted that controls on the banking sector are ineffective and, in the UK, the authorities rely on changes in the rate of interest to encourage or discourage borrowing thereby encouraging or discouraging the growth of bank deposits.

STUDENT'S ANSWER TO QUESTION 2

Account

```
(a) Bank deposits originate in two main ways: when a
    customer deposits funds and when a bank makes a loan.
    In the first case, the bank simply credits the
    customer's (name) with the amount deposited. The second
    case is more interesting for present purposes because
    banks create a deposit in the name of the borrower.
```

An important point to note is that banks are aware that, on any particular day, not all of the money deposited with them will be withdrawn. This means that banks can lend out the remainder. For simplicity, let us assume that banks require only 10 per cent of the total amount deposited with them to meet day-to-day demands from customers. Banks will therefore be able to lend out 90 per cent of all funds deposited with them.

The process does not end there. Once a bank has lent out 90 per cent of any initial amount deposited with it, this will be withdrawn and spent by the borrowers. However, each payment will be made by drawing a cheque authorising the bank deposit to be transferred to the seller of goods. His or her bank will thus receive an inflow of funds and will lend out 90 per cent of this and so on.

This process does not go on indefinitely. At each stage less and less is lent out and the limit is reached when the whole amount of the original deposit represents only 10 per cent of the deposits the banks have created. The bank deposit multiplier tells us the final amount of deposits that can be created from an initial deposit of funds. This is written as 1/(cash ratio). In our example, the cash ratio is 10 per cent so that the bank deposit multiplier is 1/0.1 = 10. This tells us that the banking system will be able to create deposits equal to ten times the amount initially deposited with them.

(b) The Bank of England has powerful techniques for controlling the ability of the commercial banks to create credit. In the early 1980s, the Bank of England used special deposits to restrict the lending of the commercial banks. Special deposits are deposits placed with the Bank of England which cannot be withdrawn by the commercial banks. They are repaid at the discretion of the Bank of England but the point is that when special deposits are made, the commercial banks experience a loss of liquidity which restricts their ability to make loans because funds that are deposited with them must be paid to the Bank of England and cannot therefore be lent to customers.

Another technique is open market operations. Here, the Bank of England buys or sells securities in the open market depending on whether it wishes to increase or decrease liquidity in the banking system. When the Bank of England sells securities in the open market, these are paid for by a transfer of bank deposits from a commercial bank to the Bank of England. As a result, the operational deposits of the commercial bank fall and again this implies a reduction in their liquidity. As liquidity falls the commercial bank will be compelled to restrict its lending.

❝ Rather vague ❞

❝ The B of E did not use Special Deposits in the 1980s — now abandoned altogether ❞

❝ Some good points but a vague explanation of the credit creating process — a simple numerical example would help. The main technique for controlling the creation of bank deposits in the 1980s was varying the rate of interest in order to change the demand for bank loans. ❞

OUTLINE ANSWERS

Question 3

(a) You could begin your answer to this question by explaining the main reason why there are several definitions of money, i.e. that different assets have different degrees of liquidity. This is important becaue of the effect changes in the money supply have on the macro economy. You could then go on to outline the components of the different official measures of the money supply currently monitored in the UK. It is important to distinguish between **narrow money** and **broad money**. The former is a measure of immediate spending potential in the economy whereas the latter includes a range of liquid and relatively illiquid assets all of which influence expenditure.

(b) You could begin your answer by briefly explaining the quantity theory of money (see p. 240) and thus highlighting the importance of obtaining an accurate measure of the money supply. The main issue to consider here is which monetary aggregate most accurately mesures spending potential in the economy. This is a matter of dispute among economists. Some economists believe measures of narrow money are more important because they foreshadow relatively swift changes in expenditure. Other economists argue that narrow money might fluctuate but, in the long run, changes in expenditure are the result of changes in many factors. Changes in wealth are particularly important and broad money more accurately measures this. You must explain these points in some detail stressing the importance of velocity. At the end of the day, if it is agreed that money matters, then it is clearly important to agree on what constitutes money!

Question 4

You could begin your answer by outlining the role of the Bank of England. In the UK, the Bank of England is constitutionally part of the government and the main implication of this is that the government is free to set fiscal policy secure in the knowledge that the Bank will adopt an accommodating monetary policy. In particular, the Bank will ensure that the government's borrowing requirement is met.

See also Ch. 13, p. 250

Some economists argue that the problem with this, is that it allows the government to vary its economic policy in response to short-term developments and makes it difficult for other economic agents (firms and individuals) to plan future levels of expenditure accurately since it implies that aggregate demand, the exchange rate, the rate of interest and inflation will all fluctuate. This adversely affects economic growth.

The main argument in favour of an independent central bank is that it could be given a specific role, in particular controlling the rate of inflation. An independent central bank would not be obliged to accommodate the government's expansionary or contractionary policies and it is alleged that this would give greater economic stability. In particular, it is now widely accepted that price stability and a low rate of inflation confer substantial benefits on the economy. You should outline these benefits (see pp. 258–259).

Further reading

Griffiths and Wall, *Applied Economics: An Introductory Course* (6th edn), Longman 1995. Ch. 17, The UK Financial System; Ch. 18, Money.

Harrison et al, *Introductory Economics*, Macmillan 1992: Ch. 23, Money and the Creation of Bank Deposits; Ch. 24, The Monetary Sector; Ch. 25, Monetary Control.

REVIEW SHEET

1 Define the following:

Liquidity: _____

_____

Sight deposits: _____

_____

2 List four functions of money.

(a) _____

(b) _____

(c) _____

(d) _____

3 Explain how money encourages specialisation to take place in an economy.

_____

_____

_____

4 List four characteristics of money.

(a) _____

(b) _____

(c) _____

(d) _____

5 Assuming a 10 per cent ratio, describe the impact of a £1,000 cash deposit on a bank's balance sheet.

_____

_____

_____

_____

_____

_____

6 Define financial intermediation.

_____

_____

_____

7 Why does financial intermediation arise? Suggest two reasons.

(a) _____

_____

(b) _____

_____

8 Describe six functions of the Bank of England.

(a) _____

(b) _____

(c) _____

(d) _____

(e) _____

(f) _____

9 Explain what is meant by discounting.

_____

_____

_____

10 Describe five functions of the discount market.

(a) _____

(b) _____

(c) _____

(d) _____

(e) _____

11 List the assets of the clearing bank in decreasing order of liquidity.

_____

_____

12 What do we mean when we say that there is an inverse relationship between liquidity and profitability?

_____

_____

13 Describe each of the following:

Bills of exchange: _____

_____

Treasury bills: _____

_____

Certificates of deposit: _____

_____

Narrow money measures: _____

Broad money measures: _____

_____

14 Briefly describe how each of the following aspects of monetary policy are conducted by the Bank of England on behalf of the government.

Open market operations: _____

_____

Interest rate policy: _____

_____

Calls for special deposits: _____

_____

Funding: _____

_____

Monetary base control: _____

_____

THE VALUE OF MONEY

GETTING STARTED

In itself, money has no intrinsic value. It derives value because it is acceptable in exchange for goods and services. The value of money is therefore determined by the prices of goods and services purchased with money. Clearly, if all prices in the economy rise, then a given amount of money will exchange for (or buy) fewer goods and services. In this case, the value of money has fallen. Conversely, if all prices in the economy fall, the value of money has risen.

This seems simple enough, but the problem is that over any given period of time not all prices in the economy move in the same direction or by the same amount. Some prices rise and others fall. Some rise by more than others, and so on. In practice, therefore, it is difficult to measure changes in the value of money, and economists use a technique involving **index numbers** to estimate changes in an average of prices. Not all price changes are considered, merely those of most significance to the average person.

The cause of changes in the value of money, i.e. the cause of price changes, is a subject which has long been discussed by economists. The earliest attempt to explain the cause of changes in the value of money is the **quantity theory of money**. The earliest version of this theory proposed a direct relationship between changes in the money supply and changes in the price level; but it is the more refined version, associated with Irving Fisher, that is usually considered most significant.

QUANTITY THEORY OF MONEY

ESSENTIAL PRINCIPLES

Fisher's quantity theory of money is based on the **equation of exchange**. This is usually expressed in the following way:

$$MV_t = PT$$

where M = the total money stock
V_t = the transactions velocity of money, i.e. the number of times each unit of currency is spent over a given period of time
P = the average price level
T = the total number of transactions which take place over a given period of time.

However, T is difficult to measure since it includes second-hand and intermediate transactions. For policy purposes therefore, a more useful formulation of the equation of exchange is:

$$MV_y = PY$$

where M = the total money stock
V_y = income velocity of circulation or the number of times each unit of currency is used to purchase final output in any given period of time
P = average price of final output
Y = the total volume of real output produced in a given period of time.

Since P is the average price of final output and Y is the total volume of final output, PY is simply another way of expressing GNP.

Whichever formulation we consider, the equation of exchange is nothing more than an identity or a truism. Both sides of the equation must, by definition, always be identical. MV_t is total spending in the economy and PT is total receipts in the economy. By definition, total spending in one period must equal total receipts in the same period. Similarly, GNP in any particular period is equal both to total final expenditure, MV_y, and to the value of receipts, PY, from the sale of final output.

Despite this, the equation of exchange forms the basis of the quantity theory. Fisher and other classical economists assumed that the economy had an in-built tendency to establish equilibrium at full employment. They therefore believed that the total volume of transactions was fixed in the short run by the amount that can be produced at full employment. Additionally, they also assumed that the velocity of circulation was determined independently of changes in the money supply and changed so slowly over time that it could be treated as a constant. Accepting both these propositions leads to the conclusion that M varies directly with P.

> The quantity theory relates money supply directly to prices

However, this still does not provide an adequate explanation of how the price level is determined. A further assumption, frequently made by monetarist adherents to the quantity theory, is that the authorities can control the money supply. Thus, the basic prediction of the quantity theory becomes one in which changes in M cause changes in P, and that there can be no change in P independently of a prior change in M. Although, as we shall see later, the quantity theory has been reformulated, most notably by Friedman, Fisher's version remains the basis of all monetarist thinking.

INDEX NUMBERS

We have seen that changes in the value of money imply a change in the average price level. Changes in the average price level are measured by **index numbers** and, in the UK, the most publicised index is the index of retail prices.

INDEX OF RETAIL PRICES

The retail price index (RPI) purports to measure changes in the cost of living experienced by an average household over a particular period of time. The technique is simple enough. A representative sample of the population provides a detailed record of their expenditure over a given period, usually a month, and this is used to estimate the expenditure pattern of the 'average' household. This estimate of expenditure is used to derive the *items* to be included in the index and the *weights* assigned to them; the weight being based on their relative importance. Those items which account for a large proportion of total expenditure over the period are assigned a higher weight than items which account for a smaller proportion of total expenditure. Table 13.1 illustrates the basic principles involved in computing the RPI.

		Year 1			Year 2		
Item	Weight	Price	Index No.	Weighted No.	Price	Index No.	Weighted Index No.
A	4	£1.00	100	400	£1.50	(£1.50/£1 =) 150	(150x4 =) 600
B	2	£2.00	100	200	£2.50	(£2.50/£2 =) 125	(125x2 =) 250
C	3	£5.00	100	300	£6.00	(£6/£5 =) 120	(120x3 =) 360
D	1	£4.00	100	100	£6.00	(£6/£4 =) 150	(150x1 =) 150
	10			1000			1360
Index of prices = 1000/10 = 100					Index of prices = 1360/10 = 136		

Table 13.1 Finding the retail price index

In the base year (Year 1) each commodity is assigned an index number of 100. The weighted index number of each commodity is then obtained by multiplying the index number by the weight. Adding up all the weighted index numbers and dividing by the sum of the weights, gives the value of the price index. In the example provided, the value of the price index in the base year is 100. (In fact, this will *always* be the value of the index in the base year, because each commodity is assigned a value of 100. In calculating a weighted price index in the base year we are therefore effectively multiplying 100 by the sum of the weights and then dividing the answer by the sum of the weights.)

“ Finding the retail price index ”

In the next period (Year 2) the index number of each commodity is simply the price of the commodity in Year 2 expressed as a percentage of its price in Year 1. So we see that the price of commodity A in Year 2 is 150 per cent of its price in Year 1, and so on. Again, this is multiplied by the relevant weight for each commodity, and the total of all the weighted index numbers which results, is divided by the sum of the weights to give the price index, i.e. the average weighted value of all price changes in Year 2. In this case, the price index in Year 2 is 136 indicating that the average family has experienced a rise in the cost of living of 36 per cent between Year 1 and Year 2.

Problems of interpreting changes in the RPI

Changes in the RPI are the most widely used measure of changes in the rate of inflation in the UK. However, for several reasons changes in the RPI might not accurately measure changes in the rate of inflation:

“ The need for caution in interpreting changes in the RPI ”

■ A retail price index such as that illustrated in Table 13.1 measures changes in retail prices experienced by the **average family**. However, different families will have different patterns of consumption, which might deviate substantially from that used to construct a price index. For example, families with children consume different goods and services than families with no children. Similarly changes in the prices of goods and services affect people differently. For example, non-smokers are unaffected by changes in the price of tobacco, and changes in the mortgage rate only affect home-buyers.

■ Over time **patterns of consumption** change. For example, more fish is now consumed and less red meat than a decade ago. Consumption of alcohol has increased in the last decade and so on. If an index is to be accurate, the weights must be altered to reflect these changes.

■ Care must also be taken to monitor changes in the types of institution used by consumers. Here again patterns have changed, with small independent retailers declining in importance and supermarkets increasing in importance. Data on prices charged in **different retail outlets** must reflect expenditure by consumers in them if an index is to be accurate.

■ Over time the **quality of goods** changes. For example, pocket calculators are now more reliable and have a greater range of functions than models available only a few years ago. Simply monitoring price changes ignores such quality improvements.

- **New goods** become available and again the index must be altered to take account of these if it is to be accurate. For example, few houses had a home computer or a video in the 1970s and yet now, they are quite common.
- Particular problems arise over interpreting changes in the RPI caused by changes in the rate of interest. When the rate of interest changes, the cost of mortgage repayments changes and this causes fluctuations in the RPI. It is now customary to refer to **headline inflation** as the rate of inflation calculated from changes in the RPI *excluding* mortgage repayments.

In practice weights in the RPI and the range of goods monitored are altered to allow for the changes mentioned above. This undoubtedly improves the accuracy of the RPI in the short term, though it makes comparisons over long term periods less precise.

THE TAX AND PRICE INDEX

" An alternative index "

The RPI measures changes in the cost of living. But what people can buy with their earnings depends on the deductions from their pay, in particular those made in respect of income tax and national insurance contributions, as well as on the average level of prices when take-home pay is spent. The **tax and price index** shows how the purchasing power of income is affected by changes in both direct taxes and prices.

Changes in prices, as measured by the RPI, have a weight of about 75 per cent in the tax and price index, while changes in income tax and national insurance contributions account for the remainder. Like the RPI, the tax and price index is a composite index reflecting the weighted experience of groups of households with different tax liabilities. The tax and price index is therefore an attempt to reflect what has happened to the purchasing power of the average household's take-home pay.

DEMAND-PULL INFLATION

Demand-pull inflation occurs when there is excess demand for real output at the existing price level. In other words, aggregate demand exceeds aggregate supply. We have analysed this situation in terms of the inflationary gap in Chapter 9 but the assumption there was that prices remain constant. The 45° line used to explain the Keynesian model of income determination is effectively the aggregate supply curve of the economy. In practice, an excess of aggregate demand over aggregate supply at the existing price level, which cannot be fully accommodated by an expansion of output, will result in the price level being pulled upwards until aggregate demand and aggregate supply are brought into equality.

The process is sometimes likened to an auction. In the early stages of bidding for an item, demand usually exceeds supply, and price is pulled upwards until demand equals supply. Similarly, in the real world, if demand exceeds the limited amount of output available at the current price level, then the price level rises. However, when the economy is producing at less than full capacity, and there are substantial amounts of unemployed resources, it is likely that a rise in demand will be accommodated by an expansion of output, with little or no effect on the average price level. But, as the economy approaches full employment it becomes increasingly difficult for output to respond, and in these circumstances excess aggregate demand is at least partly manifested in higher prices. Once full employment is reached, however, any increase in aggregate demand is entirely reflected in higher prices. Because of this, demand-pull inflation is particularly associated with economies which are at, or near, full employment. The effect of increases in aggregate demand on output and the price level is illustrated in Fig. 13.1.

In Fig. 13.1, AS_S is the initial short-run aggregate supply curve and AD is the initial aggregate demand curve. AS_L is the long-run aggregate supply curve. The price level is initially P and the equilibrium level of income is Y_n, the 'natural' or 'full employment' level. Now, an increase in aggregate demand shifts the aggregate demand schedule to AD_1 causing the price level to rise to P_1 and output to rise to Y_1. In response to rising prices, trade unions will demand compensatory increases in pay. Firms are likely to grant these because there will be labour shortages. If all other things remain the same, this will shift the short-run aggregate supply curve to AS_{S1} and, in consequence, the price level rises to P_2 but output returns to the natural rate Y_n. There has simply been

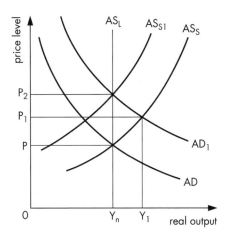

Fig. 13.1 The effect of an increase in aggregate demand

a once and for all increase in the price level. However, as higher wages are transformed into higher expenditure, prices will again be forced upwards and so the cycle continues of rising demand, rising costs, rising demand, and so on, which implies demand-pull inflation.

COST-PUSH INFLATION

Cost-push inflation occurs when pressure on prices results from an exogenous rise in costs. Since the share of national income paid to labour is about 70 per cent of the total of all incomes paid, wage increases in excess of productivity increases have been an important source of rising costs. Any depreciation of sterling will also have an important impact on costs in the UK (see pp. 293–296), since the UK depends heavily on imported raw materials.

An exogenous increase in costs, whatever its source, raises firms' costs at all levels of output. After an increase in costs, any given level of output will therefore only be supplied at a higher price. Although individual firms might be willing to absorb an increase in costs by cutting profits, it will be impossible for *all* firms to do this. Therefore, the aggregate supply curve shifts upwards. With an unchanged level of aggregate demand, the effect of an exogenous increase in costs on output and the price level is shown in Fig. 13.2.

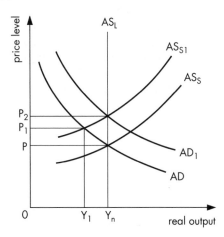

Fig. 13.2 The effect of an exogenous increase in costs

To understand the effect of an exogenous rise in costs let us consider Fig. 13.2. Again, we begin with AD as the original aggregate demand curve, AS_S as the original short-run aggregate supply curve and AS_L as the long-run aggregate supply curve at the 'natural' output level Y_n. P is the equilibrium price level and OY_n the equilibrium level of real output. Now, if there is an exogenous increase in wage rates unmatched by an increase in productivity, the aggregate supply curve will shift to AS_{S1}. The price level will rise to P_1 and real output will fall to Y_1. However, the higher wage rates will shift the aggregate demand curve to AD_1 and long-run equilibrium will be restored when output has returned to the natural rate. Note that, in long-run equilibrium, the price level has increased to P_2. This, of course, is a one-off increase in the price level. Cost-push inflation occurs when costs go on rising and one way in which this might happen is when, in response to the higher price level, trade unions again demand (and are successful in obtaining) wage increases for their members in excess of any increase in productivity. In this way, the spiral of rising costs, rising prices, rising costs and so on goes on, which implies cost-push inflation.

Because of the importance of wages in firms' costs, economists have coined the term **wage-push inflation** to indicate a situation when the main source of cost increases is wage increases in excess of productivity increases. Again, this is more likely to occur at higher levels of employment; as shortages of skilled labour develop, unions are usually more able to negotiate higher pay awards.

THE INFLATIONARY SPIRAL

In practice, it is not always easy to distinguish between cost-push and demand-pull inflation. For example, a rise in costs which pushes up prices will also result in higher factor incomes. At least part of these will be spent domestically and the extra demand, especially if there is a shortage of capacity, is likely to pull prices up still further. These price increases imply a fall in the real income of wage earners. It is likely that trade unions will demand compensatory pay rises, giving a still further push to inflation.

In practice, the inflationary spiral will not go on indefinitely. There are several reasons for this. The tax and benefit system acts to stabilise the economy automatically; increased expenditure on imports and a reduction in exports will raise leakages and cut injections, etc. Nevertheless, because of the potentially adverse effects of inflation, especially on the balance of payments, governments have actively pursued policies to reduce the rate of inflation rather than merely to allow the process to peter out in the fullness of time. These policies are discussed in Chapter 17.

THE PHILLIPS CURVE

The relationship between unemployment and inflation is generalised in the **Phillips curve**. In its original form, this curve indicated a negative correlation between the rate of change of *wages* and the level of unemployment. The impressive feature of the Phillips curve was that the relationship it identified had been remarkably stable for a continuous period of almost a hundred years. Soon after the original Phillips curve was identified, it was quickly discovered that there was also a significant, and stable, negative correlation between the rate of change of *prices* and the level of unemployment. Moreover, it was widely believed by policy makers that because the relationship had been stable for almost a hundred years, it would remain stable in the future. It therefore appeared to offer policy makers a range of policy choices. A particular level of unemployment could be traded off against a particular rate of inflation. For example, a lower level of unemployment implied a higher rate of inflation, and vice versa. This inverse relationship between unemployment and the rate of inflation is shown in Fig. 13.3.

> ❝ Relating unemployment to inflation ❞

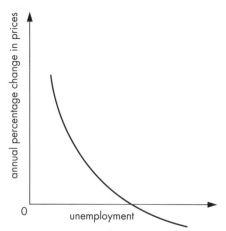

Fig. 13.3 The Phillips curve

However, the appeal of the Phillips curve was not just in its apparent stability. The Phillips curve also played a role in identifying the **causes of inflation**. High rates of inflation at low levels of unemployment supported both the demand-pull and cost-push explanations of inflation. At low levels of unemployment, buoyant demand would pull up prices, while trade unions would be in a strong bargaining position from which they could negotiate relatively high pay awards. Buoyant demand in the economy would lower employers' resistance to pay demands since rising costs could more easily be passed on as higher prices. In contrast, at high levels of unemployment, demand in the economy would be less buoyant and the bargaining position of unions weaker.

THE BREAKDOWN OF THE PHILLIPS CURVE

For over a decade, economic policy in the UK was implicitly based on the Phillips curve. However, it became apparent in the late 1960s that the relationship identified by Phillips was not as stable as at first believed. Figure 13.4 shows the course of inflation and unemployment in the UK since 1969.

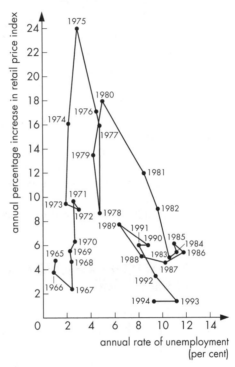

Fig. 13.4 Breakdown of the Phillips curve

It is clear that a higher rate of inflation than previously, is now consistent with any given level of unemployment. Various reasons have been advanced to account for this. Some economists claim that the Phillips curve has simply moved outwards from the origin; some possible reasons for this are examined below. However, an alternative explanation is provided by the monetarists who claim that the Phillips curve was never more than a short-run phenomenon that had no long-run validity. This view is examined in the following section.

Causes of the breakdown of the Phillips curve

■ **Increased unemployment and welfare benefits** One possible explanation for the breakdown of the Phillips curve is the increasing availability of unemployment and welfare benefits. These reduce the financial pressure on the unemployed to obtain work. In this sense, there is a greater willingness to accept unemployment. Taking longer to find alternative employment would cause an increase in the unemployment figures. The statistics may then show that any *given* level of aggregate demand, and therefore rate of inflation, is associated with a *greater* level of unemployment than previously. This would shift the Phillips curve rightwards and outwards, changing the inflation–unemployment relationship in the way observed in Fig. 13.4. This is arguably not so much a cause for concern, as an indication that social policies designed to alleviate the financial hardships of unemployment are actually working.

❝ Possible reasons for the Phillips curve breaking down ❞

■ **Demographic changes** It is likely that the demographic changes which have taken place during the post-war period have had a significant impact on the labour market, affecting the relationship between inflation and unemployment. For example, in the post-war period, the female activity rate rose almost annually until about 1977, and although it has declined slightly since then, there are still currently some 10.5 million women in the labour force. Labour turnover among women is considerably higher than among men. As a result, any *given* level of aggregate demand, and therefore rate of inflation, may again be associated with a *greater* level of unemployment than previously. This also would lead to a rightward and outward shift in the Phillips curve.

- **Union militancy** Another possible factor is that trade union militancy has increased, so that unions have felt less constrained in their wage demands by the threat of unemployment than previously; wage and price inflation would then be higher at any *given* level of unemployment. Union militancy may have been encouraged by the belief that governments will pursue policies which prevent rising labour costs from leading to unemployment. It is this belief which the medium-term financial strategy seeks to discourage (see Chapter 17).

- **Unemployment becoming a less reliable indicator of labour market pressure** It has been suggested that the inflation—unemployment relationship implied by the Phillips curve is really a relationship between inflation and the pressure of demand in the labour market, with the level of unemployment providing a proxy measure of the pressure of demand in the labour market. The argument is that the fundamental relationship between inflation and pressure in the labour market still exists, but that the level of unemployment no longer provides an accurate proxy measure of that pressure. The **growth of the black economy** tends to support this notion; at any *given* level of official unemployment there may now be *greater* labour market pressure than previously. This might partly account for the apparent breakdown of the Phillips curve.

THE EXPECTATIONS-AUGMENTED PHILLIPS CURVE AND THE NATURAL RATE OF UNEMPLOYMENT

In the long run, the monetarists believe that there is *no* stable relationship, or trade-off, between different rates of inflation and unemployment. The monetarists suggest that changes in wage rates and prices only influence workers and employers in so far as they are perceived to be changes in *real* wages or in *real* prices. Thus, a rise in money wage rates will have no lasting impact on the economy if it is accompanied by an equivalent rise in prices, and vice versa.

Natural rate of unemployment

66 **The natural rate of unemployment** 99

Furthermore, the monetarists believe that there is a natural rate of unemployment to which the economy will tend, in the long run. In fact, the natural rate of unemployment is defined as the rate that exists in the long run when the supply of, and the demand for, labour are in equilibrium. Any attempt by the authorities to reduce the level of unemployment *below* the natural rate will be unsuccessful in the long run, and will simply result in a higher rate of inflation. In detail, the argument is explained in terms of Fig. 13.5. For simplicity it is assumed that unemployment is initially at the natural rate U_n, that actual and expected inflation is zero, i.e. the real wage is expected to remain constant, and that there is no change in productivity so that prices and wages change by the same proportion.

$P^e = 0\%$ is the short-run Phillips curve that exists when the actual and expected rate of inflation are zero.

$P^e = 4\%$ is the short-run Phillips curve that exists when the actual and expected rate of inflation are 4%, and so on.

If the government attempts to reduce the level of unemployment to U_1 by an expansion of the money supply by 4 per cent, the intitial result will be an increase in aggregate demand. Eventually, this will pull prices up (by 4 per cent if the quantity theory holds), and this implies a rise in the real profits of producers. They will therefore expand output, and in order to attract more workers they will raise the wage rate; to retain

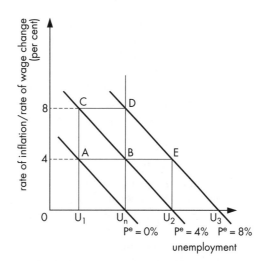

Fig. 13.5 The expectations-augmented Phillips curve

higher profits per unit of output, employers will raise wages *by less than* the increase in prices. Workers will not immediately perceive this fall in their real income, because the expected rate of inflation is zero; they will therefore interpret the higher money wage awards as an increase in real wages. The economy will therefore move to point A.

However, this does not represent a long-run equilibrium situation, since it is based on **money illusion**. Once workers realise that, far from rising, their real wage has actually fallen, they will demand pay rises at least sufficient to restore their real wage. But when wages and prices have both risen by 4 per cent, the real profits of producers will revert to their original level and they will no longer have any incentive to produce the higher level of output. They will therefore cut back production to their equilibrium level and unemployment will increase.

However, while the economy moves up the short-run Phillips curve $P^e = 0\%$ it does not move back down it simply because unemployment rises. The expansion of the money supply ensures that the price level remains at the higher level. In terms of the equation of exchange, since V_y and Y are constant, an increase in M must lead to an increase in P. Thus equilibrium is restored when the economy moves to point B.

The expected and actual rate of inflation is now 4 per cent and the appropriate Phillips curve is therefore $P^e = 4\%$. Any further expansion of the money supply, for example, by another four percentage points, will initially take the economy to point C. However, the reduction in unemployment only occurs because the actual rate of inflation is different from the *expected* rate. Once workers realise that their expectations were incorrect, the advantage to producers from the higher rate of price inflation will disappear and equilibrium will be restored when the economy moves to D. Because of this, it is suggested that, in the long run, the Phillips curve is *vertical* at the natural rate of unemployment. Any attempt to reduce unemployment permanently below the natural rate will simply result, in the long run, in an accelerating rate of inflation. It is for this reason that the monetarist approach is sometimes referred to as the **accelerationist theory of inflation**.

The conclusion of the monetarist interpretation of the Phillips curve is that inflation is entirely a monetary phenomenon caused by an excess supply of money, in other words, by an increase in the money supply which is greater than the average rise in productivity. Hence the belief that control of the money supply is *all* that is required to reduce inflation. For example, in terms of Fig. 13.5, if the economy is at point D and the government wishes to restore average prices to the level that existed before there was any expansion of the money supply, it must reduce the money supply by 8 percentage points. If it did this, all at once, the economy would initially move to U_3, as the fall in prices that results from the lower money supply reduces real profits and leads firms to cut back output and to lay off workers. Once expectations of inflation are adjusted to the lower level (here 0%) there would be lower wage settlements and real profits would be restored to their former levels. In response to this, output would rise and unemployment would fall as more workers were taken on. Equilibrium would be restored when unemployment was re-established at the natural rate, i.e. at point U_n.

It is, of course, possible to achieve the same reduction in inflation, that is from 8 per cent to zero, without such heavy unemployment. All that is required is for the government to reduce the money supply in *stages* until the total reduction is 8

The vertical Phillips curve

percentage points. For example, if the government reduces the money supply by 4 percentage points, the economy will move from D through point E to point B. If the money supply is then reduced by a further 4 percentage points the economy will eventually establish equilibrium at U_n. Again, the total reduction in the rate of inflation is 8 percentage points but, in this case, it is achieved with a temporary increase in unemployment of only $U_2 - U_n$ compared with an increase of $U_3 - U_n$ when the money supply is reduced in one action by 8 percentage points.

Despite this, accepting the natural rate hypothesis does not imply that governments are powerless to influence the level of unemployment in the long run, i.e. reduce the natural rate. It simply implies that unemployment cannot be *permanently* reduced by expanding aggregate demand. In order to reduce unemployment below the current natural rate, governments must act on those factors which determine the natural rate of unemployment, i.e. factors affecting the long-term supply of, and demand for, labour at any given real wage rate. These factors include the mobility of labour, the techniques of production, the extent of welfare benefits, restrictions in competition and so on. These are usually referred to as **supply-side factors** and they are discussed on pages 341–343.

THE RATIONAL EXPECTATIONS HYPOTHESIS

The monetarist analysis presented above is based on the assumption that changes in the *actual* rate of inflation precede changes in the expected rate. It is, however, possible that if governments publicly announce that the rate of growth of the money supply is to be reduced to a certain level, this will then influence expectations of inflation. In other words, to the extent that the government's target rates of growth for the money supply are publicised and are believed, then **rational expectations** about the future rate of inflation may be formed. If this leads to lower pay awards, inflation can be reduced without significantly affecting unemployment. Indeed, if the economy is initially at point D (the natural rate of unemployment with 8 per cent inflation) in Fig. 13.5, a reduction in the money supply of 8 percentage points will, provided rational expectations lead to pay awards falling by exactly the same proportion, lead to a movement *straight down* the vertical Phillips curve to point U_n.

MONETARISM

WHAT IS MONETARISM?

At its simplest level, monetarism is a set of beliefs about the way in which changes in the money supply affect other macroeconomic variables such as the rate of inflation and nominal national income. These beliefs are based on an impressive volume of statistical information which shows a highly significant correlation between changes in the money supply and changes in the rate of inflation. However, the statistics only show an *association* between these two variables. They do not show that one is *caused* by the other. Nevertheless, the monetarists are unshakeable in their belief that changes in the money supply are the *only* cause of changes in the rate of inflation. While there are many varieties of monetarism, this belief is common to them all. The following discussion is an outline of the basic principles of monetarism which provide the theoretical underpinnings for this belief.

> " Association is not necessarily cause! "

THE DEMAND FOR MONEY

All monetarists accept the early quantity theory of money which focuses on the importance of changes in the money supply. However, the revival of monetarism as an economic doctrine stems largely from Friedman's re-statement of the quantity theory. This differs from the early quantity theory in that it focuses attention on the importance of the demand for money to hold.

Friedman's re-statement of the quantity theory
In his re-statement, Friedman suggested that the demand for money is determined by the same general factors which influence the demand for other goods and services. However, of all the factors Friedman considered, only the level of income, the price

level and the *expected* rate of inflation, had any significant effect on the demand for money. Furthermore, Friedman claimed that the relationship between the demand for money and its determinants was highly *stable* over time. This is extremely important since such stability could not exist unless the *velocity of circulation* was also relatively stable. An increase in the demand for money to hold will reduce its velocity of circulation and vice versa. Therefore, if it can be shown that the demand for money is stable, velocity is also stable.

It is important to understand that in arguing that velocity is stable, the monetarists are not arguing that it is constant. Instead they have always claimed that velocity changes only slowly over time and in a predictable way. In this sense, it is stable from one period to the next. We shall see later that this has important implications for policy purposes.

For simplicity, it is sometimes suggested that Friedman's view implies that the demand for money is a stable function of nominal national income. While not strictly correct, this does not seriously misrepresent Friedman's view. In the long run, the *actual* rate of inflation and the *expected* rate of inflation coincide and hence the main determinants of changes in the demand for money are changes in the actual rate of inflation, i.e. changes in the price level, and changes in real income, i.e. changes in nominal GNP. Monetarists therefore argue that when there are changes in the *supply of money*, this will lead to changes in nominal GNP which will bring the demand for money into equilibrium with the supply.

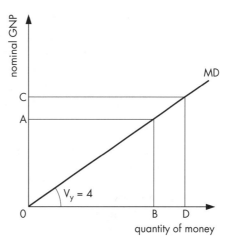

Fig. 13.6 The demand for nominal money

Explanation of theory

Figure 13.6 is used is used as a basis for explanation. If the demand for money is constant at 25 per cent of GNP then Vy must equal 4. If the initial level of GNP is £200m then, assuming supply and demand for money are in equilibrium, the quantity of money demanded (and supplied) will be equal to £50m. If the money supply now increases, nominal GNP will increase and hence demand for money will also increase. For example, if the *money supply* increases by £10m, equilibrium can only be restored when the *demand for money* increases by £10m. If V_y is unchanged, this implies an increase in nominal GNP of £40m. This must happen because if the money supply increases and all other things remain the same, people will be holding excess money balances relative to the amount they demand. The excess will be spent and will cause nominal GNP to increase until demand for money is brought into equilibrium with the increased supply of money.

However, this simple approach is ambiguous because an increase in *nominal* GNP can consist entirely of an increase in real income, prices unchanged, or entirely of an increase in prices, real income unchanged, or a combination of both. The monetarists claim that, in the short run, nominal GNP will consist of an increase in *both*. However, in the long run, they argue that the level of real income is determined by institutional factors such as the capital stock, the mobility of labour, the rate of technological progress and so on. Such factors are *not* influenced by changes in the money supply. While it is possible that changes in the money supply will bring about changes in real income in the short run, such changes will only be transitory and, in the long run, real income will return to the level that would have existed *before* the increase in the money supply. Hence, an increase in the money supply above the rate of growth of real income will, in the long run, simply lead to higher prices.

This, of course, explains why, in the short run, unemployment falls below the natural rate as the money supply increases. As demand and prices rise, firms expand output and unemployment falls. Hence the economy moves up the appropriate short-run Phillips curve. However, as expectations of inflation adjust to the higher rate, output reverts to that level which would have existed if there had been no increase in the money supply, and unemployment reverts to the natural rate.

The transmission mechanism

The route through which the effect of a change in the money supply is transmitted to the economy is referred to as the **transmission mechanism**. The monetarists argue that an increase in the money supply will leave people holding excess money balances at the existing level of GNP. Consequently, spending will increase as people divest themselves of unwanted holdings of money. The important point is that the monetarists claim that this increased spending will be on a whole range of goods and services. (This contrasts with liquidity preference theory which implies that it will be spent on securities.) As demand increases, output and prices will rise until people are *persuaded* to hold the increased money supply in order to finance the increased value of their transactions. In other words, nominal GNP goes on rising until the increase in the supply of money is matched by an increase in the transactions demand for money, so that supply and demand for money are brought back into equilibrium.

Crowding out

The term 'crowding out' refers to the extent to which an increase in public sector expenditure can only take place at the expense of private sector expenditure. The monetarists claim that, in the long run, crowding out occurs on a one-for-one basis. As we have seen, the monetarists argue that any increase in public expenditure financed by an increase in the money supply, will have *no* effect on *real* GNP in the *long run*. However, because public expenditure is at a higher level and because aggregate expenditure (real GNP) is unchanged, then private sector expenditure must have been crowded out.

The monetarists also claim that crowding out occurs even when public sector expenditure is financed by *borrowing from the non-bank public* so that there is no change in the money supply. Their argument is that increasing borrowing by the public sector will force up interest rates, because of increased competition for funds. The main impact of higher interest rates will fall on private sector investment, although there will also be some reduction in expenditure on consumer durables. Again, increased public sector expenditure crowds out private sector expenditure.

The view that an increase in public sector expenditure crowds out private sector expenditure by an equivalent amount, even when money supply is constant, can easily be explained in terms of the identity $MV_y = PY$. Since the monetarists argue that V_y is constant, and since there has been no change in M, then PY, i.e. GNP, must also be constant. However, public sector expenditure has *increased*, so that private sector expenditure must have fallen by an equivalent amount within the constant GNP. In other words, an increase in public sector expenditure, even when financed by borrowing from the non-bank private sector, does not change the level of GNP; it simply changes its structure because public expenditure increases and private expenditure falls.

The monetary rule

The monetarists therefore believe that increasing the money supply has no long-run effect on the level of real GNP; it simply leads to higher prices. They also believe that attempts to manage the economy by using demand management techniques, increase uncertainty. This in turn makes it difficult for business to plan, and leads to less investment in research and development, in capacity, and so on. Because of this the monetarists suggest that governments should abandon attempts to manage the level of aggregate demand, and should instead aim for a *steady* rate of growth of the money supply in order to achieve a particular rate of inflation. Again, their basic argument can be explained in terms of the identity $MV_y = PY$. If Y grows at an average 5 per cent per annum and V_y by 1 per cent per annum, then a government aiming to achieve an annual inflation rate of 2 per cent must achieve a growth of the money supply of approximately, but no more than, 10 per cent. (You can check this by substituting in $M = PY/V_y$.)

 Linking money supply to inflation

MONETARISM AND KEYNESIANISM COMPARED

There is in fact a great deal of agreement between monetarists and Keynesians. They *both* accept the equation of exchange, and broadly agree on the determinants of the demand for money. However, they disagree on which factors are *most* significant in affecting the demand for money. This is clear in the following differences between the two schools.

THE TRANSMISSION MECHANISM

Monetarists' view

The monetarists believe that an increase in the money supply leads to an increase in demand for *all* goods and services, with financial assets (securities, etc.) being just one in a range of items on which expenditure will increase. In other words, financial assets are not regarded as unique, in the sense of being close substitutes for money. An increase in the money supply willl therefore lead to a direct increase in spending on goods and services, rather than just on financial assets. Nevertheless, any part of the extra money supply that is spent on securities will raise security prices, i.e. reduce interest rates. However, money demand is assumed by monetarists to vary with the level of national income and not with the rate of interest, so that little or none of the extra money supply is absorbed into idle balances as interest rates fall, i.e. demand for money is interest rate inelastic. Consequently, all that the fall in interest rates will do is to encourage further consumer spending on goods and services, and of course investment expenditure.

In summary, the monetarists argue that an increase in the money supply leads to an increase in aggregate expenditure because:

- increased holdings of money will mainly be spent on goods and services;
- an increase in the money supply will lead to lower interest rates which encourages further consumer (and investment) spending.

In the long run, because of its effect on aggregate expenditure, an increase in the money supply has a relatively large effect on GNP.

Keynesians' view

Keynesians maintain that the demand for money is, in general, responsive to changes in the interest rate. They argue that financial assets are a close substitute for money and that an increase in the money supply will lead to increased expenditure on these. This will raise security prices, and the fall in interest rates that this implies will lead to a *more than proportional* increase in the demand for money, as people are persuaded to hold larger idle balances. The rate of interest continues to fall until supply and demand for money are brought into equilibrium. However, because demand for money is interest rate elastic, an increase in the money supply leads to a less than proportional fall in the rate of interest.

Furthermore, the Keynesians argue that aggregate expenditure is interest rate inelastic; any given change in interest rates therefore leads to a less than proportional change in expenditure. For example, an increase in the money supply is, via a fall in the rate of interest, mainly absorbed into idle balances and consequently has little impact on aggregate expenditure. This implies that an increase in the money supply has relatively little effect on GNP. The opposite is true when the money supply is reduced. Because of this, the Keynesians argue that monetary policy is not a very powerful tool of economic management.

In summary, the Keynesians believe that the effects of changes in the money supply are transmitted to the economy via changes in the rate of interest, but that overall there is little impact on GNP.

> " Comparing Keynes and the monetarists "

THE VELOCITY OF CIRCULATION

Implicit in the monetarist transmission mechanism is the belief that the velocity of circulation is unaffected by changes in the money supply. Hence a change in M leads to a proportional change in GNP in the long run.

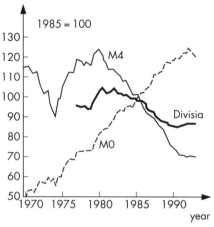

Fig. 13.7 The velocity of M0, M4 and Divisia

Source: Bank of England Quarterly Review, February 1993

However, the Keynesians do not accept that the velocity of circulation is unaffected by changes in the money supply. For example, they argue that because an increase in the money supply has relatively little effect on GNP then, because of the identity of $MV_y = GNP$, V_y must fall when the money supply increases, and vice versa. For the Keynesians, the extreme case occurs when the rate of interest is so low that the demand for money is infinitely elastic. This is the so-called **liquidity trap** (see Ch. 11) and in these circumstances an increase in the money supply has *no effect* on the rate of interest at all and consequently no effect on the level of GNP. This can only occur when, for each change in the money supply, there is an exactly off-setting change in the velocity of circulation; i.e. when an increase in the money supply is completely absorbed into idle balances.

It is worth noting that because the monetarists deny that the velocity of circulation can change in response to changes in the money supply, they also deny the existence of any liquidity trap. The available empirical evidence is inconclusive. In the short run, velocity fluctuates and appears quite unstable. In the longer run, it appears to follow a clearly identifiable trend. However, even here the evidence is ambiguous. Prior to about 1982, broad money velocity followed an identifiable upward trend. Since then (see Fig. 13.7) it has followed a downward trend!

CROWDING OUT

We have seen that the monetarists believe that crowding out takes place on a one-for-one basis.

However, the Keynesians argue that this will only be true when the government increases its expenditure at a time when the economy is at full employment. At levels below this, an increase in government expenditure will draw more resources into employment, raising real GNP and real expenditure, so that private investment expenditure need not fall. One important reason why this happens, according to the Keynesians, is that the government borrows and spends funds that would otherwise have been saved. In other words, borrowing to finance government expenditure transfers funds from lower velocity users to higher velocity users. The resulting increase in aggregate demand then results in an increase in aggregate supply.

 ## THE MULTIPLIER

The monetarists believe that the value of the multiplier is relatively low. For example, if crowding out takes place on a one-for-one basis, then increased government expenditure financed by borrowing from the non-bank private sector has a zero multiplier effect.

The Keynesians, on the other hand, argue that the multiplier will have a relatively high value.

The empirical evidence that is available tends to support the view that the multiplier has a relatively low value (see Ch. 9).

STABILITY OF THE ECONOMY

The Keynesians believe that aggregate demand, and therefore employment, is subject to sharp fluctuations, so that the government has an important role to play in stabilising aggregate demand.

In contrast to this, the monetarists believe that the economy is inherently stable, at least in the long run, with aggregate demand and employment not being subject to sharp fluctuations. Because of this, the monetarists claim that stabilisation policy is not only unnecessary, but may actually have a *destabilising* effect on the economy, causing greater short-run fluctuations in GNP than would otherwise have occurred. Where increased government expenditure leads to an increase in the money supply, it will result in higher prices which will further increase uncertainty.

CHANGES IN THE MONEY SUPPLY AND CHANGES IN THE PRICE LEVEL

The monetarist argument is that a change in the price level can only be caused by a change in *money supply,* and that a change in the money supply is all that is required to cause a change in the price level.

The Keynesian position is that a change in the *velocity of circulation* can cause changes in the price level which are independent of changes in the money supply. Nevertheless, the Keynesians agree that changes in the money supply are correlated significantly with changes in the price level. However, they do not accept that this implies causation. They argue that the money supply is determined endogenously and simply responds passively to changes in the demand for money and therefore to changes in the price level.

APPLIED MATERIALS

An article in the *Bank of England Quarterly Bulletin*, August 1993, includes a section on the **velocity of circulation of money**. Economists are very interested in velocity because the use of a money supply target depends on velocity being predictable. If velocity is predictable then controlling money growth should ensure that nominal income (GNP or GDP) grows at a target rate and, in particular, that a target rate of inflation can be achieved. This explains why economists have expended so much effort searching for a stable measure of velocity. Figure 13.7 earlier shows the velocity of M0, M4 and Divisia money with respect to nominal GDP.

Over the longer term, M0 has followed a clearly identifiable upward trend and, despite short-run fluctuations, its value seemed predictable. However, since the second quarter of 1992, its value has been falling. M4, on the other hand, has behaved erratically over the period shown. Between 1980 and 1990, its value tended downwards but has been relatively stable since then. It is too early to say whether these changes in the velocity of M0 and M4 are permanent or simply temporary aberations. Either way, for the moment, their behaviour raises serious questions about their usefulness.

Divisia velocity has fluctuated but of the three measures of velocity, it has exhibited greater stability over the period covered by the data. Nevertheless, its behaviour remains too erratic at present for use in establishing a money growth target and the search goes on for a stable and predictable measure of velocity.

An article in *Finance and Development*, March 1992, discusses the case for an **independent central bank**. Considerable attention has been devoted to this in recent years and, with plans to create an independent European central bank in the run up to EMU (see Ch. 12), this is an important issue.

Central bank independence implies that monetary policy is set by salaried officials and is free of government interference. In other words, governments relinquish their involvement in planning and implementing monetary policy. This, in turn, requires that governments do not hold an account with the central bank. If such an account exists, as it does in the UK, governments can overdraw their account at will and, in this way, exert considerable influence over growth of the money supply.

The problem is that variations in money growth have a crucial influence on the rate of inflation, in the long run, but might confer transient short-run benefits. In other words, there might be short-run benefits from variations in monetary policy. Because of electoral considerations, politicians might be tempted to seek short-run gains from varying monetary policy and sacrifice long-run price stability. There is another problem: variations in monetary policy, especially when they are unanticipated, make it difficult for firms and individuals to plan their future expenditures. The consequence is inefficiency in the allocation of resources.

There are two extreme views concerning the conduct of monetary policy. Some economists advocate fixed, binding *policy rules* for the conduct of policy. The main problem with this is that it does not allow the policy makers to adapt to monetary shocks such as an oil price rise. Because of this, other economists advocate *discretion* in the conduct of monetary policy. It is sometimes suggested that there is a middle ground. One example of this is where governments announce a target rate of growth for the money supply. The problem with this is that such targets are not binding and governments might not always find it convenient to implement policies to ensure their target growth for the money supply is met.

The argument in favour of central bank independence is that the credibility of monetary policy, and hence its ability to achieve and maintain longer run price stability at a lower cost in terms of output and employment, would be improved if policy formulation were in the hands of salaried officials. It was argued on p. 244 that a reduction in the rate of inflation will cause a short-run increase in the rate of unemployment unless expectations of inflation adjust rapidly. An independent central bank would certainly have no incentive to depart from achieving its goal of price stability and would therefore be able to favourably influence expectations. For example, the Bank would be able to implement rapid changes in the rate of interest in response to unanticipated changes in the growth of the money supply which jeopardised long-run price stabililty and which the Bank wished to neutralise. It is true that not all low inflation countries have an independent central bank, but it is also true that, in general, the more independent the central bank, the greater the success in achieving a low rate of inflation.

However, central bank independence is not without problems. One problem is that it might create a 'democratic deficit'. If central bankers are not subject to political control, then in what sense are they accountable to the people they serve? It is possible that they might pursue an unacceptable monetary policy, choosing to reduce inflation faster at a higher cost in terms of jobs, than the general public and their elected representatives, the government, would choose.

EXAMINATION QUESTIONS

1 (a) Explain the possible causes of inflation. *(12)*

(b) Why have UK governments found it so difficult to control inflation? *(13)*

(AEB June 1993)

2 (a) How is the value of money measured? *(12)*

(b) How substantial are the problems involved in measuring changes in the value of money? *(13)*

(UCLES November 1992)

3 Are the benefits that are said to arise from the control of inflation worth the costs involved in achieving that control?

(ODLE June 1992)

4 (a) What is meant by the natural rate of unemployment? *(20)*

(b) Examine how the natural rate of unemployment might be reduced. *(40)*

(c) Analyse the likely consequences of attempting to reduce unemployment below its natural rate. *(40)*

(ULEAC June 1993)

ANSWERS TO EXAMINATION QUESTIONS

TUTOR'S ANSWER TO QUESTION 1

(a) **Inflation** is usually defined as a persistent rise in the general level of prices. The rate of inflation as measured by the percentage increase in the price level might vary from period to period, but inflation implies that the average price level moves continuously upwards.

It is widely acknowledged that, in the long run, inflation is caused by excessive money growth and that the quantity theory of money provides a powerful explanation of the inflationary process. In its simplest form, the quantity theory of money can be derived from the income equation of exchange which can be written as:

$$MV_y = PY$$

where M = some measure of the money supply
V_y = the income velocity of circulation, that is, the average number of times each unit of currency is spent on final output
P = the average price of final output
Y = real income, i.e. the volume of final output.

Now, it must always be correct that MV_y is identical to PY since MV_y represents total expenditure on final output and PY represents the value of final output. However, it is alleged that the **velocity of circulation** is determined, in the long run, by institutional factors such as the frequency with which wage payments are made, and so will change relatively slowly over time. It is also alleged that real output tends towards an equilibrium natural rate which is again determined by institutional factors such as the rate of investment and the mobility of labour. Again, these factors change only slowly over time. It is true that V_y and Y might fluctuate in the short run but, in the long run, their trend values will be fairly stable and predictable. This implies a direct correlation between M and P, in the long run.

This is the basis of the quantity theory of money which states that, in the long run, a change in M is both a necessary and a sufficient condition for a change in P. In other words, it is alleged that, if all other things remain the same, a change in M will cause a proportionate change in P. In other words, a change in M will always cause a change in P, but there can be no change in P without a prior change in M.

The prediction of the quantity theory is therefore that inflation is caused by excessive money growth. Excessive, in this sense, implies that the growth of MV_y is greater than the growth of Y so that the price level is forced upwards in order to satisfy the equality between MV_y and PY. The route through which a change in M leads to a change in P is simple. When money growth increases, economic agents will experience an increase in real money balances and, in consequence, they will increase their spending. Initially, as stocks fall, firms will be encouraged to increase output. However, an increase in output above the natural rate is only transitory and, in the long run, as output returns to the natural rate, the full impact of increased money growth will fall on the price level.

A different view of inflation is that it is caused by excess demand at the existing price level. An increase in money growth might be one source of increased demand, but it is argued by some economists that it is not the only source — especially in the short run. Rising demand might stem from a depreciation of the exchange rate. As the exchange rate falls, demand for exports will rise and there will be a switch of demand in favour of domestic substitutes. Increased demand might also stem from a reduction in the savings ratio, an increase in investment or an increase in government expenditure.

The effect of an increase in demand can be explained in terms of Fig. 13.8.

In Fig. 13.8, AS_S is the initial short-run aggregate supply curve and AD is the initial aggregate demand curve. AS_L is the long-run aggregate supply curve. The price level is initially P and the equilibrium level of income is Y_n. Now, an increase in aggregates demand shifts the aggregate demand schedule to AD_1 causing the

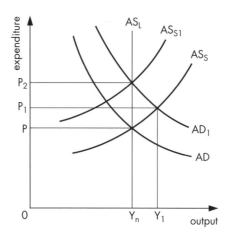

Fig. 13.8 The effect of changes in aggregate demand and aggregate supply on price and output in the short run and the long run

price level to rise to P_1 and output to rise to Y_1. In response to rising prices, trade unions will demand compensatory increases in pay. Firms are likely to grant these because there will be labour shortages. If all other things remain the same, this will shift the short-run aggregate supply curve to AS_{S1} and, in consequence, the price level rises to P_2 but output returns to the natural rate Y_n.

Rising costs are sometimes alleged to be the cause of inflation. Costs might rise for any of several reasons but, because labour costs form the largest proportion of total costs, these are sometimes singled out as the primary source of pressure on costs. In recent years, legislation, falling membership and the recession have all weakened the power of trade unions in the UK so that less emphasis has been placed on their role in the inflationary process. However, there is no doubt that, historically, wage increases in excess of productivity increases have been cited as an important cause of inflation.

The UK also has a high dependency on imported raw materials so that depreciation of sterling on the foreign exchanges has been cited as a source of cost pressure. As sterling depreciates, the domestic price of imports rises. In so far as raw materials and semi-finished goods are imported, firms experience rising costs which feed through to consumers in the form of higher prices.

The demand and cost views of the inflationary process are not at odds with the quantity theory, but if the predictions of this theory are accepted then the effect of excess demand and rising costs on the price level can only be sustained if the money supply rises. This is precisely what many economists argue has happened. The effect of increased aggregate demand and increased costs on the price level has been *accommodated* by an expansionary monetary policy.

(b) One reason why UK governments have found it so difficult to control the rate of inflation is that governments reap benefits from inflation and there are heavy costs associated with adopting an anti-inflationary policy. Because of this, there is some doubt about the commitment of UK governments to such a policy. When the real rate of interest, i.e. the difference between the nominal rate of interest and the rate of inflation, is negative, inflation redistributes income from lenders to borrowers. In real terms, borrowers pay back less than they borrow. The government, as the biggest borrower of all, gains most from this process of redistribution.

The government also gains because of **fiscal drag**. Inflation leads to rising nominal incomes and rising nominal expenditure. The former leads to rising income tax receipts while the latter leads to rising VAT receipts. This enables governments to finance a higher level of nominal expenditure without recourse to borrowing or tax increases. For both of these reasons, it has been alleged that governments might not be totally committed to an anti-inflationary policy.

There are also costs associated with a policy aimed primarily at the control of inflation. The traditional technique for restraining inflation is to depress aggregate demand. However, inflation only falls when the economy slows up and unemployment rises. It has been argued that this represents an economic waste in the sense of lost output, but it is also politically unpopular. For these reasons, governments have sometimes conducted policy as though they were confronted with a conflict of objectives. A high level of demand supposedly protected employment and stimulated economic growth but ultimately generated inflation and led to a balance of payments deficit. Deflation reversed these and again it is argued that the existence of these costs weakened the resolve of different governments to tackle inflation.

A more modern view is that, in the long run, the level of unemployment tends towards an equilibrium natural rate and raising aggregate demand simply generates a higher rate of inflation in the long run. This implies that government attempts to 'manage' the economy so as to achieve a lower level of unemployment have in fact simply generated a higher rate of inflation. It is possible that because of relatively low mobility of labour, a generous system of welfare benefits and so on, the UK has a relatively high natural rate of unemployment. Because of this, even the temporary gains from inflation might appeal to governments and the relatively high cost in terms of unemployment of reducing inflation might discourage a policy of disinflation.

In this sense, the success of Germany and New Zealand in reducing inflation is partly attributed to the fact that their respective central banks are independent of government. In other words, neither government can manipulate the money supply to achieve short-term economic aims. Both central banks are charged with responsibility to ensure a low rate of inflation and restrict money growth so as to achieve this objective. In the UK, the Bank of England has no such independence and therefore there is no institution which can protect the value of the currency against the short-term aims of government.

Those economists who accept that inflation is caused by cost pressures might argue that inflation has proved so stubborn in the UK partly because of the way in which unions bargain for wage awards. There is a *cycle* of wage negotiations and it is sometimes argued that the existence of 'pace-setters' at various points in the cycle set the going rate for others to match or better. If wage awards were negotiated on a *particular day* this problem would be removed. The other main source of cost pressure, rising import prices, might stem from the persistent tendency of sterling to fall on the foreign exchanges. However, here again government commitment to a strong anti-inflationary stance would halt this.

There are several possible reasons why, until fairly recent years, UK governments have achieved little success in the control of inflation. However, there is little doubt that a major factor has been lack of commitment on the part of governments to such a policy.

STUDENT'S ANSWER TO QUESTION 2

> **Good**

(a) The value of money varies inversely with the price level. As the average level of prices rises, the value of money falls and vice versa. Economists measure changes in the value of money by reference to changes in the average price level.

The official measure in the UK of changes in the average price level is the retail prices index (RPI). This is computed by monitoring changes in the price of a representative basket of goods. However, some items in the basket are purchased more frequently than others and therefore simply to calculate a straight average of price changes would give a misleading indication of the impact of each individual price change on the average consumer. Each item in the basket is therefore accorded a weight to reflect the proportion of income spent on that good. A numerical example will illustrate the main points.

Suppose there are two goods in the representative basket, good A and good B. Suppose further that good A costs £6 and good B costs £2 and that good B is purchased twice as frequently as good A. From one year to the next if the price of good A rises by 20 per cent and the price of good B rises by 50 per cent, the effect of this on the average price level can be illustrated in the table below.

	Good	Price	Weight	Index No	Weighted Index No	
Year 1	A	£6	6	100	(6 x 100 =)	600
	B	£2	4	100	(4 x 100 =)	400
			10			1000

Index of prices in Year 1 = 1000/10 = 100

	Good	Price	Weight	Index No	Weighted Index No	
Year 2	A	£7.20	6	$\frac{£7.20}{£6.00}$ = 120	(6 x 120 =)	720
	B	£3.00	4	$\frac{£3.00}{£2.00}$ = 150	(4 x 150=)	600
			10			1320

Index of prices in Year 2 = 1320/10 = 132

> 66 Good — you have provided a numerical example to illustrate your points 99

The example above implies that the price of an average basket of goods has increased by 32 per cent between Year 1 and Year 2. This implies that the value of money has fallen by 32 per cent between Year 1 and Year 2.

> 66 Perhaps other price indices – e.g. Tax and Price Index might be mentioned 99

(b) There are many reasons why changes in the RPI might not provide an accurate guide to changes in the value of money. An important factor limiting its usefulness in this context is that it is computed from a basket of goods which is unlikely to be consumed by all families. Families with young children, for example, will consume an entirely different range of goods to pensioners for example. For some people, price changes will have no significance if they do not consume the goods. Changes in the price of tobacco has no effect on non-smokers!

> 66 Good point 99

Not only are different age groups likely to consume a different range of goods, different families are also likely to spend different amounts on the same goods. For example, a relatively wealthy family will spend more on furniture than a relatively poor family and so on. A relatively wealthy family is likely to consume a better quality range of products than a relatively poor family and the prices of such goods might change by a different proportion to less expensive items.

There is another problem because patterns of consumption are not static. Over time, people change the range of goods they consume and this again will make estimates of changes in the value of money less accurate.

> 66 Excellent answer to part a) of question; part b) might have been developed a little further. Other types of price index could have been considered in part a) and b). 99

OUTLINE ANSWERS

Question 3

This is a straightforward question that simply requires a discussion of the costs and benefits associated with the control of inflation. The costs of inflation are easily summarised and controlling the rate of inflation would either eliminate or reduce these costs.

■ Inflation causes a serious misallocation of resources and prevents the price mechanism from discharging its role efficiently. When the price of one good rises this is a signal to producers that society desires more of that particular good and resources will be competed away from alternatives. However, when inflation causes a *general* rise in prices, it is impossible for producers to distinguish this from a rise in the price of a particular good. Because of this producers will increase the output of certain goods when price is rising in the mistaken belief that society requires more of that particular good.

- Resources are used inefficiently because inflation necessitates the production of new price lists, slot machines need altering and so on.

- Inflation makes it difficult to plan future changes in output and investment decisions which will adversely affect economic growth. It also makes it more difficult to tender for work.

- Inflation redistributes income, for example from lenders to borrowers, which might discourage saving. It tends also to encourage investment in non-productive assets which provide a hedge against inflation. This diverts resources into the production of non-productive assets and away from the creation of real capital goods which would make possible a higher level of output in the future.

- Inflation tends to be associated with a balance of payments deficit because it increases the competitiveness of imports in the domestic economy and reduces the competitiveness of exports in the international economy.

The only technique which has a proven record in the control of inflation is *deflation* and many economists now argue that, since deflation inevitably implies a reduction in money growth, it is the latter which is responsible for any reduction in the rate of inflation. Avoid exploring this debate; you are simply asked to discuss the costs of controlling inflation, and these are easily summarised:

- The most obvious cost of reducing inflation is rising unemployment. You could discuss this in terms of the Phillips curve and go on to argue that if the Phillips curve is vertical, in the long run, any unemployment as a result of deflation is transitory. You could then go on to explain that the short-run costs of unemployment depend on how severely the policy of deflation is applied and whether the authorities prefer to bring inflation down in stages.

- Deflation also implies a reduction in output and this implies a cut in the standard of living. Again, if there is an equilibrium natural rate, any reduction in output will be transitory.

Question 4

(a) There are various definitions of the **natural rate of unemployment** but it is important to stress that the natural rate of unemployment is that rate which gives equilibrium in the labour market. It is determined by the structural rigidities in the economy and is immune to changes in aggregate demand.

(b) There are various ways in which the natural rate might be reduced and for high marks you will need to examine several in detail. It is usually argued that the main way in which the natural rate can be reduced is to increase incentives in the labour market. Various options have been suggested here. One is to cut unemployment benefit so as to reduce the real wage of the unemployed. Another possibility is to reduce direct taxation so as to increase real disposable income for those in employment thus increasing the attractiveness of employment. It would be useful to discuss briefly the measures actually taken by UK governments in this area. A different approach is to reform the labour market so as to reduce the power of the trade unions. Again it would be useful to briefly discuss the measures actually taken by UK governments in this area. Rigidities in the labour market might be reduced by increasing the flow of information on job opportunities and by increasing the provision of training for the unemployed. Various institutional changes, such as abolishing the Wages Councils which establish minimum rates of pay for certain occupations might be discussed. It is also possible that increased privatisation, by allowing greater freedom of market forces in the economy, might reduce the natural rate.

(c) This section of the question requires a discussion of the long-run Phillips curve (see p. 247). It is important to explain the reasoning behind the vertical Phillips curve and, in so doing, to argue that any attempt by governments to reduce unemployment *below* the natural rate will simply result in higher inflation in the long run.

Further reading

Begg, Fischer and Dornbusch, *Economics* (3rd edn), McGraw-Hill 1991: Ch. 28, Inflation.

Glaister, *The Causes and Control of Inflation* (2nd edn), Longman 1989.

Glaister, *The Meaning, Measurement and Consequences of Inflation* (2nd edn), Longman 1989.

Griffiths and Wall, *Applied Economics: An Introductory Course* (6th edn), Longman 1995: Ch. 19, Inflation; Ch. 20, Unemployment.

Harrison et al, *Introductory Economics*, Macmillan 1992: Ch. 27, Measuring Changes in the Value of Money; Ch. 28, Inflation.

Stanlake, *Macro-economics: An Introduction* (4th edn), Longman 1989: Ch. 15, The quantity of money and the price level; Ch. 16, Output, demand and the price level; Ch. 17, Inflation.

REVIEW SHEET

1 Write down an equation for the quantity theory of money.

2 Use your equation to explain the relationship between M and P.

3 Describe the index of retail prices (RPI) and how it is calculated.

4 Identify five problems in interpreting the economic meaning of changes in the RPI.
   (a)
   (b)
   (c)
   (d)
   (e)

5 Describe the tax and price index.

6 Draw a diagram to illustrate demand-pull inflation.

7 Use your diagram to help you explain the causes of demand-pull inflation.

8 Draw a diagram to illustrate cost-push inflation.

9 Use your diagram to help you explain the causes of cost-push inflation.

_____

_____

_____

10 What is meant by the Phillips curve?

_____

_____

_____

11 Draw the Phillips curve.

12 Offer four reasons why the Phillips curve has broken down.

(a) _____

(b) _____

(c) _____

(d) _____

13 Define the natural rate of unemployment.

_____

_____

14 Using a diagram to help you, explain why some economists believe that the long-run Phillips curve is vertical at the natural rate of unemployment.

Explanation:

_____

_____

15 Describe the monetarist view of the transmission mechanism (rise in money → rise in aggregate demand).

_____

_____

_____

16 Describe the Keynesian view of the transmission mechanism.

_____

_____

_____

_____

INTERNATIONAL TRADE AND PROTECTION

ABSOLUTE ADVANTAGE

COMPARATIVE ADVANTAGE

THE TERMS OF TRADE

PROTECTION

APPLIED MATERIALS

GETTING STARTED

International trade arises for many reasons, but the most obvious one is that different countries have different factor endowments, and the international mobility of these factors is severely limited. International trade therefore makes available to consumers in one country, products which are only produced in other countries.

However, the fact is that the vast majority of goods and services which countries buy from abroad they could produce domestically for themselves. The main reason they are imported is that they can be produced with greater relative efficiency by foreign firms than by domestic firms. This is the crux of the matter: countries might be capable of producing the same goods, but they are unlikely to produce them with equal efficiency. The **law of comparative advantage** implies that countries gain when they specialise in the production of those goods and services in which they have the greatest relative efficiency. These can be traded for the other goods and services they require.

One of the main advantages of **international specialisation** is that by concentrating on the production of those goods and services in which it does have the greatest relative efficiency, a country may even increase its absolute level of efficiency. For instance, larger outputs will make possible economies of large-scale production. If these cost reductions are passed on to the consumers, then the gains from specialisation will be reflected in lower prices. It is also argued that if there are no restrictions on investment, funds will flow to those activities which offer the greatest return. Because of this, it is sometimes suggested that international specialisation will, in the long run, bring about a more efficient utilisation of world resources.

Although the potential gains from international trade are vast, countries invariably impose **restrictions on trade**. There are various reasons for this, but not all are supported by economic analysis. Great care must be taken in assessing the validity of economic arguments advanced in support of protection since they are sometimes based on subjective factors, or on a misunderstanding of the long-run effects of restricting trade.

ESSENTIAL PRINCIPLES

For simplicity our analysis of international trade is limited to the simple case: two countries producing the same two goods. However, the conclusions can be generalised and applied to a world consisting of many countries producing many commodities.

ABSOLUTE ADVANTAGE

A country is said to have an **absolute advantage** in the production of a commodity when it is more efficient than other countries at producing that commodity, i.e. when it can produce more of a commodity than other countries using the same amount of resources. When two countries each have an absolute advantage in different commodities, total world output can be increased (and both countries can gain) when each country specialises in the production of those commodities in which it has an absolute advantage.

COMPARATIVE ADVANTAGE

Even where a country has an absolute advantage in the production of both commodities, trade can still be mutually beneficial so long as each country has a **comparative advantage**. Table 14.1 is used as a basis for explanation.

	TONNES OF WHEAT THAT CAN BE PRODUCED FROM X RESOURCES	NUMBER OF CARS THAT CAN BE PRODUCED FROM X RESOURCES
Country A	40	10
Country B	20	8

Table 14.1

Country A has an absolute advantage in the production of both wheat and cars since, with a given amount of resources, it can produce more of both goods than Country B.

However, if we examine the domestic opportunity cost ratios it is clear that each country has a relative, or comparative, advantage in the production of one commodity.

In **Country A**, the domestic opportunity cost ratio is such that 4 tonnes of wheat must be given up for each car produced.

In **Country B** the domestic opportunity cost ratio is such that only 2.5 tonnes of wheat must be given up for each car produced. A country has a comparative advantage in that product for which it has a **lower domestic opportunity cost ratio** than its competitor. Country B, therefore, has a comparative advantage in the production of cars since, for each car that is produced, less wheat is sacrificed in B than in A.

Country A by the same reasoning has a comparative advantage in the production of wheat. For each tonne of wheat produced Country A must sacrifice 0.25 cars, whereas in **Country B** each tonne of wheat produced 'costs' more, i.e. 0.4 cars.

It is easy to show that, if both countries specialise in the production of the good in which they have a comparative advantage, the combined output of both goods will be greater than when each country produces both goods. We can show this by taking a *marginal* change. If A produces 1 tonne *extra* wheat (comparative advantage in wheat), it gives up 0.25 cars. If B produces 1 tonne *less* of wheat (comparative advantage in cars) it *gains* 0.4 cars. So with wheat production unchanged, there has been a net 'gain' of 0.15 cars by specialising according to comparative advantages.

However, specialisation and trade can only be mutually beneficial if the **terms of trade**, i.e. the rate at which one good exchanges for another, lie somewhere between the respective domestic opportunity cost ratios. This is easily demonstrated. For example, if the terms of trade are that one car exchanges for 3 tonnes of wheat, this reduces the cost of cars in terms of wheat for Country A, and reduces the cost of wheat in terms of cars for Country B. Hence any given amount of one good foregone gives both countries more of the other good after trade than is possible from domestic production.

ASSUMPTIONS

In discussing the possibility of trade in terms of absolute and comparative advantage, several assumptions have been made. Some have been explicitly mentioned, but others have not. These are important because the absence of such conditions in the real world will considerably reduce the possible gains from trade. The main assumptions on which our discussion of absolute and comparative advantage is based are set out below.

Perfect factor mobility

We have assumed that countries can shift resources from the production of one good to the production of another good. In practice, there is likely to be a certain amount of factor immobility which will prevent this, especially in the short run.

❝ Some important assumptions ❞

Constant costs

In assuming constant costs, we are discounting the possibility of lower unit costs as output expands, for instance because of economies of scale, or higher unit costs as output expands, because of diseconomies of scale. In practice, constant costs are unlikely to be the case and it is much more realistic to suppose that a country may only have a comparative advantage in the production of a particular commodity up to a certain level of output. If production expands beyond this point, then rising costs will reduce or even remove altogether the country's comparative advantage.

Technical change

Changes in technology bring about changes in productive efficiency. Because of this, a country might have a comparative advantage in the production of a particular commodity at one point in time; but this might be lost to another more technologically advanced country at a different point in time.

Barriers to trade

Countries do not always trade freely with each other. The existence of restrictions on trade clearly limits the scope for specialisation between countries.

Divergence between real values and money values

It has been assumed that the money prices of goods accurately reflect their domestic opportunity costs. For example, where the domestic opportunity cost ratio was four tonnes of wheat for one car, we have implicitly assumed that the *price* the consumer pays for a car is four times the price paid for a tonne of wheat. In a world of perfect competition where price is equated with marginal cost, this will be the case; but in the real world, where prices are distorted by imperfect competition in factor and product markets, as well as by taxes and subsidies, it is unlikely to be the case. Since consumption and production decisions are based on *money values* rather than real values, if money prices are out of line with real costs, it may no longer be possible for countries to gain from trade by specialising in the production of those commodities in which they have a real (comparative cost) advantage.

THE TERMS OF TRADE

The terms of trade are the rate at which one nation's output exchanges against another nation's output. In the previous examples, we assumed only two countries, each trading a single product. However, in the real world, where many countries trade many different commodities, it is not so easy to estimate the terms of trade. In practice, the prices of commodities traded are measured by an index of prices. The **terms of trade index** is the ratio of an index of export prices to an index of import prices. Thus, the terms of trade index can be calculated as:

❝ Calculating the terms of trade ❞

$$\frac{\text{index of export prices}}{\text{index of import prices}} \times 100$$

In the base year, the value of the terms of trade index will be 100, i.e. $100/100 \times 100$. Changes in the terms of trade are measured by changes in the value of this index.

FAVOURABLE AND UNFAVOURABLE MOVEMENTS IN THE TERMS OF TRADE

A movement in the terms of trade is said to be **favourable** whenever export prices rise relative to import prices, i.e. whenever the terms of trade index rises. Care must be taken here because this does not necessarily imply that the terms of trade index has a value of greater than 100! If the terms of trade index in one year is greater than its value the previous year, then there has been a favourable movement in the terms of trade. Conversely, a movement in the terms of trade. is said to be **unfavourable** whenever the terms of trade index falls

Favourable movements in the terms of trade are so called because they imply a 'favourable' change in the opportunity cost of imports in terms of exports. For example, if export prices rise while import prices remain constant, a *given volume of exports* will exchange for a *greater volume of imports*. In other words, a favourable movement in the terms of trade makes possible an increase in real income. Because of this the *prices effects* of an increase in the terms of trade are said to be favourable when export prices rise faster than import prices (or when export prices fall more slowly than import prices). Unfavourable movements in the terms of trade occur when the opposite is true.

Interpretation
Great care must be taken over interpreting a favourable or unfavourable movement in the terms of trade. It is the *price* changes which are favourable or unfavourable. The overall effect on revenue from exports or expenditure on imports of a favourable movement in the terms of trade might actually be disadvantageous. This is because changes in revenue and expenditure consist of price *and* volume changes. A favourable movement in prices might have an adverse effect on the volume of exports sold, or on the volume of imports bought. For example, where demand for exports is elastic, a rise in the price of exports may result in a more than proportionate reduction in the volume of exports sold. In this case, the so-called favourable movement in the terms of trade might actually cause a balance of payments problem!

PROTECTION	## TYPES OF RESTRICTION ON TRADE

Despite the potential gains from trade, countries sometimes adopt measures to restrict international trade. There are various types of restriction including the following.

Tariffs
These are simply taxes placed on import commodities. Where a tariff is levied on a commodity its price is increased in the domestic economy. Tariffs may be *specific*, i.e. lump sum, in nature, or *ad valorem*, i.e. proportional to the value of the article. They can be applied individually to particular products or across the board.

Quotas
These are a volume restriction on imports. Specific limits are placed on the quantity of particular products that can be imported. Again, they can be applied selectively or across the board.

Subsidies
❝ Types of protection ❞
By subsidising exported commodities, their competitiveness can be increased in foreign markets. Subsidising domestic products lowers their price and so reduces competition from imports.

Exchange controls
By restricting the supply of foreign currency to particular purchases, governments are able to exercise a great deal of control over which commodities are imported, and in what quantities.

The new protectionism
The new protectionism encompasses a variety of restrictions some of which are difficult to identify as a restriction on trade. Some common *non-tariff* barriers used as protective measures in recent years are listed here:

- ■ **Voluntary export restraints (VERs)**   These are agreements between two countries such that one country agrees to limit exports of particular goods to another country for a specific period of time. One example of this is the Japanese agreement to limit the export of cars to the UK.

- **Government contracts** It is possible that governments deliberately place contracts with domestic producers as a means of restricting imports.
- **Customs procedures** In some countries customs procedures are deliberately excessive. The most often quoted example is that of France who insisted that imports on video equipment must pass through an office in Poitiers, many miles from the ports of entry. With a staff of only eight this undoubtedly resulted in a delay of several weeks in the import of video recorders.
- **Health and safety standards** Strict standards can be imposed on imports such as restrictions on the ingredients of foods or the exhaust emission levels from cars to protect domestic industry.

MOTIVES FOR PROTECTION

There are several arguments for protection but, at the present time, most economists consider these arguments to be quite weak.

To aid economic recovery

It has been argued that if domestic industry is protected, demand will switch from imports to domestic goods and services and this will raise output and employment in the domestic economy. This, in particular, is the view of the **Cambridge Economic Policy Group**. However, protection imposes a welfare loss on consumers (see pp. 267–268), might encourage inefficiency in protected firms and could lead other countries to retaliate which would damage exports thus offsetting any gains in terms of output and employment. Exports might also fall if protection in the UK leads to a reduction in incomes abroad (because imports into the UK have fallen) leaving foreigners with less ability to purchase British output.

To remove a balance of payments deficit

❝ Reasons for protection ❞ Here again it is suggested that widespread protection can remove a balance of payments deficit. The argument is similar to that outlined above but the point is that protection does not remove the cause of the deficit which is lack of competitiveness. Often this might be lack of non-price competitiveness in areas such as quality, reliability, delivery, design, inefficient marketing and so on!

To reduce structural unemployment

In this case, protection is directed to a single industry. It has the same possible effects as that previously outlined with respect to protecting industries to aid economic recovery. However, in this case it is less likely to reduce incomes abroad because protection is only granted to a single industry, but more likely to encourage inefficiency in that industry.

To protect an infant industry

It is sometimes suggested that, in the early stages of growth, infant industries require protection from foreign competition. However, it is almost impossible to identify potentially successful infant industries and bearing the risks of financing infant industries is the function of the entrepreneur. Entrepreneurs will finance infant industries when they believe they will be successful in the long run. If they are not prepared to do this the prospects of success must be thought poor.

Strategic reasons

Another possible motive for protection is that it is considered desirable to produce certain essential goods, such as food and energy, domestically rather than become dependent on another country for their supply. In these circumstances, supply might be withheld to exert political pressure. Strategic factors are one reason for the CAP operated by the EU.

PROTECTION AND CONSUMER WELFARE

The effect of a tariff on consumer welfare can be considered in terms of Fig. 14.1.

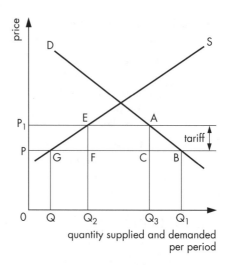

Fig. 14.1 The effect on consumer welfare of a tariff

Domestic supply and demand are represented by S and D respectively. The world price of this commodity is OP and supply of this commodity in the domestic economy is perfectly elastic at the ruling world price, assuming there is no restriction on imports. Sales in the domestic economy are therefore OQ_1 with OQ being supplied by domestic producers. If the government now imposes a tariff of PP_1, the price of this commodity in the domestic market rises to OP_1, total consumption falls to OQ_3 and domestic output increases to OQ_2. The welfare effects of the tariff are a loss to consumers, i.e. a loss of consumer surplus, equal to PP_1AB. However, this is not the total welfare loss to society since PP_1EG of the surplus is transferred from consumers to producers and ACFE is transferred from consumers to the Exchequer as tax revenue. However, the areas ABC and EFG represent pure welfare loss because there is no offsetting gain to any other group in the economy.

PREFERENTIAL TRADING ARRANGEMENTS

Preferential trading arrangements involve trading concessions among members party to the agreement which are denied to non-members. There are several types of preferential trading arrangement.

- **Trade Preference Associations**   Each country reduces barriers to trade with other members of the association but makes no concessions to non-members.
- **Free Trade Area**   In this case, all barriers to trade between members are eliminated but each member country can operate its own protectionist policy against non-members, should it wish to do so.
- **Customs Union**   Here all barriers between participants are eliminated and a common external tariff is erected against imports from *outside* the customs union.
- **Common Market**   In this case, all barriers between participants are eliminated, a common external tariff is erected against imports from outside the common market and certain common policies, particularly with respect to movement of capital and labour, are implemented.

TRADE CREATION AND TRADE DIVERSION

One of the main issues associated with preferential trading arrangements such as customs unions, is whether they lead to trade creation or trade diversion. Table 14.2 is used as a basis for explanation.

| | Rate of tariff imposed by Country A | | |
Cost of wheat in:	0	2	5
Country A	6	6	6
Country B (before customs union)	5	7	10
Country B (after customs union)	5	5	5
Country C	2	4	7

Table 14.2 The effect of customs unions

Before any customs union is formed, country A has a tariff of 2 against all imports of wheat. If country A imports wheat, it will purchase it from the cheapest source, country C. However, if the tariff is 5, country A will grow its own wheat because the domestic cost is 6 compared with a cost of 7 if wheat is imported from country C. Now suppose Countries A and B form a customs union and that country A maintains its tariff of 5 against imports from outside the union. The result is *trade creation* because wheat is imported from country B which is a lower cost producer than country A. This is beneficial because resources in country A are then freed to move to where they can be used more efficiently whereas country B is using resources in producing wheat where it has a comparative advantage compared with country A. However, if the tariff is set at 2 in country A *before* the customs union is formed, then the customs union, with a tariff of 5 against imports from outside, will cause country A to switch from a low cost supplier, country C, to a high cost supplier, country B. In this case, trade is diverted to a less efficient supplier, i.e. B compared to C.

Trade creation is desirable because it represents increased world trade. Because of this, global economic efficiency is increased. However, if trade is not additional, but represents a shift away from lower cost suppliers outside the preferential trading area to higher cost suppliers inside, global economic efficiency declines.

APPLIED MATERIALS	In recent years, there has been a marked trend towards the emergence of **regional trading blocs**. An article in the *British Economy Survey* Vol 22, No 2, Spring 1993 provides some data on the extent of trading blocs and considers some of the reasons for their emergence. Table 14.3 is reproduced by permission.

TRADING GROUP	
Total of countries in trading groups listed below	*82.10*
European Community (12)	41.00
Canada-United States Free Trade Area	17.14
European Free Trade Association	6.65
Association of South-East Asian Nations	4.44
Latin American Integration Association	3.03
Bangkok Agreement	2.66
Gulf Co-operation Council	2.02
Australia-New Zealand Closer Economic Relations Trade Agreement	1.48
Southern Cone Common Market	1.13
Arab Common Market	0.95
Arab Maghreb Union	0.89
Andean Common Market	0.72
Southern African Customs Union[2]	0.65
Economic Community of West African States	0.63
Preferential Trade Area for Eastern and Southern African States	0.28
Caribbean Common Market	0.20
Economic Community of Central African States	0.19
West African Economic Community	0.17
Central American Common Market	0.17
Economic and Customs Union of Central Africa	0.14
Mano River Union	0.12
Organisation of Eastern Caribbean States[3]	0.02

Table 14.3 Preferential trading groups' shares of world merchandise trade (%, 1990)[1]

1 The trade (exports, imports or total trade) for each group is the sum of the trade of the individual members of the group, including trade with countries both within and outside the group. Trading groups' shares of world trade do not sum to the total for all countries in the listed groups (first line) as some countries are members of more than one group and data for each country is counted only once in this total.
2 Not including member territories that are not countries
3 Not including the British Virgin Islands
Source: International Monetary Fund, *Direction of Trade Statistics Yearbook.* 1991.

Clearly regional trading blocs are important in world trade. One possible reason for their emergence is that they are perceived to lead to trade creation and are therefore considered beneficial. Another possibility is that by creating a larger internal market, regional trading blocs give participating countries access to a larger market and this might encourage increased efficiency through greater economies of scale.

The emergence of regional trading groupings might indicate frustration at the slow progress made by GATT in liberalising world trade. In the case of less developed countries, it is possible that regional trading blocs provide a means of reducing dependence on the industrialised countries, particularly for manufactured products. There is the additional advantage for the poorer countries of increasing their bargaining power *vis-à-vis* the industrialised countries.

An article in *Finance and Development*, September 1993, entitled *Trade Reform in Latin America and the Caribbean*, describes and analyses the effects of the trade reforms which have taken place in this area in recent years. Some of their findings are set out in Table 14.4.

Country (pre-reform year, post-reform year)	Average unweighted legal tariff rates (per cent)		Tariff range (per cent)		Coverage of Quantitative Restrictions (QRs) on imports (per cent of tariff lines, unless otherwise noted)*		Openness of Economy (imports + exports as percent of GDP, 1980 prices)	
	Pre-reform	Post-reform	Pre-reform	Post-reform	Pre-reform	Post-reform	Pre-reform	Post-reform
Argentina (1987, 1991)	42[P]	15	15–115[P]	5–22	62[1]	A few	38.57	54.32
Bolivia (1985, 1991)	12[M]	8	NA	5–10	NA	Minimal	57.51	83.97
Brazil (1087, 1992)	51	21	0–105	0–65	39	Minimal	21.17	25.27
Chile (1984, 1991)	35	11	35	11	Minimal	0	44.96	56.34
Colombia (1984, 1992)	61	12	0–220	5–20	99	1	28.23	32.66
Costa Rica (1985, 1992)	53[P]	15[P]	0–1400[P]	5–20	NA	0	58.66	78.97
Ecuador (1989, 1992)	37[P]	18	0–338[P]	2–25[2]	100	0	48.73	50.34
Guatemala (1985, 1992)	50[P]	15[P]	5–90	5–20	6[1,3]	0[3]	31.31	35.56
Honduras (1985, 1992)	41[P]	15[W,P]	5–90	5–20	NA	0	62.82	61.76
Jamaica (1981, 1991)	NA	20	NA	0–45	NA	0[4]	105.51	163.49
Mexico (1985, 1990)	24[W]	13[W]	0–100	0–20	92[1]	20[1]	22.63	34.31
Paraguay (1988, 1991)	NA	16	NA	3–86	NA	A few	51.01	63.14
Peru (1988, 1992)	NA	17	0–120	5–25	100	0[4]	30.37	41.58
Trinidad & Tobago (1989, 1991)	NA	41[P]	NA	0–103[P]	NA	A few [5]	124.89	141.21
Uruguay (1987, 1992)	32	18	10–55	12–24	0	0	38.04	45.10
Venezuela (1989, 1991)	37	19	0–135	0–50	40	10 [6]	49.25	53.29

Table 14.4 Some indicators of trade regimes before and after reform

Source: World Bank (various reports, staff estimates, and ANDREX).
* Even where tariff line coverage is small, domestic production coverage may be significant.
P: including tariff surcharges; M: import-weighted average tariff; W: production-weighted average tariff.
[1] Of domestic product
[2] Ecuador also has a specific tariff of 40 per cent on automobiles.
[3] Guatemala has significant QRs for health and safety reasons; pre-reform, they covered 29 per cent of domestic manufacturing production.
[4] Some QRs do exist for health and safety reasons.
[5] On agricultural products only.
[6] Another 8 per cent of tariff items are restricted because of health reasons; pre-reform, the number was 5 per cent.
NA: Not available.

Table 14.4 shows that nominal protection, as indicated by average tariff rates, has fallen substantially as a result of trading arrangements in these countries and there has also been a considerable reduction in quantitative import restrictions. Not surprisingly, Table 14.4 also shows that there has been an increase in the openness of the economies covered, as measured by the sum of real exports and imports as a ratio of GDP.

The article also goes on to consider several important lessons of the reforms:

■ **Trade reforms are successful if they are bold and extensive** Wide-ranging, vigorously implemented reforms send a powerful signal of the direction of government policy and liberate that policy from narrow, vested interests.

■ **Successful trade reforms require a supportive macroeconomic environment** Trade reforms in all of the countries were initiated and maintained in the context of tight monetary and fiscal policies. Such policies are necessary, not only to reduce real expenditures and improve the balance of payments, but also to ensure that the accompanying real devaluations are non-inflationary.

■ **Successful trade reforms are, in general, preceded or accompanied by a depreciation of the real exchange rate** Real devaluations ensure the sustainability of trade reforms by offsetting the excess demand for tradeables that reforms induce.

■ **Trade reforms are more likely to succeed when economies are growing**
The increased import/export performances in Latin America and the Caribbean
following the implementation of reforms are not due solely to trade liberalisation.
The concurrent economic recovery, which raised incomes and stimulated foreign
borrowing, also stimulated import/export growth.

EXAMINATION QUESTIONS

1 The following is an adaption of an extract from P. Torday, *The Independent*, 13
November 1990.

The Achilles Heel in GATT
The General Agreement on Tariffs and Trade was founded in 1948 under the
auspices of the United Nations as 23 countries began to revive free trade after World
War II.

GATT's aims were to liberalise trade in industrial goods and so improve the
prospects for growth in world trade. At the time, direct tariffs on industrial goods
averaged some 40 per cent, partly a legacy of the war, but also a reflection of the
1930s, one of the most protectionist periods this century.

Today, some 96 countries are members and a further 28 countries apply GATT
rules on an informal basis.

GATT's crowning achievement was to bring down industrial tariffs to an average
4.7 per cent since its inception, when rates averaged 40 per cent. In addition to
direct cuts in customs charges in manufactured goods, GATT has also attempted to
reduce the so-called 'non-tariff' barriers to trade. It has also tried to curb the
practice of countries 'dumping' goods below cost in overseas markets.

However, two key trends are emerging. One is the shift in trading patterns
towards regional trading blocs such as the EU and the Caribbean Free Trade Area.
The other is the growth in new areas of trade such as services.

Perhaps the most contentious issue in new trading areas is agriculture. During
the 1980s, there was increasing recourse to subsidising farm exports by the EU,
which the US countered with measures of its own. As world prices fell, subsidies
rose and the struggle for other markets intensified. This has caused acrimonious
discussion in the current round of GATT negotiations.

In practical terms, if the current round of GATT negotiations fails there is a fear
that, in areas such as agriculture and services, a trade war will ensue and
protectionist laws proliferate.

(a) What is meant by 'non-tariff' barriers to trade? *(2)*
(b) Examine the economic reasoning behind GATT's attempt 'to revive free trade
after World War II' and 'liberalise trade in industrial goods'. *(6)*
(c) Examine the consequences of a trade war and protectionist measures in areas
such as agriculture and services. *(6)*
(d) Examine the implications of 'the shift in trading patterns towards regional
trading blocs'. *(6)*

(ULEAC June 1992)

2 Evaluate the economic arguments for the creation of the Single European Market.
Given these arguments, why might members of the EC (EU) oppose free trade
among all countries of the world?

(JMB 1992)

3 Discuss whether customs unions such as the European Community (European
Union) help or hinder the development of world trade in accordance with the
principle of comparative advantage.

(AEB November 1992)

4 (a) How can a domestic market be protected? *(7)*

(b) If a country had a protected domestic market what would be the likely effect on its balance of trade? *(8)*

(c) Do you think that domestic market protection is to the disadvantage of most people in the country? *(10)*

(UCLES June 1992)

5 Explain carefully the theory of comparative advantage. Is the theory of any use in explaining the pattern of world trade?

6 Analyse and evaluate the possible causes and consequences of a deterioration in a country's terms of trade.

ANSWERS TO EXAMINATION QUESTIONS

TUTOR'S ANSWER TO QUESTION 1

(a) Tariffs are a tax on imports of goods. **Non-tariff barriers** include a range of other restrictions such as quotas, domestic government purchasing policies and the imposition of safety and technical standards which give preferential treatment to domestic firms.

(b) Restrictions on trade limit the extent to which countries can specialise and exploit the gains from comparative advantage. These gains can best be illustrated with a numerical example. Using the same quantity of resources, assume two countries, A and B, can produce two goods, X and Y, in the quantities shown below:

	Good X	Good Y
Country A	10	8
Country B	8	4

The domestic opportunity cost ratio in country A is 1X: 0.8Y and in country B it is 1X: 0.5Y. It is clear that country A has an absolute and comparative advantage in the production of good Y because for each unit of X given up, it gains 0.8Y whereas country B gains only 0.5Y for each unit of X given up. On the other hand, although country B has an absolute disadvantage in the production of good X, it has a comparative advantage in the production of that good because for each unit of Y given up, country B gains 2X whereas country A gains only 1.25 of good X for each unit of Y given up. It can be shown that when countries specialise in the production of those goods where they have greatest *comparative advantage*, total world output will increase and, so long as the rate of exchange lies somewhere between the domestic opportunity cost ratios, both countries can achieve a higher level of consumption through trade than would otherwise be possible.

At the end of World War II, many restrictions on trade were in place which prevented countries from exploiting the gains from specialisation and trade. GATT was created to persuade countries to dismantle these so that specialisation and trade would be encouraged. The implication is that living standards would be increased as a result.

(c) Potentially the most serious result of a trade war and the emergence of protectionist measures is that it will discourage specialisation and trade. This, as we have seen above, will inhibit economic growth and will limit the extent of any improvement in the standard of living. In any war, there are gainers and losers, and a trade war in agriculture would initially lead to lower prices for consumers but lower incomes for farmers and growers. In a free market, this would lead to a cut back in production. However, if protectionist measures are adopted, depending on the form such measures take, imports will be restricted or taxed while domestic output will be subsidised in an attempt to prevent domestic output falling. In the short term, this might preserve levels of employment but, in the longer term, unemployment will rise as resources are diverted to inefficient uses. If domestic output is subsidised, taxes will need to be increased to finance these. If imports are taxed or restricted, this will cause rising prices which might lead to wage demands and be a source of inflation. There is a further problem because protectionism inevitably encourages inefficiency in the protected sectors and this again will inhibit economic growth.

(d) Regional trading blocs might either increase or reduce efficiency in the allocation of resources depending on whether they lead to trade creation or trade diversion. **Trade creation** occurs when the creation of a regional trading bloc results in additional trade from a lower cost source than at present whereas **trade diversion** occurs when the regional trading blocs results in trade being diverted from a low cost source to a higher cost source.

Another possibility is that, by creating a larger market, a regional trading bloc will encourage the growth of firms who will be able to exploit the available economies of scale. To the extent that this happens, productive efficiency will increase which might result in lower prices for consumers.

It could be argued that regional trading blocs represent a stage on the road to global free trade. When regional trading blocs are created, smaller countries become part of a group which will have a stronger negotiating position when bargaining for any reduction in barriers to trade with larger economies or other trading blocs.

STUDENT'S ANSWER TO QUESTION 2

> 66 An interesting and relevant introduction 99

The Single European Market aims to remove barriers to the free movement of capital and labour within the EU. It also aims to free those markets where restrictions still exist, such as in the trade of non-life insurance services, road haulage, and air transport, and which therefore limit the extent of competition with the EU. Trade generally is to be encouraged by abolishing any remaining exchange controls and abolishing frontier controls.

> 66 Good point 99

The Single Market will confer many benefits on EU members. By removing restrictions within the EU, the allocation of resources will be improved. For example, by opening up insurance services to competition there will be more choice available to savers. However, it is argued that the removal of restrictions will have other benefits and will have a favourable impact on economic growth, inflation and employment.

There are several reasons why these benefits might materialise. By removing restrictions on trade, there will obviously be an increase in competition in EU markets. This will no doubt provide a spur to efficiency, but a greater benefit will stem from the increased scope for specialisation and trade which the removal of restrictions will facilitate. There are tremendous gains from trade summed up in the **law of comparative costs** which states that countries will gain when they specialise in the production of those goods where they have greatest comparative advantage. When countries impose barriers to trade, this prevents specialisation and countries are compelled to produce some goods where they are relatively inefficient compared with foreign firms. When restrictions are dismantled, resources can move to their most efficient uses.

> 66 Can you provide a numerical example or diagram to show the gains from trade? 99

There is another benefit, usually referred to as a **dynamic advantage**, from the removal of barriers to trade.

66 Good — could develop
further 99

The Single Market has a population of some 325 million and the increased size of the market will enable firms to grow and reap economies of scale. This implies falling average costs of production, which will make lower prices possible.

The Single Market will therefore improve efficiency and, in this way, will stimulate economic growth, raise employment and reduce inflation below levels that might otherwise have been achieved. Despite these advantages, EU members might have many reasons for opposing a complete liberalisation of trade with the outside world. One major reason is that many other countries outside the EU have barriers which limit their imports. These can take many forms, such as the tariffs erected by other trading blocs, but the fastest growing restrictions are those associated with the new protectionism. If the EU reduces barriers against imports from the rest of the world it would open up its own markets while access to markets in other countries was restricted.

66 Need to explain 99

Protection might also be important for strategic reasons. One of the main aims of the CAP is to ensure that Europe is self-sufficient in the production of food. Only through protection can this aim be achieved because this is the only way of guaranteeing the relatively high food prices that will encourage self-sufficiency.

66 Good 99

The EU might also wish to maintain barriers with the rest of the world in order to protect intra-EU employment. There seems little doubt that, in the long run, there are gains from free trade. However, the long run might be very long indeed and the adjustment in terms of reallocating resources might be very painful and involve higher levels of unemployment and a slower rate of economic growth. Freer trade within the EU will not involve such heavy adjustment costs because trade between members is increasingly intra-EU trade.

66 Relevant point — but
perhaps take further 99

There are strong economic reasons why, despite the gains from free trade, EU members would wish to maintain barriers. However, it could be argued that the creation of trading blocs such as the EU are a step towards free world trade in accordance with the principles of comparative advantage.

66 Many good qualities about this essay — but the general points need to be taken a little further on occasions. The use of diagrams/numerical examples/case studies etc. could all help to re-inforce your points. 99

OUTLINE ANSWERS

Question 3

You could begin by defining a **customs union**. Basically free trade exists between members of the union, they maintain a common external tariff against imports into the union and they adopt certain common policies such as the CAP of the EU.

You could then go on to explain the **principle of comparative advantage**, perhaps including a numerical example to illustrate this principle. Whether a customs union helps to encourage trade in accordance with the principle of comparative advantage depends partly on whether the union leads to **trade creation** or **trade diversion**. You could explain this using a numerical example such as the one given on p. 268. However, you might also explain that, even if the union leads to trade diversion, it is possible that, in the long run, trade will develop in accordance with the principle of comparative advantage. The union will have greater power to negotiate reductions in barriers to trade with other countries than any single member of the union.

Question 4

(a) The main instrument's of protection are discussed on pp. 266–267.

(b) The answer to this part of the question is uncertain. If all other things remain the same, protection will almost certainly lead to a short term improvement in the balance of trade. In the longer run, if protection leads to inefficiency and higher prices, the balance of trade will deteriorate. (You should explain why protection might lead to inefficiency and higher prices.) However, even in the short run, if other countries retaliate and impose protective measures of their own, the effect on the balance of trade depends on the extent of protection and on the elasticity of demand for exports and imports. You should explain this point in some detail.

(c) Again the answer to this part of the question depends on the assumptions we make. If an infant industry is protected and grows into an internationally competitive firm, protection will benefit all. However, protection will almost certainly lead to higher domestic prices, either directly because of a tariff or indirectly because import restrictions lead consumers to buy higher priced domestic substitutes. On the other hand, by transferring demand away from foreign competition to domestic substitutes, domestic employment might be protected. Perhaps the greatest argument against protection is that it encourages inefficiency so that, in the long run, resources are misallocated and the effect of this will be higher prices and lower employment.

Question 5

It is useful to begin by distinguishing between **absolute** and **comparative advantage**. You could then go on to explain, using a numerical example, how countries gain from specialisation and trade. The pattern of world trade at least partly confirms the theory of comparative advantage with some countries specialising in certain goods and services: coffee from Brazil, electronic equipment from Japan, nitrates from Chile; Switzerland specialises in banking, Zambia in copper and so on. However, countries produce a variety of goods and services which seems to conflict with the law of comparative costs. One reason for this is that the law is based on certain assumptions which might not hold in the real world. These assumptions must be discussed. Another reason why the law might fail to predict the pattern of world trade is that countries might not wish to trade with some countries for political reasons or they might not wish to specialise for strategic reasons.

Question 6

You could begin with a definition of the **terms of trade** followed by a numerical example to distinguish between *favourable* and *unfavourable* movements in the terms of trade.

A change in the terms of trade implies a change in export prices and/or import prices. Several factors might bring this about:

- A relatively high (or low) **rate of inflation** in the exporting country compared with importing countries will cause changes in the terms of trade. For example, an excess of aggregate demand over aggregate supply, or costs rising faster than productivity will raise the value of the terms of trade index because it will cause a rise in domestic, i.e. export prices.

- **Exchange rate changes** will also affect the value of the terms of trade index. For example, when a country's currency depreciates, the domestic price of its exports will be unchanged, but the domestic price of its imports will increase. Depreciation will therefore reduce the value of the terms of trade index; appreciation reduces the domestic price of imports, and therefore raises the terms of trade.

- **Changes in commodity prices** can also have a powerful effect on the terms of trade. When their price is bid up on world markets, or when producing countries restrict supply and force up price, the terms of trade index of the exporting countries will rise; for importing countries the terms of trade index will fall. A slump in commodity prices has the opposite effect.

■ Changes in the terms of trade might be caused by **bottlenecks** in the supply of exports or imports. For example, a bottleneck may occur when demand for exports increases, perhaps because of an increase in the national income of a major buying country, but exports cannot respond to increased demand because of a shortage of skilled labour or some other input. In these circumstances export prices will rise relative to import prices, and the terms of trade will rise. The opposite occurs when demand for imports increases and supply is inelastic.

Further reading

Begg, Fischer and Dornbusch, *Economics* (3rd edn), McGraw-Hill 1991: Ch. 32, International Trade and Commercial Policy.

Griffiths and Wall, *Applied Economics: An Introductory Course* (6th edn), Longman 1995: Ch. 26 Protectionism.

Harrison, *International Trade and Finance*, Longman 1987: Ch. 1, The Gains from International Trade; Ch. 2, Restrictions on Trade.

Harrison et al, *Introductory Economics*, Macmillan 1992: Ch. 30, International Trade; Ch. 31, Free Trade and Protection.

Stanlake, *Introductory Economics* (5th edn), Longman 1989: Ch. 27, International Trade.

REVIEW SHEET

1 Briefly explain the following theories.
Theory of absolute advantage:

Theory of comparative advantage:

2 Present a numerical example to show two countries and two products, with each country having a comparative advantage in one product.

Product Country		

3 Use your table to show net gains from specialisation according to comparative advantages.

4 Define the terms of trade.

5 Explain why a rise in the terms of trade may not always benefit a country.

6 Identify four types of protection.
(a)

(b)

(c)

(d)

7 Briefly explain four arguments to support the use of protection.

(a) _____

_____

(b) _____

_____

(c) _____

_____

(d) _____

_____

8 Present a diagram and use it to show the effect of a tariff on consumer welfare.

Explanation: _____

_____

_____

_____

_____

_____

_____

9 Outline the main features of the 'Single Market' of the European Union.

_____

_____

_____

_____

_____

_____

_____

10 Assess some of the likely benefits from the 'Single Market' for UK firms.

_____

_____

_____

_____

_____

_____

_____

_____

_____

_____

GETTING STARTED

Chapter 14 looked at the gains from international trade. Over any given period of time, the total financial dealings of one country with the rest of the world are recorded in its balance of payments account. However, just as individuals can sometimes spend more than they currently earn and finance this by borrowing, so countries can sometimes spend more than they currently earn. When this happens a country imports a greater value of goods and services than it exports, we say it has a **balance of payments deficit**. When the value of exports exceeds the value of imports a country is said to have a **balance of payments surplus**. Although a balance of payments deficit is often taken as cause for concern and a surplus a sign of economic strength, one advantage of a deficit is that it allows residents of one country to consume more than they currently produce, thereby raising current living standards.

In the real world, international trade and payments are only possible if there is an international means of payment. Although most currencies can be converted into other currencies via the foreign exchange market, most international trade is financed through the use of **vehicle (or reserve) currencies**. These are simply currencies that are acceptable as a means of settling international indebtedness. The American dollar is the main vehicle currency, though sterling and the Deutschmark are also used as vehicle currencies.

CHAPTER

15

THE BALANCE OF PAYMENTS AND EXCHANGE RATES

THE BALANCE OF PAYMENTS

THE RATE OF EXCHANGE

FLOATING EXCHANGE RATES

FIXED EXCHANGE RATES

FIXED AND FLOATING EXCHANGE RATES COMPARED

THE EUROPEAN MONETARY SYSTEM (EMS)

REAL AND EFFECTIVE EXCHANGE RATES

INTERNATIONAL LIQUIDITY

EXCHANGE RATE CHANGES AND BALANCE OF PAYMENTS ADJUSTMENT

POLICIES TO DEAL WITH A BALANCE OF PAYMENTS DEFICIT

APPLIED MATERIALS

THE BALANCE OF PAYMENTS

66 Visible + Invisible =
Current 99

ESSENTIAL PRINCIPLES

A country's balance of payments is simply an annual record of its financial dealings with the rest of the world. In practice, all transactions which make up the balance of payments are either autonomous transactions or accommodating transactions.

- **Autonomous transactions** are those which take place for their own sake. They reflect voluntary decisions to buy, sell, lend or borrow.
- **Accommodating transactions** are those which are necessary because the net value of all autonomous transactions yields either a deficit in the balance of payments (outflows exceed inflows) or a surplus (inflows exceed outflows).

In the UK, all international transactions are recorded in the current account of the balance of payments and/or the capital account (now referred to as **Transactions in UK assets and liabilities**) of the balance of payments. The accounts are constructed on the principle of double entry bookkeeping thus ensuring that the accounts always balance in accounting terms. One entry shows the original transaction, the other shows the way in which it was financed. For example, the purchase of cars from Japan would be recorded as a visible import in the current account. It would also be recorded in the capital account as perhaps a loan from an overseas bank if this is how the deal was financed.

THE CURRENT ACCOUNT

This account records dealings in:

- visible trade, i.e. exports and imports of goods, and
- invisible trade which consists mainly of trade in services.

As Table 15.1 shows, the visible balance (–£10,290m) when added to the invisible balance (£3,969m) gives the current balance (–£6,321m).

Trade balance

The state of the **visible balance**, or **trade balance**, is of great importance because it indicates the extent to which the UK depends on the rest of the world for the goods it consumes. We shall see on pp. 296–298 that a lack of international competitiveness has been a major factor in the decline of the manufacturing sector, usually referred to as **deindustrialisation** in the UK in recent years. When visible imports exceed visible exports, it is still of course possible for this deficit to be offset by a surplus on invisibles since it is the sum of the visible balance and the invisible balance which gives the current balance.

State of the current account

The state of the **current account** is of great importance because it indicates a nation's net surplus or deficit in its trading with the rest of the world. The UK has often had a deficit on the trade balance which has been more than offset by a surplus on the invisible account giving an overall surplus on the current account. However, the extent of the current account deficit in recent years has been a particular cause for concern. More is said about this below.

THE CAPITAL ACCOUNT (CHANGES IN UK EXTERNAL ASSETS AND LIABILITIES)

This section of the balance of payments account records capital movements between the UK and the rest of the world. Such capital movements are undertaken by governments, firms and private individuals, and may be short term or long term. Capital outflows are given a negative sign in the accounts, and capital inflows a positive sign.

Long-term capital flows

These consist of:

- direct investment
- portfolio investment
- other external assets (liabilities) of central government.

CURRENT ACCOUNT			
Visible trade			
Exports		103,413	
Imports		113,703	
Visible balance			−1,0290
Invisible trade			
General government	412		
	−2,808		
		−2,396	
Sea transport	3,658		
	−3,643		
		15	
Civil aviation	3,927		
	−4,397		
		−470	
Travel	7,165		
	−9,825		
		−2,660	
Financial and other services	16,540		
	−6,039		
		10,501	
Interest profit and dividends	1,763		
	−1,897		
		−134	
Private sector and public corporations	75,906		
	−75,443		
		463	
Transfers			
General government	4,894		
	−5,943		
		−1,049	
Private sector	1,900		
	−2,200		
		−300	
Invisible balance			3,969
Current balance			−6,321

CAPITAL ACCOUNT (Transactions in UK assets and liabilities)		
Direct investment overseas	−10,261	
Portfolio investment overseas	−30,908	
Total UK investment overseas		−41,169
Direct investment in UK by overseas residents	12,045	
Portfolio investment in UK by overseas residents	16,627	
Total investment in UK by overseas residents		28,672
Net foreign currency transactions of UK banks		12,592
Net sterling transactions of UK banks		−4,385
Deposits with and lending to banks abroad by UK non-bank private sector		−3,580
Borrowing from banks abroad by:		
UK non-bank private sector		13,032
Public corporations		−49
General government		−65
Official reserves (additions to − drawings on +)		−2,662
Other external assets of UK non-bank private sector and public corporations		−4,707
General government		−894
Other external liabilities of UK non-bank private sector and public corporations		10,710
General government		−2,246
Net transactions in assets and liabilities		6,321
Balancing item		1,072

Table 15.1 UK Balance of Payments (£m) 1992

Direct investment and Portfolio investment

Direct investment refers to the creation of real physical assets, such as factory buildings, whereas *portfolio investment* refers to purely financial transactions, such as the purchase or sale of equity in joint stock companies. Other external assets (liabilities) of UK government includes such items as subscriptions to international organisations, e.g. contributions to the EU budget or overseas aid. Table 15.1 shows that almost £13,000m *more* was invested overseas by UK residents than was invested in the UK by overseas residents.

66 **Types of capital flow** 99

Short-term capital flows

These consist of lending by, or borrowing from, banks as well as private lending and deposits overseas. Entries into these sections of the capital account arise mainly because of transactions in the current account. For example, the import of goods might be paid for by running down a bank deposit held in a bank abroad. However, it might also represent the purchase and sale of short-term instruments by foreign nationals with surplus funds to invest. For example, overseas residents might purchase Treasury bills, commercial bills of exchange, or local authority bills and these purchases would lead to an *inflow* of foreign currency. They might also deposit funds in bank accounts in London for convenience. These short-term capital flows are purely monetary flows since, they do not involve the creation of physical assets. Because of this they are highly liquid and are sometimes referred to as **hot money** since they can be moved from one country to another very rapidly in response to expected changes in interest rates and/or exchange rates. The volatile nature of hot money can be a source of pressure on a country's exchange rate and, as we shall see, can be a problem for the authorities.

CHANGES IN THE OFFICIAL RESERVES

These arise because any deficit or surplus on the current account is not completely offset by other transactions in the capital account. A negative entry indicates that the authorities have used part of the reserves to bring the balance of payments into balance and vice versa. It is important to note, however, that the change in the reserves is not necessarily identical to the balance of payments deficit or surplus, because the authorities sometimes borrow from abroad to finance a deficit.

THE BALANCING ITEM

The balance of payments account records the effect on foreign currency earnings and expenditure of millions of transactions. In calculations of this magnitude there are bound to be errors and omissions; the balancing item records the collective value of these. Its value is known because the Bank of England's records show the net result of all foreign currency transactions. A positive value, as in Table 15.1, indicates that there have been unrecorded net exports and a negative figure that there have been unrecorded net imports.

BALANCE IN THE BALANCE OF PAYMENTS

66 Distinguish accommodating from autonomous transactions 99

Because the balance of payments always balances, this does not imply that it never gives cause for concern. When discussing deficits or surpluses in the balance of payments, attention focuses on the current account because it is this account which records autonomous transactions. **Autonomous transactions** in the capital account simply ensure that the deficit is financed or the surplus disposed of. Balance in the accounts is achieved by **accommodating transactions** and, in the case of deficit countries at least, there is a limit on the ability of the authorities to sustain these. For instance, a deficit leads to an outflow of foreign currency reserves which are limited in value, or borrowings from abroad which are also limited by foreign perceptions of credit-worthiness, etc. Clearly, balance of payments deficits cannot be sustained indefinitely.

THE RATE OF EXCHANGE

Exchange rates are the rate at which one country's currency can be exchanged for other currencies in the foreign exchange market. There are various kinds of exchange rate system, but for simplicity economists identify two broad types: **floating exchange rates** and **fixed exchange rates**. The determination of exchange rates in each of these is considered in turn, but first we must clarify what is often a source of confusion over the use of terminology.

- In markets where exchange rates *float*, an increase in the external value of a currency is referred to as **appreciation** and a decrease in the external value of a currency is referred to as **depreciation**.

- In markets where exchange rates are *fixed*, when the authorities raise the external value of the currency to a higher fixed parity we refer to **revaluation**. A change to a lower fixed parity is referred to as **devaluation**.

FLOATING EXCHANGE RATES

Where exchange rates are allowed to float freely, the value of one currency in terms of others is determined by the operation of market forces, i.e. the interaction of demand for, and supply of, that currency in the market for foreign exchange.

DEMAND

Demand for foreign currency arises out of the desire to purchase another country's exports or to invest abroad. For example, the demand for sterling in the foreign exchange market arises partly from the desire of foreigners to purchase UK goods and services, or to invest in the UK. Like all normal demand curves, the demand for sterling varies inversely with its price. The reason for this is simple. Consider the external value of sterling in relation to American dollars; at a rate of exchange of £1 = $2, it is clear that £100 export from the UK costs an American importer $200. If the rate of exchange falls to £1 = $1.80, the same £100 export now costs an American importer only $180. At the lower price more British exports will be demanded. Consequently, as the rate of exchange falls, there will be a rise in the quantity of sterling demanded on the foreign exchange market to pay for these exports.

SUPPLY

Similarly, the supply of sterling on the foreign exchange market arises from the demand of UK importers for goods and services produced abroad, or from the desire to invest abroad. For example, in order to buy American exports UK importers will require dollars. These can be obtained through the foreign exchange market where sterling is exchanged for dollars. So the supply of sterling on the foreign exchange market is derived from the demand for imports into the UK, and from the need to purchase foreign currencies to finance UK investment overseas.

The supply curve
The supply curve for sterling (or any other currency) on the foreign exchange market will also be normal-shaped, with the supply of sterling varying directly with its international price. For example, if the current rate of exchange is £1 = $1.50, a $300 American export will cost an importer in the UK £200. However, if the rate of exchange increased to £1 = $1.60, the same good costing $300 in America would now have a price in the UK of £187.50. In other words, as the rate of exchange rises, the price of imports falls. At the lower domestic price we can assume that more imports will be demanded. It follows that as the rate of exchange increases there will be a rise in the quantity of sterling supplied to the foreign exchange market.

The equilibrium rate
In a free market, exchange rates will be determined by the interaction of demand for, and supply of, the currency. The rate established will be the **equilibrium rate** and there can be no deviation from this unless the *conditions* of demand or supply change. Figure 15.1 illustrates how the exchange rate for sterling against dollars is determined.

66 Finding the equilibrium rate 99

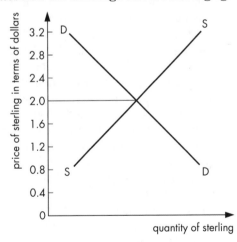

Fig. 15.1 The equilibrium rate of exchange

Figure 15.1 shows that, with demand and supply conditions given by DD and SS, the equilibrium exchange rate is £1 = $2. At any rate of exchange below this there will be a shortage of sterling and its exchange value will rise. At any rate above this, there will be a surplus of sterling and its exchange value will fall.

Factors influencing floating exchange rates
Demand for sterling is represented by DD and supply of sterling is represented by SS in Fig. 15.2. For simplicity, it is assumed that demand for, and supply of, sterling are both elastic so that as the sterling exchange rate rises, there is an increase in the quantity of sterling supplied and a reduction in the quantity of sterling demanded.

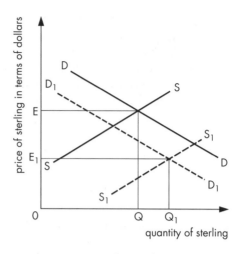

Fig. 15.2

Given the supply and demand conditions illustrated, the rate of exchange will settle at E; no other exchange rate can exist in the long run.

To answer the question of what factors determine the foreign exchange value of the pound sterling, it is therefore necessary to explain what determines the supply of, and demand for, sterling on the foreign exchange market. In fact, the state of the **current account** is usually seen as a major determinant of the exchange rate in the long run. If all other things remain equal, a current account *surplus* implies excess demand and appreciation for a country's currency and vice versa. However, the current account is important in another way. In particular, it indicates a country's ability to finance its overseas expenditures with overseas earnings. A current account surplus is therefore taken as a sign of economic strength and will attract investment from overseas residents seeking to place their funds in a strong currency. Countries with a strong current account therefore tend to have strong exchange rates, i.e. their currency is likely to appreciate against (some) other currencies.

Whether a country's current account is in surplus or deficit depends on several factors. One of the most important is undoubtedly **relative inflation rates**. When the rate of inflation in one country is high relative to its trading competitors, if other things stay the same, its exports will become less competitive on world markets and imports will become more competitive in the domestic economy. In terms of Fig. 15.2 this implies a reduction in demand for sterling from DD to D_1D_1 (as overseas residents demand fewer exports) and an increase in supply of sterling from SS to S_1S_1 (as UK residents demand more imports). In other words, the current account deteriorates and sterling depreciates on the foreign exchange market. The notion that relative inflation rates exert a powerful influence on the rate of exchange is embodied in the **purchasing power parity theory** which states that exchange rates will adjust until a unit of one currency exchanges for an amount of foreign currency which buys exactly the same basket of goods abroad that can be purchased in the domestic economy with a unit of currency. This can be expressed as $e = P/P^f$ where e is the exchange rate, P is the domestic price level and P^f is the foreign price level. However, strict purchasing power parity is unlikely to be observed because many goods are purchased domestically but are not traded internationally. Only the latter will affect the exchange rate. Nevertheless, there is little doubt that, in the long run, relative inflation rates are an extremely important determinant of exchange rates.

Another factor that influences the current account is **comparative advantage**. When technological change leads to the creation of different goods and services or changes the efficiency with which these can be produced by different countries, this can bring about changes in the state of the current account and result in some countries moving from surplus to deficit or deficit to surplus in certain key areas. The strength of Japan in producing motor cars and electronic equipment is a major reason for its strong current account surplus. For the UK, however, several sectors which were formerly strong in comparison with other countries have now declined in importance and this decline has not been fully offset by growth of other sectors.

Purchasing power parity and comparative advantage are undoubtedly the major *long-run* determinants of the sterling exchange rate and they exert this influence because of their effect on the **current account**. However, in the *short run*, the influence of other factors will be the major determinant of the sterling exchange rate and will exert their influence through changes in the **capital account**. The foreign exchange market responds quickly to expectations of future developments and short-term funds, or **hot money**, can be invested or withdrawn in response to favourable or unfavourable expected changes in the exchange rate. For example, an expected change in the price of oil is likely to have an immediate effect on the sterling exchange rate with an expected reduction in oil prices causing sterling to depreciate against other currencies and vice versa. Again this can be explained in terms of supply and demand. An expected depreciation of sterling will cause a reduction in demand for sterling as potential investors will prefer to invest in other currencies. It will also cause an increase in the supply of sterling as investors withdraw their funds from the UK and invest in other currencies. The combined effect will cause sterling to depreciate. Similarly, an expected change of government can cause depreciation of sterling if the foreign exchange market expects the new government to adopt monetary and fiscal policies that will cause a higher rate of inflation.

However, the major factor causing short-run changes in the sterling exchange rate is the **rate of interest** available on funds invested in the UK relative to rates available in other countries. An unanticipated increase in the rate of interest in the UK relative to that available in other countries will, if all other things remain the same, cause an appreciation of sterling and vice versa. This is simply because, if all other things remain the same, the increased return from investing in sterling will cause an inflow of funds (an increase in demand for sterling) and a reduced outflow of funds (a reduction in supply of sterling) as UK residents cut investment abroad.

The effect of an unanticipated reduction in the rate of interest on sterling can be illustrated in terms of Fig. 15.2. Supply of, and demand for, sterling are initially represented by SS and DD respectively and the rate of exchange is E. If all other things remain the same, an unanticipated reduction in UK interest rates shifts the demand curve for sterling to D_1D_1 and the supply curve of sterling to S_1S_1 and, as a result, the sterling exchange rate depreciates to E_1.

However, as previously explained, the foreign exchange market responds rapidly to **changes in expectations**. Because of this, changes in the rate of interest might not have an identifiable effect on the rate of exchange. For example, if the current account is *expected* to show a relatively large deficit, sterling would tend to depreciate in anticipation of the adverse figure being published. Because depreciation is expected, investors will attempt to withdraw their funds before depreciation thus avoiding the capital loss implied by depreciation. However, the government might not wish to see sterling depreciate and to avoid this might raise the rate of interest. In fact (to avoid any change in the exchange rate) interest rates will have to increase until the higher return from investing in the UK exactly matches the expected capital loss from depreciation.

In the long run, the main influence on the sterling exchange rate is the current account and this is determined mainly by the **rate of inflation** in the UK relative to inflation rates in competitors' countries. Changes in comparative advantage also have an effect in the long run. However, in the short run, changes in the rate of interest are the main influence on the sterling exchange rate.

FIXED EXCHANGE RATES

It is possible for governments to fix the external value of their currency in relation to other currencies. A fixed exchange rate is maintained by intervention through central banks in the foreign exchange market. Such intervention is designed to offset changes in the conditions of supply or demand in the foreign exchange market which would otherwise cause fluctuations in exchange rates. The way in which exchange rate stability is maintained by intervention is explained using Fig. 15.3.

Assume that the rate of exchange between sterling and dollar is fixed at £1 = $2 and that supply and demand conditions for sterling are initially represented by SS and DD respectively. If the UK demand for imports now increases, there will be an increase in the supply of sterling on the foreign exchange market shown by the shift in the supply to S_1S_1. This will cause downward pressure on the sterling exchange rate and in a free market its value would fall to around £1 = $1.60. However, because the authorities are committed to maintaining the exchange rate for sterling at £1 = $2, they will be forced to buy the excess supply of sterling (AB) that exists at this exchange rate, using dollars from the foreign exchange reserves. The *increased demand* for sterling is shown by an outward movement of the demand curve to D_1D_1 which exactly offsets the increase in supply and prevents any movement in exchange rates.

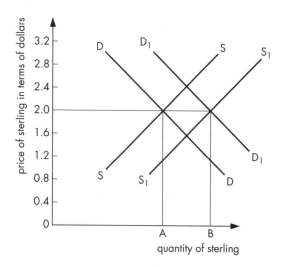

Fig. 15.3 Maintaining a fixed exchange rate

Whatever the cause of pressure on fixed exchange rates, the authorities must take action which *exactly offsets* changes in the conditions of supply or demand in the foreign exchange market if fixed parity values between different currencies are to be maintained. (You should check your understanding of this by considering what action the authorities would take to neutralise the effect of an increase in demand for sterling on the foreign exchange market.)

FIXED AND FLOATING EXCHANGE RATES COMPARED

ADVANTAGES OF FLOATING EXCHANGE RATES

Automatic adjustment to balance of payments disequilibrium

The main advantage of floating exchange rates is undoubtedly that it provides an *automatic* mechanism for the maintenance of balance of payments equilibrium. Thus, if demand for imports by the UK is rising relative to the rest of the world's demand for UK exports, there will be an *excess supply* of sterling on the foreign exchange market. This will cause the sterling exchange rate to depreciate, reducing the price of exports in foreign markets and raising the price of imports in the domestic market. As exports become cheaper foreigners will buy more of them, and as imports become more expensive fewer will be bought by domestic residents. It is therefore argued that currency depreciation will prevent the emergence of deficits on the balance of payments; equally, that currency appreciation will eliminate any emerging surplus.

66 Advantages of a floating rate 99

In practice, movements in exchange rates do not always eliminate deficits and surpluses as simply as implied here, and this aspect of exchange rates is examined more fully on pp. 293–296.

Greater freedom to pursue domestic goals

Because floating exchange rates make the balance of payments self-correcting, it is sometimes argued that governments are free to pursue whatever policies they wish in the domestic economy. Specifically, governments are more free to pursue policies designed to achieve full employment and economic growth. Under fixed exchange rates, a 'dash for growth' may result in an increase in imports—a balance of payments crisis—and therefore a deflation of domestic demand to curb imports. This is the familiar 'stop-go' cycle. The argument here is that the exchange rate will *automatically* fall to eliminate any emerging deficit and to reduce the need for any deflation of domestic demand. Again, this is something of an over-simplification, but there is general agreement that floating exchange rates give governments greater freedom of action in the domestic economy.

Economies in the use of foreign exchange reserves

Suppose there is pressure on the pound under a fixed exchange rate system, as was the case in Fig. 15.3 In this case, the Bank of England would no longer have to intervene to buy sterling with its gold and foreign exchange rate reserves in order to maintain the par value of £1 = $2. Under a floating system, the Bank of England can simply let the pound depreciate to £1 = $1.60, and will not have to purchase the excess supply of sterling AB. As a result, the Bank of England need not maintain gold and foreign exchange rates to as high a value under a floating system than under a fixed system.

Less speculative activity

The suggestion here is that a speculative movement of funds out of a currency could actually result in a *loss* under a floating system – unlike the fixed exchange rate system where no losses are incurred. With a fixed exchange rate system, the pressure builds up in one direction; for example, a country with a balance of payments deficit can hardly revalue its currency. All it can do is retain its present par value or devalue. In the first case, the speculator does not lose, should he/she have moved his/her money out of the currency; in the second case, he/she makes a speculative gain.

Suppose a speculator has £100m and that the initial rate of exchange is £1 = $2. If the UK has a balance of payments deficit he/she may move out of sterling for fear of devaluation. He /she now has $200m. If the UK does devalue to, say, £1 = $1, then he/she can return to sterling after the devaluation and receive $200m, i.e. a capital gain of $100m. If he/she is wrong and sterling resists devaluation, he/she can return to sterling and receive £100m, i.e. no loss, except for transactions costs (brokerage fees, etc.). This speculative activity was a major factor in sterling's withdrawal from the ERM and in the collapse of the ERM a year later. (see pp. 289–290 and p. 298).

The situation is different under a floating rate system because the possibility of a *loss* exists. If sterling moves in the opposite direction, i.e. appreciates to £1 = $4 say, then returning the $200m to sterling will only give £50m, a loss of £50m. The greater risk of losing via speculative activity under floating rates will, it is argued, result in *less* speculative activity.

These arguments constitute a powerful case for floating exchange rates. However, there are disadvantages and these are discussed below.

DISADVANTAGES OF FLOATING EXCHANGE RATES

Increased uncertainty

It is sometimes suggested that floating rates increase uncertainty in international trade. The possibility of changes in the external value of different currencies might deter long-term international investment or might make firms reluctant to negotiate long-run trade contracts with different countries. There is much greater certainty when foreign exchange rates are fixed.

Increased speculative activity

66 **There are also disadvantages!** 99

We have seen that an argument in favour of a floating system is that it allegedly deters speculative activity as there are now possibilities of losses. But there are also greater opportunities for gains, given the greater number of changes taking place in exchange rates. This might encourage speculative activity under floating exchange rates.

Increased volatility of exchange rates

Frequent short-run changes in exchange rates can have serious repercussions in the domestic economy. Where exchange rates float, flows of capital into a currency, attracted by higher short-term interest rates, can cause some currencies to appreciate; while flows of capital out of a currency can cause it to depreciate. When a country's currency appreciates, its exports become less competitive in world markets, and industries which produce import substitutes find it more difficult to compete in the domestic economy because imports become relatively cheaper. Conversely, when a country's currency depreciates, export and import competing industries boom. Where appreciation or depreciation is caused by a fundamental change in the pattern of world consumption or changes in a country's comparative advantage, these changes in exchange rates might be necessary and desirable. However, where exchange rates float, fluctuations can be caused by speculative flows in response to changes in short-term interest rates. Because of factor immobility such currency changes can lead to a serious misallocation of resources and cause unemployment. Where rates of exchange are fixed, intervention by the authorities in the foreign exchange market will avoid short-run fluctuations. Fundamental changes in supply or demand conditions for particular currencies can be accommodated by a change from one fixed parity to a lower or higher fixed parity, as appropriate.

IS SPECULATION DESTABILISING?

It was implied in the previous section that speculation can destabilise floating exchange rates. However, it can be argued that far from destabilising exchange rates, speculation acts as a *stabilising* influence! Remember that speculators buy when prices are low and sell when prices are high in order to realise speculative gains. They therefore add to demand when price is falling, thereby limiting the extent of any price reduction, and add to supply when price is rising, thereby limiting the extent of any price rise. The effect of speculation is therefore to limit the extent of movements in exchange rates.

Another way in which speculation might have beneficial effects is when speculators correctly anticipate the effect on exchange rates of any change in policy by the authorities. For example, a reduction in the rate of interest would normally lead to a depreciation of the exchange rate. However, when a reduction in the rate of interest is anticipated by speculators they will sell currency and thus move the exchange rate in the direction that it would have moved anyway. But since speculators sell currency at different times, the argument is the exchange rate will adjust more smoothly than the abrupt change that will follow an unanticipated reduction in interest rates.

Notwithstanding these arguments, capital flows are now so vast, and so easily converted from one currency into another, that it is possible for exchange rates to overshoot their underlying equilibrium rate because of speculation. **Overshooting** has serious implications for domestic industry such as a reduction in demand for exports because of an overpriced exchange rate. Because of this, to the extent that speculation causes overshooting, it should be considered harmful.

DIRTY FLOATING OR MANAGED FLEXIBILITY

Although fixed exchange rates were maintained between most of the world's major currencies for over 25 years after World War II, for most of the period since 1972 rates of exchange have been allowed to float. However, this does not necessarily imply that floating rates of exchange are superior to fixed rates, since there has been no commitment to allow exchange rates to float freely. The system that now exists is effectively a compromise between fixed and floating rates. The authorities often intervene to neutralise short-run pressure on exchange rates, but market forces now play a more important role in the determination of exchange rates. This exchange rate system is usually referred to as **managed flexibility**, although because the authorities do not always make it clear that they are using the reserves to support a currency's external value, the system is sometimes referred to as **dirty floating**.

EUROPEAN MONETARY SYSTEM (EMS)

There are two main strands to the EMS: the ERM and ecu. The ERM is the **exchange rate mechanism** whereby participating countries agree to maintain exchange rates *vis-à-vis* other participating countries within specified limits of the agreed central parity. Before the turmoil that beset the ERM in 1992–93, the agreed margins of fluctuation for most participating currencies was $\pm 2\frac{1}{4}$ per cent of the central parity. For Italy and the UK, the margins of fluctuation were ± 6 per cent. The agreed margins of fluctuation are currently ± 15 per cent of the central parity, though the Dutch have agreed that the guilder will continue to fluctuate against the Deutschmark by only $\pm 2\frac{1}{4}$ per cent.

The **ecu** is the European currency unit. The value of the ecu is determined by a weighted average basket of EU member currencies. Its value against any currency in the EMS is therefore relatively stable when compared with any other bilateral exchange rate. Because of this, the ecu is increasingly used as a unit of account and a great deal of private sector borrowing involves issuing bonds denominated in ecus. Thus for example, before the turmoil of 1993, the value of the Deutschmark against the ecu was 1 ecu = DM 2.05586. This implies that a firm which issued a 1,000,000 ecu bond could convert this into DM 2.05586m and, as long as the ERM continued to function as normal, this would be very close to the amount that would need to be repaid when the bond matured regardless of how sterling fluctuated against the Deutschmark. This facilitates borrowing abroad because firms are more certain of the amount they will have to repay when their debt matures. All countries participating in the ERM are given a *central rate* against the ecu and this is used to establish any bilateral exchange rate.

" Operation of the ERM "

For example, when sterling participated in the ERM its central rate was 1 ecu = £0.696904. From the Deutschmark rate given above, we can calculate what the central parity of sterling against the Deutschmark was, i.e. dividing 2.05586 by 0.696904 gives £1 = DM 2.95.

As well as having a margin of fluctuation against every other currency in the system, each currency in the ERM must, of course, have the same margin of fluctuation against the ecu. However, the margin of fluctuation against the ecu is used to generate a divergence indicator. When a currency diverges against its ecu rate by the agreed limit, there is a presumption that the authorities will intervene to prevent any further upward or downward movement of their currency against other currencies. In other words, intervention on the foreign exchange market commences *before* the limits of fluctuation are reached.

THE UK AND THE ERM

Why did the UK join the ERM?

The Government took the UK into the ERM in October 1990. At that time, the UK economy was moving into recession, inflation was rising and interest rates were at record levels. It was argued that, by joining the ERM, the Government would send a clear signal to those involved in fixing prices and wages that it was determined to adopt a strong anti-inflationary stance. In other words, if rising prices resulted in a loss of competitiveness, the exchange rate would not be adjusted downwards to restore competitiveness. The result of inflationary wage demands would therefore be unemployment as higher prices resulted in falling sales. It was hoped that this message would be clearly understood and that inflation would fall as the pace of wage settlements slowed.

66 Reasons for the UK joining the ERM 99

It was also argued that membership of the ERM would facilitate a cut in interest rates. There was a widely held view that interests rates in the UK were relatively high to prevent sterling from depreciating on the foreign exchanges. Such a depreciation might add a further twist to the inflationary spiral in two ways. First, rising import prices would lead directly to an increase in the RPI and would also have lagged effect as rising raw material and energy prices worked their way through to final prices. Second, falling export prices might encourage rising sales and profits in the export sector, which would weaken the resistance of exporting firms to wage demands from their employees. The likely effect of this would be to increase average pay awards in other sectors of the economy and so push up the rate of inflation. It was argued that inside the ERM interest rates could be cut, thus promoting economic recovery without causing a fall in the sterling exchange rate.

The consequences of UK membership of the ERM

The UK entered the ERM at a central rate of £1 = DM 2.95. Immediately after entry, UK interest rates were cut and continued to decline into 1991. Inflation also fell sharply and it appeared that the tough anti-inflationary stance adopted by the government and underlined by entry into the ERM had the desired effect of reducing wage increases. However, despite initially appearing fairly strong, the current account quickly deteriorated. As a result, sterling depreciated towards the floor of its ERM band and the UK government was forced to increase interest rates to prevent sterling falling through the floor.

Defending the exchange rate had a disastrous effect on the domestic economy. Higher interest rates deepened the recession for several reasons. One particular problem was that the property market remained depressed and this partly accounted for low levels of consumer spending. When people buy a house, they also tend to buy many new consumer durables. In addition, when the property market is depressed, the building industry is depressed and this adversely affects incomes and expenditure. Relatively high interest rates tend to depress investment across all sectors, and spending on consumer durables falls. Consumer spending is particularly important since it encourages production in consumer goods industries and, because of this, encourages investment.

Moreover, sterling was over-valued in the ERM and this placed exports at a competitive disadvantage in European markets. Imports from Europe, on the other hand, were increasingly competitive in the UK economy. Here again the effect was to deepen the recession in the UK.

UK withdrawal from the ERM

Events leading up to UK withdrawal from the ERM

By September 1992, it was clear that the value of sterling against its central rate was unsustainable without relatively high interest rates. However, it was also clear that recovery from recession was impossible without a cut in interest rates. The UK authorities tried unsuccessfully to persuade the Bundesbank to cut German interest rates which would facilitate a cut in UK interest rates by the same margin. However, the Bundesbank refused to cut German interest rates because of concern over the rate of growth of their own money supply. The result was that the markets increasingly came to expect a realignment of currencies in the ERM which would involve a devaluation of sterling. Wave after wave of speculative attacks followed until sterling's membership of the ERM was suspended in September 1992. (see pp. 298–299).

The collapse of the ERM

It is widely argued that reunification of Germany and, in particular, the way it was financed, was the major factor explaining the collapse of the ERM. The German authorities chose to finance reunification by borrowing rather than by raising taxes and the result of this was a rapid increase in the German money supply. As demand increased and prices rose, the Bundesbank increased interest rates to constrain money growth. On the foreign exchanges, this caused the Deutschmark to appreciate and, to ensure their currencies remained within the ERM band, other countries were forced to follow suit. The inevitable result was a deepening of the recession in Europe and increasingly the markets formed the view that a realignment of ERM parities was inevitable to allow a cut in interest rates. There was massive speculation against the weaker currencies in the system until it eventually collapsed. Italy and the UK have withdrawn from the ERM and, with the exception of Holland, those countries that remain in the ERM now maintain their currencies within relatively wide margins of fluctuation (± 15 per cent) against their central parity.

The future of the ERM

At the present time, the future of the ERM is uncertain. It is possible that, as the markets settle down, currencies will be returned to narrow bands of fluctuation against their central parity. The system will then operate as if nothing had happened. However, this is unlikely. The reunification of Germany has demonstrated that the ERM is vulnerable to economic shocks and although there will never be another reunification of Germany, there will certainly be other economic shocks in the future. Markets have learned, if they did not already know, that the ERM is like any other fixed exchange rate system; it can be destabilised by speculative flows and therefore gives speculators a one-way bet against weaker currencies.

Possible developments involving the ERM

It might be argued that one way to prevent speculative flows is to reintroduce capital controls which would raise the cost of speculation. However, this is also unlikely because it would reduce the gains from the single market and, in any case, if the markets felt devaluation was inevitable, the potential gains would outweigh the costs incurred as a result of capital controls.

Another option might be to proceed directly to **economic and monetary union (EMU)** and eliminate exchange rates altogether. When there is a single currency, there is no possibility of speculative activity. However, this has provoked considerable resistance in many countries.

The only other viable option is a **soft ERM** with wide bands of fluctuation and a greater willingness to adjust exchange rates as economic circumstances change. The problem is to agree on how wide the margins of fluctuation against the central parity should be. The margins must be wide enough to eliminate the one-way option that fixed exchange rates give to speculators, but narrow enough so as to retain the advantages of fixed exchange rates. Admittedly, with wide bands of fluctuation, exchange rates would move but at least the authorities could intervene to iron out the day-to-day fluctuations in the foreign exchange markets that arise as a result of the normal leads and lags in currency payments.

The real problem with a soft ERM would be the extent to which the authorities are committed to maintaining the fixed exchange rate. In the long run, a necessary condition to maintain any fixed exchange rate is that countries must have a similar rate of inflation. If the unemployment costs of reducing inflation to levels achieved in low-inflation countries are considered too high by the authorities in high-inflation countries then devaluation will almost certainly be the preferred option.

ECONOMIC AND MONETARY UNION (EMU)

EMU defined

Economic union implies the creation of a single market without barriers to trade, common competition and regional policies and co-ordination of macroeconomic policy-making. **Monetary union** involves irrevocably fixed exchange rates and the eventual establishment of a common currency.

Advantages and disadvantages of EMU

Much has been written about the desirability of EMU and its main *advantages*:

- **Greater specialisation and trade**   The elimination of barriers to trade will encourage greater specialisation and trade which will benefit all participants in the union.

- **Real resource savings**   The establishment of a common currency would eliminate the need to convert currencies in order to settle international indebtedness. This would free resources for alternative uses and one official estimate suggests that the savings from this alone would be equal to about 4 per cent of Community GDP. Resources would also be saved because it would no longer be necessary for central banks to hold reserves of foreign currency.

 Benefits of EMU

- **Greater efficiency in the allocation of resources**   With a single currency it is argued that there will be an improvement in the allocation of resources. One reason for this is that capital will move to where rewards are greatest. Another reason is that price differences will no longer be masked from consumers because they are in different currencies. This will increase competition and consumers will tend to buy in markets where goods are cheapest.

The *disadvantages* of EMU are equally easily summarised:

- **Loss of policy sovereignty**   The main problem with EMU is that it becomes impossible for a country to pursue its own monetary and exchange rate policies. A community-wide monetary policy would be implemented by the Community's central bank. The problem is that there is no guarantee that what is good for the Community would be good for each individual country. It might be possible for a country to do better outside of the union than inside it because it will be possible to vary monetary policy to achieve its own economic goals and use the exchange rate to ensure its goods remained competitive in domestic and international markets.

66 Problems of EMU 99

The importance of economic convergence

The Maastricht Treaty which was ratified in late 1993 laid down several *convergence criteria* that must be met before it would be possible for a country to proceed to EMU:

- A Member State will have participated in the narrow band of the ERM without severe tensions for at least two years and will not have initiated a devaluation of its bilateral central rate for at least the same period.

- A Member State will have an average rate of inflation for the twelve months preceding examination that does not exceed the rate in that of the three Member States with the lowest inflation by more than 1.5 percentage points.

66 Convergence criteria 99

- A Member State will have an average long-term rate of interest for the twelve months preceding examination that does not exceed the rate in that of the three Member States with the lowest rate of interest by more than 2 percentage points.

- The ratio for the planned or actual government deficit to GDP is fixed at 3 per cent.

- The ratio for government debt to GDP is fixed at no more than 60 per cent.

Stable currencies are clearly a crucial element in any move to EMU. This explains the importance of being in the narrow band of the ERM. It also explains the importance of similar rates of inflation and similar rates of interest. Convergence over the size of the budget deficit is important because it will be crucial in establishing convergent rates of money growth which is important if similar rates of inflation and similar rates of interest are to be achieved. Finally, the debt to GDP ratio is important because if this is rising, it will drive up interest rates and this might destabilise the exchange rate.

For many countries, convergence is still a long way off and the turmoil in the ERM of 1992 and 1993 has undoubtedly slowed down the momentum towards EMU. Whether the pace will increase as the foreign exchange markets settle down remains to be seen but there is clearly less enthusiasm for EMU now than there once was.

REAL AND EFFECTIVE EXCHANGE RATES

Throughout this chapter, we have ignored any ambiguity over our definition of exchange rate changes. Indeed, there is no ambiguity when exchange rates are fixed, because when one country changes the external value of its currency it does so by an equivalent amount against the currencies of all its trading partners. For example, when sterling was devalued by 14.3 per cent in November 1967, this was the rate of devaluation against all currencies. However, when exchange rates float it is possible for a currency to be appreciating against some currencies and depreciating against others. Alternatively, it might depreciate against some currencies by a greater amount than against other currencies, and so on. A more sophisticated measure of the exchange rate is then necessary in order to assess whether a particular currency is appreciating or depreciating.

One way would be able to take a straightforward *average* of the way one currency has moved against all other currencies. However, this would be unsatisfactory because some exchange rate changes are more important for a country than others. A second possibility would be to construct a **trade weighted index**. Such an index for the UK, for example, would show the value of sterling measured against an average of all other currencies weighted according to their importance as a trading partner. Here again, this is not entirely satisfactory because it takes no account of the fact that the UK does not only trade bilaterally with its partners, but also competes against them in world markets. It is necessary to take this fact into account when measuring the importance of exchange rate movements for a country's balance of payments.

❝ **Effective exchange rate** ❞

There is no universally accepted measure of the effective exchange rate for a currency, but the method used at the moment takes *both* factors mentioned above into consideration. So, in the case of the **effective exchange rate** for sterling, the weight attached to the dollar and to the Japanese yen are both greater than the share of UK exports to, or imports from, these countries. This is because both of these countries are important competitors for the UK in many world markets.

In summary, we can say that at present effective exchange rates are designed to answer the following question: 'What uniform percentage change in the sterling exchange rate against every other currency would have had the same effect on the UK's trade balances as the set of changes that have actually taken place?'

The real exchange rate

The **real exchange rate** is an index which takes account of differences in international rates of inflation on the competitiveness of exports and imports. For example, if sterling appreciates against the dollar by 5 per cent, this does not necessarily imply that UK goods will be 5 per cent more expensive relative to American goods. This will only be the case if there is no inflation in the UK or America. In this case, a 5 per cent appreciation in the *nominal* sterling exchange rate also implies a 5 per cent appreciation in the *real* sterling exchange rate. However, if there is a difference of inflation in one or both countries, changes in the nominal exchange rate will be different from changes in the real exchange rate. The real exchange rate is usually expressed as

❝ **Real exchange rate** ❞

$$e^r = \frac{eP}{P^*}$$

where e^r is the real exchange rate, e is the effective exchange rate, P^* is an index of foreign prices and P is an index of the domestic price level.

We can now see what happens to the *real* exchange rate if there is inflation in the UK of 10 per cent, inflation in other countries of 4 per cent and a 10 per cent depreciation of sterling. If we assume the effective exchange rate depreciates from 100 to 90, the result of these changes is ($90 \times 110/104 = 95.19$) a depreciation in the real effective exchange rate of about 4.81 per cent. In other words, some of the 10 per cent depreciation in the effective exchange rate of sterling has been *offset* by the higher relative inflation in the UK. The *real* exchange rate has depreciated by much less than 10 per cent (here 4.81 per cent).

When the value of the *real* exchange rate falls (either because of a relatively much lower domestic rate of inflation, a relatively higher rate of inflation abroad or because of a fall in the effective exchange rate), British goods become more competitive and vice versa.

INTERNATIONAL LIQUIDITY

International liquidity refers to the supply of internationally acceptable assets, i.e. those assets acceptable in settlement of an international debt. The main component of international liquidity is, of course, vehicle or reserve currencies such as the American dollar, but gold and Special Drawing Rights (SDRs) are also acceptable in settlement of a debt. SDRs are in an asset created by the International Monetary Fund (IMF) specifically to be used as international liquidity and, subject to certain restrictions, they are acceptable by all IMF member countries.

The growth of international liquidity is an important issue. If international liquidity does *not* grow at the same rate as the value of international trade, this will restrict the growth of trade. We have already noted the importance of specialisation and trade for the growth of output and therefore the growth of world living standards. An adequate supply of world liquidity is essential if trade is to continue to grow.

EXCHANGE RATE CHANGES AND BALANCE OF PAYMENTS ADJUSTMENT

Whether changes in the exchange rate succeed in removing a balance of payments deficit or surplus depends on many factors. We concentrate here on those factors which determine whether a downward movement in the exchange rate, i.e. devaluation or depreciation, will succeed in removing a balance of payments deficit. For simplicity, the use of the term depreciation here will refer to either. Whether revaluation or appreciation will succeed in removing a balance of payments surplus depends on the opposite set of factors.

Depreciation exerts its most powerful impact on the current account of the balance of payments. Before we formally consider the circumstances in which it will remove a balance of payments deficit, therefore, it is important to be clear about the way in which depreciation affects the prices of exports and imports. When a currency depreciates it reduces the *foreign price of exports*. For example, if sterling depreciates against the dollar from £1 = $1.20 to £1 = $1.10, then the price of a car exported to America which costs £10,000 in the UK falls from $12,000 before depreciation to $11,000 after depreciation. The sterling price of the car is unchanged: depreciation reduced the foreign price.

> 66 Impacts of depreciation 99

The situation is reversed for imports. Depreciation raises the *domestic price of imports*. Again, if sterling depreciates from £1 = $1.20 to £1 = $1.10, the price of a good imported by the UK which costs $2,400 in America rises from £2,000 to £2,181.80. The dollar price of the good is unchanged: depreciation raises the domestic price.

There are two broad approaches to the balance of payments adjustment: the **elasticities approach** and the **absorption approach**. Each is considered in turn.

THE ELASTICITIES APPROACH

This approach stresses the effect of *relative price changes* on the balance of payments. It implies that whether depreciation will remove a balance of payments deficit or not depends primarily on the price elasticity of demand for exports and for imports, since it is this above all else that determines the net change in the flow of funds to the current account following depreciation. If demand for exports is elastic (i.e. greater than one), depreciation will lead to a rise in foreign currency earnings because the proportionate increase in quantity sold will be greater than the proportionate reduction in price. However, the foreign price of imports is unchanged so that any reduction in the quantity bought will lead to a reduction in foreign currency expenditure. In other words, if elasticity of demand for imports is greater than zero, then depreciation will lead to a *fall in* foreign currency expenditure on imports.

The Marshall–Lerner condition

“ The Marshall–Lerner
elasticity condition „ „

The importance of these elasticities of demand are generalised in the **Marshall–Lerner condition**. This implies that depreciation will lead to an improvement in the balance of payments if the sum of the price elasticities of demand for exports and imports exceeds unity. The following example clarifies this.

Example: For simplicity the balance of payments is presented in foreign currency values. Assume sterling depreciates against the dollar by 10 per cent from £1 = $1.20 to £1 = $1.08. Thus export prices (which are denominated in foreign currency) fall in the ratio 0.12/1.20, i.e. a fall of 10 per cent. Import prices, on the other hand, (which are denominated in sterling) rise in the ratio 0.12/1.08, a rise of 11.1 per cent. (This is easily verified. A good costing $1.20 in America costs a UK importer £1 before depreciation and £1.11 after depreciation, an increase of 11.1 per cent.) If the elasticity of demand for exports is 1.6 and the elasticity of demand for imports is 1.5, the effect on the balance of payments of this depreciation is easily demonstrated.

Initial balance of payments position

Exports ($M)	Imports ($M)
2,000	2,100

Sterling depreciates by 10 per cent

$$\text{Elasticity of demand} = \qquad \text{Elasticity of demand} =$$

$$1.6 = \frac{\%\,\Delta QX}{\%\,\Delta PX} \qquad\qquad 1.5 = \frac{\%\,\Delta Qm}{\%\,\Delta Pm}$$

therefore $\%\,\Delta QX = 16\%$ therefore $\%\,\Delta Qm = 16.65\%$

After depreciation

Exports ($M)	Imports* ($M)
2,145.6	1,750.35

*The relationship between total revenue (expenditure) and elasticity of demand was discussed in Chapter 4. Care must be taken when measuring the change in import expenditure, however, because the foreign price of imports is unchanged. This implies that a 16.65 per cent reduction in quantity demanded will lead to a 16.65 per cent reduction in foreign currency expenditure on imports. It is a good idea to work out several examples of your own to satisfy yourself of the importance of the Marshall-Lerner condition.

'J' curve effect

However, over time, demand for exports and imports is much more elastic. Patterns of consumption and investment flows change in response to the price changes brought about by depreciation. Because of this, depreciation only leads to an improvement in the balance of payments in the long run. The initial deterioration and subsequent improvement in the balance of payments is usually referred to as the 'J' curve effect. The adverse initial impact on the balance of payments is often thought to average around 18 months or so. The general effect is illustrated in Fig. 15.4.

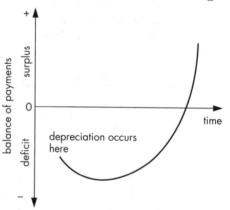

Fig. 15.4 The 'J' curve effect

It seems that, so long as the elasticity conditions are favourable, depreciation will lead to an improvement in the balance of payments position. However, elasticity conditions are unlikely to be favourable in the short run. It takes time for people to adjust their patterns of consumption and to change their investment plans. The result is that depreciation *initially* leads to an increased balance of payments deficit. Foreign currency spending on imports is largely unchanged, because much the same quantity of imports are consumed at an unchanged foreign price. On the other hand, foreign currency earnings fall because much the same volume of exports are sold at a lower foreign price. Hence, initially, the balance of payments deteriorates after depreciation.

THE ABSORPTION APPROACH

This analysis of balance of payments adjustment is based on the income accounting identity.

$$Y = C + I + G + X - M$$

which can be rewritten as

$$Y - (C + I + G) = X - M$$

i.e. $\quad Y - A = X - M$

Where A = domestic absorption.

This implies that the balance of payments of a country is equal to domestic income minus domestic expenditure (or *absorption*). A deficit on the balance of payments will exist when the country absorbs more goods and services than it produces, i.e. when (C + I + G) exceeds Y.

It follows from this that depreciation or devaluation can only succeed if it increases domestic output (income) relative to absorption, or reduces absorption relative to domestic output (income). The absorption approach therefore places much more emphasis on the *level of domestic demand* as the main determinant of the balance of payments position rather than on relative price levels.

The absorption approach shows that, when there is full employment in the economy, it is impossible to raise domestic output (income) and therefore it is necessary to deflate the domestic economy in order to reduce absorption and to release resources for export production. However, elasticities are still important. Simply depressing domestic demand does not guarantee that the resources released will be transferred into export production, though it is usually effective in reducing demand for imports.

GENERAL PROBLEMS OF ADJUSTMENT

Despite the general predictions of these two approaches to the balance of payments adjustment, there are other factors which have an important influence on the effect of depreciation. Essentially both approaches are *static*. In the real world, there are other dynamic factors to consider. These include the following.

Income effects
If depreciation succeeds in reducing the flow of imports, it will bring about a reduction in the national income of those countries whose exports, which are the counterpart of these imports, have fallen. As income in these countries falls, their own ability to import from the depreciating country will fall. This will have a particularly significant effect where demand for imports in these countries is *income elastic*. Additionally, it is possible that falling national income will tend to reduce the pressure on prices and make exports from these countries more competitive. This will be particularly important where demand for their exports is *price elastic*. Because of these income (and price) effects in the foreign country even if export revenues rise for the domestic country after depreciation, they might subsequently fall. Similarly, any reduction in domestic imports might be subsequently reversed. To the extent that income (and price) effects operate in this way, depreciation will not necessarily be successful in the long run.

Domestic inflation
A potentially serious problem following depreciation is domestic inflation, especially where imports consist of raw materials. Rising import costs can quickly erode any price advantages conferred by depreciation, resulting in a continuing deficit on the balance of payments.

66 **Problems for an exchange rate depreciation** 99

Price adjustments

Just as inflation can wipe out the gains from depreciation, administered price changes can have the same effect. In the export market, instead of offering lower foreign prices following depreciation, there is some evidence that firms raise domestic prices and in so doing retain foreign prices at the pre-depreciation level. For example, following depreciation of sterling from £1 = $1.20 to £1 = $1.08, a product costing £10,000 in the domestic market would cost a foreign importer $12,000 before depreciation and (all other things remaining the same) $10,800 after depreciation. However, if the domestic price was increased from £10,000 to £11,111, depreciation would have an imperceptible impact on the foreign price.

Exporters

Exporters might have many reasons for wishing to maintain price stability. It avoids the threat of retaliation by foreign firms and the possibility of a damaging price war. Where a multi-national corporation has subsidiaries in many countries it might wish to avoid competition between these by administering price changes to offset those brought about by depreciation. Probably most important of all, however, is that by raising domestic prices (and keeping the foreign price constant) firms are able to increase profits. The same volume of goods and services are sold but at a higher price. For whatever reason, to the extent that prices are adjusted in the way described above, the effect will be to mitigate the gains from depreciation.

POLICIES TO DEAL WITH A BALANCE OF PAYMENTS DEFICIT

Broadly, there are three courses open to deficit countries: depreciation of the currency, deflation of the domestic economy, or some form of direct restriction on imports. In practice, countries are unlikely to adopt only one of these to the exclusion of the others and might even adopt a combination of all three.

- **Depreciation** This involves lowering the exchange rate with the aim of increasing receipts from abroad and reducing expenditures on imports. The success of this policy in removing a deficit therefore depends on the elasticities of demand for exports and imports. However, it also depends on whether rising import prices leads to a higher domestic rate of inflation. If this happens, the relative advantage conferred by depreciation will quickly be eroded.

“ Dealing with a balance of payments deficit ”

- **Deflation** Deflating the level of aggregate demand works in two ways:
  - As demand and output fall, the ability to buy imports falls.

  - In the longer term, deflation reduces the domestic rate of inflation, and so increases the competitiveness of exports.

  The attraction of this policy is that if it is severe enough, deflation will always remove a balance of payments deficit. The disadvantage is that it works by depressing domestic income, which lowers living standards and increases unemployment. Moreover, deflation does not offer a permanent means of removing a balance of payments deficit — unless the level of demand is permanently depressed. As soon as demand is expanded the deficit will reappear.

- **Restricting imports** Restrictions on imports can take several forms: tariffs, quotas, subsidies on domestic products and so on — although none of these is an option available to the UK because of its membership of the EU. Such measures will probably be successful in the short run but have considerable disadvantages. They might provoke retaliation, lead to higher prices and encourage inefficiency overall, resulting in a less efficient allocation of resources (see Ch. 14).

APPLIED MATERIALS

RECENT CHANGES IN THE UK BALANCE OF PAYMENTS

Figure 15.5 shows how the visible balance, the invisible balance and the current account have changed over recent years.

Throughout the period shown, the invisible account remained in surplus. In the early part of the period there was also a surplus in visible trade which was mainly due to a surplus from trade in oil. However, for the UK, the trade balance has traditionally been weak and for most of the period shown there have been substantial deficits which

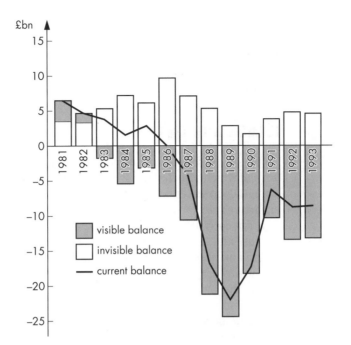

Fig. 15.5 The visible and invisible balance, and the current account 1984–92 (*Source*: HMSO)

have not been offset by invisible surpluses. The current account has therefore been in deficit since 1986.

The state of the trade balance is extremely important since changes in exports and imports have an important bearing on the real economy and in particular on output and employment. In the longer run, a persistent deficit, if it cannot be offset by a surplus on invisibles, will have serious implications. It will handicap the conduct of macroeconomic policy. Its effects will be to increase instability of exchange rates and/or interest rates as the UK becomes dependent on inflows of hot money to finance the deficit (cf. UK experience in the ERM — see pp. 299–300). Higher interest rates are also likely to cause a reduction in real investment and therefore in economic growth. The current account deficit might also be financed by increased sales of assets to overseas firms and residents which, in the long run, will lead to an increased outflow of interest, profits and dividends.

Of course, a deficit on visible trade is not necessarily a problem. For example, if the deficit is caused by imports of capital goods which might be expected to increase productivity, a deficit might be thought desirable. The problem for the UK is that this is not the case. Imports of capital goods are relatively small compared to imports of consumer durables. The current account deficit is most certainly a cause for concern!

Another recent trend in the UK balance of payments is the extent to which trade is increasingly European. Figure 15.6 shows how the proportion of imports and exports *vis-à-vis* Europe have grown at the expense of trade with the rest of the world. This, of

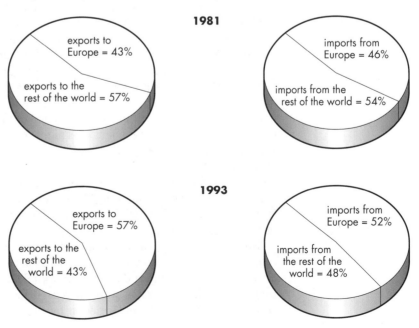

Fig. 15.6 Geographical changes in UK visible trade 1981–93 (*Source*: HMSO)

course, is precisely what might be expected. As restrictions in the European block are dismantled, it is inevitable that trade will grow, but the trend has probably been increased by the emergence of other trading blocs such as the North American Free Trade Association. The UK's increasing trade with Europe underlines the importance of stability in the European foreign exchange market.

TURMOIL WITH THE ERM

An article in the *OECD Economic Outlook*, May 1993, outlines the reasons for the turmoil which afflicted the ERM in 1992. It also outlines the lessons that can be drawn from the crisis and provides a case study of the problems of sustaining a fixed exchange rate.

From early 1987 until June 1992, the ERM experienced an unprecedented period of stability and the only realignments of currencies during this period were technical in nature and occurred because the Italian lira moved to the narrow band of the ERM and because the Spanish peseta, the UK pound sterling and the Portuguese escudo all joined the system. The stability of the ERM was underpinned by parallel cyclical movements in most Community countries and there was increasing convergence on a broad range of macroeconomic fronts including the rate of inflation and the crucial interest rate differential.

Towards the end of 1991 and into 1992, there were early signs of the turmoil that was to come. Sterling had drifted to the bottom of its ERM floor, the Finnish markka, which had been informally linked to the ecu, was devalued in November, and interest rates in all European countries with the exception of the UK had been increased. Nevertheless, the markets remained fairly calm until the Danish 'no' vote in the Maastricht referendum on 2 June 1992. This caused the markets to question the reality of an early route to EMU and, with it, the likelihood of greater economic convergence.

Increasingly, macroeconomic *divergence* was becoming apparent. The fiscal situation in Italy was becoming critical. By 1992, the public sector deb/GDP ratio had risen to around 100 per cent and in spring, the budget deficit exceeded its target. The implied increase in money growth signalled to the markets higher inflation and downward pressure on the lira.

Another important trend began in March, when the dollar depreciated sharply on the foreign exchanges. While this affected competitiveness in general, it was particularly significant for the UK and deepened what was already a severe recession. This fuelled growing criticism of the Government's policy and increased pressure for a cut in interest rates. However, in mid-July, hopes of an early cut in interest rates were dashed when the Bundesbank raised the discount rate because the growth in M3 (a measure of broad money) exceeded its target range and this further increased pressure on sterling.

Pressure on sterling intensified to the extent that on August 28, the EU finance ministers issued a statement ruling out any realignment of currencies in the ERM. This was a blatant attempt to calm the markets. However, the markets were unconvinced and turbulence increased to the point when, in early September, the EU finance ministers issued another statement again ruling out any realignment of the ERM.

However, the markets remained unconvinced and the continuing weakness of the dollar precipitated the crisis. In early September, the ecu-pegging of the Finnish markka was terminated after massive capital outflows. The Swedish krona came under pressure next and, at one point, overnight interest rates were raised to 75 per cent. Attention then switched to the lira and, by September 11, it was subject to massive speculative attacks because dealers anticipated a devaluation. Their expectation proved correct and, during the weekend of September 12 and 13, a realignment was agreed in which the lira was devalued by 3.5 per cent and the Bundesbank gave a commitment to lower interest rates. Within days, it had cut its crucial Lombard rate by three quarters of 1 per cent.

However, these measures did not satisfy the markets and, after the French referendum on Maastricht, pressure intensified and there were speculative attacks against the lira, sterling and the pesata with dealers sensing the possibility of a further realignment. Interest rates were increased in Italy and Spain, but the depth of the recession discouraged similar action by the authorities in the UK. Despite massive intervention to preserve the foreign exchange value of sterling, the battle was lost and on 16 September, sterling was temporarily withdrawn from the ERM.

One point that is clear from these events is that, if there is macroeconomic divergence between countries, dealers will come to expect a change in exchange rates. Under a fixed exchange rate system, they have a one-way option and, without exchange controls, the speculative flows that can be mobilised can result in irresistible pressure unless the authorities are prepared to allow interest rates to rise to whatever level is necessary to curb pressure.

EXAMINATION QUESTIONS

1   Explain what is meant by the balance of payments deficit and whether or not a deficit on the visible balance should be regarded as a problem by the Government. Discuss the factors responsible for the UK's foreign trade record in recent years and evaluate their importance for the future economic performance of the economy.

(JMB 1993)

2   (a) Distinguish between a country's terms of trade and its balance of trade.   *(10)*
    (b) Discuss how both might be affected by a fall in the country's exchange rate.

(15)

(AEB Nov 1992)

3   (a) Explain how exchange rates are determined in:
       (i) a floating rate system
       (ii) a fixed rate system   *(50)*
    (b) With reference to recent experience in the UK, examine the arguments for, and against, a floating exchange rate system.   *(50)*

(ULEAC June 1993)

4   (a) What does Fig. 15.7 show about the movement of the foreign exchange rate of
       (i) the Japanese yen and
       (ii) the dollar during the period shown?   *(2)*
    (b) With respect to Japan and the USA, examine how these movements in the foreign exchange rate could explain changes in the volume of exports and imports during the period shown in Fig. 15.8.   *(8)*
    (c) What other economic effects might these movements in the foreign exchange rate have had on either the USA or Japan?   *(6)*
    (d) Despite an appreciation of the German Deutschmark between 1986 and 1991, Germany's exports actually increased. How might this be explained?   *(4)*

(ULEAC June 1993)

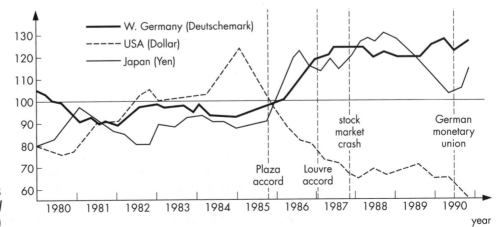

Fig. 15.7 Indices of exchange rates (1985 = 100) (*Source: The Financial Times,* 17 June 1991)

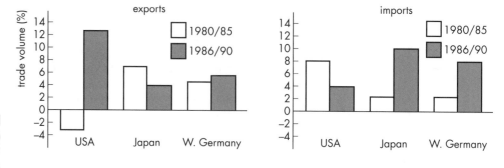

Fig. 15.8. Growth of trade – annual percentage change (in volume) (*Source: The Financial Times,* 17 June 1991)

ANSWERS TO EXAMINATION QUESTIONS

TUTOR'S ANSWER TO QUESTION 1

The balance of payments account records a country's financial transactions with the rest of the world for a given period such as a month, a quarter or a year. It includes purchases and sales of goods and services, gifts, government transactions and capital flows.

In the UK, the balance of payments consists of two broad accounts: the current account, which records trade in goods and services; and transactions in assets and liabilities, which largely consists of investment flows and loans. The current account consists of autonomous transactions whereas transactions in assets and liabilities includes accommodating transactions, i.e. those transactions necessary to finance current account transactions.

A balance of payments deficit on the visible balance implies that imports of goods exceeds exports of goods. This might not necessarily be a cause for concern for any of a number of reasons. Most obviously, a visible trade deficit might simply be a short-term phenomenon which will disappear over time. Indeed, such a deficit might occur naturally as the result of the trade cycle. When the economy is moving out of the recession imports of machinery, raw materials and semi-finished manufactures increase while exports tend to be diverted to the expanding domestic economy.

Another important factor to consider is the state of the invisible account. The UK almost invariably records a surplus on invisibles and, in this case, a visible deficit can be offset by an invisible surplus. Even if there is an overall deficit on the current account, this is not necessarily a problem if the deficit is short term. So long as the reserves can finance the deficit or there are compensating inflows of capital funds, it is unlikely that the authorities will be concerned with the visible trade deficit.

The situation is different if the deficit is persistent and rising. The deficit on the visible balance would be particularly disturbing if the invisible balance was shrinking and/or if the visible deficit was the result of increased consumer spending on imports matched by a declining preference in world markets for UK goods. For the UK, such a situation implies a declining manufacturing sector, i.e. deindustrialisation. The consequences of this might be rising unemployment and a slower rate of economic growth. In the longer term, it implies that the UK will become dependent on the rest of the world for an increasing amount of visible output with no guarantee that the rest of the world will require an increasing amount of invisible output from the UK. Since no country can borrow indefinitely, the Government might be very concerned with a visible deficit in these circumstances.

The UK's visible balance is almost invariably in the red. Towards the end of the 1980s, the deficit began to shrink after reaching record levels. Despite this, the visible deficit remains relatively high and was over £10bn in 1991. By any standards the UK has a poor record on visible trade!

It has been alleged that one reason for the poor UK performance in world markets is partly due to the fact that UK elasticity of demand for world products grows faster than world income elasticity of demand for UK products. This implies that as world income grows, world demand for UK exports will grow more slowly than UK demand for imports. This implies that the visible balance will inevitably move into deficit unless the UK economy grows more slowly than our major trading partners. The UK's poor trade performance might therefore be due to attempts to increase growth in the UK economy to levels achieved in other countries. It is further alleged that, as the UK economy grows, exports are diverted to the buoyant, and relatively secure, home market thus causing the trade balance to deteriorate.

It is sometimes suggested that the UK has concentrated production in commodity groups where demand is falling. In fact, an analysis of UK exports indicates that these are in the same broad commodity groups as our major competitors. The problem appears to be an inability to compete *within* these commodity groups. There is some evidence that, in recent years, the UK has tended to export lower quality products which embody old technologies and antiquated skills. This would certainly account for the UK's relatively poor export performance and the attractiveness of imports for UK consumers.

There is a great deal of anecdotal evidence that the UK's relatively poor export performance and relatively high import penetration ratio is at least partly due to inadequate marketing by UK firms. In particular, UK firms are frequently criticised for their poor after-sales service, poor delivery and, in certain cases, product design. Such allegations are difficult to test but if correct they would certainly have an adverse effect on the balance of trade.

It has also been alleged that many UK products are not price competitive in world markets while imports are highly competitive in the domestic market. If this is true, it would explain falling world demand for UK products and an increased preference for imports by the UK. During the UK's membership of the ERM there was certainly some suggestion that sterling was overvalued. Despite this, the evidence, though not entirely conclusive, and in any case fraught with data collection problems, suggests that lack of price competitiveness is again only a minor part of any explanation of the UK's poor trade performance in recent years.

The disappointing UK trade balance is significant for several reasons. Exports are an injection into the circular flow and imports are a leakage from the circular flow. Slow growth of exports and high growth of imports implies slow growth of aggregate demand which some economists argue might adversely affect investment, employment and economic growth. Another important consideration is that the trade balance looks to be in a situation of perpetual decline. This is disturbing because, for the UK, a deteriorating trade balance implies a declining manufacturing sector and there is no guarantee that invisibles will go on rising to offset the visible deficit. The problem for the UK will therefore be how to pay for the growing quantity of manufactures that will be imported.

In summary, whether or not a balance of trade deficit is a cause for concern depends on the nature of the deficit. If it is short term and/or can easily be financed, it is unlikely to be a problem. There is certainly some concern about the UK's trade performance in recent years. It seems that no single factor is sufficient on its own to explain UK trade performance. Instead, there are several factors each of which has had an adverse effect on the trade balance.

STUDENT'S ANSWER TO QUESTION 2

(a) The **terms of trade** are the rate at which a country's exports exchange against its imports. They are usually measured by the formula:

$$\frac{\text{Index of export prices} \times 100}{\text{index of import prices}}$$

66 An unusual way to express this 99

The terms of trade improve when the terms of trade index rises, and deteriorate when the terms of trade index falls.

66 Give an example to illustrate 99

The **balance of trade** is an account of the value of exports and the value of imports over a given period of time, such as a year. When the value of exports exceeds the value of imports the balance of trade is in

66 Mention *visibles* as opposed to *invisibles* – often called balance of visible trade 99

Good

surplus, and when the value of imports exceeds the value of exports the balance of trade is in deficit.

(b) The terms of trade and the exchange rate are related because changes in the exchange rate cause changes in the prices of exports and imports. For example, if the exchange rate is initially £1 = 1.5DM, then a good which costs £10 in the UK will cost 15DM in Germany and a good which costs 30DM in Germany will cost £20 in the UK. Now if sterling appreciates against the Deutschmark to £1 = 2DM, the good which formerly cost 15DM in Germany will now cost 20DM and the good which formerly cost £20 in the UK will now cost £15 in the UK.

Correct – but very badly expressed

It is clear from this example that an appreciation of the exchange rate will cause a rise in the price of exports and a fall in the price of imports. This implies an improvement in the terms of trade. Conversely, depreciation of the exchange rate will cause a fall in the price of exports and a rise in the price of imports. This implies a deterioration in the terms of trade.

You need to develop this point more fully

The terms of trade and the balance of trade are also related because changes in the terms of trade are likely to cause changes in the balance of trade. When the terms of trade rise, export prices rise by more than import prices and this will cause changes in demand for exports and imports. The effect of changes in the prices of exports and imports depends on the elasticity of demand. When the elasticity of demand for exports and imports is relatively small (less than one when added together) a fall in the terms of trade will cause an improvement in the balance of trade!

Good – you are talking about the Marshall–Lerner elasticity condition

In practice, whether this happens depends on whether all other things remain the same. If they do not, we cannot be sure that a deterioration in the terms of trade will improve the balance of trade. If there is full employment in the domestic economy, it will not be possible to increase the supply of exports after their prices fall and this will have an adverse effect on the balance of trade. Similarly depreciation will lead to a rise in the price of imported raw materials and this will cause an increase in final prices. Domestic inflation following depreciation will quickly wipe out any competitive advantage gained from depreciation.

Good point

Part (a) could have been developed a little further. Some good points made in part (b) – not always clearly expressed.

OUTLINE ANSWERS

Question 3

(a) (i) When exchange rates float they are determined by the forces of supply and demand. It is important to stress that, in a free floating regime, there is no interference by the authorities to influence the exchange rate. The determination of the exchange rate in a floating system is explained on p.283 and you should include in your analysis some examples of factors which will cause the exchange rate to change.

(ii) A fixed exchange rate system implies that exchange rates have a fixed value against each other, or against some commodity such as gold. There is usually some degree of flexilibity, but the point to stress is that when exchange rates are fixed, flexibility is limited and specified. You should explain the techniques available to the authorities for maintaining a fixed exchange rate.

(b) The experiences of the UK in the ERM would provide a useful case-study approach to answering this part of the question.

The main advantages of floating rates over fixed rates are as follows:

■ Floating rates offer an automatic means of eliminating balance of payments surpluses and deficits. When the UK was in the ERM, there was a massive balance of payments deficit which was deteriorating.

■ Under a floating rate regime, the balance of payments constraint on economic policy is removed. The authorities can therefore concentrate policy on the domestic economy. During UK membership of the ERM, as the balance of payments deteriorated, it was clear that sterling had become overvalued and interest rates were increased to maintain the exchange rate. This combination thrust the UK economy into recession.

■ Fixed exchange rates give speculators a one-way option. It was severe speculative flows that precipitated UK withdrawal from the ERM and subsequently precipitated the system's virtual collapse.

■ Because floating exchange rates adjust continuously to the flow of new information, adjustment is relatively smooth. When fixed exchange rates are adjusted, there is a severe shock to the economy.

■ When exchange rates float, there is no need for the government to hold such a large quantity of reserves which then become available for domestic purposes.

The main disadvantages of floating rates are equally easily summarised:

■ When exchange rates float, the adjustment mechanism might not work as smoothly as implied. There might be relatively low price elasticities of demand or relatively low elasticity of supply so that depreciation might actually exacerbate a balance of payments deficit or appreciation increase a balance of payments surplus.

■ Freed of the balance of payments constraint, governments might implement expansionary policies which overheat the economy. This possibility was frequently discussed when the UK left the ERM and there was concern over the effect of a depreciating exchange rate and falling interest rates on the rate of inflation.

■ Because the exchange adjusts continuously to the flow of new information floating exchange rates might be unstable, and it is alleged that this will hamper the growth of international trade and make it difficult for the private sector to plan investment decisions.

■ Destabilisation of the exchange rate might be increased because of speculative flows motivated in response to some international shock such as a rise in the price of oil.

Question 4

(a) Only a brief discussion is necessary here.

(i) The yen rose and fell between 1980 and mid-1982. It appreciated again at the end of 1982 and was then fairly steady until the end of 1985 when it appreciated sharply. Despite fluctuations, its upward trend continued until towards the end of 1988 when it fell sharply. It appreciated again from about mid-1990.

(ii) In general, the American dollar appreciated against other currencies until the end of 1982, when it fell slightly. It remained fairly stable throughout 1983 and then rose sharply during 1984 and into the early part of 1985. It then depreciated by almost 50 per cent by the end of 1987 and despite a slight appreciation between 1988 and most of 1989, it subsequently depreciated until the end of the period.

(b) Changes in exchange rates change the foreign price of exports and the domestic price of imports. You could explain this with a simple arithmetic example and then go on to explain the importance of elasticity of demand in bringing about volume changes in response to price changes. It is important to illustrate your points with reference to the information in Figs 15.7 and 15.8. You should also briefly mention other relevant factors such as the elasticity of supply and so on.

(c) A whole range of possibilities could be discussed here. For example the appreciation of the dollar in the early part of the period probably led to a deterioration in the current account. The growth in the volume of imports and fall in the volume of exports implies falling national income and rising unemployment. Rising unemployment and falling tax revenues implies rising government expenditures which, through its affect on the money supply, might have generated inflation. Rising import prices might also have been a source of inflationary pressure. However, as the budget deficit was brought under control and the economy slowed down, inflation would be likely to fall. The mechanism would be reversed in the latter part of the period.

(d) Clearly, demand for Germany's exports was inelastic during the period mentioned. This might partly be because of changes in the prices of competing products. For example, until about the end of 1988, imports from Japan would be rising in price. However, there are also non-price factors to consider such as design, delivery, after-sales service, product reputation and so on.

Further reading

Begg, Fischer and Dornbush, *Economics* (3rd edn), McGraw-Hill 1991. Ch. 33, The International Monetary System and International Finance.

Griffiths and Wall, *Applied Economics: An Introductory Course* (6th edn), Longman 1995. Ch. 24, Exchange Rates; Ch. 25, The United Kingdom Trade Performance.

Harrison, *International Trade and Finance*, Longman 1987: Ch. 4, The Foreign Exchange Market and Exchange Rate Systems; Ch. 5, The International Monetary System.

Harrison et al, *Introductory Economics*, Macmillan 1992; Ch. 32, The Balance of Payments; Ch. 33, Exchange Rate Systems.

REVIEW SHEET

1 Define the following:
Autonomous transactions:

Accommodating transactions:

Double-entry bookkeeping:

Trade balance:

Current account:

Long-term capital flows:

2 Present a diagram for a floating exchange rate system. Use your diagram to explain what will happen to the exchange rate if, other things remaining the same, exports increase.

Explanation:

3 Explain what will now happen to the exchange rate if capital outflows increase.

4 Briefly outline four advantages of a floating exchange rate system.
(a)

(b)

(c)

(d)

5   Briefly outline three possible disadvantages of a floating exchange rate system.

(a) _____

_____

(b) _____

_____

(c) _____

_____

6   Briefly describe the main features of the European Monetary System (EMS).

_____

_____

_____

_____

_____

7   Outline the Marshall-Lerner elasticity condition.

_____

_____

_____

8   If the Marshall–Lerner condition is fulfilled, what effect will a fall in the exchange rate have on the balance of payments?

_____

_____

_____

_____

_____

9   Explain the 'J' curve effect.

_____

_____

_____

_____

_____

10 What does the absorption approach tell us about policy for correcting a balance of payments deficit?

_____

_____

_____

_____

_____

_____

_____

_____

_____

PUBLIC FINANCE

BORROWING REQUIREMENTS

THE PSBR AND THE MONEY SUPPLY

THE NATIONAL DEBT

TAXATION

THE STRUCTURE OF TAXATION

THE INCIDENCE OF TAXATION

TAXATION POLICY

REFORM OF THE TAX SYSTEM

APPLIED MATERIALS

GETTING STARTED

In the UK, the main instrument of fiscal policy is the government's annual **budget**. Traditionally, the budget contains a record of government revenue and expenditure for the year gone by, as well as the government's plans for raising revenue to meet planned expenditure during the coming year. The main reasons for public expenditure are discussed on pages 322–323 and page 326 as well as in parts of Chapter 17.

When planned expenditure exceeds planned revenue, a budget deficit exists. This is important because it implies a net increase in injections into the circular flow of income. However, a budget deficit is financed by **borrowing**, and, in recent years, more attention has been paid to the effect of increased government borrowing on the money supply. The **National Debt** is the total accumulated sum of all outstanding government debt.

Government revenue is raised mainly from **taxation**, and it is customary to distinguish between *direct* and *indirect* taxation. One distinction is that direct taxation is collected by the Department of Inland Revenue and indirect taxation is collected by the Customs and Excise Department.

In this chapter there is quite a lot of statistical information on government revenue and expenditure. This is deliberate. Familiarity with this type of information will often prove invaluable in coping with examination questions on this topic!

ESSENTIAL PRINCIPLES

THE BUDGET

The Budget is an occasion when the Chancellor presents an account of government expenditure and revenue for the financial year about to end and presents his other estimates of revenue and expenditure for the coming financial year to Parliament.

Where it comes from	(£bn)	Where it goes	(£bn)
Income tax	64.4	Social security	83.0
National insurance contributions	42.8	Local government	71.7
Value added tax	42.1	Health	31.7
Excise duties	27.1	Defence	23.5
Corporation tax	17.6	Debt interest	22.8
Other receipts	57.4	Other borrowing	57.6
Borrowing	38.9		
Total	290.3	Total	290.3

Table 16.1 Public Money in 1992/93 (£bn)

Source: The Budget in Brief, HMSO 30 November 1993.

Table 16.1 provides a summary of the revenue raised from the different sources and the amounts spent on different categories.

However, the Budget is not simply a financial statement. It is the main instrument of economic policy and considerable significance is attached to whether the government has a budget surplus or deficit, and the size of that surplus or deficit. When the government achieves a *budget surplus*, its estimated revenue exceeds its estimated expenditure and this surplus can be used to redeem part of the National Debt. However, when the government has a *budget deficit*, its planned expenditure is greater than its estimated revenue and the difference must be made good by borrowing. Such borrowing becomes part of the Public Sector Borrowing Requirement (PSBR) and adds to the National Debt.

It used to be argued that the Chancellor should deliberately aim for a budget surplus or deficit as a means of varying injections and leakages into the circular flow of income so as to achieve certain economic objectives. In particular, it was argued that if aggregate demand was insufficient to generate the full employment level of national income, the government should aim at a budget deficit so as to increase injections so raising income and employment. However, the effect of the budget on injections and leakages is no longer considered as important as its effect on the money supply. In particular, when the government has a budget deficit, the way in which this is financed can have a profound impact on the growth of the money supply. This issue is considered fully on in Chapter 12 and on pp. 308–311.

THE REGULATOR

Although rates of direct taxation can only be changed in the annual budget with Parliamentary approval, the Chancellor has much more flexibility in varying the rates of certain *indirect taxes*. Specifically, export and import duties can be changed by up to 10 per cent of the current rate and VAT by up to 25 per cent of the current rate. The Chancellor can therefore change the current rate of VAT (17.5%) to a lower limit of 13.125 per cent, or to an upper limit of 21.875 per cent without parliamentary approval.

BORROWING REQUIREMENTS

The CGBR is different from the PSBR

THE CENTRAL GOVERNMENT BORROWING REQUIREMENT (CGBR)

The main component of the CGBR is the overall budget deficit. However, the CGBR is not exactly equal to the government's budget deficit because it includes certain items of expenditure such as the National Insurance Fund which are not part of the budget. We shall later see that the size of the CGBR has an important bearing on the growth of the money supply because it is the largest component of the PSBR. This explains why the size of the budget deficit has acquired great significance in recent years.

THE PUBLIC SECTOR BORROWING REQUIREMENT (PSBR)

The PSBR is the total amount the public sector needs to borrow from the private sector and from overseas for the year ahead. It therefore consists of borrowing by the central government, by the local authorities and by the public corporations. However, care must be taken here because part of central government borrowing is on-lent to other institutions within the public sector. To the extent that the CGBR is on-lent in this way, it reduces the amount the rest of the public sector needs to borrow from the private sector and from overseas. In other words, it has already been included in total public sector borrowing. Only that part of borrowing by local authorities and public corporations that has *not* been on-lent by the central government adds to the PSBR. The structure and financing of the PSBR for 1992/93 are summarised in Table 16.2.

The structure of the PSBR (£m)		
Central government borrowing requirement:		
on own account	42,402	
for on-lending to local authorities	−7,267	
for on-lending to public corporations	1,185	
CGBR		36,320
Local authorities' net borrowing from markets	1,481	
Public corporation's net borrowing from markets	−1,100	
PSBR		36,701
The financing of the PSBR (£m)		
Borrowing from banks and building societies	8,520	
Other financial institutions	20,569	
Industrial and commercial companies	−1,659	
Personal sector	6,245	
Overseas sector	3,026	
PSBR		36,701

Table 16.2 The Structure and Financing of the PSBR (1992/93)

Source: Financial Statistics, HMSO, No 381, Jan 1994 and *Bank of England Quarterly Bulletin*, November 1993.

THE PSBR AND THE MONEY SUPPLY

The most publicised aspect of the PSBR is its effect on the money supply and, in particular, its relationship with *broad money*. In practice, the effect of an increase in the PSBR on the money supply is uncertain since its impact on broad money may be offset in whole or in part by a change in any of the other components which make up broad money. Nevertheless, the authorities remain convinced that there is a central link, and it is possible to identify some of the ways in which the PSBR might lead to an increase in broad money.

The extent to which the PSBR leads to an increase in broad money depends on the way in which the PSBR is financed. In fact, there are several methods of financing the PSBR:

Ways of financing the PSBR

- by borrowing from the non-bank private sector;
- by borrowing from the banking system;
- by borrowing from overseas or in foreign currency; and
- by issuing more cash (notes and coin) to the public.

The effect of these different methods of financing the PSBR on broad money is now considered in turn.

BORROWING FROM THE NON-BANK PRIVATE SECTOR

When the PSBR is financed by borrowing from the non-bank private sector, there will be no direct effect on broad money. The sale of debt to the non-bank private sector simply transfers bank deposits from the private sector to the public sector. When the government spends this money, deposits move back to the private sector and the money supply is unchanged.

BORROWING FROM THE BANKING SYSTEM

However, the same is not true when the PSBR is financed through the banking sector. When the banking sector buys public sector debt, their purchase will be paid for by a reduction in operational deposits at the Bank of England. At this stage, there has been no change in the money supply. One asset has simply been substituted for another and the liabilities of the banking sector are unchanged. However, the government has additional deposits and when these are spent the funds will flow back ino the banking sector. This will increase the assets and liabilities of the banking sector, and extra bank deposits are included in broad money. Each additional deposit in government hands, as a result of selling public sector debt to the banking sector, represents an increase in the money supply. The direct effect of sales of public sector debt to the banking sector is therefore an equivalent increase in bank deposits and hence in broad money.

The *direct* effect on broad money of the banking sector purchasing public sector debt is the same whether short-term debt or long-term debt is purchased. However, the *indirect* effects are likely to be very different.

Short-term debt

When the banking sector buys **short-term debt** such as Treasury bills, their operational deposits at the Bank of England decrease, but there is no overall change in their liquidity position. They have simply substituted one liquid asset for another liquid asset. When the government spends its additional deposits and they flow back into the banking system, the money supply will increase in the way described above. However, the overall liquidity of the banking sector will have increased with the receipt of extra bank deposits, and the banks will increase their lending to the discount market (so as to meet legal requirements) and to private customers. The increased liquidity of the banking sector might therefore lead to a multiple expansion of bank lending. The extent to which this happens depends partly on the availability of willing borrowers and partly on acquiescence by the authorities. In other words, we are assuming that the authorities take no off-setting action to 'mop up' the excess liquidity. The ways in which this might be done are discussed in Chapter 12. If there is a multiple expansion of bank deposits, financing the PSBR by the sale of short-term debt to the banking sector might ultimately lead to a more than proportional increase in the money supply.

Long-term debt

The situation is different when the banking sector buys **long-term debt**. In this case, their operational deposits at the Bank of England decrease and their investments increase. In other words, they have exchanged a liquid asset (operational deposits) for an illiquid asset (investments). When the government spends the deposits it has borrowed and they flow back into the banking system, the money supply will increase. However, to the extent that these deposits are lent to the discount market as money at call, there will simply be a restoration of the banking sector's original liquidity position. In other words, although the money supply increases via extra bank deposits, there will be no significant change in the overall liquidity position of the banking sector and no multiple expansion of the money supply.

Clearly, if the authorities aim to control the growth of the money supply, the issue of long-term securities is preferable to an increase of short-term securities. However, it is not always possible or desirable to sell long-term debt and in these circumstances the authorities are compelled to sell short-term debt.

BORROWING FROM OVERSEAS OR IN FOREIGN CURRENCY

When the government borrows from overseas or in foreign currency, the receipts must be paid into the Exchange Equalisation Account at the Bank of England in exchange for an equal value of sterling. The sterling balance is then paid into the government's account at the Bank of England. When the government spends these deposits, cheques will be drawn against them, and when they are cleared operational deposits at the Bank of England will increase and broad money will have increased. However, if there is unsatisfied demand for loans and the government does not sell securities to the non-bank private sector so as to reduce operational deposits, there will also be a multiple increase in the money supply as bank lending increases.

BORROWING BY ISSUING MORE CASH TO THE PUBLIC

Finally, to the extent that the PSBR is financed by an increase in the issue of notes and coin, the money supply will increase. This is rather obvious since one of the components of broad money is notes and coin in circulation with the public. However, the Bank of England makes no attempt to control the issue of notes and coin and simply responds passively to the public's demand for cash. This has never been an important means of financing the PSBR, at least in recent years, so that issuing more notes and coin has had little impact on the growth of broad money.

THE NATIONAL DEBT

The national debt is the total accumulated sum of all outstanding central government debt. Table 16.3 shows that in 1993, its value stood at £223,877m. It also shows the relative importance of different securities which make up the national debt.

Distribution			
Market holdings			
Domestic holders	£m		
Public corporations and local authorities	2,101		
Banking sector	11,378		
Building societies	4,426		
Institutional investors	91,671		
Overseas holders			
International organisations	694		
Central monetary institutions	9,000		
Other	15,508		
Other holders	25,202		
Total market holdings		201,873	
Official holding		22,004	
Total sterling debt			223,877
Composition			
Treasury bills	5,349		
Government stocks	162,642		
Non-marketable debt	55,886		
Total composition			223,877

Table 16.3 The distribution and composition of the national debt (£m)

Source: Bank of England Quarterly Bulletin, November 1993.

In the UK, most of the national debt is held by domestic residents. This is referred to as **internal debt**. That part of the national debt held by non-UK residents is referred to as **external debt**. Table 16.3 shows that at the end of March 1993 about $11^1/_4$ per cent of total national debt was held externally.

THE BURDEN OF THE NATIONAL DEBT

It is sometimes alleged that the existence of the national debt imposes a *burden* on the community. This argument takes many forms, but the one most often quoted is that a burden is imposed via the community being taxed to meet interest payments on the debt. When any part of the debt is redeemed, this too must be met out of current tax receipts. The implication is that the overall level of taxation would be lower if the national debt did not exist.

In fact, the suggestion that a burden is transferred to the present generation from previous generations is largely groundless and does not stand up to close examination. The main issues are summarised below.

- When the government borrows, it does so to increase its own expenditure above current tax yields. To borrow from its own residents implies that the rest of society is cutting back on consumption, i.e. saving, with the resources released being transferred to the public sector. In fact, as Table 16.3 shows, approximately 90 per cent of internal debt is in private hands (market holdings) so that increases in the national debt have largely implied a cut in private consumption. To the extent that society cuts its consumption, the burden of government borrowing falls on the generation alive at the time the borrowing takes place. It is then that consumption is cut in order to release resources for the public sector.

- Although interest payments on the national debt are met out of tax revenue this does not necessarily imply the existence of a burden. The generation which receives interest payments from holding the national debt is also the generation which pays taxes to meet those interest payments. To the extent that the national debt is held internally, there is simply a redistribution of income within the community. Taken as a whole, the community is neither better off nor worse off. The same argument applies when any part of internal debt is redeemed.

Nevertheless, there are three ways in which the national debt can impose some cost on the present generation: externally held debt, administration costs and effect on initiative.

Debt held externally

To the extent that national debt is held *externally*, it does impose a burden on present and future generations. When the government borrows abroad, the nation as a whole is able at that time to import more than it exports. In other words, borrowing from abroad makes it possible for domestic consumption to exceed domestic output. However, subsequent interest payments on the debt, together with its final redemption, give foreigners claims on domestic output which can only be met from exports. In this case, domestic consumption will be less than domestic output. A burden has therefore been transferred to future generations who must cut their consumption because of debts incurred in the past. In this sense, external debt imposes a very real burden on future generations.

Administration costs

There are costs of administering the national debt which are paid out of current tax receipts. If the national debt did not exist, these costs would not be incurred and instead of administering the debt, resources could be put to other uses. However, the cost of administering the national debt amounts to less than £200m which is a small proportion of GNP (see Table 8.1, Ch. 8). Nevertheless, this is the opportunity cost society bears.

Effects on initiative

The higher levels of taxation necessary to meet interest payments on the debt might have a disincentive effect on effort and initiative. If this is the case, it will reduce GDP below the level that woud otherwise be attained. It will also adversely affect the rate of economic growth. The ways in which higher taxation might have a disincentive effect are discussed on pp. 316–318 but the empirical evidence on the existence of disincentive effects is controversial.

All that can be said with certainty is that external debt does impose a burden on the community. Nevertheless, it is important to keep the extent of this burden in perspective. Table 16.3 shows that only about $11\frac{1}{4}$ per cent of the national debt is held externally. Furthermore, the real value of this, like the real value of all debt, is eroded by inflation. Because of inflation, a smaller volume of output is given up when the debt is redeemed than is gained when it is incurred. Currently the sterling national debt has fallen to just over 30 per cent of GDP compared with a figure in excess of 100 per cent 30 years ago.

Finally, in assessing the extent of any burden, it is necessary to consider the use to which borrowed funds have been put. If they have been put to some productive use, such as improving the infrastructure, then far from passing on a burden to future generations, the capacity for greater future output is created.

TAXATION

THE CANONS OF TAXATION

In 1776, Adam Smith set down four **canons of taxation**. These are still important today and provide a set of conditions against which any tax can be judged. The canons of taxation are:

66 **The canons of taxation** 99

- **Certainty** The type and timing of taxes should be known with certainty to those paying them
- **Convenience** A tax should be as convenient as possible for the tax payer
- **Economy** A tax should be as cheap to collect as possible, or in more modern jargon, we might say a tax should be as cost-effective as possible
- **Equity** Taxation should be as equitable as possible in the sense that there is equality of sacrifice.

More recently, another principle of taxation has been added: a tax system should be **consistent** with the overall aims of economic policy. If it was not, the implementation of a tax could be counter-productive. An example of consistency between taxation and economic policy is the way the tax system acts as an *automatic stabiliser*. Specifically, when demand in the economy is buoyant and taxes and income are rising, tax revenues rise more than proportionately as people are drawn into the tax net or the higher tax bracket and more goods on which VAT is levied are purchased. This automatically limits the effect of rising demand on inflation. When demand is falling, the opposite occurs limiting the effect on unemployment. The benefit system also automatically stabilises the economy. When incomes are rising, the payment of social security benefits falls and vice versa.

THE STRUCTURE OF TAXATION

Taxation in the UK is usually classified as *direct* or *indirect*. Direct taxes are collected by the Department of Inland Revenue, and in the main are levied on incomes and transfers of capital. Indirect taxes, on the other hand, are collected by the Customs and Excise department. They are sometimes referred to as expenditure taxes since they are levied mainly on spending. However, the traditional distinction between direct and indirect taxes is that the incidence, or burden of a direct tax is borne by the person on whom the tax is levied. This burden cannot be transferred to another person or party. However, as we shall see, the burden of an indirect tax can often be passed on to a third party.

DIRECT TAXES

The main direct taxes levied in the UK are summarised below.

Personal income tax

For tax purposes, in the UK, both earned and unearned income are treated together. Tax is levied on gross income minus various allowances, such as the single person's allowance. After all deductions have been made, taxable income was subject to the following rates in 1993—94.

Rate %	Taxable income (£)
20	0–2,500
25	2,501–23,700
40	over 23,701

66 **Types of direct tax** 99

One feature of income tax in the UK is that it is **progressive**, i.e. the marginal rate of taxation is greater than the average rate. However, care must be taken here because the higher rates of tax only apply to increments above the upper limit of each tax band. Therefore, for example, someone with a taxable income of £30,000 pays income tax at the rate of 20 per cent on the first £2,500, 25 per cent on the next £21,200 and 40 per cent on the remainder.

Corporation tax

This tax is levied on company profits, whether earned at home or abroad, after deducting allowances such as interest on loans. However, dividends to shareholders are not tax deductible, and corporation tax is levied on profits before any part is distributed to shareholders. The rates of corporation tax in 1993/94 stood at 25 per cent for firms with taxable profits under £250,000 and at 33 per cent for firms with taxable profits over £1,250,000. Intermediate rates of corporation tax operate between these two levels.

Petroleum revenue tax (PRT)

This is levied at different rates on the net incomes from each field in the North Sea after deducting royalties and operating costs. In fact, there are three elements of North Sea oil and gas taxation. A **royalty** of $12\frac{1}{2}$ per cent is levied on the value of the well-head deposits of oil and gas. **PRT** is then levied on company incomes, and finally, **corporation tax** is levied on company profits.

Capital gains tax

This tax is levied on the increase in the value of capital assets between the time of purchase and the time of sale. There are exemptions such as a person's main dwelling of residence, life assurance policies and so on. In addition, there is a non-taxable allowance which stood at £5,800 in 1993/94. Only capital gains in any year above this basic allowance are subject to taxation though capital losses can be offset against any gains. The rate of capital gains tax depends on the rate at which income tax is paid. For those who pay income tax at the basic rate, capital gains tax is levied at 25 per cent and for higher rate tax payers it is levied at 40 per cent.

Inheritance tax

This is a tax levied on transfers at time of death and is levied at the constant rate of 40 per cent on the excess of any transfers above £110,000. Inheritance tax is therefore a proportional tax.

INDIRECT TAXES

Indirect taxes can either be specific or *ad valorem*. **Specific taxes** have a fixed money value per unit, whereas *ad valorem* **taxes** are levied as a percentage of value. In this case, the amount paid in tax varies directly with the value of purchases subject to taxation.

The main indirect taxes levied in the UK are VAT and the excise duties on tobacco, oil and alcohol. These are summarised below.

Value added tax (VAT)

66 Types of indirect tax 99

In terms of revenue raised, this is undoubtedly the most important of all indirect taxes in the UK and accounted for over 17 per cent of the total tax yield in 1993/94. It is a proportional or *ad valorem* tax and is currently levied at the rate of 17.5 per cent. The mechanics of VAT are set out in Table 16.4.

VALUE ADDED (£)		PURCHASE PRICE TO SELLER EXCLUDING VAT (£)	PURCHASE PRICE INCLUDING VAT (£)	SELLING PRICE EXCLUDING VAT (£)	VAT LIABILITY (£)	VAT CREDIT (£)	VAT DUE (£)
100	Manufacturer imports raw materials	0	0	100	17.50	0	17.50
100	Manufacturer sells to wholesaler	100	117.50	200	35.00	17.50	17.50
50	Wholesaler sells to retailer	200	235.00	250	43.75	35.00	8.75
150	Retailer sells to customer	250	293.75	400	70	43.75	26.25
Cost to customer = £470 of which VAT = £70							

Table 16.4 The mechanics of VAT

Basically, firms supplying products on which VAT is levied add VAT to the total value of their output, but deduct VAT already paid on inputs. In other words, tax is levied only on the *value added* at each stage of production.

Not all commodities are subject to VAT. Certain stages in the production of particular commodities are exempt from VAT, while others are zero-rated. Where an exemption applies, traders do not charge VAT on their own output, but are unable to claim back any VAT charges on their inputs as in the case of postage, rent and insurance. Where commodities are zero-rated no VAT is levied and traders can claim back from the customs and excise department any VAT already paid on their inputs as in the case of exports, children's clothing and food (except meals eaten out).

Excise duties

These are levied on domestic and imported goods with the aim of raising revenue. Of all the excise duties, most revenue is raised from tobacco, oil and alcohol. In all three cases, excise duty is a large proportion of purchase price and the large sums raised from sales of these products is therefore an indication that demand for them is relatively inelastic. It is certainly true that in recent years increases in price caused by higher excise duty have had little lasting impact on consumption!

THE INCIDENCE OF TAXATION

Economists refer to the question of who actually bears the burden of taxation as the **tax incidence**. Despite this, it is not always easy to identify the person or organisation on whom the tax incidence usually falls. In some cases, it is possible for those who make tax payments to the authorities to pass the burden of taxation on to others. This is especially true in the case of indirect taxation as Fig. 16.1. shows.

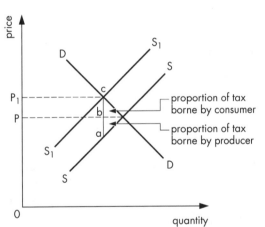

Fig. 16.1 The incidence of an indirect tax

The imposition of a tax on sales equal to ac per unit shifts the supply curve for this commodity vertically upwards by the amount of tax, i.e. from SS to S_1S_1. Price rises from OP to OP_1. However, the price increase is less than the full amount of the tax, showing that producers pass on only part of the burden of the tax. In this case, consumers bear bc of the tax incidence, and producers bear ab.

For any given product, there is a distribution of the tax burden after the imposition of an indirect tax, i.e.

$$\frac{\text{consumers' share of tax burden}}{\text{producers' share of tax burden}} = \frac{\text{elasticity of supply}}{\text{elasticity of demand}}$$

So, if the supply is more elastic than demand, the consumers' share of the tax burden will exceed the producers' share, and vice versa.

TAXATION POLICY

We can broadly identify three main reasons why governments levy taxes:

- to finance the provision of public goods and services
- to provide a powerful tool of economic management policy
- to redistribute income and wealth.

The first of these has already been considered and the second and third are examined in Chapter 17. There is no doubt that taxation policy in the UK achieves all three aims. However, there is a great deal of controversy about whether present policy is the most efficient means of achieving these aims. The remainder of this section is devoted to a discussion of these areas of controversy.

For taxation to be economically efficient, it should not lead individuals or companies to change their behaviour, except where such changes are the intended result of taxation. Since the majority of taxes are raised to provide the government with revenue, this implies that, in general, taxes should extract money from the economy in as neutral a way as possible. In fact, there are several reasons why such neutrality might not be achieved.

TAXATION AND INCENTIVES

The way in which taxation affects incentives is probably the most controversial of all the issues surrounding the operation of tax policy. This is mainly because it is difficult to test any of the hypotheses in such a way that the results clearly indicate how taxation affects incentives. Nevertheless, several possibilities can be identified.

THE LAFFER CURVE

The Laffer curve is illustrated in Fig. 16.2 and shows how tax revenue and tax rate are related.

> **A case for limiting tax rates**

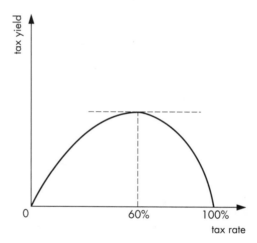

Fig. 16.2 The Laffer curve

If there is no taxation, i.e. the tax rate is zero, tax revenue must also be zero. At the other extreme, if the tax rate is 100 per cent, tax revenue will again be zero because all production except that required for subsistence will cease. The tax rate of 100 per cent totally removes the incentive to work. Between these two extremes, different rates of taxation have a different effect on production. The problem for the authorities is to set the tax rate at that level which maximises tax revenue and therefore minimises the disincentive effect. Some studies for the UK suggest that a composite tax rate, i.e. including direct and indirect taxes as well as social security payments, of 60 per cent will maximise tax revenue. The composite tax rate in the UK is currently estimated at about 40 per cent, implying that higher taxes would have no disincentive effect. This is completetely at odds with the government's belief, and that of most *supply side economists*, that lower taxes are necessary to increase incentives!

THE POVERTY TRAP

A potentially serious disincentive effect arises when individuals are caught in the poverty trap. The **poverty trap** does not, as it is often thought, denote the existence of poverty. Indeed, it is the result of efforts to relieve poverty by providing benefits.

Basically, the poverty trap arises because benefits are withdrawn the higher up the income scale a family moves. With higher income, therefore, a family faces both a rising tax bill *and* the reduction or withdrawal of its social security benefits. In cases where people pay income tax at the rate of 25 per cent and national insurance contributions at the rate of 9 per cent, the marginal rate of tax is 34 per cent. However, when the rate at which benefits are withdrawn is added to this, the *effective* marginal rate of tax is much higher and in certain income ranges it can exceed 100 per cent!

THE UNEMPLOYMENT TRAP

The **unemployment trap** is similar to the poverty trap in that its existence is due to the availability of benefits. However, whereas the poverty trap affects those in employment, the unemployment trap affects those who are unemployed. In some cases, the benefits available while unemployed are equal to or greater than the after-tax income that would be earned by accepting employment. When an unemployed person's disposable income *falls* by accepting employment, the effective marginal rate of tax on earnings is over 100 per cent. The effect of this is to create a serious disincentive for those who are currently unemployed to seek employment. Furthermore, the implication is that any attempt to price the unemployed into jobs by cutting wages actually worsens the unemployment trap. Indeed, one reason put forward for taxing unemployment benefit is to reduce the extent of the unemployment trap by lowering the *effective* rate of benefit.

> ❝ Know about unemployment and poverty traps ❞

TAXATION AND THE INCENTIVE TO WORK

It has been suggested that relatively high rates of income tax reduce the incentive to increase earnings through working overtime, accepting promotion and so on. There is also a view that high rates of taxation encourage a certain amount of absenteeism by reducing the loss of earnings which results from being absent. However, the available evidence on these matters is inconclusive and it is just as possible that relatively high rates of taxation will provide an incentive to work. This would be the case where individuals aim at a *given level* of after-tax income, and need to work overtime, accept more responsibility and so on, in order to achieve it.

TAXATION AND INVESTMENT

Taxation reduces the net return from investment and so might discourage enterprise and risk taking. This is particularly likely when shareholders pay income tax at progressive rates. Returns on high-risk investment are variable, and over any given period the total tax paid by shareholders is likely to be greater in this case than when returns are fairly constant from one year to the next. This would happen because higher dividends paid in those years when profits permitted, would push shareholders into higher taxable bands for income tax purposes.

STIMULUS TO INFLATION

It has sometimes been suggested that the nature of income tax in the UK might increase inflationary pressure. The argument centres on the way relatively high rates of inflation and progressive taxation affect real income. Where pay awards rise in line with retail prices and workers continue to pay the same proportion of their income in taxation, real income will be constant. However, if wage awards push earnings into higher taxable bands, the *proportion* of income paid in tax will rise and real income will fall. The higher average rate of tax which results from incomes rising in a progressive tax system is referred to as **fiscal drag**. If workers demand further pay rises in response to falling real incomes the process will repeat itself; prices will rise still further and real income will fall as earnings are pushed into still higher taxable bands. In other words, prices will rise faster than after-tax income.

Example

The following example illustrates the problem. Assume that the first £2,000 of earnings is untaxed. Thereafter the following rates of taxation apply.

TAXABLE EARNINGS (£)	TAX RATE
1–1,000	30 per cent
1,001–2,000	40 per cent
2,001–3,000	50 per cent
Over 3,000	60 per cent

Table 16.5

If gross income rises from £5,000 in Year 1 to £7,000 in Year 2, we can see in Fig. 16.3, how the amount paid in taxes rises.

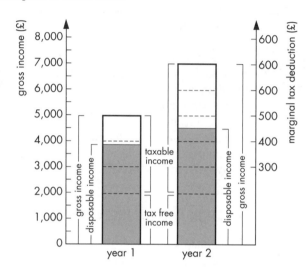

Fig. 16.3 Rise in taxes paid

Gross income increases by 40 per cent (2,000/5,000), but disposable income, or net income, increases by only 21 per cent (800/3,800). Suppose now that prices increase over the same period by 25 per cent. Disposable income at *constant prices* will fall from £3,800 in Year 1 to £3,680 (i.e. £4,600 × 100/125) in Year 2. In other words, *real income* will fall by over 3 per cent despite a rise in *gross income* of 40 per cent. (Non-taxable allowances and taxable bands are usually increased in the budget partly to avoid this effect, but where they are not adjusted in line with inflation some groups will experience a fall in real income.)

Fiscal drag

This process whereby individuals are forced into higher tax bands because of rising income is referred to as **fiscal drag**. Governments have sometimes been accused of using fiscal drag as a means of financing their expenditures. If higher expenditures generate inflation they can be financed without increasing the rates of taxation because inflation will draw people into higher tax brackets and therefore increase government revenue from taxation.

REFORM OF THE TAX SYSTEM

A NEGATIVE INCOME TAX

This proposal is sometimes referred to as a reverse income tax and aims to reduce the effect of the poverty and unemployment traps on the financial incentive to work.

Minimum income guarantee

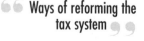 Ways of reforming the tax system

There are many variations of the basic idea. One involves the establishment of a minimum income guarantee (the poverty line) which is fixed in cash terms according to the circumstances (number of dependents, etc.) of each particular family. The cash benefit, i.e. the **minimum income guarantee**, would be paid in full to those without any other form of income. It would therefore replace the present social security system. Thereafter tax would be levied on the whole of a person's earned income.

Example   The operation of this system is explained using Fig. 16.4. We assume that the minimum income guarantee is £4,000 and that earned income is taxed (via loss of cash benefit) at the constant rate of 50 per cent.

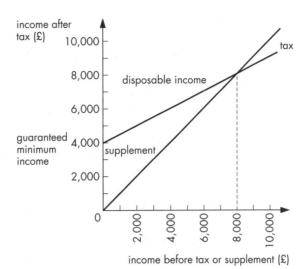

Fig. 16.4 Minimum income guarantee

When the family has no other income, it receives the full minimum income guarantee of £4,000. For each additional £1,000 earned, the rate of cash benefit falls by £500. This is equivalent to a marginal rate of tax of 50 per cent. The break-even point is £8,000. When family income reaches this level no cash benefit is received and no income tax is paid. For incomes above this level a positive rate of tax applies.

Tax credits

A slightly different proposal involving the establishment of tax credits has received most official support in the UK. Under this system, tax credits would replace non-taxable allowances and all tax payers would be given a tax credit irrespective of income. All income would then be assessed for tax without exempting any initial amount. If the tax credit exceeds the tax payable, the difference will be paid in cash support; if the tax liability exceeds the tax credit, the difference is due in tax payment.

Example   This system of taxation is easy to operate and therefore cheap to administer. For example, if the tax rate is 25 per cent, then an individual with a *tax credit* of £40 per week and no other source of income would receive £40 per week in state benefit. If this person now accepted employment at a *wage* of £40 per week, their tax liability would be (0.25) £40 = £10 per week. This person would therefore receive £30 per week in state benefit (i.e. the tax credit minus the tax liability) giving a total weekly income of £70. At a wage of £160 per week this person would receive no state benefit nor pay any tax since their tax credit exactly matches their tax liability. Positive income tax would only be paid when wages exceed £160 per week.

CHANGING THE TAX BASE

There are three tax bases: wealth, income and expenditure. However, there are practical problems associated with the taxation of wealth and, in recent years, emphasis on tax reform has concentrated on shifting the tax base away from income and on to expenditure. In other words, it has been suggested that less revenue should be raised from taxing incomes and more from taxing expenditures. Let us consider the relative advantages and disadvantages of each tax base.

Direct taxation advantages

66 **Benefits of direct tax** 99

- **Redistribution of income**   Direct taxation is a powerful tool for redistributing income more equally. This is especially true of personal income tax which is levied at progressive rates so that those on higher incomes pay proportionately higher taxes than those on lower incomes.
- **Economy of collection**   The major direct taxes such as income tax and corporation tax are relatively cheap to collect since they are deducted at source.
- **Automatic stabilisation properties**   Because income tax is a progressive tax, it functions as an automatic stabiliser. When the economy is buoyant and incomes

rise, the proportion of income taken in taxation rises. Conversely, when economic activity is depressed and incomes fall, the proportion taken in income tax falls. This mitigates both the boom and the recession.

Direct taxation disadvantages

Problems of direct tax

- **Disincentive effects** Direct taxation is widely regarded as having a disincentive effect on effort and initiative. The poverty and unemployment traps are cited as examples of this (see p. 316). It is also possible that relatively high rates of direct taxation might lead to a reduction in mobility of labour. Similarly, it might make workers reluctant to accept promotion or overtime working. Disincentive effects are not limited to the labour market. Relatively high rates of progressive taxation might reduce the ability and willingness to save and this might result in a reduction in the rate of investment.

- **Tax avoidance** It is alleged that relatively high rates of direct taxation encourage tax avoidance and stimulate the growth of the black economy.

Indirect taxation advantages

- **Lower disincentive effect** It is alleged that indirect taxation will have a lower disincentive effect than direct taxation because it has no effect on the level of disposable income. A reduction in direct taxation and an increase in indirect taxation will have a positive effect on the unemployment and poverty traps, but it is by no means certain that an increase in indirect taxation will have no disincentive effects. After all, higher rates of indirect taxation will clearly lead to a reduction in real income and this might affect incentives.

Benefits of indirect tax

- **Allocation of resources** Indirect taxes can be used to influence the allocation of resources. This is important when the *private cost* of producing a good diverges from the *social cost* of producing the good because there are negative externalities. In general, taxing demerit goods more heavily than merit goods might reduce consumption of the former in favour of the latter. This has certainly been true of the consumption of leaded petrol compared with consumption of unleaded petrol since a different rate of tax was imposed.

- **Flexibility** VAT is more flexible than a direct tax because it can be varied by ±25 per cent of the basic rate without parliamentary approval.

- **Economy of collection** The major indirect taxes, such as VAT, are relatively cheap to collect. Indeed, the cost of collecting VAT is even less than the cost of collecting income tax!

- **Automatic stabilisation properties** Because expenditure rises when economic activity rises, VAT receipts rise. Conversely, because expenditure falls when economic activity falls, VAT receipts fall. This mitigates both the boom and the recession.

Indirect taxation disadvantages

Problems of indirect tax

- **Regressive effect** A major criticism of indirect taxation is that it operates regressively and so bears more heavily on the poorer members of the community. Since everyone who pays indirect taxation pays it at the same rate, this criticism cannot be refuted. On the other hand, it is possible to reduce the regressive effect of indirect taxation by exempting from taxation altogether, or levying a lower rate of tax on, certain items of expenditure which are particularly important to lower income groups. For example, at present, no VAT is levied on food to be prepared and consumed in the domestic household.

- **Effect on inflation** An increase in the rate of indirect taxation leads to an increase in the RPI. Even when an increase in indirect taxation is accompanied by a reduction in direct taxation, economic agents might *perceive* their real income to have fallen. This might encourage demands for higher wages and further increase inflationary pressure.

We now turn to the advantages and disadvantages of a wealth tax.

Wealth tax advantages

❝❝ Benefits of a wealth tax ❞❞

- **Equity considerations**   There is no doubt that the possession of wealth adds to a person's standard of living. For example, income, in the form of rent or interest, is often earned on accumulations of wealth. An egalitarian principle is that those who have more should pay more. On equity grounds, economic theory supports the imposition of a wealth tax because the law of diminishing marginal utility implies that successive increments of wealth confer a declining amount of utility. However, in practice a wealth tax might not operate equitably; see below – *Problem of defining wealth* and *Possibility of evasion*.

- **No disincentive to effort or initiative**   It is argued that wealth depends on *past*, rather than *present*, effort and initiative. A wealth tax is therefore unlikely to have a disincentive effect. On the contrary, effort and initiative might even be encouraged by the desire to achieve a higher level of consumption, which, if wealth is taxed, can only be obtained via higher current income.

In summary, a wealth tax would raise revenue for the government but might be expected to have a largely neutral impact on the economy as regards incentives. However, this argument is not strong, and doubt has been expressed that effort and initiative would not be adversely affected. It is conceivable that individuals might accumulate less wealth and therefore be content with a lower level of current income if wealth were taxed.

Wealth tax disadvantages

❝❝ Problems of a wealth tax ❞❞

- **Problem of defining wealth**   In practice it is difficult to define wealth and even more difficult to value it. Many assets such as jewellery and works of art would have their value fixed arbitrarily, while the value of other forms of wealth such as pension rights or future earnings depends on assumptions about future inflation, interest rates, survival prospects, and so on.

- **Possibility of evasion**   There is also likely to be widespread evasion since wealth owners would have a powerful incentive to conceal their holdings of taxable assets. It would therefore not only be difficult to define wealth, it would be virtually impossible to measure it accurately. This would make the tax inequitable in its operation since the wealth of some individuals is more readily identified and assessed than that of others. For example, it is difficult to value shares in joint stock companies and, as recent experience has shown, even the value of property can fluctuate. Other forms of wealth, such as the possession of antiques and art treasures, are difficult to identify and, in the absence of selling them, impossible to value.

- **Problem of payment**   Other problems would arise in paying the tax. If wealth owners were forced to sell off part of their assets to meet their tax liability this might depress asset prices. There would then be problems of reassessment, with assets failing to realise the value ascribed to them for tax purposes. There might also be a general reluctance from people to purchase assets whose price is likely to fall because of market sales and on which future tax would be levied.

- **Cost**   A final argument against a wealth tax is that it would be difficult to administer and expensive to collect.

LOCAL TAXATION

In the late 1980s, the system of local taxation was changed from a system of rates, which were a tax on property values, to the **community charge**, which was a tax levied, with certain exceptions, on persons aged eighteen and over. The reasons for the change were that because rates were levied on property values they were unrelated to current income. In addition, it was estimated that rates tended to be paid by house-owners rather than all adult members of a household. This implies that many people consumed local services but made no contribution towards their cost.

However, there were severe problems with the community charge, or *poll tax* as it came to be known. The tax was particularly regressive since it was entirely unrelated to income. The cost of collecting the tax was relatively high and there was widespread evasion (unlike rates which were relatively cheap to collect and were difficult to evade). There were also vast differences in the rate of tax levied between authorities.

The current system of local taxation is the **council tax**. This is part a tax on property values and part a personal tax. For purposes of tax assessment, properties are graded into bands reflecting different values. Those in the higher bands attract a higher rate of tax. However, the rate of tax is based on the assumption that each house contains at least two adults. If a house contains only one adult, the resident will pay only 75 per cent of the tax bill.

AUTOMATIC STABILISERS

An article in the *OECD Economic Outlook*, No. 53, June 1993, deals with the role and use of **automatic stabilisers**. Taxation and government expenditure function as automatic stabilisers, i.e. they vary automatically in a counter-cyclical way. As the economy moves into recession, tax revenues fall, thus reducing the tax leak from the circular flow of income, and government expenditure on transfer payments rises, thus increasing injections into the circular flow of income. The mechanism works in reverse during the boom phase of the cycle.

Public sector deficits have increased markedly in nearly all OECD countries since 1990, in line with the downturn in economic activity. However, the extent of automatic stabilisers varies across countries reflecting, in particular, the overall size of the public sector, the progressivity of the tax system, the sensitivity of different tax bases to movements in economic activity, the generosity of unemployment benefit schemes and the extent to which unemployment fluctuates with output.

Automatic stabilisers and the tax system

The **structure** of the tax system has a significant impact on the size of the automatic stabilisers. The higher the average tax rate from a cyclically sensitive source, the larger will be the automatic stabiliser. For example, when taxation is lost because an employee is made redundant, the extent of stabilisation depends on the average rate of tax on labour income. The **progressivity** of the tax system is also an important determinant of the size of the automatic stabilisers. The more progressive the tax system, the greater the extent of stabilisation. The **sensitivity** of the individual tax bases is the final factor affecting the size of the automatic stabilisers on the revenue side. This will be influenced by several factors, such as the size of the marginal propensity to consume which is a major determinant of VAT revenues.

Automatic stabilisers and expenditure

Unemployment benefits are the principle source of fluctuation in government expenditure. As a rule of thumb, unemployment changes about half as rapidly as output; a one per cent fall in the level of output raises government expenditure by about 0.1 per cent. The ratio is greater in those countries (such as Canada, Austria, Denmark, Sweden and Switzerland) where the ratio of unemployment benefit to earnings is relatively high, than in countries (such as the United States, Japan and the UK) where the ratio of unemployment benefit to earnings is relatively low.

The impact of automatic stabilisers on government borrowing

The impact of the automatic stabilisers varies significantly between countries but their most important determinants are the size of the public sector in an economy and the importance of tax revenues. In particular, the higher the share of tax revenues in the economy, the greater is the sensitivity of government income to fluctuations in GDP. Fluctuations in revenues account for a much larger share of automatic stabilisers than fluctuations in expenditure which are only responsible for about one fifth of the increase in government borrowing in a recession.

The effect of automatic stabilisers on cyclical fluctuations in output

OECD estimates suggest that the automatic stabilisers reduce the cumulative output loss during a recession by about one half. Among the smaller European countries, the degree of *output smoothing* provided by the automatic stabilisers only matches that achieved in the major European countries when the automatic stabilisers are particularly large — as in Denmark, Norway and Sweden. In the United States and Japan, the stabilisers have much greater effect on the economy despite their smaller size, reflecting the below-average openness of these two countries.

Some policy issues

1 The difference in the size of the automatic stabilisers between OECD countries might mean that, in the face of similar deflationary forces, there could be more pressure for *discretionary fiscal action* in countries with low stabilisers. Conversely, countries with large automatic stabilisers might wish to offset some of the increases in borrowing if government debt and borrowing are already high.

2 Countries with significant fluctuations in general government borrowing for a given change in output tend to be those European countries where fiscal measures (automatic or discretionary) have the least impact on output. Until output returns to its trend level, there is a risk that the borrowing caused by automatic stabilisers may (through increased financing costs) turn cyclical deficits into structural deficits, especially when output is low relative to previous trends and there is doubt about future trends in output growth and the speed of the recovery.

3 Tax-based automatic stabilisers have the advantage that they are rule based. They respond quickly to changes in economic activity and, importantly, generate *expectations* of future reversals that may limit the impact of greater public borrowing on long-term interest rates. Discretionary changes in expenditure that compensate for relatively low automatic stabilisers have to be carefully designed if they are not to create permanent increases in expenditure and deficits that adversely impact on long-term interest rates. The effect of automatic stabilisers on government borrowing is more likely to be ignored by markets if they are confident, not just of a reversal of the borrowing but of eventual repayment of the cyclical borrowing — so that cyclical effects cancel out over the complete cycle. This, of course, assumes that output lost during the recession is regained during the boom, otherwise the automatic stabilisers might not be fully reversed during the upswing.

4 During the 1980s, revenues from automatic stabilisers were used to reduce tax rates rather than public debt. As a result the increase in the debt ratio that occurred in the early 1980s recession was never fully reversed. The temptation to do this in the future must be avoided if public debt is to be reduced.

EXAMINATION QUESTIONS

1 'Between 1979 and 1993, the UK tax system became less progressive.'
    (a) Explain this statement using relevant examples. *(40)*
    (b) Analyse the possible effects of these tax changes. *(60)*
          (ULEAC June 1993)

2 Explain why we need taxes and outline the requirements of a good tax. Compare the community charge, the council tax, and a local income tax as means of raising revenue to finance local government.
          (JMB 1993)

3 (a) With reference to public expenditure, distinguish between current expenditure, capital expenditure and transfer expenditure. *(30)*
    (b) What factors may explain changes in
        (i) the total level?
        (ii) the composition of expenditure over time? *(40)*
    (c) Examing the problems involved in attempting to control public expenditure.
                (30)
          (ULEAC June 1993)

4 Using economic analysis and relevant examples, discuss the relative merits and demerits of direct and indirect taxes.

ANSWERS TO EXAMINATION QUESTIONS

STUDENT'S ANSWER TO QUESTION 1

(a) A progressive tax is defined as a tax where the marginal rate of tax exceeds the average rate of tax. The aim is to ensure greater equality in the distribution of income. In most countries, the taxation of income is progressive and an example will illustrate how a progressive tax and a regressive tax work.

Example 1: A progressive tax

Income (£)	Rate of tax (%)	Amount paid in taxation (£)
5,000	20	1,000
10,000	30	3,000
20,000	40	8,000

Example 2: A regressive tax

Income (£)	Rate of tax (%)	Amount paid in taxation (£)
5,000	20	1,000
10,000	15	1,500
20,000	10	2,000

In the first example, as income rises the proportion paid in taxation rises, whereas in the second example as income rises, the proportion of income tax paid in taxation falls although the absolute amount paid in taxation still rises.

Taxation of expenditures might also be either progressive or regressive. For example, by ensuring that goods and services purchased by low income groups are exempt from VAT, this expenditure tax will operate progressively because the wealthier members of society will pay proportionately more in taxation than lower income groups. On the other hand, when VAT is levied at a flat rate on most goods and services, it will bear more heavily on the lower income groups who will pay proportionately more in taxation than the wealthier members of society. In the UK, VAT is progressive because certain items such as medicines are zero-rated, but it has become less progressive since 1979 because the basic rate of VAT has been increased from 15 per cent to 17.5 per cent. It is less progressive still because since the end of 1993, it has been levied on domestic fuel at 8 per cent. This makes VAT less progressive because everybody consumes domestic fuel.

In the UK, in 1979, the top rate of income tax was 83 per cent. Since then it has steadily been reduced and currently stands at 40 per cent. This tax has become less progressive. Corporation tax has also been reduced from a top rate of 52 per cent to 25 per cent. This could be regarded as regressive, since it is the wealthier members of society who own profit-making organisations and taxation of profits has been reduced.

(b) The changes in taxation outlined above have had several effects. It is usually argued that by reducing the progressive nature of income tax there will be an improvement in incentives. It is true that by allowing people to keep more of their own money, the incentive to obtain employment will be increased. In the 1970s,

Good, but take definition further

A good idea to present a numerical example

Good

A relevant point

Good

Overall many good points raised in part (a)

⁶⁶ Rather general ⁹⁹

⁶⁶ Rather general ⁹⁹

income tax was so high that the UK suffered from an unemployment trap when people were better off out of work than in work. It is also possible that a lower corporation tax might have increased the incentive to invest. In the UK, there has been no sharp increase in investment as corporation tax has fallen but we have no way of knowing what investment would have been if corporation tax had not been reduced.

⁶⁶ Yes ⁹⁹

The tax changes outlined in section (a) above have probably led to a reduction in the growth of the black economy. This is jobs done in exchange for cash so as to avoid paying income tax. By reducing the rates of income tax, there is less incentive to run the risk of tax evasion.

⁶⁶ Any evidence? ⁹⁹

One detrimental effect of these tax changes is that they will have increased the extent of inequality in the distribution of income. Indeed, the years since 1979 have been characterised by increasing inequality caused partly by tax changes.

⁶⁶ Part (a) is good; part (b) is too general. You need to talk in a little more detail about poverty and unemployment traps, Laffer curve, etc. Try to use economic analysis and empirical studies to support your points.⁹⁹

OUTLINE ANSWERS

Question 2

Governments need taxes for several reasons. Most obviously, tax revenue is used to finance government expenditure on goods and services, salaries and transfer payments. It is not sufficient to mention these. You will need to discuss briefly the reasons why governments undertake expenditure. Taxes are also necessary to influence the allocation of resources. By taxing certain demerit goods, such as cigarettes, governments can discourage their consumption. Taxes are also used to influence the distribution of income and to achieve certain macroeconomic objectives, such as the control of inflation.

The attributes of a **good tax** are discussed on p. 313.

One way of answering the last part of the question is to compare the different types of local taxation against the criteria listed for a good tax. The **community charge** and **council tax** satisfy the convenience criteria since there are various ways in which they can be paid, e.g. in full or by regular instalments. There is some doubt about whether they satisfy the certainty criterion because some individuals or households are unaware of their tax liability until fairly close to the time at which they become liable for payment. On the other hand, many individuals or households are notified in advance of their tax rates. It might be argued that since the community charge was fixed at the same rate across boroughs it was equitable. However, it is usually argued that because there are differences in incomes within boroughs, the tax was inequitable. There were also considerable differences between boroughs. The community charge would have no effect on incentives and therefore was broadly consistent with government policy.

The **council tax** is based on the capital value of each house on the assumption that it contains two adults. If the property contains only one adult then he or she will pay only 75 per cent of the bill of a two-household property. Discounts are given for certain people such as the handicapped or those in full-time education.

There is no doubt that the council tax is regressive since properties of below average value will attract a proportionately higher rate of tax. It is, however, more equitable than the community charge since the amount of tax payable will, up to a limit, rise with the value of the house. Again, this tax is unlikely to have any effect on incentives and is therefore broadly consistent with government policy. There is less likelihood of evasion and therefore it is likely to be cheaper to collect than the community charge.

A **local income tax** would be most convenient of all since it would be deducted at source. Because the tax would be progressive, it would satisfy the equity criteria. It would also probably be the most economical of the three taxes to collect since it would be deducted at source. However, evasion would be a greater problem than with the council tax because of the black economy. It might also be inconsistent with government policy because of its effect on incentives.

Question 3

(a) **Current expenditure** is regular recurring payments made by the Government on such things as salaries, e.g. of teachers and the armed forces. It also includes other items, such as maintenance of buildings and highways.

  Capital expenditure refers to public sector investment including the construction of new roads and buildings, such as a new hospital.

  Transfer expenditure refers to payments made not in exchange for any output. They are simply payments made which redistribute income. Examples include pensions, interest on debt, student grants and social security payments.

(b) (i) One broad point to emphasise is that the total level of government expenditure will depend on the type of economic system considered. In centrally planned economies, government expenditure will be greater than in market economies!.

  Another relevant factor is the rate of inflation. As inflation rises, the absolute level of government expenditure will rise. If all other things remain the same, as people live longer, the provision of pensions and increased expenditure on health care will drive up government expenditure.

(ii) The changing political stance of the government is important and, in the UK, we have seen efforts to reduce the size of the public sector in recent years as privatisation has increased. Government expenditure will change as the trade cycle moves the economy from recession to boom because tax revenues will fall and social security payments will rise.

  Political considerations are also important. For example, since the Eastern bloc economies have collapsed, the public are more prepared to accept cuts in the defence budget. Conversely, as law and order has declined the public seem to prefer increased expenditure in this area. Again, the effect of an ageing population will be relevant.

(c) There are many problems involved in attempting to control public spending. All governments have international obligations over which they have little control, e,g, the UK's contribution to the EU budget. In addition, it is very difficult to cut back investment programmes once they are under way. In the medium term, reductions are possible because governments need not necessarily embark on new programmes. The government is also committed to providing health care, pensions, education and unemployment benefit. Again, it is difficult to change these in the short run but, by institutional changes, it is possible for the government to encourage people to provide many of these for themselves. For example, the tax system could be (and currently is) used to encourage increased private expenditure on providing private medical insurance and private pensions, etc.

Question 4

You could begin by defining **direct** and **indirect taxes**. In general, direct taxes are levied on the incomes of individuals and firms and on transfers of wealth. Indirect taxes, on the other hand, are levied on specific goods and services and must be paid by the consumer or producer of these goods or services.

  You could then go on to discuss the relative *merits* and *demerits* of direct and indirect taxation. It is frequently alleged that the relatively high rates of personal income tax in the UK have a powerful disincentive effect on effort and initiative. You could discuss the **poverty** and **unemployment traps**, lower mobility of labour, the possibility that risk-taking and investment will be discouraged and so on. Using income and substitution effects you can demonstrate that sometimes when an individual is offered higher wages they will work fewer hours! Taxing profits through corporation tax might reduce the finance available to firms for investment in R&D as well as additional capacity both of which can affect the future growth of output as well as the quality and competitiveness of UK products. These are major reasons for the UK government's reduction in corporation tax (in stages) from 52 per cent when it first took office to 32 per cent (25 per cent for smaller companies).

It is usually argued that an increase in indirect taxes, such as VAT, would have fewer disincentive effects than an increase in direct taxation; this is one of the main arguments for shifting the burden of taxation away from direct taxes in favour of indirect taxes. However, this is by no means certain. For example, the higher prices implied by higher indirect taxes will reduce income and make leisure cheaper in terms of goods foregone. (Again you can demonstrate this in terms of income and substitution effects.) Despite this, indirect taxes have other advantages over direct taxes which should be discussed, e.g. they can be used selectively to discourage consumption of demerit goods; they are more flexible, and rates can be changed within certain limits by the Chancellor without parliamentary approval, i.e. without waiting for the Budget; and they are cheaper to collect and easier to understand. You should also mention that they both function as automatic stabilisers.

Nevertheless, direct taxation has advantages over indirect taxation which must also be considered. The progressive nature of income tax makes it particularly useful in redistributing income more equally (indirect taxes tend to act regressively because they represent a larger proportion of the expenditure of lower income groups); higher rates of indirect taxation have an immediate effect on the retail price index, and this might lead to demands for higher wages and set in motion an inflationary spiral.

Further reading
Begg, Dornbusch and Fischer, *Economics* (3rd edn), McGraw-Hill 1991: Ch. 16, Taxes and public spending: the government and resource allocation.
Griffiths and Wall (eds), *Applied Economics: An Introductory Course* (6th edn), Longman 1995: Ch. 15, Public expenditure; Ch. 16, Taxation.
Harrison et al, *Introductory Economics*, Macmillan 1992: Ch. 35, Public Finance and Taxation.

REVIEW SHEET

1 Define the following terms:

The Budget: _____

_____

_____

The regulator: _____

_____

_____

Public Sector Borrowing Requirement (PSBR): _____

_____

_____

The national debt: _____

_____

_____

2 Explain why the national debt might be regarded by some as a burden?

_____

_____

_____

3 List four canons of taxation.

(a) _____

(b) _____

(c) _____

(d) _____

5 Distinguish between direct and indirect taxes.

Direct: _____

_____

_____

Indirect: _____

_____

_____

6 Describe briefly the five main direct taxes in use in the UK.

(a) _____

(b) _____

(c) _____

(d) _____

(e) _____

7 Describe briefly the two main indirect taxes in use in the UK.

(a) _____

_____

(b) _____

_____

8 Use a diagram to explain why an indirect tax imposed on a product with a perfectly inelastic demand will tend to fall entirely on the consumer.

Explanation:

9 Draw the 'Laffer curve'. What relevance does it have for policy?

Explanation:

10 Explain what is meant by the following:

The unemployment trap:

The poverty trap:

Fiscal drag:

11 Briefly explain the advantages and disadvantages of a wealth tax.

12 Present a diagram and then use it to show how a negative income tax might operate.

GETTING STARTED

In 1944, the UK government published a White Paper on Employment Policy which stated that: "The Government believe that, once the war has been won, we can make a fresh approach, with better chances of success than ever before, to the task of maintaining a high and stable level of employment without sacrificing the essential liberties of a free society." Since then, there has been a change in the approach to achieving this objective, but there is no doubt that it remains an important long-term goal of all political parties. However, governments have other objectives which at times have taken precedence over employment levels as the main short-term goal. In recent years, considerable importance has been attached to reducing the annual rate of inflation. At other times, the balance of payments deficit has been the most pressing problem, and so on.

The overall aims of economic policy have not changed, but the means of achieving these aims has. For most of the post-war period, governments pursued their aims by managing the level of aggregate monetary demand. Such an approach is essentially Keynesian, since it implies manipulating the level of aggregate demand (i.e. $C + I + G + X - M$) so as to influence nominal income (Y). This approach is usually referred to as **demand management**.

More recently, and certainly since the late 1970s, the emphasis has changed from managing aggregate demand to what has come to be termed **supply-side economics**. At its simplest, supply-side economics is the use of microeconomic incentives to achieve microeconomic goals. Supply-side economics thus reflects the view that the macroeconomic system can only operate efficiently if each microeconomic market (the labour market, the capital market and so on) operates efficiently. The emphasis of macroeconomic policy has therefore shifted away from simply managing the overall level of aggregate demand, to the pursuit of policies which enable each microeconomic market to operate efficiently.

CHAPTER

17

MANAGING THE ECONOMY

THE AIMS OF ECONOMIC POLICY

INTERDEPENDENCE OF AIMS

INSTRUMENTS OF POLICY

THE MEDIUM-TERM FINANCIAL STRATEGY (MTFS)

CURRENT MACROECONOMIC POLICY

PRIVATISATION

DEREGULATION

APPLIED MATERIALS

ESSENTIAL PRINCIPLES

THE AIMS OF ECONOMIC POLICY

The economic aims of the government can be briefly stated as the maintenance of full employment, a relatively low and stable rate of inflation, equilibrium in the balance of payments and economic growth. Each is now considered in turn.

FULL EMPLOYMENT

We have already seen that all governments are concerned with employment levels, but the 1944 White Paper was careful to make no specific mention of how full employment was to be defined. Similarly, governments express their concern to bring unemployment levels down, but have chosen not to define full employment. In fact, the concept of full employment is difficult to define because the minimum level of unemployment that can be achieved at any particular time is constantly subject to change and cannot be zero because as the demand for various goods and services changes, so does the demand for the labour which produces them (see Chapter 10). The level of employment that can then be achieved will depend on the distribution of that demand between different goods and services and on the mobility of labour. The more that demand is concentrated on labour intensive goods and services and the more mobile the population, the lower the level of unemployment that can be achieved. The government's aim in this area is therefore to achieve some level of employment which it considers acceptable. We shall see later that because its aims are not independent of one another, what is considered to be an acceptable level of unemployment is to a certain extent dictated by the priority governments give to achieving their other economic aims.

66 Governments try to achieve several objectives at the same time 99

Natural rate of unemployment

A different definition of full employment is the level which exists when unemployment is at the **natural rate**. However, the natural rate of unemployment is extremely difficult to estimate and any estimates that are produced would be subject to a wide margin of error. A further complication is that the natural rate is not constant from one period to the next but will change as those factors which determine it change (see Chapter 13).

Types of unemployment

Traditionally, there are several types of unemployment:

- **Seasonal unemployment** is, as its name suggests, caused by the changing seasons. For example, fewer building and agricultural workers are required in the winter than in the summer. Probably the only 'cure' for this type of unemployment is to encourage mobility of labour so that as workers become unemployed, their chances of obtaining re-employment are increased.

- **Frictional unemployment** is sometimes referred to as *search unemployment* because it stems from a mismatch between the workers who become unemployed and the jobs that are available in the economy. Every month some 3–4 hundred thousand workers join the unemployment register and a similar number leave the register because they have found employment. Because of this, frictional unemployment is not regarded as a problem.

- **Structural unemployment** is caused by a reduction in the demand for a product, i.e. it is caused by a change in the *structure* of demand. For example, the increased use of plastic instead of steel has caused a long-term reduction in demand for steel and a reduction in the number of steel workers employed; increased competition from abroad has caused a reduction in demand for ship-building in the UK. Structural employment is often localised because of the decline of an industry which is localised. This is true of steel, ship-building, cotton, coalmining and so on. One way of dealing with this type of unemployment is to encourage mobility of capital (so that industry moves to those areas with the severest unemployment problems) and mobility of labour (so that workers move to where vacancies exist or are retrained in the skills that are required in the area where they live).

■ **Cyclical unemployment** is due to a downswing in the trade cycle. In any economy, there are regular recurring changes in the pattern of aggregate demand, sometimes rising, sometimes falling. This is referred to as the **trade cycle**. When demand falls there is a general reduction in demand for labour and unemployment. It used to be argued that governments could cure this type of unemployment by demand management. However, the belief now is that any reduction in unemployment as a result of demand management will only be temporary and will ultimately lead to higher inflation.

■ **Voluntary unemployment** is said to exist when people are unwilling to accept employment at existing real wage rates. It is argued that at any moment in time there is a natural rate of unemployment to which the economy will tend. At the natural rate, many workers could find employment but only at a lower wage than they require. It has been suggested that governments could deal with this type of unemployment by cutting benefits paid to the unemployed. However, in general, the suggestion is that the natural rate can be reduced by supply-side policies, such as the various training initiatives. If the natural rate can be reduced by retraining workers, this implies that not everyone who is unemployed at the natural rate is voluntarily unemployed!

PRICE STABILITY

This is another important objective of governments, although price stability does not imply a commitment to zero inflation. Changing supply and demand conditions for various products will lead to price changes in the various product markets; this is, of course, an inevitable feature of any economy where the price mechanism operates. Additionally, although academic opinion is divided, there is considerable support for maintaining a moderate rate of inflation rather than aiming to eliminate it altogether. A moderate rate of inflation, it is argued, will provide a spur to investment because it will give producers 'windfall' profits. However, while there is widespread support for maintaining a moderate rate of inflation there is certainly no agreement about what constitutes such a rate, although 1.5–2 per cent has been suggested. Again, all that can be said is that it is for the government to decide what rate is acceptable, given the constraints imposed by its other aims. We should note that when the government is aiming to reduce the rate of inflation, its choice of policy will at least be partly determined by whether inflation is due to excess demand (demand-pull inflation) or to rising costs (cost-push inflation).

EQUILIBRIUM IN THE BALANCE OF PAYMENTS

This is not a concept that can be easily defined. However, since all imports must ultimately be paid for by exports, one definition is that the *flow of autonomous debits be equalled by the flow of autonomous credits*. At any moment in time, a country might have a surplus or deficit in its balance of payments so that autonomous debits and credits will not necessarily be equal. The concept of equilibrium must therefore be related to some time period over which a balance should be achieved.

There is a further problem, in that a balance between debits and credits will also depend on the exchange rate system which operates. When exchange rates *float*, balance between autonomous transactions is guaranteed; at least it is under certain circumstances such as a 'pure' float. But when exchange rates are *fixed*, autonomous transactions must either be encouraged or discouraged if balance is to be achieved. We have seen that attempts to manage the exchange rate have serious implications for policy in the domestic economy. Balance of payments equilibrium might therefore be said to exist when, over a given period of time, autonomous transactions cancel out in such a way that does *not impede* the government's efforts to achieve its other policy aims.

ECONOMIC GROWTH

Another important aim of governments is to manage the economy in such a way that economic growth will be fostered. There are many definitions of economic growth. It is sometimes taken to mean the growth of capacity of productive potential for the economy as a whole because, in the long run, this is the only way of increasing the size of real GDP. This definition implies an outward movement of the economy's production possibility curve. However, the usual definition of economic growth is an increase in real GNP.

Policy objective

Economic growth has been given high priority as a policy objective, because if the growth of output exceeds the growth of population, per capita income will rise, i.e. the standard of living will rise. In the longer term, the compound effect on output of a constant rate of growth is impressive. For example, if output grows every year by 2 per cent, GDP will double in approximately 36 years; but if the growth of output can be increased to 3 per cent each year, output will double in approximately 24 years!

Factors influencing growth

66 **Ways of growing more rapidly** 99

- **Capital Stock**   One of the most important factors which influences economic growth is the quantity of capital per worker. The greater the capital : labour ratio, the higher the productivity of labour. This is important because if there is no change in the number of workers employed, an increase in productivity implies a higher level of GDP, i.e. economic growth.

- **Technological Progress**   It is not only the quantity of capital employed that affects economic growth, it is also the quality of capital, and this depends on technological progress. The productivity of capital can be increased if machinery is updated so that firms use the latest technologies available. This might mean scrapping existing machinery but the higher productivity will make it profitable for firms to do this. Since technological advances are encouraged when there is investment in research and development, greater expenditure on this will encourage economic growth.

- **The Quantity and Quality of the Labour Force**   This is another factor which is important in determining economic growth. The quantity of labour is determined by the population but countries with the highest populations do not have the highest economic growth. The important point is for countries to aim at the 'optimum population'. This is simply that level of population which maximises average product. When countries are not maximising average product they are either underpopulated or overpopulated and economic growth could be increased by moving to the optimum level.

  The quality of labour depends on education and training. An educated labour force is easier to train and is likely to be more adaptable and enterprising. In addition, a highly trained labour force is likely to be more mobile and this can have an important bearing on the growth of productivity.

Benefits of growth

66 **Some benefits of faster growth** 99

- **Higher Standard of Living**   The main benefit is that it makes possible a higher standard of living. This is especially important in the UK because, at the present time, the UK has an ageing population, i.e. the average age of the population is rising and there is a rising proportion of retired people in the population. When someone retires they continue to be a consumer but cease to be a producer. This means they consume what others produce. It is therefore important to achieve economic growth if living standards are not to fall.

- **Greater Investment**   Another reason why economic growth is necessary is that it makes investment in scientific research possible. This is particularly important in medicine where new vaccines prevent the spread of disease and new treatments make it possible to cure people of certain illnesses which only a few years ago claimed many lives; smallpox and TB are two examples.

Costs of Growth

- **Negative Externalities**   Despite this there are costs of economic growth — especially environmental costs. There is no doubt that in the past the drive for greater economic growth has resulted in an increase in pollution. This pollution

❝ Some costs of faster growth ❞

has many different consequences. It might simply be annoying because dumping toxic waste into a river makes it impossible to swim in that river. However, there are more serious consequences. There is overwhelming evidence that using lead in petrol has caused brain damage in certain young children. Acid rain, caused mainly by power stations that burn fossil fuels in the UK, is blamed for creating over ten thousand dead lakes in Scandinavia and many dead forests. Recently, economists and politicians have argued that economic growth leads to harmful externalities such as 'global warming' due partly to the destruction of the Amazon rain forest. Power is of course necessary for economic growth, but these externalities are clearly undesirable.

When considering the costs and desirability of economic growth, an important point to consider is that greater economic growth provides the means of dealing with the externalities it creates. It is a question of how society wishes to utilise its available resources. It might choose to use the benefits of increased productivity to increase consumption per head. On the other hand, society might allocate its resources into cleaning up the environment and to producing the technology that imposes fewer externalities on society.

- **Opportunity cost** To the extent that greater economic growth results from increased investment, there is an opportunity cost to consider. Increased investment requires abstention from current consumption and so the current population makes a sacrifice that makes a higher standard of living possible in the future.

INTERDEPENDENCE OF AIMS

❝ Conflicts can occur ❞

The use of demand management to achieve these economic aims led to a major policy dilemma for successive governments. The problem was that it proved impossible to achieve all aims simultaneously, so that governments faced a conflict of policy objectives. We have already seen in Chapter 13 that the use of high levels of aggregate demand to achieve full employment often conflicted with price stability. However, it also conflicted with the balance of payments objective. As demand in the economy increased and incomes rose, so the demand for imports also rose. This was partly to be expected because of the high marginal propensity to import in the UK. However, the adverse impact of increased demand on the balance of payments was reinforced by higher domestic prices which made imports more competitive in the domestic market and exports less competitive in foreign markets. There is no doubt that increased home demand also resulted in goods initially produced for export being diverted to the domestic economy, where demand and prices were rising and where transport costs to market were lower. As a result, the level of unemployment a government could achieve was determined in part by the rate of inflation it was prepared to accept, and in part by its need to achieve balance of payments equilibrium. At times, full employment was the major aim while, at others, it was sacrificed to the more pressing problems of containing inflation and restoring equilibrium to the balance of payments.

The stop-go cycle

This switch of policy objectives became known as the **stop-go cycle**. The stop phase of the cycle occurred when aggregate demand was reduced to combat inflation and/or the balance of payments deficit. As the economy slowed down and unemployment developed, these particular problems seemed to disappear; the government would then embark on the *go* phase of the cycle, expanding aggregate demand to bring unemployment down. As unemployment fell, the problems of inflation and the balance of payments deficit would re-emerge, and the cycle would be repeated. It has been argued that the stop-go cycle can be explained as the consequence of governments trying to reduce the level of unemployment below the natural rate. Each injection of demand temporarily reduced unemployment, but ultimately resulted in a higher rate of inflation and no permanent reduction in unemployment as the economy returned to the natural rate.

During the 1960s and 1970s, in an attempt to break out of this cycle, governments ceased to rely solely on managing the level of aggregate demand to achieve their aims, and began to make greater use of incomes policy and exchange rate adjustment as policy instruments. It was not until 1979, with the election of Mrs Thatcher as Prime Minister, that there was any radical change in the conduct of policy. These changes and the conduct of current macroeconomic policy are discussed further below.

Demand management also led to another problem. Successive governments believed that economic growth could be encouraged by greater investment and that this was more likely to be forthcoming when aggregate demand was rising. The reason for this was simple: rising demand would create a growing market in which the additional output that resulted from increased investment could be sold. However, the management of demand to encourage growth was rarely, if ever, the major policy objective of the authorities; more often price stability and balance of payments equilibrium took precedence over other aims. It is possible that the variable and unpredictable nature of aggregate demand discouraged the private sector from investing because it increased uncertainty.

INSTRUMENTS OF POLICY

FISCAL POLICY

This consists of variations in government income and expenditure. The main fiscal stance of the authorities is implied in the annual budget when the government outlines its income and expenditure plans for the coming financial year.

For many years after 1945, fiscal policy was the instrument used to bring about major changes in aggregate demand. Until the mid/late 1970s comparatively little attention was paid to the size of the PSBR. Indeed, the size of the PSBR was regarded as a *consequence* of fiscal policy and not a *target* in itself. In other words, the government set its expenditure and taxation levels to achieve that particular level of GDP which it considered consistent with its various economic objectives. It therefore regarded its own budget deficit as simply a residual which had to be financed in order to achieve that level of GDP.

However, in the UK after about the mid-1970s, the emphasis of policy shifted away from demand management techniques. There was a growing belief that, in the long run, by varying aggregate demand governments had actually increased instability in the economy and made it more difficult for firms and individuals to make long-run decisions about consumption and investment. It was alleged that this had led to a serious misallocation of resources and had adversely affected economic efficiency in general and economic growth in particular. In consequence, the role of fiscal policy was downgraded and emphasis switched to monetary policy. Fiscal policy remained important because of the effect of the central government's budget deficit on the PSBR, and through this on growth of the money supply. During the early part of the 1980s, the stance of the government was decidedly monetarist! In the 1990s, monetary policy remains important but monetary growth is only one of a number of variables and, in particular, the rate of exchange is now closely monitored by policy makers.

MONETARY POLICY

Governments can use various policy instruments

This consists of policies designed to influence the supply of money and/or its 'price', i.e. the rate of interest. As an instrument of demand management, monetary policy was regarded as subordinate to fiscal policy (until the mid–late 1970s). Whereas fiscal policy could bring about major changes in aggregate demand, the potency of monetary policy was questioned and it was relegated to the role of 'fine-tuning' the economy. In other words, its role was to bring about minor changes in aggregate demand which could not be achieved with fiscal policy. For example, the view was taken that when the economy approached the target level of output, it might be necessary to adjust aggregate demand slightly upwards to achieve the employment target, or downwards to avoid any excess pressure which might generate inflation. Fiscal policy was considered unsuitable for such fine-tuning, because it produced major changes in aggregate demand and it also takes longer to exert its full effect; on the other hand, monetary policy was considered capable of achieving the minor adjustments required.

Since the mid-1970s, and especially during the 1980s, the role of monetary policy was elevated and it now plays a major part in the conduct of economic policy. This is discussed in more detail later in this chapter.

EXCHANGE RATE POLICY

Apart from a brief period when sterling was part of the ERM, the sterling exchange rate has been floating since 1972. As a result, exchange rate changes have been more frequent than when sterling had a fixed parity. Market forces were allowed greater freedom in determining exchange rates in the hope of freeing domestic policy from having to achieve a particular balance of payments position. To the extent that exchange rate changes offset a relatively high rate of inflation in one country compared to others, the balance of payments will prove less of a constraint thus freeing economic policy to be directed to achieving other economic objectives.

In practice, exchange rates are influenced by many factors, not all of which are related to the underlying trends in the economy. For example, towards the end of the 1970s and for part of the 1980s, sterling had a tendency to appreciate partly because of the inflow of North Sea oil revenues. It has been argued that the strength of sterling seriously hampered the competitiveness of exports and consequently led to higher domestic unemployment. However, towards the end of 1984 and the early part of 1985, high interest rates in the US contributed towards sterling depreciating sharply on the foreign exchanges; it reached an all-time low against the dollar in February 1985 of less than £1 = $1.04.

Because of the variety of factors that can cause changes in external currency values when exchange rates float freely, the authorities are likely to stick to 'dirty' or 'managed' floating. As a result they might still be compelled to pursue policies in the domestic economy which prevent severe short-run fluctuations or which smooth the process of adjustment upwards or downwards. Moreover, because of the effect of changes in the exchange rate on the domestic economy, the government have sometimes opted to set an exchange rate target and have directed economic policy to achieving that target rate. This was most obviously the case between 1990 and 1992 when sterling was part of the ERM. Since leaving the ERM sterling has fluctuated more widely though the government is not prepared to allow sterling to float freely, and has stated categorically that it will intervene if depreciation of the exchange rate threatens the objective of price stability.

INCOMES POLICY

The final instrument the authorities have at their disposal is a *statutory* incomes policy, although they have sometimes preferred to negotiate a *voluntary* policy. In the UK, the term 'incomes policy' has often been synonymous with wages policy, since it has mainly applied to wage increases. Although incomes policy can be used to redistribute income it has mainly been applied as an anti-inflationary measure in the UK. By establishing a norm for wage increases, incomes policy has sought to ensure that wage awards accord more closely with the growth of output, i.e. productivity. If wages and productivity grow at the same rate, wage increases will have no effect on costs of production. Consequently they will have little, if any, effect on inflation.

Incomes policies in the UK
In the UK, incomes policies have not been particularly successful as a long-run anti-inflationary measure, although there is no doubt that they have sometimes been successful in the short run. One reason for their lack of success is that the norm has tended to be regarded as a minimum wage award on which more powerful unions have built further claims. Even when policy has been applied with the force of law so that wage increases have been limited, as soon as controls have been relaxed there has tended to be a 'catching up' phase with wage awards well above the growth of output. Despite this, in 1993/94, the government placed a restriction of $1^1/_2$ per cent on public sector pay awards, though there were exceptions including the salaries of MPs! By restricting public sector pay, it was anticipated that private sector pay awards would also fall and through this there would be a favourable effect on the rate of inflation. Pay awards did in fact fall and to this extent the policy was successful.

Objections to incomes policies
Nevertheless, perhaps the main objections to incomes policy are that, by establishing a norm, they have reduced the incentive for workers to increase productivity and that,

by removing flexibility in wage differentials, they have led to lower mobility of labour. The price mechanism works in the labour market as well as in product markets and, by limiting the growth of wages in those occupations which are expanding and which require more workers, incomes policy reduces the incentive for workers to move. Again, this could limit the growth of productivity.

Because of these factors, the present government believes that, in the long run, incomes policy has no particular advantages but that it does have serious disadvantages. However, this view is not shared by all and it is probable that incomes policy will again be used as a policy instrument at some stage in the future.

THE MEDIUM-TERM FINANCIAL STRATEGY (MTFS)

The conduct of economic policy changed decisively in 1980 when MTFS was introduced. The aims of the MTFS were to reduce the rate of inflation and to reduce the proportion of resources taken by the public sector. Inflation was to be reduced primarily by a reduction in the rate of growth of the money supply and the reduction in the proportion of resources taken by the public sector was to be achieved by a reduction in the absolute size of the PSBR, as well as by reducing it as a percentage of GDP. It was thought that reducing the PSBR would not only reduce the extent of crowding out, it was also anticipated that it would lead to lower interest rates because of the implied reduction in the demand for funds.

DECISIVE POLICY CHANGE

66 An important change in policy 99

This was a decisive change in policy in two ways. First, it implied that the government accepted that the rate of growth of the money supply determined the rate of inflation so that control of inflation could only be achieved by controlling the money supply. It also implied an acceptance that the private sector used resources more efficiently than the public sector and therefore that economic growth was more likely to be encouraged by reducing the size of the public sector.

GOVERNMENT ECONOMIC POLICY

It was because of the increased emphasis on controlling the rate of money growth that the Conservative government of the early 1980 was referred to as 'monetarist'. In policy terms, it has meant that monetary policy now occupied the dominant role in the government's economic strategy and that fiscal policy was no longer used as an instrument of short-term demand management. Instead, considerably more importance was attached to the effects of fiscal policy on the money supply and, as we shall see, on incentives. A view reinforced by the privatisation programme and the process of deregulation (see p. 343).

However, in more recent years, the importance of monetary policy has been downgraded, though it remains an important instrument of economic policy. In short, monetary policy has been assigned the long-term objective of price stability, but if this objective is threatened, in particular by adverse short-run movements in the exchange rate, monetary policy will be assigned to correcting these short-run movements. Remember, when the exchange rate depreciates, domestic prices will almost certainly be forced upwards.

The government has formalised its commitment to price stability, and the long-term goal of monetary policy is to achieve a target range for the underlying rate of inflation of 1–4 per cent by the end of the current parliament. The emphasis has been placed firmly on the lower end of this target range and a rate of 2 per cent or less is the preferred goal. In pursuit of this objective, the government has retained a target range for the growth of M0 (narrow money) of 1–4 per cent and has also adopted a monitoring range for the growth of M4 (broad money) of 3–9 per cent. These targets are to run annually for the whole period covered by the Medium Term Financial Strategy, i.e. until 1997/98.

Since the suspension of sterling in the ERM, the exchange rate has also become a major concern because of its effect on prices. No formal target has been announced for the exchange rate and it seems that the authorities will adopt a pragmatic approach.

There is no doubt they will intervene if price stability is threatened, but there is also no doubt that while the economy is in recession they will also consider the effect of intervention on output and employment so long as such intervention does not prejudice the objective of price stability.

In addition, there is still considerable emphasis attached to reducing the size of the PSBR because of its effect on money growth and interest rates, and because the view that the private sector uses resources more efficiently than the public sector still prevails. Indeed, the rapid expansion of the PSBR in the 1990s has forced the government to make cuts in public expenditure and raise taxes even when there are signs of a fragile recovery from the recession. Nothing could more vividly illustrate the government's commitment to reigning in the PSBR! It is something of a paradox that the reason the PSBR has expanded rapidly is mainly due to the depth of the recession which has caused tax revenues to fall and social security payments to increase.

Operation of MTFS

Originally, the MTFS involved setting declining targets for the growth of broad money and for the PSBR. These targets were not, of course, independent of each other and as we have seen, changes in the PSBR can bring about changes in broad money. However, as the MTFS has evolved, targets ceased to be published for broad money and M0 (narrow money) became the focus of attention. In the latest version of the MTFS, M0 remains the most prominent money aggregate though a monitoring range for M4 has also been established.

Despite its evolution, the basic principles on which the MTFS is based have remained unchanged:

- Growth is generated by private sector initiative and entrepreneurship, *not* by government action. The role of the government is to help to establish the right climate for the private sector to thrive.

- The essential condition for sustained growth is low inflation. This is vital if competitiveness is to be maintained.

- The only way to increase the country's long-term growth rate is by improving the supply performance of the economy. This means increasing the role of the private sector, doing away with unnecessary regulations and establishing competitive and open markets.

As we shall see, the role of monetary policy within this framework is to achieve and sustain price stability. It is now recognised that a key element in achieving price stability is to convince economic agents (individuals and firms) that inflation is defeated and will remain at a relatively low rate. It is anticipated that this will be taken into consideration by those involved in setting wages and prices and that the unemployment consequences of higher wage settlements will be avoided.

While sterling was in the ERM, monetary policy was dictated by the need to maintain the exchange rate within the agreed parity band, Since sterling's withdrawal, this certainty of policy no longer exists. The government has made it clear that it intends to identify the build-up of inflationary pressure at an early stage and to take appropriate action. The government has adopted a three-pronged approach to providing information to economic agents on the future course of monetary policy:

- A *Monthly Monetary Report* is published which summarises the outcome of the regular meetings which take place between the Chancellor of the Exchequer and Governor of the Bank of England. This report contains an assessment of all the various indicators of the state of the economy, inflation and monetary growth, which are used as the basis for monetary policy judgements. Adverse movements in these indicators will give a hint of a possible tightening of monetary policy.

- The Treasury now publishes a detailed account of the reasoning behind changes in interest rates. The aim is to explain the particular factors which led the government to decide on a change in interest rates. Over time it is hoped that these announcements will demonstrate a clear and consistent basis for the government's decisions on monetary policy.

- The Bank of England's *Quarterly Bulletin* now includes a commentary on progress towards the government's inflation objective. The report is designed to offer a comprehensive guide to inflation – not only reporting on past performance but of likely future developments. This will enable economic agents to assess the Bank of England's record in achieving its objectives and, in this way, the aim is to establish credibility for the Bank in maintaining a low rate of inflation.

PROBLEMS OF MTFS AS A POLICY STRATEGY

There are several problems with the MTFS as a policy strategy. One obvious criticism is that there is still no conclusive proof that controlling money growth will guarantee control of inflation. Any policy based on this approach is an act of faith rather than a proven policy option. There is also some doubt that controlling the PSBR will give sufficient control over the rate of money growth. For example, if the government is committed to maintaining a particular rate of exchange, a balance of payments surplus can cause an increase in money growth. (Net receipts from abroad imply an increase in foreign currency receipts which the authorities are committed to converting into sterling at the existing exchange rate through the Exchange Equalisation Account.) Similarly the link between the PSBR and the rate of interest is not clear. For example, if increased borrowing by the authorities is matched by an autonomous increase in savings, i.e. an increase in savings motivated by an increased desire on the part of the community to save, there is no reason why interest rates should necessarily rise. Moreover, if government spending financed by a higher PSBR increases the receipts of firms in the private sector and, as a result, these firms cut down their own borrowing, a higher PSBR does not necessarily imply a higher total demand for loans. Because of this, it is again uncertain how an increase in the PSBR will affect the rate of interest.

ADVANTAGES OF MTFS

Despite these problems, one advantage of the MTFS is that it gives clear indication of the government's intent. This provides firms, in particular, with the information they require to plan effectively. It also provides useful information for those involved in negotiating wages.

CURRENT MACROECONOMIC POLICY

One reason for distinguishing between macroencomic policy and economic policy in general is because of the increased emphasis on microeconomic or supply-side policies to achieve macroeconomic goals. In brief, the main instrument for the implementation of macro policy is monetary policy, which is currently directed towards reducing inflation. Supply-side policies, on the other hand, are directed to achieving increased efficiency and a reduction in unemployment by improving incentives and removing restrictions which inhibit efficiency. Supply-side policies are discussed on pp. 341–343, but it is clear that the authorities aim to improve macroeconomic performance by increasing aggregate supply, rather than by adjusting aggregate demand.

The methods used to implement monetary policy have changed since the MTFS was first unveiled. Rather than controlling the rate of money growth, greater emphasis is now placed on the use of interest rates not only to control the growth of spending, but also to influence the exchange rate which has become an important instrument in the pursuit of economic goals and, in particular, changes in the exchange rate have an important influence on the rate of inflation.

THE IMPORTANCE OF THE EXCHANGE RATE

The way in which the rate of interest and the exchange rate can be used to control inflation is simple. A relatively high rate of interest raises the exchange rate and therefore reduces the domestic price of imports. In an economy like the UK, with its dependence on imported raw materials and its relatively high marginal propensity to import generally, this helps to reduce inflation. However, this policy is also likely to have a favourable effect on inflation in another way. The relatively high exchange rate implies that exporters must either reduce the sterling price of their goods, or accept a reduction in sales because of the higher export price. If the sterling price is reduced, this leads directly to a reduction in the rate of inflation. If sales are reduced this will probably encourage moderation in wage settlements and therefore indirectly contribute to a lower rate of inflation. This is precisely what happened when sterling joined the ERM in 1990 at what clearly turned out to be an over-valued exchange rate. To maintain the exchange rate, interest rates were forced steadily upwards and the economy moved deeper and deeper into recession. As the economy slowed up and unemployment rose, the pace of wage settlements fell and this, in turn, led to falling inflation. When sterling left the ERM, the exchange rate depreciated sharply and, although it has since recovered, its value remains well below its ERM rate. In addition, interest rates have fallen sharply and there are signs that the stimulus to the economy from these developments, and the lower rate of inflation, might create an up-turn in economic activity.

However, as we have seen, high interest rates have an immediate adverse effect on the retail price index because of their impact on mortgage costs. As the RPI rises, it could lead to increased demands for higher wages which, if achieved, will further increase inflation.

SUPPLY-SIDE ECONOMICS

The aim of supply-side policy is to remove obstacles which prevent or discourage people and firms from adapting quickly to changing conditions of market demand and changing techniques of production. It is argued that the implied increase in efficiency will encourage economic growth. Two aspects of supply-side policies — privatisation and deregulation — are considered under separate headings.

❝ Supply-side policies ❞

The emphasis on supply-side policies stems from a belief that, if markets can be made to operate more efficiently, this will encourage economic growth and employment without adding to the risk of inflation. We can see the effect of an increase in efficiency on aggregate supply in Fig. 17.1.

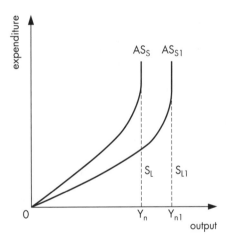

Fig. 17.1

If all other things remain the same, an increase in efficiency at all levels of output will shift the short-run aggregate supply curve from AS_S to AS_{S1} and the long-run aggregate supply from S_L to S_{L1}. Any given level of output now has a lower supply price, and a greater amount of output can be produced at full employment than previously. In the absence of any improvement in efficiency, attempts to achieve economic growth and full employment by increasing aggregate demand will not be sustainable, because they will generate inflation and a balance of payments deficit.

The various methods by which the government has attempted to improve the supply side of the economy can be discussed under the following headings.

Taxation

Measures have been introduced to ensure that, in general, people are better off in work than out of work. In particular, the basic rate of income tax has been reduced from 33 per cent in 1979 to a current level of 25 per cent, with the first £2,000 of taxable income taxed at a rate of 20 per cent. Further reductions are planned in the future, although in practice the total tax take has increased. The threshold above which people start paying tax has also been increased by more than the rate of inflation. Additionally, unemployment benefit is now taxed. It is hoped that, among other effects, this will have a positive effect on the unemployment trap.

Corporation tax has also been reduced from 52 per cent to a lower rate of 25 per cent for smaller firms and a rate of 33 per cent for larger firms. The aim here is to encourage firms to invest in more productive capital by reducing the taxation of profits.

The labour market

Alongside these changes, the government has introduced training schemes, the most important of which is the YTS which provides one-year and two-year training placements for 16- and 17-year-olds respectively who leave school or college (or who cannot find employment). On completion of their YTS scheme, an estimated 60 per cent of trainees find employment or go into further education.

Other labour market measures

Other important labour market measures are the Employment Acts of 1980 and 1982 and the Trade Union Act of 1984 which have attemped to safeguard the interests of individual employees and to encourage more effective democracy within trade unions. Some of the main measures introduced were:

■ removal of legal immunities both for picketing, other than by employees at their place of work, and for secondary industrial action;

■ introduction and strengthening of the rights of employees dismissed for refusing to join closed shops;

■ removal of legal immunities from civil actions so as to make trade unions subject to injunctions and damages when they are responsible for unlawful industrial action; and

■ removal of legal immunities from civil action in any industrial action which has not been agreed in advance by a secret ballot of the membership.

The aim of this legislation has been to create a more flexible labour market, since it is believed that lack of flexibility is one of the major reasons why real wages have risen to levels which reduce employment.

The capital market

A whole range of controls have been abolished in the capital market. For example, in 1979, exchange controls were abolished and, in 1982, hire-purchase controls were abolished. The aim is to improve efficiency by allowing savings to go where there is the best combination of risk and return.

The **Big Bang** also increased competition in the capital market. The Stock Exchange now permits dual capacity trading, i.e. it allows firms to simultaneously act as principle on their own account and as agents for their clients. Fixed commissions by brokers have also been abolished and full ownership of Stock Exchange firms by non-members (permissable since March 1, 1986) is now permissable. All of these changes are seen as major ways of improving competition and, through this, efficiency.

Markets for other goods and services

Again, a whole range of measures have been introduced and, while they vary in significance, their aim is to create the conditions in which the freer play of market forces can stimulate the economy to work more efficiently. Two measures are particularly important: **The Competition Act** (1980) and the programme of **privatisation** and **deregulation**. The former gives the Monopolies and Mergers Commission (MMC) power to investigate individual firms suspected of operating 'anti-competitive practices'; they are referred to the MMC by the Director-General of Fair Trading. The latter reflects the government's view that economic performance can be improved by subjecting firms and whole industries to the full rigours of the market — although the proceeds of privatisation have also helped to reduce the PSBR. The implicit assumption is that organisations in the public sector are sheltered from competition and that this leads to inefficiency. Whether this is true or not is debatable, but it certainly is true that, on average, the rate of return on capital employed in nationalised industries has for many years been lower than the rate of return in the private sector, while price increases have in general been higher.

In the financial sector, the **Building Societies Act (1986)** has enabled them to compete more effectively with the retail banks. In particular, they are now able to offer cheque books and cheque guarantee cards. Several now also offer cash point facilities. Other provisions of the Act allowed the building societies to abandon their status as Friendly Societies and form themselves into public limited companies as the Abbey National has recently done. Building Societies are now also able to make unsecured loans up to certain limits for purposes other than house purchase and to compete for funds on the wholesale markets. In 1986, a limit of 20 per cent of total borrowed funds was originally set on the amount that could be borrowed from the wholesale markets. However, in 1988, this was raised to 40 per cent further increasing their ability to compete with retail banks.

PRIVATISATION

The term **privatisation** is usually taken to imply the transfer of assets from the public sector to the private sector. In this sense, privatisation refers to a change in the ownership of assets. However, privatisation can cover other activities, e.g. ceasing to provide such activities as refuse collection through the public sector and putting them out to private contract. Despite this, it is the transfer of assets from the public sector to the private sector which has attracted most attention and on which we focus in this section. Furthermore, although this might include activities such as the sale of council houses, it is the sale of nationalised industries as well as industries in which the state has a major shareholding with which we will be concerned.

One point to be aware of, at the outset, is that privatisation is not simply a British phenomenon; it is happening in many countries throughout the world — USA, France, Germany, Spain, Singapore, Jamaica, Chile, Turkey and many other countries have privatisation programmes.

REASONS FOR PRIVATISATION

The reason for privatisation in the UK are typical:

- A major aim of privatisation is to increase efficiency in the allocation and utilisation of resources.

 **Some reasons for privatisation**

- Another aim is to increase the extent of share ownership, partly for political reasons in the UK at least, but also because it is thought to affect the allocation and utilisation of resources.

- In the case of the UK, privatisation has been a major factor in cutting down borrowing by the government. Lower borrowing by the government has been a major part of the government's macroeconomic strategy.

Let us consider each of these in turn:

Efficiency in privatised firms

Privatisation might encourage efficiency in privatised firms for several reasons. One is that there will be less government interference in pricing and investment decisions by these firms. Another reason is that there will be increased competition following privatisation.

It is certainly true that governments have often deliberately prevented nationalised industries from increasing their prices as a means of tackling inflation, and have altered investment in different industries as a means of varying aggregate demand. As privatised organisations, firms will be able to plan more effectively. However, efficiency in the allocation of resources might also be improved. We have already seen that when prices are prevented from rising, too much is consumed in relation to the optimum. Furthermore, it has been argued that increased investment in the nationalised industries has crowded out private sector investment, and the higher rate of return achieved in the private sector is taken as evidence that investment is more efficient when undertaken by the private sector.

However, there seems little evidence of increased competition following some privatisations. Indeed, some organisations such as British Gas have been sold as monopolies to increase their attractiveness to shareholders. It might be claimed that the government had little alternative since some industries are quite clearly *natural monopolies* and that, in any case, as private sector organisations, they must compete for funds on the capital market with other private sector organisations. Nevertheless, critics have argued that monopolies do not have to be efficient to be profitable, and that profitability is the main determinant of a firm's ability to raise funds on the capital market. Furthermore, it would have been possible to sell these industries as regional units which would be allowed to compete for business in each other's regions as to some extent has happened when electricity and water were privatised.

Increase in number of shareholders

Turning to the second aim of privatisation, the government has clearly had success in increasing the number of shareholders with over 25 per cent of the adult population in the UK owning shares in 1994. It has been argued that this will encourage efficiency because management are now accountable to shareholders with a vested interest in the efficiency and profitability of the companies in which they hold shares. However, few shareholders attend the AGM when the Board of Directors is elected and when they must account for the policies of the previous 12 months.

Raising revenue

As for the third aim of privatisation, there is no doubt that the government has achieved success in raising revenue through privatisation as Table 17.1 shows. The major privatisations have raised around £37 billion in revenue for the Treasury.

Major sales since 1979	Date	£m
British Petroleum*	1979, 1983 and 1987	8,054
British Aerospace	1981 and 1985	389
Cable and Wireless	1981	1,020
Amersham International	1982	64
National Freight Consortium	1982	5
Britoil	1982 and 1985	1,053
Associated British Ports	1983 and 1984	97
Enterprise Oil	1984	382
British Telecom	1984 and 1991	3,682
British Gas	1986	5,600
British Airways	1987	390
Royal Ordnance	1987	186
Rolls-Royce	1987	1,080
British Airports Authority	1987	1,275
Rover Group*	1988	150
British Steel	1988	2,425
Water and Sewerage Companies	1989	3,470
Electricity Industries	1990/91	7,549
	Total	36,871

Table 17.1 Proceeds from privatisation

* Private sector company.

Nevertheless, it has been suggested that the government might have met with even more success if it had not underpriced some of the shares it has issued. For example, shares in British Telecom were issued at a price of £1.30, but by the end of the first day's trading they were quoted at £1.73, thus depriving the government of potentially an extra £1,295 million revenue.

However, deciding on the price at which to issue shares so as to ensure that a sufficient quantity is sold is a notoriously difficult problem. Some have criticised the government for not issuing shares by tender. This was certainly a possibility open to the government, but was rejected probably because it was felt that this would not attract small investors, with little or no experience of buying shares, to anything like the extent required to increase significantly the number of share-owning individuals.

DEREGULATION

Deregulation is the term used to describe the process of dismantling state regulations on the activities of the business sector. Like privatisation, deregulation is a worldwide phenomenon though, in this chapter, we are only concerned with deregulation in the UK. It is useful to note, however, that while privatisation and deregulation sometimes overlap, as when an industry is denationalised and is also opened up to competition, this is not always the case. Before we consider the issue of deregulation, the reasons for regulating industry in the first place are considered.

THE REASONS FOR REGULATION

It is usually suggested that the main reason for regulation is to safeguard the **public interest**, although what constitutes the public interest differs from case to case. For example, the banks have been subject to regulation mainly because of the possibility of default, if there was a sudden large withdrawal of deposits by customers. A bank that was unable to honour withdrawals might well precipitate a run on other banks as well as itself. Air transport, as well as buses and coaches, have been subject to regulation for **safety reasons**. Television and radio broadcasting have been regulated, partly because it was felt that competition would reduce the quality of reception by causing interference. The regulation of agriculture has been partly to ensure that harmful chemicals are not used to increase yields, and partly to ensure that, as an industry, agriculture survives so that food supplies cannot be cut off by a foreign supplier.

Despite these cases, the most complete regulations are those governing the nationalised industries which are given sole rights of supply. One of the most important arguments for nationalisation was that in some cases such as gas, water and electricity, a **natural monopoly** existed, and that nationalisation was necessary to ensure the public were not exploited by a private monopolist.

APPLIED MATERIALS

THE REASONS FOR DEREGULATION

The major reason for deregulation is that it is now thought that the public interest is better served by competition and that regulations not only restrict competition, but also impose higher costs on the firms subject to regulation. However, another factor is technological advances which have sometimes made deregulation essential if an industry is to survive the growth of foreign competition. For example, technological advances made automated dealing possible on the world's stock exchanges which substantially reduced the cost of transacting business. Technological progress also made it possible for a dealer in one financial centre, such as London, to transact business with another dealer in a different financial centre somewhere else in the world, with the latest dealing rates available on screen. When minimum dealing rates were abolished in New York, this precipitated reform of the London Stock Exchange (the Big Bang), because almost overnight it became cheaper to buy and sell securities in New York than in London! Without reform the London Stock Exchange would have ceased to be one of the world's leading financial centres.

If you refer back to the reasons for imposing regulations on industry, it is hardly surprising that it has been suggested that efficiency in the allocation of resources is now given priority over safety standards. In fact, there is no evidence that this is true and safety is still an important issue. What is different, is the view that efficiency in the allocation of resources is better promoted by competition than by government controls on the behaviour of industry!

UNEMPLOYMENT IN THE UK

Figure 17.2 shows that unemployment in the UK increased steeply in the early part of the 1980s but fell from its peak of 3.5 million in 1986 to 1.7 million in 1990, before rising to 2.8 million by 1993, falling again to 2.3 million in 1995. One reason for the increase in unemployment was that the working population increased more rapidly than job opportunities. Figure 17.2 provides some information on the changes in the working population, the numbers unemployed and the increases in self-employment that have occurred in recent years.

TRAINING

An article in the *British Economy Survey*, Vol. 22, No. 1, Autumn 1992 outlines the importance of training and discusses the training initiatives currently operating in the UK. Training is important in improving mobility of labour and reducing skill shortages, and is therefore crucial to the success of an economy. However, training is a merit good (see Ch. 2) and will be underprovided in relation to the optimal level if it is financed

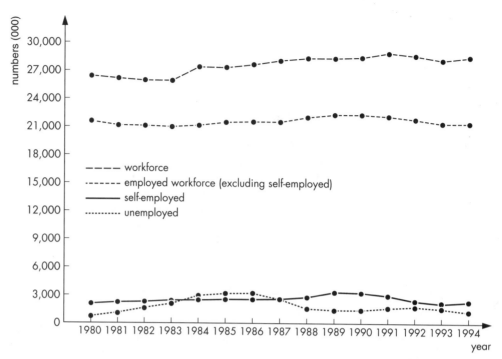

Fig. 17.2 Unemployment in the UK
(*Source:* HMSO)

entirely through the private sector. This is why governments have become increasingly involved in measures to increase the availability of training. The different initiatives currently available in the UK are summarised below.

- **Training and Enterprise Councils (TECs)** Currently there are 82 TECs in England and Wales and 22 Local Enterprise Councils (LECs) in Scotland. These are responsible for administering many existing training programmes including the YTS. Though funded by the Government, the TECs are business-led and have senior executives from industry on their boards. Their function is to meet the training, enterprise and vocational education requirements of local communities.

- **Employment Training (ET)** This scheme provides training for the long-term unemployed and those at a disadvantage in the labour market, such as single parents or those with some kind of disability. The scheme runs for six months and the unemployed are allocated to training agents and continue to receive benefits plus a training allowance for this period.

- **High Technology National Training (HTNT)** This scheme is operated within the ET for those with the ability to acquire high-level skills.

- **Youth Training Scheme (YTS)** This scheme offers two years of training to any 16-year-old and one year of training to any 17-year-old not in full-time education. The emphasis is on training at employers' premises. However, there are no regulations on the type of training that should be given and, in some cases, serious questions have been asked about the quality of training given.

- **Training Credits (TCs)** By 1996, it is anticipated that every school-leaver will have the offer of a training credit. The recipient can exchange this for training or education of his or her choice. The aim is to increase the choice available to school-leavers and to encourage employers to offer high-quality training.

EXAMINATION QUESTIONS

1 How do you explain the fact that monetary targets are no longer the prime focus of economic policy in the UK?

(ULEAC June 1993)

2 Explain whether or not you regard economic growth as a desirable objective of economic policy for any government. Compare the obstacles to achieving a satisfactory rate of growth in the UK with those in countries such as Ethiopia or Chile.

(JMB June 1993)

3 (a) Outline the various supply-side policies which have been introduced in the United Kingdom during recent years. *(10)*
   (b) Discuss the extent to which these supply-side reforms have influenced the performance of the economy. *(15)*

(AEB June 1993)

4 How does the analysis and classification of unemployment contribute to our understanding of how to deal with it? Compare government training schemes, increases in aggregate demand and cuts in real wages as ways of dealing with unemployment.

(JMB June 1993)

ANSWERS TO EXAMINATION QUESTIONS

TUTOR'S ANSWER TO QUESTION 1

In the early 1980s. economic policy in the UK was characterised by monetary targeting. This simply means that the government established a target rate of growth for the money supply and directed the instruments of monetary policy to achieving this target.

Monetary targeting was introduced because of the strong monetarist stance adopted by the government. By 1980, inflation in the UK had reached 18 per cent and its control had become the main focus of economic policy. It was widely believed that inflation was caused by excessive money growth and that it could only be controlled by reducing money growth. The quantity theory of money became the doctrine that underpinned economic policy and the medium term financial strategy (MTFS) was introduced in the budget of 1980.

The MTFS established declining target rates of growth for broad money, narrow money and for the PSBR for the next several years ahead. It was felt that, by publishing monetary targets for several years in advance, the private sector would be provided with information that could be taken into account when negotiating wage increases or implementing price changes. This was considered to be an important part of the government's anti-inflationary strategy which it was hoped, through its effect on expectations, would bring down the rate of inflation at a faster rate than would otherwise be achieved.

Money growth was to be controlled by raising interest rates to damp down demand for money and thereby curb the growth of bank deposits. In addition, partly because of the belief that changes in the PSBR led directly to changes in money growth, declining targets were established for the PSBR. Furthermore, the PSBR was no longer to be financed by sales of debt to the non-bank private sector. The exchange rate was also allowed to float more freely thus reducing the need for intervention which, because of the implications for the domestic money supply of intervention, would make it easier for the government to achieve its target.

From the very start, there were problems with the MTFS. For example, the link between the PSBR and money growth is far from clear and is certainly not a mechanistic one. There is some doubt, therefore, whether controlling the PSBR is an effective instrument for controlling money growth. More fundamentally, there was no agreement on what money aggregate was the appropriate one to target for controlling the rate of inflation. Some economists felt broad money was the appropriate aggregate, whereas others stressed the importance of narrow money. For the authorities, a dilemma existed because these aggregates sometimes move in opposite directions. As the MTFS evolved, targets for broad money were dropped and some economists cite this as the reason why inflation rose towards the end of the decade. However, the damage to the MTFS was done and rising inflation discredited monetary targeting.

Initially, the policy of monetary targeting appeared to be successful in reducing the rate of inflation, which fell from a rate of almost 20 per cent in 1980 to an annual rate of 4.5 per cent by 1983. However, the economy was plunged into deep recession and unemployment went on rising to what were then post-war record levels. This weakened confidence in the MTFS because it raised doubt over whether inflation had been brought down by falling money growth or whether it was simply the result of deflation.

Over the longer term, interest rate policy did not prove as effective in restraining money growth as was originally anticipated. Indeed, in the early 1980s, private sector borrowing increased rapidly and only subsided when interest rates rose to in excess of 15 per cent at the end of the decade. This increased debt servicing charges to such an extent that expenditure fell, followed by a fall in the rate of inflation. Raising interest rates therefore proved to be an effective anti-inflationary weapon, but not in the way envisaged by the MTFS. Instead of controlling inflation by constraining money growth, inflation was brought under control by restricting expenditure and throwing the economy into deep recession.

Moreover, in the latter half of the 1980s, as inflation began to increase the favourable effect on expectations of policy pronouncements on money growth disappeared. In the event, it proved to be increasingly difficult to meet target rates of growth for the money supply and towards the end of the decade policy statements played down the role of monetary targets. Indeed the exchange rate emerged as the key weapon against inflation and policy concentrated on maintaining this at a relatively high rate. The main instrument for maintaining a relatively high exchange rate was the rate of interest which was also maintained at a relatively high rate. This combination, especially after the UK joined the ERM, again plunged the economy into recession and, despite announcements that controlling the rate of inflation is the main long-term aim of policy, there is little doubt that attention has now shifted to stimulating the real economy as a medium-term objective. This implies a relaxation of efforts to control money growth along with a low interest rate and low exchange rate policy to stimulate expenditure on domestic output.

Monetary targeting has been downgraded in the UK because it is perceived to have been ineffective in controlling the rate of inflation. There might be many reasons for this. Some economists maintain that excessive money growth is not the only cause of inflation. If this view is correct, a policy of monetary targeting is bound to fail. Other economists argue that monetary targeting was not pursued vigorously enough and this accounts for the failure of monetary targeting.

STUDENT'S ANSWER TO QUESTION 2

> **Real or nominal**

> **Could present a production possibility curve to illustrate!**

Economic growth can be defined as an increase in GNP. A policy to increase economic growth is a very desirable policy for governments to pursue as long as undesirable side-effects can be avoided. Economic growth is desirable because, as GNP rises, there is an increase in the amount of goods and services that can be consumed by the population and therefore the standard of living rises.

There are other advantages of economic growth. It is only through economic growth that greater investment in research and development can be financed. This leads to an increase in the range of products a country can produce. It also makes possible scientific advances which have led to cures being developed for many illnesses which were previously untreatable. Vaccines have been developed to prevent the spread of others.

The problem with policies to increase economic growth is that they often impose externalities on the economy. These are the undesirable side-effects of production. The

<table>
<tr><td>Good – here you mean negative externalities</td><td>most obvious externality associated with economic growth is pollution. As production increases, more fossil fuels are burned and this increases the amount of acid rain that falls on the countryside. This causes dead lakes and forests. On an international scale, this is a very serious problem because one country often burns fossil fuels but, as clouds move across countries, acid rain falls in a different country.</td></tr>
</table>

> **66** Good – here you mean negative externalities **99**

most obvious externality associated with economic growth is pollution. As production increases, more fossil fuels are burned and this increases the amount of acid rain that falls on the countryside. This causes dead lakes and forests. On an international scale, this is a very serious problem because one country often burns fossil fuels but, as clouds move across countries, acid rain falls in a different country.

More generally, pollution, as a result of economic growth, has caused a hole in the ozone layer which in turn has led to global warming. This is a very serious development which, if unchecked, will eventually lead to the polar ice caps melting and flooding on a massive scale. The implications are tremendous since many people would be made homeless while there would be a global shortage of food.

> **66** Good point **99**

The main source of economic growth is increased investment. This requires an increase in savings by the community because capital accumulation is impossible without abstention from current consumption. In other words, there is an opportunity cost associated with greater investment even though, in the long run, it is worth paying this cost! It is easier for the population of the UK to increase the amount saved because they are relatively wealthy compared with the residents of Ethiopia and Chile.

> **66** Good **99**

It is very difficult for people in these countries to save because many of them are caught in the vicious circle of poverty which means all of their income is spent on consumption to keep them alive. Because of this, savings, and therefore investment, are both low and this limits economic growth.

> **66** A relevant point **99**

There is another problem because it is easier for the UK to attract outside investment – especially from countries outside the EU seeking access to EU markets. For example, Japan has invested heavily in the UK to avoid EU restrictions on imports from outside the EU. There is no such incentive for other developed countries to invest in countries such as Ethiopia or Chile where the return on their investments will be quite low. In other words, funds can be invested more profitably elsewhere.

Foreign firms are also more likely to invest in the UK because their investments are more secure. The UK is a democracy whereas countries such as Chile and Ethiopia are ruled by dictators. These countries are often politically unstable and this discourages foreign investment.

> **66** Many good points raised. Perhaps a little more economic analysis could have been presented — e.g. production possibility curve, aggregate demand and supply diagram, 45° diagram, etc. A few more facts/studies could be used to support your points in places.' **99**

OUTLINE ANSWERS

Question 3

(a) You could begin with a broad definition of supply-side policies. Since the beginning of the 1980s, there have been many supply-side reforms implemented in the UK. These are detailed on pp. 341–343.

(b) Supply-side policies might have influenced the performance of the UK economy in several ways. At the micro level, there have been price reductions in certain markets, partly as a result of increased competition following privatisation and deregulation. Greater competition might also have led to a reduction in inefficiency in privatised organisations.

At the macro level, this will have had a favourable effect on the rate of inflation. There have been tremendous improvements in manufacturing productivity. Again, this might be partly the result of increased competition but it is also likely to be at least partly due to trade union reforms which have curbed union power and lessened the incidence of strikes. This will have improved the competitiveness of UK goods abroad (as well as in the domestic economy) which, despite the deficits of recent years, will have had a favourable effect on the balance of trade.

On the other hand, in the latter part of the 1980s, the savings ratio declined. One reason for this was that there was an increase in borrowing, partly due to financial deregulation and privatisation. It was this increase in borrowing that led to the consumer boom and an up-turn in the rate of inflation. This had an adverse effect on the balance of trade.

The Stock Exchange reforms have enabled it to compete with other financial centres in the world, particularly New York and Tokyo, and this has had a beneficial effect on the invisible account.

The reduction in direct taxation might have had a favourable effect on incentives. To the extent that this is correct, the natural rate of unemployment will have fallen.

Question 4

Economists sometimes identify various types of unemployment. (See pp. 332–333 for a discussion of these.) Having discussed the various types of unemployment, you can go on to look at the various policy options suggested in the question. You will need to show how an increase in aggregate demand will lead to an increase in output and employment. However, if the natural rate hypothesis is accepted, this is only a temporary outcome and as output and unemployment return to the natural rate, the only long-term results of an increase in aggregate demand is an increase in the rate of inflation.

One of the main determinants of the natural rate is the extent of mobility of labour. The greater the adaptability of the working population, the higher the natural rate of output and the lower the natural rate of unemployment. However, if the conventional classification of unemployment is accepted, mobility of labour would also alleviate unemployment. You will need to show why and how mobility of labour, and therefore an increase in government training schemes, will affect output and employment.

A cut in real wages would increase the demand for labour because, if all other things remain the same, it implies an increase in real profits. However, if the real wage is at the equilibrium level, unemployment will be at the natural rate and a cut in the real wage, while increasing the demand for labour, will lead to a reduction in the supply of labour. The result will be an increase in unemployment. Only if real wages are above the equilibrium level will a cut in the real wage lead to an increase in employment. This is easily illustrated diagrammatically and it would be useful to go on and do this.

Further reading

Wall and Griffiths (eds), *Applied Economics: An Introductory Course* (6th edn), Longman 1995: Ch. 27, Managing the economy.

Harrison et al, *Introductory Economics*, Macmillan 1992: Ch. 36, Stabilisation Policy; Ch. 37, Supply-side Policies in the UK.

Lipsey and Harbury, *First Principles in Economics* (2nd edn), Weidenfeld and Nicolson 1992; Ch. 43, Macroeconomic Controversies.

REVIEW SHEET

1 Identify four key aims of economic policy, briefly explaining each aim.

(a) _____

_____

(b) _____

_____

(c) _____

_____

(d) _____

_____

2 Show how trying to fulfil any two aims simultaneously might bring about policy conflict.

_____

_____

_____

_____

3 Identify four key instruments of economic policy.

(a) _____

_____

(b) _____

_____

(c) _____

_____

(d) _____

_____

4 What is meant by supply-side economics?

_____

_____

_____

_____

5 Present a diagram to show how supply-side economics might be used to increase national output without stimulating inflation.

6 Use your diagram to explain the process involved.

_____
_____
_____
_____
_____
_____

7 Outline the practical policies which might be considered supply-side.

_____
_____
_____
_____
_____

8 What is meant by privatisation?

_____
_____

9 Consider the three main arguments used to support privatisation.

(a) _____
_____
_____

(b) _____
_____
_____

(c) _____
_____
_____

10 Consider the arguments in favour of regulation of industry.

_____
_____
_____
_____
_____

11 Consider the arguments in favour of deregulation of industry.

_____
_____
_____
_____
_____

12 Describe recent changes in the patterns of employment and unemployment in the UK.

_____
_____
_____
_____
_____